H. Charlton Bastian

The Beginnings of Life

Vol. 1

H. Charlton Bastian

The Beginnings of Life

Vol. 1

ISBN/EAN: 9783741174599

Manufactured in Europe, USA, Canada, Australia, Japa

Cover: Foto ©Andreas Hilbeck / pixelio.de

Manufactured and distributed by brebook publishing software (www.brebook.com)

H. Charlton Bastian

The Beginnings of Life

THE BEGINNINGS OF LIFE.

VOL. I.

'Il y a eu une époque où notre planète ne possédait aucun germe de vie organisée ; donc la vie organisée y a commencé sans germe antérieur. Toutes les apparitions nouvelles qui ont eu lieu dans le monde se sont faites, non par l'acte incessamment renouvelé d'un Être Créateur, mais par la force intime déposée une fois pour toutes au sein des choses.'—*Ernest Renan.*

'The utmost possibility for us is an interpretation of the process of things as it presents itself... to our limited consciousness. . . . There is no mode of establishing the validity of any belief except that of showing its entire congruity with all other beliefs.'—*Herbert Spencer.*

THE
BEGINNINGS OF LIFE:

BEING

SOME ACCOUNT OF THE NATURE,

MODES OF ORIGIN AND TRANSFORMATIONS

OF

LOWER ORGANISMS.

BY

H. CHARLTON BASTIAN, M.A., M.D., F.R.S.

Fellow of the Royal College of Physicians;
Professor of Pathological Anatomy in University College, London;
Physician to University College Hospital;
Assistant Physician to the National Hospital for the Paralysed and Epileptic.

IN TWO VOLUMES.

VOL. I.

WITH NUMEROUS ILLUSTRATIONS.

London

MACMILLAN AND CO.

1872.

[All rights reserved]

OXFORD:
By T. Combe, M.A., E. B. Gardner, and E. Pickard Hall
PRINTERS TO THE UNIVERSITY.

PREFACE.

RATHER more than three years ago, in the course of some investigations upon the microscopical characters of the blood of persons suffering from acute diseases, my attention was first thoroughly given to the great question of the Origin of Life. And as so much depended upon the proper solution of this problem—not only for Science generally, but even with reference to the scientific basis of Medicine—I determined to undertake some investigations and endeavour to revise the grounds of opinion upon the subject.

I did investigate, and in consequence was after a time compelled to renounce my old prepossessions, and adopt views concerning the origin of 'living' matter which are as yet only very partially accepted in the world of science. The state of professional opinion on these questions, moreover, was such that it would have been unsuitable for me to have taught new doctrines based upon facts ascertained during these investigations, without having fully and publicly stated the grounds upon which I had adopted them.

At much personal sacrifice, therefore, I resolved to attempt to produce a statement of the facts which should carry conviction to the minds of others. And although at first wishing to do this in a work much smaller than that which I now submit to the public, it was soon found that more elaboration would be needed. The scope of the subject itself, moreover, widened so rapidly—biological problems of such enormous importance were opened up—that I at last felt compelled to pursue the investigation in a manner a little more commensurate with the magnitude of its dependent issues.

The First Part of this work was written and printed nearly three years ago. It was intended to show the general reader, more especially, that the logical consequences of the now commonly accepted doctrines concerning the 'Conservation of Energy' and the 'Correlation of the Vital and Physical Forces,' were wholly favourable to the possibility of the independent origin of 'living' matter. It also contains a review of the 'Cellular Theory of Organization,' which was written and was in type before I had had the pleasure of reading Prof. Stricker's essay on 'Cells.'

In the Second Part of the work, under the head 'Archebiosis,' the question as to the present occurrence or non-occurrence of 'spontaneous generation' is fully considered. And in spite of all the difficulties—in great part imaginary—which have hitherto interfered with the acceptance of a positive solution of this problem, it seems to me one which is now not difficult to solve. It must be considered to turn almost wholly upon the possibility of the *de novo* origin of Bacteria; since if such a mode of origin can be proved for them, it must also be conceded for other allied fungoid and algoid units. Evidence which is of the most convincing character when looked at from all sides, now shows that Bacteria are killed by a temperature of 140°F. Yet similar organisms will constantly appear and rapidly multiply within closed flasks containing organic fluids, although the flasks and their contents have been previously exposed for some time to a temperature of 212°F. The latter fact has been admitted by almost all experimenters — including even Spallanzani and Pasteur — and the inference from it must be quite obvious to those who accept this or any lower temperature as the thermal limit of organic life. In experiments yielding positive results, they would have to admit that the progenitors of the new, and more or less rapidly multiplying brood must have been evolved *de novo* within the previously superheated flasks. So that, even if nothing more could be said, the positive results which can almost invariably be obtained in experiments conducted with this temperature, should suffice, in the present state of science, to show that living matter may arise *de novo*—more especially when such a conclusion is also supported by the utter break-down of the opposing Panspermic hypothesis. But much stronger evidence can be adduced; since numerous similarly successful results have been obtained by Pasteur himself, by Pouchet, Mantegazza, Wyman, Cantoni, Ochl, and others— although the closed flasks and their contents had been subjected to the influence of still more destructive temperatures, ranging from 212°F to rather over 300°F. Several of such experiments are now recorded for the first time; and their results cannot be reasonably explained except on the supposition that the living things obtained from the closed flasks had been developed from newly-evolved living matter.

The probabilities in favour of this interpretation of the experimental evidence become, moreover, stronger and stronger in proportion as the problem is viewed by the light derived from various kinds of general evidence, which I have adduced in different parts of this work.

We know that the molecules of elementary or mineral substances combine to form acids and bases by virtue of their own 'inherent' tendencies; that these acids and bases unite so as to produce salts, which, in their turn, will often again combine and give rise to 'double salts.' And at each stage in this series of ascending molecular complexities, we find the products endowed with properties wholly different from those of their constituents. Similarly, amongst the carbon compounds there is abundance of evidence to prove the existence of internal tendencies or molecular properties, which may and do lead to the evolution of more and more complex chemical compounds. And it is such synthetic processes, occurring amongst the molecules of colloidal and allied substances, which seem so often to engender or give 'origin' to a kind of matter possessing that subtle combination of properties to which we are accustomed to apply the epithet 'living.'

The experimental evidence which I have brought forward not only goes to prove that living matter may originate in this natural manner, but that, like other kinds of matter, it comes into being by virtue of the operation of the same laws and molecular properties as suffice to regulate its 'growth.' Would it not be deemed absurd if we were to assume, as a necessity, the existence of one set of agencies in order to bring about the origination of crystalline matter, and of another set for inducing and regulating the growth of crystals? And may it not also be deemed just as absurd and unnecessary that any such demands should be made in reference to the origin of living matter and the growth of organisms?

Both crystalline and living aggregates appear to be constantly separating *de novo* from different fluids, and both kinds of matter now seem to be naturally formable from their elements. It so happens, however, that one of the fundamental properties of living matter—that is to say, its power of undergoing spontaneous division—is constantly entailing results which, owing to their being of a more obvious nature, have long and unduly monopolized the attention of biologists and of the world in general. And yet the existence in living matter of this power of spontaneous division, by which processes of 'reproduction' are brought about, is rendered somewhat less exceptional and mysterious when we consider that a fragment of crystalline matter artificially severed from the parent mass will, under suitable conditions, grow into a crystal similar to the original form. The reproduction of similar matter takes place in each case; and surely the mere fact that the initial reproductive separation may occur 'spontaneously' in the case of living matter, is no argument against the probability that such matter may, like crystalline matter, also come into being by an independent elemental mode of origin.

Our experimental evidence, therefore, merely goes to prove that such an elemental origin of living matter *is* continually taking place at the present day,—that it still comes into being, in fact, by the operation of the same laws, and in the same manner as the majority of scientific men and a large section of the educated public believe that it must have originated in the early days of the earth's history—when 'living' compounds first began to appear upon the cooling surface of our planet. And if such synthetic processes took place then, why should they not take place now? Why should the inherent molecular properties of various kinds of matter have undergone so much alteration? Why should these particular processes of synthesis now be impossible, although other processes of a similar nature still go on?

Whilst no attempt has ever been made to justify or explain such a supposed arbitrary curtailment of natural laws, it happens most fortunately that the ascending series of molecular combinations, to which we have already referred, does not end with the birth of 'living' matter. Steps which were previously beyond the reach of our senses, become, in some newly-discovered terms of the series, capable of ocular demonstration. Whilst invisible colloidal molecules are supposed to combine and undergo re-arrangements in order to produce specks of new-born living matter, such specks of living matter may be actually seen to combine, fuse, and undergo molecular re-arrangements so as to lead to the origin of Fungus-germs, of Amœbæ, of Monads, or of Ciliated Infusoria; and, in the same manner, larger and still more complex living units of an algoid nature may actually be seen to fuse and become altered externally, whilst they undergo those obscure and mysterious molecular re-arrangements whereby they are converted into the embryos of large and complex Rotifers.

Visible phenomena of Synthetic Heterogenesis thus serve, as it were, to demonstrate the mode in which, by invisible processes, the simplest living units may arise. So that after watching all the steps of the more complex phenomena, we may find it less difficult than we should otherwise have done to believe in the occurrence of the simpler process of Archebiosis—more especially when its occurrence is attested by facts and probabilities of the highest independent value.

Again, we know that simple mineral substances may exist in different allotropic conditions, just as numerically-similar combinations of different elements may exist in two or more isomeric states. But, if mere differences in molecular arrangement may cause sulphur or arsenic, on different occasions, to present wholly different appearances and properties; or if a similar alteration in molecular arrangement may lead such salts as mercuric iodide to pass easily from one to another mode of crystallization, it should not be very difficult for us to believe that living matter might also, with comparative ease, undergo somewhat analogous molecular rearrangements, and that such changes might also entail some modifications in the form and other attributes of the living aggregate. And now, as matter of fact, we have to state that the occurrence of Heterogenetic Transformations amongst lower living things and in portions of higher living things have been almost as well attested as the occurrence of allotropic and isomeric modifications amongst different kinds of not-living matter.

Unmistakeable processes of Heterogenesis have been watched over and over again by some of the best observers, amongst whom may be named Turpin, Kützing, Reissek, Hartig, Gros, Pringsheim, Pineau, Carter, Nicolet, Pouchet, Schaaffhausen, Braxton Hicks, and Trécul. And yet the careful investigations of these well-known naturalists have, upon this particular subject, been either wholly disregarded or publicly repudiated by some leading biologists who—not having worked over the same ground themselves—rashly trust to their own theoretical convictions, rather than to the positive observations of so many workers. How unwarrantable this conduct has been, almost any competent person—however sceptical—may learn for himself, if he will but devote two or three months to the careful study of the changes which are apt to take place in the substance of many of the fresh-water Algæ, or in those beautiful green animalized organisms known by the name of Euglenæ, some of whose marvellous transformations were faithfully described more than twenty years ago in the highly valuble but much neglected memoir of Dr. Gros.

The time is doubtless not far distant when it will be a source of much wonder that those who had already heartily adopted the Evolution philosophy could—even in the face of facts long ago known—stop short of a belief in the present and continual occurrence of Archebiosis and Heterogenesis. Do not the very simplest forms of life abound at the present day? And, would the Evolutionist really have us believe that such forms are direct continuations of an equally structureless matter which has existed for millions and millions of years without having undergone any differentiation? Would he have us believe that the simplest and most structureless Amœba of the present day can boast of a line of ancestors stretching back to such far-remote periods that in comparison with them the primæval men were but as things of yesterday? The notion surely is preposterously absurd; or, if true, the fact would be sufficient to overthrow the very first principles of their own Evolution philosophy. Again, may we not see at the present day all those minute shades of difference by which the primordial fissiparous act of reproduction gives place to the more and more specialized forms of bisexual reproduction? Even this could scarcely occur unless the excessively changeable forms of life which supply us with these various transitions were continually seething into existence afresh. Instead of having to do with a pretty accurate picture of the original process of evolution, each sectional mosaic of which has been faithfully transmitted for millions of years with little or no variation, we probably stand face to face with processes that have been independently repeated billions and billions of times—and repeated in a more or less similar manner, simply because the processes themselves have always been the results of the conjoint action of the same external forces in conflict with similar material properties or tendencies. Like causes should produce like results: so that the primordial living units of to-day should undergo changes which are, in the main, similar to those passed through by the units of living matter which first came into being upon the surface of our globe.

Again, we find that the comparatively low forms of life in which all these developmental transitions are embodied, instead of being almost unchangeable—as they ought to be if there were any truth in the contradictory doctrines to which we have already referred —are variable in the highest degree. They pass through the most diverse and astounding transformations, and, as we have endeavoured to show in the Third Part of this work, such organisms are often seen to be derived from matrices wholly unlike themselves.

In fact, these lower forms of life—corresponding pretty closely with the Protista of Prof. Haeckel—form an enormous and ever-growing plexus of vegetal and animal organisms, amongst which transitions from the one to the other mode of growth take place with the greatest ease and frequency. Here Heterogenesis is constantly encountered, and variability reigns supreme, so that those assemblages of definitely recurring individuals, answering to what we call 'species,' are not to be found amongst them. They are essentially transitory and variable forms, which I have proposed to name 'Ephemeromorphs.' Regularly recurring or homogenetically produced types, both animal and vegetal, are, however, constantly arising out of this great ephemeromorphic plexus, either by direct and sudden processes of transformation or by some intermediate and cyclical processes of so-called 'alternate generation.'

And until such assemblages of repeating individuals make their appearance—that is, until Homogenesis becomes the rule—the 'laws of heredity' can scarcely be said to come into operation. Hence the complexly-interrelated individuals, constituting this vast underlying plexus of Infusorial and Cryptogamic life, must remain wholly uninfluenced, so far as their form and structure is concerned, by what Mr. Darwin has termed 'Natural Selection.' Such vegetal and animal organisms, however, gradually tend to become more and more complex. An ascending development takes place, and as this occurs, the causes which originally sufficed to determine their form and structure, and which for a time continue to induce deviations, become less and less capable of bringing about structural modifications during the life of the individual. Changes have now to be perfected in a succession of individuals; and thus is the operation initiated of those subtle and more slowly modifying agencies which have been so admirably illustrated by Mr. Darwin.

Throughout this work, whilst I have been anxious to consider the various aspects of the subject with as much thoroughness as was necessary in order to be able fairly to attempt to establish the truth of the principal doctrines now advanced, I have also tried to simplify the problems as much as possible. A limitation was, moreover, necessitated by the pressing nature of those more strictly professional duties, on account of which I was first induced to enter upon these investigations, and in the midst of which the work has been carried on. A rich harvest, therefore, remains for many other workers who may wish to develop the subject in all its collateral bearings.

These volumes being, in great part, the record of a series of current investigations—each section of which was written whilst the next division of the subject was being investigated—some forbearance may, perhaps, not unfairly be claimed for certain literary defects and inconsistencies, which were to some extent unavoidable. For although this order was definitely planned, yet it has happened that more than three-fourths of the work was actually printed before the new investigations detailed in the latter part were made—and certainly at a time when I had scarcely hoped ever to witness such transformations as I have since been able to follow.

I am deeply impressed with the conviction that we are but upon the threshold of our acquaintance with these marvellous heterogenetic transformations, the discovery of which already affords material for revolutionizing the old foundations of botanical and zoological science. But the path now opened must be followed up by other workers—by faithful and competent observers who are willing zealously to watch and wait through eager hours whilst Nature unfolds her secret processes—by those true students who, instead of being blinded by any existing theories, are content to regard them as useful and modifiable aids to further progress.

QUEEN ANNE STREET, CAVENDISH SQUARE,
May 22, 1872.

CONTENTS.

Index   page xxi

PART I.

The Nature and Source of the Vital Forces, and of Organisable Matter.

CHAPTER I.

The Persistence of Force: Correlation of the Vital and Physical Forces   .. .. *Pages* 1–49

CHAPTER II.

The 'Vital Principle': Nature of Life   50–79

CHAPTER III.

Nature of Organizable Materials and of lowest Living Things 80–128

CHAPTER IV.

Relations of Animal, Vegetable, and Mineral Kingdoms: Theories of Organization   129–168

CHAPTER V.

Modes of Origin of Reproductive Units and of Cells   .. 169–239

PART II.

Archebiosis.

CHAPTER VI.
Meanings attached to term 'Spontaneous Generation' .. 243-264

CHAPTER VII.
Mode of Origin of Primordial Living Things: Nature of Problem 265-305

CHAPTER VIII.
The Limits of 'Vital Resistance' to Heat 306-343

CHAPTER IX.
The Experimental Proof: Untenability of Pasteur's Conclusions 344-399

CHAPTER X.
Physical and Vital Theories of Fermentation 400-427

CHAPTER XI.
Additional Proofs of the Occurrence of Archebiosis .. 428-475

LIST OF ILLUSTRATIONS.

Fig.		Page
1.	Animals found in tufts of Moss and Lichen	106
2.	*Hydra viridis* on Duckweed (Roesel)	112
3.	Representatives of Monera (Haeckel)	119
4.	Animal Cells (Kölliker)	145
5.	Unicellular Organisms	152
6.	Formation of Spore in Vaucheria (Hassall)	174
7.	Development of Zoospores in Achlya (Unger)	180
8.	Development of Spores in Ascomycetous Fungi (Corda)	183
9.	Development of 'Cells' in internodes of Chara (Carter)	187
10.	Reproduction of Protomyxa (Haeckel)	194
11.	Development of Reproductive Units in Amœba (Nicolet)	198
12.	Early Forms of Ova in *Ascaris mystax* (A. Thomson)	201
13.	Graafian Follicles of a Mammal (Coste)	203
14.	Portions of the Ovary of the Thrush (A. Thomson)	205
15.	Segmentation of the Yolk after Fecundation (Kölliker)	209
16.	Development of white blood-corpuscles	216
17.	Some of the Primordial Forms of Life: Bacteria, Torulæ, &c.	272
18.	Other Early Forms of Life from Organic Infusions	274
19.	Oscillatoriæ and other Simple Fresh-water Algæ (Hassall)	276
20.	The 'Micrococci' and 'Cryptococci' of Hallier	284
21.	Sarcina from Saline Solutions	287
22.	Different Developmental Stages of 'Spores' (?) found in an Ammonic Carbonate Solution	290
23.	Organisms found in Infusions of Hay with Carbolic Acid	356

LIST OF ILLUSTRATIONS.

Fig.		Page
24.	Bacteria, Vibriones, and Leptothrix Filaments found in an Infusion of Turnip ..	358
25.	Organisms found in a Simple Solution of Ferric and Ammonic Citrate ..	364
26.	Organisms found in a Solution of Ferric and Ammonic Citrate, with minute fragments of wood ..	365
27.	Fungus from a Solution of Potash and Ammonia Alum with Tartar-emetic ..	367
28.	Torulæ from a Solution of Ammonic Tartrate and Sodic Phosphate ..	369
29.	Fungus from a Solution of Ammonic Tartrate and Sodic Phosphate ..	371
30.	Organisms from a Neutralized Infusion of Turnip ..	442
31.	Protamœbæ, Monads, Torulæ, &c., from an Infusion of Common Cress ..	444
32.	Torulæ from a Neutralized Infusion of Turnip ..	447
33.	Pediastrex from a Solution containing Iron and Ammonic Citrate, &c. ..	448
34.	Green and Colourless Organisms from a Solution of Iron and Ammonic Citrate ..	450
35.	Greenish, Desmid-like Organisms found in a Fluorescent Solution of Iron and Ammonic Citrate ..	453
36.	Spore-like bodies from a Solution of Ammonic Carbonate and Sodic Phosphate ..	462
37.	Bacteria and Spore-like bodies found in a Solution of Ammonic Carbonate and Sodic Phosphate ..	463
38.	Fungus found in a Solution of Ammonic Tartrate and Sodic Phosphate ..	466

INDEX.

(Pages of the Appendix are referred to by Roman Numerals.)

ACHLYA, production of zoospores in, i. 179.
Acinetæ, developmental relationships of, xciv.
Actinophrys, mode of origin of, ii. 381; transformation of Euglenæ into, ii. 456; conversion of, into Ciliated Infusoria, ii. 485; subsequent development of, ii. 505; resolution of Rotifers into, ii. 523; transformation of, into Tardigrades, ii. 524; into Nematoids, ii. 535.
Agardh, on zoospores in Conferva, i. 171.
Agassiz, on relation of Ciliata to Planaria, cvii.
Air, germs in, ii. 6, 7, 264-288.
Algæ, transitions between Fungi and, ii. 159; relations of, to Pediastreæ and Desmids, ii. 160; spores of, ii. 376; interchangeability of Lichens and, ii. 452; lower, relations of, to Lichens, liii-lviii; variability of, lix-lxii; relations of, to Mosses, lxiii-lxvi; to Fungi, lxxvi.
Algoid corpuscles, resolution of Euglenæ into, ii. 412; transformation of, ii. 443; origin of Rotifers from, ii. 510.
Alternate Generation, ii. 564; relations of, to other processes, ii. 566; nature and mode of origin of, ii. 570.

Ammonic Tartrate, preparation of, xvi; crystals of, containing germs, xvi; examination of crystals of, xvii; spores in crystals of, xviii.
Amœbæ, germ-formation in, i. 197; digestion in, ii. 132; interchangeability of Monads and, ii. 218; encystment of, ii. 221; resolution of, into Bacteria, ii. 222; production of, in Moss-radicles, ii. 376; modes of origin of, ii. 381, 388; origin of, in Vaucheria, ii. 395; in Nitella, ii. 404; from Chlorophyll corpuscles, ii. 408; transformation of Euglenæ into, ii. 456; formation of, in Protonema, lxx; relations of, to Fungi, lxxix; to other Infusoria, xc; relations of, to Actinophrys, xcv.
Amylobacter, origin of, ii. 318; conversion of crystalline mass into, ii. 322.
Animal heat, origin of, i. 24; increased by muscular activity, i. 29; increase of, during nerve-activity, i. 40.
Animals, functions of, related to those of plants, i. 129; forms of, interchangeable with those of vegetals, ii. 431, 434.
Antiseptic system of treatment in disease, cxxv.
Arcellinæ, 486; transformation of, into Ciliated Infusoria, ii. 487.

VOL. I.   c

Archebiosis, meaning of, i. 232, 244; views of vitalists antagonistic to, i. 248; theory of, ii. 108; experiments bearing upon, i. 355-370, 434-468, xxx-lii; relation of, to other processes. (Table) ii. 545, 546.
Arlidge, Dr., on Phytozoa, lxxxi.
Ascarides, development of ova of, i. 200.
Astasiæ, modes of origin of, ii. 390, 392, 420; heterogenetic changes in, ii. 434; relations of, to Protococcus, lxxxiii; Dr. Gros on transformations of, lxxxv.

Bacon, Lord, on Heat, i. 6.
Bacteria, views concerning modes of origin of, i. 268; microscopical examination of, i. 294; origin of, compared with that of crystals, i. 298; vital resistance of, to heat, i. 317; living in air, ii. 2, 6, 7; desiccation of, ii. 3-5; different views concerning, ii. 134; variations in development of, ii. 137-140; relations of, to Torulæ, ii. 140-146; in pellicle, ii. 207; production of, from Amœbæ, ii. 222; from embryonal spheres, ii. 401; from Euglenæ, ii. 442; developmental tendencies of, xxii.
Bacteridia, i. 275.
Baer, Von, on development in plants and animals, ii. 125.
Barry, De, on Myxogasteres, lxxix; on development of zoospores in Cystopus, lxxx.
Bathybius, i. 122.
Beale, Dr. Lionel, views concerning living units, i. 153-158; on germs within cells and tissues, ii. 342; Panspermic theory of, ii. 358.
Béchamp, M., Bacteria in cells, ii. 343.
Béclard, M., on development of heat during muscular activity, i. 29.
Bennett, Prof. Hughes, on cellular theory of organization, i. 160, ii. 344; cellular crystals, ii. 59.

Berkeley, Rev. M. J., on nature of Fungi, ii. 153; on Botrytis infestans, ii. 341; development of mushrooms, ii. 433; relations of Fungi to Algæ and Lichens, lxxvi; variability of Fungi, lxxvii; relations of animal and vegetable life, lxxx.
Biocœnosis, nature of, i. 234, (Table) ii. 545, 546.
Biocrasis, ii. 193; nature of, i. 233; heterogenetic, ii. 62, (Table) ii. 545, 546.
Biodiæresis, nature of, i. 233, (Table) ii. 545, 546.
Bioparadosis, nature of, i. 234, (Table) ii. 545, 546.
Birds, their specialized organization, ii. 627.
Black-death, cxxix.
Blood, constituents of, as sources of energy, i. 48; heterogenetic changes in, ii. 332; (Sang de rate) nature of, ii. 362; diseases of, cxii, cxvii.
Bonnet, Charles, on Panspermism, i. 259; theories concerning germs, ii. 266.
Boussingault, M., on vital forces, i. 21; source of nourishment in plants, i. 135.
Braun, Alexander, on formation of seed in Phanerogamia, i. 190; the cell, i. 216; formation of seed-cell in Œdogonium, i. 177.
Brébisson, M. de, on origin of Mosses from Conservæ, ii. 454.
Brongniart, M. Ad., on succession of life on the earth, i. 137-141.
Brownian-movement, i. 318.
Buffon, theory of life, ii. 174.
Burdach, on Heterogeny, i. 246, 261.

Calculi, artificial formation of, ii. 60-65.
Cancer, non-specific nature of, cxiii, cxvii; germs of, cxiii; spread of, cxv; comparable with spread of epidemic diseases, cxviii.

Cantoni, Professor, experiments of, with superheated flasks, i. 436; with bent-neck flasks, ii. 9.
Carpenter, Dr., on correlation of forces, i. 18, 21; continuity of types of Foraminifera, ii. 104; views of, concerning individuality, ii. 553; on Foraminifera, ii. 611; epidemic diseases, cliii.
Carter, Mr. H. J., on development of gonidial-cell in Characere, i. 187; heterogenetic changes in gonidial-cell, ii. 378; transformations in Spirogyra, ii. 387; mode of origin of Otostoma, ii. 479; transformations of Ciliated Infusoria, ii. 497; relations of Amœbæ to Astasiæ, lxxxix.
Cells, formation and nature of, i. 144-158; formation of gonidial-cell in Characeæ, i. 187; Independent origin of, in Phanerogamia, i. 190; as products of development, i. 216; origin of, in Blastemata, i. 220-231; another mode of origin of, i. 231; heterogenetic changes in, ii. 338-345.
Cellular theory, discussion of, i. 143-168.
Chara, M. Nicolet on transformations in filaments of. ii 474; origin of Ciliated Infusoria from protoplasm of, ii. 478.
Characeæ, on development of gonidial-cell in, i. 182. (See *Nitella*.)
Child, Dr., on original evolution of organic life, i. 92; experiments on fermentation, i. 416.
Chlorococcus vesicles, transformation of, into Oxytricha and Plæsconia, ii. 467; aggregations of, into 'winter-egg' of Hydatina, ii. 514; relation of, to Lichens, liii; developmental changes of, liv; production of, from Protonema, lxviii; relation of, to Gleocapsa, lxix.
Chlorophyll, influence of, in metamorphic changes, ii. 435.

Chlorophyll-corpuscles, of Nitella, transformations of, ii. 407; of Euglenæ into Enchelys, ii. 410; of Moss-radicles into Monads, ii. 411; of Vaucheria and Nitella into Desmids, ii. 418.
Cholera, Dr. Aitken on, cxxix, cxxxviii.
Clenkowski, views concerning Acinetæ and Vorticellæ, xciv-xcvi.
Ciliated Infusoria, mode of origin of, ii. 238, 288; reproduction of, ii. 290-297; relation of, to the pellicle, ii. 299; other influences affecting, ii. 302; digestion in, ii. 132; direct transformation of Euglenæ into, ii. 450; production of, from Monads and Amœbæ, ii. 472; origin of, from protoplasm of Chara, ii. 478; from animal matrices, ii. 482; from eggs of Gasteropods and Rotifers, ii. 488; convertibility of forms of, ii. 492; ascending transformations of, ii. 500; encystment of, ii. 500; variations in habitat of, ii. 535; varied modes of reproduction of, xcvii-cv; successive forms of, in infusions, cvi; relations of, to Planaria, cvii.
Closterium, production of, from Euglenæ, ii. 446.
Cobbold, Dr., on Psorosperms, ii. 353.
Cohn, Professor, on Bacteria, i. 270; on constitution of Pellicle, i. 278; on origin of Empusa, ii. 310; experiments with Stephanosphæra, lxxxi; observations on transformations of Protococcus, lxxxii; succession of Ciliata in Infusions, cvi.
Colloidal matter, bodies emerging from solutions of, ii. 65.
Colloids, Professor Graham on distinction between crystalloids and, i. 88; properties of, i. 89; instability of, i. 86; interchangeability of crystalloids and, ii. 38; nature of, ii. 52.

Comparative Experiments, bearing upon occurrence of Archebiosis, xxx-lii.
Conclusions, ii. 633-640.
Confervæ, origin of Mosses from, ii. 451.
Consciousness, i. 42; not co-extensive with Mind, i. 43; changes in sphere of, i. 44; degree of correlation with nerve-action, i. 45; quantitative value of, i. 46.
Contagion, theory of, ii. 360; mode in which brought about, cxviii; early views concerning, cxix.
Contagious element, action of, in parasitic diseases, ii. 361-365.
Contagiousness, degrees of, cxiv. cxxxv; explanation of, cxlviii.
Contractility of muscle, i. 26; dependent on blood-supply, i. 28.
Corda, on Peziza, i. 184.
Crystalline matter, causes of differences in form of, ii. 87; cellular forms of, ii. 59.
Crystalloids, distinction between colloids and, i. 88; interchangeability of states of colloids and, ii. 38.
Crystals, origin of, compared with that of lowest organisms, i. 298, ii. 71-85; Mr. Rainey on formation of modifications of, i. 302; formation of, under different conditions, ii. 55-65; size of, depends upon rate of collocation, ii. 69; influence of conditions on forms of, ii. 87, 113; development of, ii. 114.

Darwin, Dr. Erasmus, views on Organization, ii. 518.
Darwin, Mr., on Natural Selection, ii. 572, 576; influence of new conditions upon species, ii. 580, 591; not a believer in Progressive Development, ii. 590; convertibility of peach and nectarine, ii. 596, 598; Correlated Variability, ii. 601; Pangenesis, ii. 601;

affiliation of existing organisms, ii. 606; variability of lower organisms, ii. 607; stability of species through long periods, ii. 609.
Davaine, M., on Bacteridia, i. 275; observations on Sang de rate, ii. 362.
Davy, Sir Humphrey, on Heat, i. 8.
Decolourization, process of, in development of Nematoids and Rotifers, ii. 532.
Desmids, modes of origin of, ii. 412, 416, 418, 443, 446, 451; mode of reproduction of, ii. 420; convertibility of, into Diatoms or Algæ, ii. 455.
Diatoms, origin of, ii. 412, 416, 418, 441, 444, 453; mode of reproduction of, ii. 420; terminal forms of a divergent series, ii. 455.
Diseases of skin, parasitic, ii. 346; blood-changes in, ii. 361; nature of, cxi; causes of, cxi; of general nature, ii. 360, cxii; of special nature, cxiii. Epidemic, mortality from, cix; importance of, cx; problems as to origin of, cx, cxlv, cli-clv; nature of, cxvii, cxlix; relations of, to Cancer and Tubercle, cxvii; spread of, cxviii; doctrines concerning, influenced by views on Fermentation, cx, cxx, cxlix; predisposing causes of, clii; independent origin of, clii; contagious, how related to non-contagious, cxxx; classification of, cxlvi; how differing from general parasitic diseases, cxlvii.
Distomata, direct development of some, explained, ii. 571.
Dumas, M., functions of animals and plants compared, i. 130, 142.
Dysentery, cxxxviii.

Ehrenberg, on multiplication of Infusoria, i. 262.
Embryonal areas of pellicle, nature and developmental transforma-

tions of, ii. 198-254; spheres, changes in, ii. 401.
Empusa, nature of, ii. 330.
Entozoa, ii. 309.
Ephemeromorphs, nature of, ii. 559; relation of, to crystals, ii. 571; not influenced by Natural Selection, ii. 572; causes which regulate their structure, ii. 620; have no long line of ancestors, ii. 606; Foraminifera to be included amongst, ii. 613.
Epochs, Geological, forms of life in, ii. 621.
Erysipelas, cxxxiv.
Estor, M., Bacteria in cells of animals, ii. 342.
Euglenæ, modes of origin of, ii. 411; heterogenetic transformations of, ii. 434; into fungus-germs, ii. 416; into Monads, ii. 440; into Diatoms, ii. 441; into Algoid corpuscles, ii. 442; external vesiculation of, ii. 436, 440; minor modifications of, ii. 443; transformation of, into Diatoms, ii. 444; into Desmids and Pediastreæ, ii. 446; into Vaucheria filament, ii. 449; into Actinophrys and Amœbæ, ii. 456; direct transformation of, into Ciliated Infusoria, ii. 459; into Oxytricha and Trichoda, ii. 462; into Vorticella, ii. 464, 504; into Amœbæ and Actinophrys, ii. 505; into Rotifers, ii. 506, 518, 525; into Tardigrades and Nematoids, ii. 525; into Nematoids, ii. 527; relations of, to Protococcus and Oscillatoriæ, lxxxii; on transformations of, lxxxv.
Evolution, hypothesis of, i. 92; artificial, i. 92; of complex chemical compounds, ii. 24; simple, ii. 121; compound, ii. 122.

Faraday, on indestructibility of force, i. 15.
Fermentation, cause of, related to origin of life, i. 400; Liebig's physical theory of, i. 403; vital theory of, held by Pasteur and others, i. 404; presence of oxygen not essential for initiation of, i. 416; conclusions on subject of, i. 420; three principal modes of, i. 423; analogy of, to vital processes, i. 425, ii. 186; occurrence of, in bent-neck flasks, ii. 12; two degrees of, ii. 14; theories of, in their bearing upon Contagious Diseases, cxlix.
Fevers, Intermittent and Remittent, cxxxv; Yellow, cxxxvii; Typhoid and Relapsing, cxl; Typhus, cxl, cxlii, cliv; Scarlet, cxliii, cliv.
Flagellum of Monads, development of, ii. 212.
Fluidity, state of, ii. 42.
Food, relation of, to vital forces, ii. 183; putrid articles of, cxliv.
Foraminifera, ancient descent of, ii. 104; nature of, ii. 611; types of, explanation of apparent persistence of, ii. 613.
Force, inseparability of matter and, i. 5; indestructibility of, i. 14; origin and distribution of, in living bodies, ii. 181.
Fox, Dr. Tilbury, on Parasitic skin-diseases, ii. 347.
Fox, Dr. Wilson, experiments on inoculability of Tubercle, cxiv.
Frankland, Prof., on vital and physical forces, i. 22, 54; mode of preparation of experimental flasks, ii. 438.
Fungi, relation of, to Bacteria, ii. 134; to Amœbæ and Monads, ii. 157; to Algæ and Lichens, ii. 159; mode of origin of microscopic, ii. 338; presence of, in closed cavities, ii. 340; influence of conditions on development of, ii. 111; exogenous origin of, from Euglenæ, ii. 436; in solutions containing silicates, xi-xiii; relations of, to Algæ and Lichens, lxxvi; to Amœbæ, lxxix; variability of, lxxvii.

INDEX.

Fungus-germs, mode of origin of, i. 183, ii. 203; development of, in Ammonic-carbonate solution, i. 288; vital resistance of, to heat, i. 315; origin of, in pellicle, from segmentation of Amœbæ, ii. 226; origin of, from embryonal areas, ii. 233; in blood, ii. 331; from milk-globules, ii. 310; from embryonal spheres, ii. 401; resolution of Euglenæ into, ii. 436; independent origin of, within closed flasks (see *Archebiosis*, experiments relating to).

Gavarret, M., on source of energy in animals, i. 23, 48; mode of action of muscle, i. 30.
Gay-Lussac, views of, concerning fermentation, i. 416.
Gemmæ, ii. 520.
Gerhardt, on fermentation, i. 416.
Germ-cells, ii. 96.
Germs, existence of, in air, ii. 305, 338; two theories concerning, ii. 266; M. Pasteur on unequal distribution of, ii. 273; M. Pouchet and others on atmospheric, ii. 275-288; distribution of those of Rotifers and Nematoids, ii. 535; absence of, in crystals, xv; abundance of, in old crystals, xxv; presence of, in crystals of Ammonic Tartrate, xvi, xviii; mode of origin of, xix, xxi, xxiii, xxv-xxix; absence of, in newly-formed crystals, xxi, xxiv.
Germ-theory of disease, cxx-cxxvii.
Glanders, cxxxii.
Gleocapsa, origin of, ii. 411.
Gomphonema, origin of, ii. 442.
Gonidia, variation in modes of growth of, ii. 164; of Algæ, Lichens, and Mosses, indistinguishable from one another, lxxiii.
Gonidial-cell, heterogenetic changes in, ii. 378.
Goodsir, Prof., on centres of nutrition, i. 146.

Graham, Prof., on colloids, i. 89, ii. 53.
Grant, Prof., views concerning evolution of living things, ii. 165; cause of organization, ii. 584.
Gregarinæ, nature of, xcii; relations of, to Amœbæ, xci; to Psorospermæ, xcii.
Gros, Dr., transformations of chlorophyll corpuscles of Euglenæ, ii. 410; origin of Desmids and Diatoms, ii. 412; heterogenetic changes in Astasiæ and Euglenæ, ii. 434; transformation of Euglenæ into Diatoms, ii. 444; into Micrasterias and Arthrodesmus, ii. 448; into Confervæ, ii. 451; origin of Mosses from Confervæ, ii. 453; direct transformation of Euglenæ into Ciliated Infusoria, ii. 459; origin of Vorticella as outgrowth from algoid filaments, ii. 470; process of Pangenesis in Rotifers, ii. 484; origin of Ciliated Infusoria from Rotifer-eggs, ii. 488; ascending transformations of Ciliated Infusoria, ii. 500; transformation of Actinophrys into Ciliated Infusoria or Rotifers, ii. 505; of winter-spore of Volvox into Rotifers, ii. 506; of Euglenæ into Rotifers, ii. 507; of Euglenæ into Nematoids, ii. 537; origin of Entozoa, ii. 539; transformations of Euglenæ and Astasiæ, lxxxv.
Grove, Mr., on correlation of physical forces, i. 9, 18.
Gruithuisen, on fermentative changes in infusions, i. 418.
Guérin-Méneville, M., on independent origin of Muscardine, ii. 326.

Haeckel, Prof., on original evolution of Life, i. 93; Protista and divisions of, i. 115; reproduction of Protomyxa, i. 193.
Halford, Prof., on snake-poisoning, cxxviii.

Hallier, Prof., on microcococi, i. 283.
Hartig, Prof., on transformation of Phytozoa of Liverworts, lxxiv.
Harvey, William, on Heterogenesis, i. 255.
Hassall, Dr. A. H., on formation of spore of Vaucheria, i. 173.
Heat, as a mode of motion, i. 7; relation of, to mechanical energy, i. 8-12; influence of, on vital processes, i. 21; its relation to nerve functions, i. 35; vital resistance to, i. 311; resistance of spores of Fungi to, i. 316; of Bacteria and Vibriones to, i. 317, 429; dissociating effect of, on compounds, ii. 43.
Heredity, law of, ii. 94-103.
Heterogenesis, i. 245; distinction between Archebiosis and, i. 249; various modes in which it may occur, (Table) i. 252; ancient and modern views concerning, ii. 172-181; classification of varieties of, ii. 182; in products of animal secretions, ii. 310; in tissues of plants, ii. 317; frequency of, amongst lowest organisms, ii. 561; varieties of, ii. 563; origin of Monads, Fungus-germs, Ciliata, and Rotifers, by synthetic, ii. 192-263, 514-521; limits to, ii. 539; future researches connected with, ii. 540; different varieties of, (Table) ii. 545.
Hicks, Dr. Braxton, production of Amœbæ in moss-radicles, ii. 376; of Monads, ii. 410; Gleocapsa, ii. 411; variability of lower Algæ and their relations to Lichens and Mosses, lili-lxxiii.
Hildgard, Mr. T. C., mode of origin of Vorticella, ii. 470; on transformations of Ciliata, ii. 495.
Hofmeister, on free cell-formation in Phanerogamia, i. 190.
Holland, Sir Henry, on spread of Epidemic Diseases, cxix.
Homogeny, meaning of term, i. 245.
Hooping-cough, cxliii, cliv.

Huxley, Prof., on Bathybius, i. 121; on cellular theory, i. 158; doctrine concerning living matter, i. 310; views concerning Individuality, ii. 553; on persistent types, ii. 614.
Hydatina, origin of, from Chlorococcus corpuscles, ii. 514; from Euglenæ, ii. 518.
Hydrophobia, cxxx, cxxxii, cxlviii.

Individual, views concerning meaning of term, ii. 542; nature of, ii. 569.
Individuality, views concerning, ii. 553; objections to views of Dr. Carpenter and Prof. Huxley, ii. 553-556.
Influenza, ccxxix.
Iron, influence of, on new-born protoplasm, ii. 157.
Itzigsohn, on transformation of Oscillatoriæ, lxxxiii.

Johnson, Mr. Metcalfe, convertibility of Ciliated Infusoria, ii. 496; transformation of these into Rotifers, ii. 504.
Jones, Dr. Bence, on Physical Theory of Life, i. 62.

Lamarck, doctrines of, concerning Life, i. 369; cause of Organization, ii. 584.
Laticiferous vessels, alterations in globules of, ii. 318.
Lavoisier, M., on source of animal heat, i. 25.
Leptothrix filaments, description of, i. 277; development of, ii. 138, xxii.
Leucocytes, mode of origin of, i. 221.
Lewes, Mr. G. H., on neurility, i. 36; life and organization, i. 69; on multiple evolutions of living matter, ii. 75; on theories of development, ii. 168.
Lichens, origin of spores in, i. 193;

relations of, to Fungi, ii. 159; to lower Algæ, liii–lviii; to Mosses and Fungi, lxvi; Interchangeability of Algæ, ii. 412.
Liebig, Baron, on physical theory of fermentation, i. 403; analogy of fermentation to some vital processes, i. 425; formation of albuminates in plants, ii. 30.
Life, views of ancient philosophers concerning, i. 56; vitalistic theories of, i. 59; Dr. Bence Jones on physical theory of, i. 62; definitions of, i. 70–77; dependent upon certain material collocations, i. 78; not abruptly limited, i. 79; speculations concerning original evolution of, i. 93; physical theory of, reconcilable with vital phenomena, i. 104; succession of, on the earth, i. 137–142; characteristics of, displayed by protoplasm, i. 153; doctrines concerning, i. 308; destruction of, by heat, ii. 3; evolution of, ii. 103; dependence of, upon decomposition, ii. 185; theories concerning, ii. 174; variability of primordial forms of, ii. 110, 137, 143, 145.
Lindley, Dr., on reproduction of Algals by zoospores, i. 171; on zoospores in Achlya, i. 180.
Lindsay, Dr. Lauder, on relationship between Fungi and Lichens, ii. 159.
Living matter, conversion of not-living into, i. 101, ii. 77; no distinct line between not-living and, i. 127; influence of heat upon, i. 429; origin of, from colloid molecules, ii. 26; process of production of, ii. 27; the result of molecular combination, ii. 27; production of, in saline solutions, ii. 30; influence of organic impurities on evolution of, within closed flasks, ii. 33; influence of external conditions on development of, ii. 107; nature of, ii. 123; differentiation of, identical with organization, ii. 127; discontinuous growth of, ii. 138; various forms assumed by new-born, ii. 155; influence of iron upon, ii. 158; formation of, in living organisms, ii. 185; homogeneous, tends to become heterogeneous, ii. 585; heterogeneity of, principally dependent on internal polarities, ii. 586; initial differences of, ii. 592; possibility of silicon replacing carbon in, x.

Living things, definition of, i. 71; nature of matter of, i. 83, 96; origin of lowest, compared with that of crystals, i. 298; resistance of, to heat, i. 317, 429; occurrence of, in vacuo, i. 347–350; origin of, from organic matter, ii. 308; persistence of forms of lowest, ii. 104–108; modes of origin of, ii. 545; nature of lowest, ii. 557; Developmental tendencies of, ii. 558.

Longet, on contractility of muscle, i. 28.

Lyell, Sir Chas., on geological record, ii. 623.

Maddox, Dr., on atmospheric germs, ii. 283.
Malaria, cxxxv.
Man, origin of, ii. 622, 628; his advent, ii. 624; development of brain of, ii. 628, 630; his intellectual and moral nature, ii. 629; probable date of first appearance, ii. 629; limits to variation of external form of, ii. 630; improvement in race of, ii. 631; prejudices concerning origin of, ii. 631; future of the race, ii. 633.
Mantegazza, Prof., researches of, i. 261, 434.
Matter, indestructibility of, i. 3; inseparability of force and, i. 4.
Max Schultze, nature of cell, i. 150.
Measles, cxliii, cliv.
Medicine, practice of, influenced by theories, cix.

Medusæ, direct development of some explained, ii. 571.
Metamorphosis (see *Transformation*).
Meunier, M. Victor, experiments of, with bent-neck flasks, ii. 8.
Micrococci, Prof. Hallier, i. 283.
Milk-globules, conversion of, into fungus-germs, ii. 310.
Milne-Edwards, M., on Panspermism, ii. 271.
Mites, probable mode of origin of, ii. 540; reproduction in, ii. 551.
Mivart, Mr. St. G., on cause of organization, ii. 583; on internal tendencies to, ii. 601.
Molecular composition, nature of bodies dependent upon, ii. 49.
Monads, description of, i. 267; evolution of, ii. 196, 368; origin of, in pellicle, ii. 196, 212, 214; interchangeability of Amœbæ and, ii. 218; origin of, from embryonal spheres of Nitella, ii. 402; from chlorophyll corpuscles, ii. 409; from outgrowths of Euglenæ, ii. 436; resolution of Euglenæ into, ii. 440.
Monera, growth and reproduction of, i. 153.
Montgomery, on cell-forms assumed by Myeline, i. 52.
Mosses, origin of, from Confervæ, ii. 452; observations of M. de Brébisson on, ii. 454; relations of, to Lichens and Algæ, lxii-lxvi.
Moxon, Dr., on fission of Ciliated Infusoria, ii. 291.
Mucous membranes, development of organisms on, ii. 345.
Müller, O. F., on spontaneous generation, ii. 179.
Mumps, cxxxii.
Murchison, Dr., on origin of fevers, cxl.
Murphy, Mr., on origin of species in wild state, ii. 598.
Muscardine, nature of, ii. 324-330.
Muscle, contractility of, i. 26; mode of action of, i. 30; source of power in contraction of, i. 33, 54.
Mushrooms, cultivation of, ii. 433.

Naïdes, a probable origin of, ii. 540.
Natural Selection, ii. 107; Mr. Darwin on, ii. 572; meaning of phrase, ii. 572-576; limitation to influence of, ii. 573; two meanings of, ii. 574, 600.
Nectarine, convertibility of, and Peach, ii. 596, 598.
Needham, on spontaneous generation, i. 258; theory of life, ii. 174.
Nematoidea, development of ova in, i. 200; origin of, from Euglenæ, ii. 466; transformation of Actinophrys into, ii. 525; mode of origin of, from resting-spore of Vaucheria, ii. 529; reproduction in, ii. 532.
Nerve activity, source of heat during, i. 40.
Nervous system, constituents of, i. 35; functions of, dependent on blood-supply, i. 37; persistence of function after apparent death, i. 37.
Neurility, i. 36.
Newport, Mr., on vital forces, i. 17.
Nicolet, on germ-formation in Amœbæ, i. 197; modes of origin of Amœbæ and Actinophrys, ii. 382; mode of origin and transformations of Trichomonas, ii. 384; transformations in Chara filaments, ii. 474; heterogenetic origin of Rotifers, ii. 509; on Amœbæ, xc.
Nitella, transformations in, ii. 399; transformations of Chlorophyll corpuscles of, into Monads and Amœbæ, ii. 407; formation of embryonal spheres in, ii. 400; their transformations into Bacteria and Pythium corpuscles, ii. 401; into Monads, ii. 402; into Amœbæ and Actinophrys, ii. 404; into Ciliated Infusoria, ii. 404;

into complex egg-like bodies, ii. 405.
Nordmann, M., production of Ciliated buds from embryos of Gasteropods, ii. 488.

Œdogonium, mode of origin of 'seed-cell' in, i. 177.
Onimus, M., on mode of origin of leucocytes, i. 221.
Organic compounds, mode of formation of, in plants, i. 23; influence of physical forces on evolution of, ii. 38; artificial production of, i. 50, 94; views concerning, i. 81.
Organic molecules, Buffon on, ii. 174.
Organisms, desiccation of, i. 104; tenacity of life in lowest, i. 106; death of higher, i. 108; degree of individuation in, i. 111; death in lower, i. 112; classification of lowest, i. 114; vital resistance of, to heat, i. 313; multiplication of, truest test of life, i. 320; views concerning origin of, ii. 71; on independent evolutions of, ii. 75; reproduction amongst, ii. 87-103, 116; cause of reproduction of, ii. 129; origin of green, ii. 157; development of corpuscular, ii. 198; segmentation of lower, into fungus-germs, ii. 226; mode of origin of, in pellicle, ii. 235; assumptions respecting, ii. 254; origin of living units from pre-existing, ii. 308; presence of, in bent-neck flasks, ii. 8; variability of lowest, ii. 259, 557, 607; modes of death of, ii. 371; tendency of, to develop into higher, ii. 432; convertibility of lower, ii. 492, 558; influence of size of heterogenetic matrix on forms of, ii. 471; modes of reproduction in, ii. 548; frequency of heterogenesis amongst lowest, ii. 561; varieties of heterogenesis amongst, ii. 563; limits to, ii. 609, 610; lowest, of present day, their descent, ii. 617.
Organizable matter, nature and composition of, i. 83; molecular re-arrangement of, i. 97; physical explanation of process, i. 98.
Organization, discussion of cellular theory of, i. 158; molecular theory of, harmonizes with evolution hypothesis, i. 162; differentiation identical with, ii. 127; causes regulating complexity of, ii. 130; existence of internal principle of, ii. 582; internal tendencies to, ii. 591, 603; Dr. Erasmus Darwin's views on, ii. 583; Prof. Owen and Mr. St. George Mivart on cause of, ii. 583; Lamarck and Prof. Grant on cause of, ii. 584; nature of internal principle of, ii. 585; this not believed in by Mr. Spencer and Mr. Darwin, ii. 585-594; strength of internal principle shown by similarity of lowest organisms in different regions, ii. 593.
Origin of living things, experiments relating to, with calcined air, i. 337-343; different results obtained by other experimenters, i. 344; experiments relating to, with organic solutions, i. 345-360; remarks on, i. 360; experiments relating to, with saline solutions, i. 363-372; remarks on, i. 372; M. Pasteur's experiments and views concerning, i. 374-384; comparative experiments connected with, i. 385-391, ii. 18; deleterious effects of acidity of solution increased by heat, i. 392-396; experiments concerning, in superheated flasks, i. 441-470; remarks on, i. 471-475; facilitated by diminution of pressure, ii. 20; occurring in organic solutions, ii. 22, 71; theoretical views respecting, ii. 254.
Otostoma, origin and development, ii. 479; origin of, from Nitella filament, ii. 482.

Ova, in lower animals, i. 199-202; in higher animals, i. 203-211.
Owen, Prof., on cause of organization, ii. 583; internal organizing tendencies, ii. 591.
Oxytricha, origin of, from Euglenæ, ii. 462; from Chlorococcus vesicles, ii. 467; metamorphosis of Vorticella into, ii. 493; transformation of, into Trichoda, ii. 496.

Palæontological Record, interpretation of, ii. 620; imperfection of, ii. 621.
Pangenesis, Mr. Darwin's hypothesis of, ii. 98, 603; previous use of term by Dr. Gros, ii. 484;—in Tardigrades, ii. 549; peculiarities of, in Tardigrades and Rotifers, ii. 551.
Panspermism, views of Spallanzani and Bonnet on, i. 259; nature of theories, ii. 267; untenability of hypothesis of, ii. 305, 359, 367, 548.
Paramecium, evolution of, from pellicle, ii. 240-250; its conversion into Nassula, ii. 251; transformations of, ii. 496.
Parasites, higher, ii. 309, 539; lower, in blood of animals, ii. 324-337; in tissues of plants, ii. 317, 338-342; in tissues of animals, ii. 341-358; within eggs of, ii. 366.
Pasteur, M., on resistance to heat of spores of fungi, i. 316; double nature of results in experiments by, i. 340, 345, 374, 384; vital theory of fermentation, i. 404; his explanation of experiments with bent-neck flasks, ii. 11; on atmospheric germs, ii. 271-275, 286.
Peach, converted into Nectarine, ii. 596, 598.
Peacock, black-shouldered, origin of, ii. 591.
Pébrine, nature of, ii. 352, cxxii.

Pellicle, formation of, on organic infusion, i. 366; composition of, i. 277, ii. 193; formation of embryonal areas in, ii. 198; remarks concerning changes in, ii. 205; series of changes in, leading to evolution of Monads, ii. 215; other changes in, leading to evolution of Fungus-germs, ii. 231-235; evolution of Ciliated Infusoria from, ii. 237-254; changes in, throw light upon mode of origin of living matter, ii. 262; conditions favourable to production of Ciliated Infusoria, ii. 241, 299.
Penicillium, evolution of, ii. 195; conversion of milk-globules into, ii. 310.
Peranemata, origin of, from Euglenæ, ii. 459; from Rotifers, ii. 484; conversion of, into Ciliated Infusoria, ii. 485.
Peziza, Corda on formation of spores in, i. 184.
Philodinæ, mode of origin of, ii. 504.
Physcia, formation of spore in, i. 186.
Physical Forces, convertibility of, i. 13; correlation of vital and, i. 16-49, 63; action of, upon living tissues, i. 98; influence of, on evolution of organic compounds, ii. 38.
Physiological units, ii. 23, 90, 98, 603.
Phytoids, ii. 542, 553.
Pineau, M., on formation of spore in Physcia, i. 186; observations of heterogenetic changes, i. 261; on origin of Penicillium, ii. 195; of Monads, ii. 196; of Vorticellæ, ii. 252, 471; of Enchelys, ii. 238; metamorphoses of Vorticellæ into Oxytrichæ, ii. 493.
Plæsconia, origin of, from Chlorococcus vesicles, ii. 467.
Plague, cxliii.
Plants, functions of, related to those of Animals, i. 129; M. Brongniart on development of, in past

ages, i. 137; M. Saussure on, i. 139; growth of, ii. 27; occurrence of heterogenesis in, ii. 317.
Plastide-particles, i. 267, 270.
Plastides, i. 157, 267.
Polarity, Herbert Spencer on organic, ii. 23, 91; its operation in higher organisms, ii. 595; an everpotent cause of form and structure, ii. 601.
Pouchet, M., on vital force, i. 248; on spontaneous generation, i. 263; interchangeability of forms of Fungi, ii. 141; heterogenesis and vitalism, ii. 180; origin of Monads, ii. 195; of Paramecia, ii. 240; of Vorticellæ, ii. 471; atmospheric germs, ii. 275; apparatus for showing connection of Ciliata with Pellicle, ii. 300.
Pringsheim, Prof., on transformations in Algæ, ii. 374.
Pritchard, on Algæ and their allies, ii. 160; modes of succession of organisms in infusions, ii. 502; variations in habitat of Infusoria, ii. 535.
Progressive development, ii. 583, 588, 590, 602.
Protamœbæ, i. 117, 121, 125.
Protista, i. 115-126; divisions of, i. 117; modes of reproduction amongst, i. 116, 191, ii. 548.
Protococcus, relation of, to Algæ, Lichens, and Mosses, ii. 163; products of transformations of, lxxii.
Protomyxa, process of reproduction in, i. 193.
Protonema, changes of, lxvi-lxxii.
Protoplasm, properties of, i. 127; independent origin of, ii. 31, 77.
Protoplasta, i. 153; development of germs in, i. 197.
Psorosperms, ii. 352, cxxii.
Puerperal Fever, cxxxiv.
Pyæmia, cxxxiv.

Rainey, Mr., on 'molecular coalescence,' i. 51; on formation of Calculi, ii. 60; nature of starch-grains, ii. 66.
Redi, on spontaneous generation, i. 257.
Reinsch, Prof., on metamorphoses of Chlorophyll corpuscles and pollen-grains, ii. 432.
Reproduction, act of, best sign of life of Bacteria, i. 320; fundamental nature, ii. 91; limitations of process in complex organisms, ii. 95; in Rotifers, ii. 522; sexual —mode of evolution of, ii. 548, 552; ultimate nature of, ii. 561; sexual modes, commencement of, ii. 564; nature of 'alternate' processes of, ii. 565.
Reproduction, different modes of, Table facing ii. 552.
Reproductive units, mode of origin of, i. 169-214, 232.
Robin, Charles, on independent origin of Leucocytes, i. 220; blood-change in parasitic diseases, ii. 361.
Rotifers, resolution of, into Actinophrys and Peranema, ii. 484; into Arcellinæ, ii. 486; origin of Ciliated Infusoria from eggs of, ii. 488; modes of analytic heterogenesis in, ii. 489; heterogenetic modes of origin of, ii. 501-523; reproduction in, ii. 522, 549.
Rumford, Count, heat as a mode of motion, i. 7.

Samuelson, Mr. James, on atmospheric germs, ii. 280.
Sanderson, Dr. Burdon, effect of desiccation on Bacteria, ii. 5; Microzymes in air, ii. 7; experiments on inoculability of Tubercle, cxiv.
Sang de rate, M. Davaine on, ii. 362.
Sarcina, i. 286; nature of, iii; products allied to, v; bodies resembling, in silicated solution, xiv.
Schaaffhausen, Prof., on heterogenetic transformations, ii. 453, 499.

INDEX.

Schelling, theory of life, i. 77.
Schleiden, sources of nutriment of plants, i. 136.
Schulze, on Panspermism, i. 262.
Schwann, on origin of cells, i. 144; on Panspermism, i. 262; method of experimentation with calcined air, i. 337.
Scolecida, modes of origin of representatives of, ii. 539.
Séguin, M., on convertibility of forces, i. 9.
Silicates, solutions of, containing Fungi, xi-xiii; spiral fibres, xiv; bodies resembling Sarcina, xiv.
Silicon, as a possible substitute for carbon in living matter, x.
Small-pox, views on, cxxvii; origin of, cxliv; contagiousness of, cxlix.
Snake-poisoning, cxxviii, cxxx.
Snow-flakes, ii. 280.
Solution, nature of process, ii. 44.
Spallanzani, l'Abbé, on Panspermism, i. 259.
Species, meaning of term, ii. 547; mutability of, ii. 548; nothing corresponding to, amongst lower forms, ii. 568; nature of, ii. 569; influenced by change in external conditions, ii. 577-582; by use and disuse, ii. 577; to what extent influenced by natural selection, ii. 578; Darwin on influence of new external conditions upon, ii. 591; variation of, ii. 598; frequency of spontaneous variation in unknown, ii. 599; modes in which transmutations are brought about, ii. 600; Mr. Darwin's views concerning, ii. 601-603.
Spencer, Mr. Herbert, on convertibility of forces, i. 13; on meaning of persistence force, i. 14; correlation of vital and physical forces, i. 22; consciousness, i. 45; morphological development, i. 52; characteristics of living things, i. 74; elements of organizable matter, i. 84; instability of protein compounds, i. 86; original evolution of life, i. 97; artificial evolution of organic matter, i. 94; operation of physical forces upon living tissues, i. 98; evolution of living matter, i. 163; organic polarity, ii. 23; physiological units, ii. 23, 90, 98; law of heredity, ii. 94, 97; nature of evolution, ii. 130; two meanings of natural selection, ii. 573; denies existence of internal organizing tendencies, ii. 585; cause of organization, ii. 587; his explanation of existence of undifferentiated organisms in present day, ii. 587-589; physiological units, ii. 603; limits to variability of species, ii. 610.
Spermatozoa, development of, i. 213.
Sperm-cells, ii. 96.
Spiral fibres, v; where found, viii; in association with mycelium, viii; in silicated solution, xiv.
Spirillum, i. 277, ii. 139.
Spirogyra, transformations in, ii. 387-393.
Spontaneous Generation, reason for rejecting term, i. 244; views of ancient writers concerning, i. 253; other views concerning, i. 255-263; two processes included under term, ii. 172.
Spores, mode of formation of, in Œdogonium, i. 177; in Zygnemaceæ, i. 179; in Fungi and Lichens, i. 183; in Peziza, i. 184; in Hydrodictyon, i. 186; Physcia, i. 186.
Starch-grains, production of, ii. 65.
Steenstrup, on alternate generation, ii. 565.
Stein, views concerning Acinetæ and Vorticellæ, xciv-xcvii.
Survival of the fittest, ii. 575.
Syphilis, cxxxii.

Tables relating to:—(1) origin of living things, i. 252; (2) modes of origin of independent living units, ii. 515; (3) modes of reproduction with reference to the origin and gradual appearance of sexual differentiation, *Table* facing ii. 552; (4) modes of development in relation to sexual multiplication occurring during its progress, ii. 567; (5) causes which determine forms of organisms, ii. 600; (6) communicable diseases, cxlvi.

Tardigrades, origin of, from Euglenæ, ii. 466; transformation of Actinophrys into, ii. 524; reproduction in, ii. 533; Pangenesis in, ii. 549; peculiarities of Pangenesis in, ii. 551.

Theory, test of true, ii. 605.

Thomson, Prof. Allen, on development of ova in Ascarides, i. 200; on individuality, ii. 556.

Thomson, Sir William, on geological time, ii. 619.

Torulæ, i. 273; mode of origin of, in solutions, i. 281; nature of, ii. 141; development of, into Fungi, ii. 145–154; interchangeability of Bacteria and, ii. 143; origin of, within closed flasks (see *Arebrbiosis*, experiments relating to).

Transformations, in Spirogyra, ii. 374, 387; in Moss-radicles, ii. 376; in Gonidial-cell, ii. 378; of Trichomonas, ii 384; in Vaucheria, ii. 394; in Nitella, ii. 399; of Chlorophyll vesicles, ii. 415; of Chlorophyll vesicles of Vaucheria, Nitella, etc. into Desmids, ii. 418; of cell-contents of Conserva into Euglenæ, ii. 421; of Spirogyra into Astasiæ, ii. 421; of Potamogeton into Euglenæ, ii. 422; M. Kützing on, of vegetable organisms, ii. 431; Reissek on, of Chlorophyll vesicles and pollen-grains, ii. 432; of Euglenæ, ii. 436–466; of Ciliated Infusoria, ii. 492–504; of Actinophrys into Rotifers, ii. 504; of Vegetal vesicles into Rotifers, ii. 506-521; of Rotifers into Nematoids, ii. 522; of Actinophrys into Nematoids and Tardigrades, ii. 524; of Euglenæ into Rotifers, Tardigrades, and Nematoids, ii. 525; of resting-spore of Vaucheria into Nematoids, ii. 528.

Trécul, M., on development of Torulæ, ii. 147; origin of Amylobacter, ii. 318.

Tréviranus, experiments in reference to heterogeny, i. 259.

Trichoda, origin of, from Euglenæ, ii. 462; metamorphosis of Oxytrica into, ii. 496.

Trichomonas, origin and transformations of, ii. 384.

Tubercle, non-specific nature of, cxliii, cxvii; generalization of, cxvi.

Turpin, M., heterogenetic changes in milk-globules, ii. 311; mode of origin of Uredo, ii. 339.

Types, persistence of, ii. 606; persistent, Prof. Huxley on, ii. 615; explanation of persistent, ii. 616–619; dominant, ii. 621, 623; of fish and insect, ii. 624; estimation of worth of, ii. 625; vertebrate, ii. 626; elaboration of, ii. 617.

Units, physiological, ii. 23, 90, 98, ii. 603.

Variation, 'spontaneous,' meaning of, ii. 595; instances of, ii. 596–599.

Varicella, cxliii.

Vaucheria, formation of spore of, i. 173; transformations in, ii. 391; of spore of, into Nematoids, ii. 528.

Vegetable forms, interchangeability of animal and, ii. 431, 434.

Vibriones, nature of, i. 274; vital resistance of, to heat, i. 317.

Virchow, Prof., doctrines concerning, i. 148; cellular pathology, i. 158; activities of tissue-elements, i. 167.

Vital forces, correlation of physical and, i. 16–49, 60; dependent on oxidation of blood, i. 48; transmutation of physical force into, i. 67; no evidence for existence of a special, i. 83; relation of food to, ii. 183.

Vital processes, effect of light and heat upon, i. 16; amenable to physico-chemical laws, i. 54; inexplicable nature of most intimate, i. 55, ii. 256, 334; analogy of fermentation to, i. 125, ii. 186.

Vorticellæ, mode of origin of, ii. 252; from Euglenæ, ii. 464; from Algoid-vesicles and Moss-sporangia, ii. 469; other modes of origin of, ii. 469; from filaments of Nitella and Chlamydococcus corpuscles. ii. 470; by synthetic Heterogenesis, ii. 471; metamorphosis of, into Oxytricha, ii. 493; into Rotifers, ii. 502, 511; origin of, from Actinophrys, xcv; relations of, to Acinetæ, xcv; conversion of, into Actinophrys, xcv.

Wallace, Mr., on natural selection, ii. 574; on means of changing colour in feathers, ii. 597; test of true theory, ii. 604; age of human race, ii. 629; development of brain in man, ii. 630; future of human race, ii. 633.

Watson, Sir Thomas, on non-susceptibility to contagion of small-pox and measles, cxlix.

Winter-eggs, of Hydatina senta, ii. 514.

Wyman, Prof. Jeffries, experiments relating to origin of living matter, i. 435; on analogical evidence concerning origin of living matter, i. 471; on atmospheric germs, ii. 282.

Zooids, ii. 542, 583.

Zoospores, mode of origin of, in Algæ, i. 171; formation of, in Vaucheria, i. 173; in Achlya, i. 180.

PART I.

THE NATURE AND SOURCE

OF THE

VITAL FORCES,

AND OF

ORGANIZABLE MATTER.

THE BEGINNINGS OF LIFE.

CHAPTER I.

THE PERSISTENCE OF FORCE—CORRELATION OF THE VITAL
AND PHYSICAL FORCES.

Indestructibility of Matter. Forces modes of motion. The doctrine of Conservation of Energy. History of. The unit of Heat. Convertibility of Physical Forces. Indestructibility of Force. Gradual growth of doctrine of Correlation of Physical and Vital Forces. Source of Energy manifested in Plants and Animals. Doctrines concerning Animal Heat. Its real mode of Origin. Power of movement in Animals. Laws regulating muscular Contractility. The Muscle a machine in which heat transforms itself into Mechanical Energy. Comparison between Muscle and Steam-Engine. Nervous phenomena. Neurility. Sensory and motor nerves have similar functions. Dependence of Nerve action upon due supply of blood. Remarkable experiments illustrating this. Evolution of heat and increased chemical change accompaniments of Nerve action. Different functions of Nervous System. Relations of Consciousness and Mind. Correlations of Consciousness not ascertainable. Conclusions.

THE doctrine that Matter is indestructible may now be regarded as one of the most universally accepted utterances of science. It is already firmly rooted, and the belief in its truth is gradually spreading deeper and wider as education advances. All must admit that there is an immeasurable difference between mere change of form and destruction, though in past times—and even at present amongst the uneducated—the former has been often mistaken for the latter. Such misconceptions, however, were natural enough in the past, and even now they are quite in harmony with the defective general knowledge of those who still entertain them: their occurrence does not in the least tend to diminish our well-grounded belief in the indestructibility of matter.

Of late years, too, experimental investigators as well as purely speculative enquirers have alike been gradually tending towards the recognition of the complemental doctrine of the essential oneness and indestructibility of Force. Matter, they say, is indestructible, and so also is force. Forces are 'modes of motion,' and motion is continuous. The very idea of motion, however, cannot be realized in thought except it be in connection with a something which moves—though the moving body may be infinitely great or infinitely small. We may imagine *molar* motion, or motion of a mass, as exhibited by the revolution of a planet or of a sun in its orbit; and we may imagine *molecular* motion amongst the particles of a cosmical æther, even though this æther itself may be so subtle as to elude all present means of recognition. But, though motion is inseparable from matter, it is, as we have intimated, continuous or persistent, and, therefore, communicable from particle to particle. Æthereal pulses of solar derivation impinging upon the surface of our earth may produce effects which, in part, manifest themselves in our consciousness as sensations of heat; or, acting upon other bodies, organic and inorganic, may in them produce such molecular re-arrangements—such modifications of form and nature—as will suffice to alter their qualities or attributes. Matter, then, may undergo changes of form—it may be now solid, now liquid, and now an invisible gas; whilst the disguised Force or Motion, owing to such different modes of collocation of the atoms of matter, may manifest itself to us in different ways, but in its essence it remains as the underlying and indestructible cause of the attributes of matter. So that at the same time that force is indestructible, it is moreover incapable of existing alone and independently of matter. We cannot conceive force save as inhering in, and appertaining to some body; we cannot conceive a body, or matter, existing, devoid of all attributes or force manifestations. Both are mutable, both indestructible, and both, so far as we know, quite incapable of existing alone.

The growth of modern scientific opinion concerning force has necessarily had much influence in modifying the doctrines concerning Life which were formerly in vogue. During the present century the labours of earnest workers of all kinds have done much towards the overthrow of the ancient and long-predominating metaphysical conceptions of Life. Chemists, physiologists, and others have striven manfully to dispel the mists and darkness which previously enshrouded all vital phenomena, and few, we suppose, would deny that the results of their labours had sent gleams of light into corners previously unillumined. However much there may be of the mysterious and occult still remaining, *some* of the phenomena, at least, formerly looked upon as essentially 'vital'—and, therefore, well-nigh inexplicable—are now recognized as depending in great part upon purely physical processes. But before stating what are the modern conceptions of Life — what views are now possible — it will be well to glance briefly at the labours of those who have helped to build up that doctrine of the Correlation of Forces, or Conservation of Energy, whose influence has been so great in upsetting the old metaphysical conceptions to which we have referred.

It is not to be expected that the doctrine of the Conservation of Energy should have sprung fully formed from the brain of any single man. The progress of scientific thought and experiment had been gradually tending in this direction during the closing years of the last century, and the doctrine has since been built up and perfected by the labours of many workers and thinkers. The germs of it are, however, to be found, stated with remarkable clearness, even more than two centuries ago, in the writings of Lord Bacon, who says in the twentieth Aphorism of his 'Novum Organum:' —' When I say of motion that it is the genus of which heat is a species, I would be understood to mean, not that heat generates motion (though both are true in certain cases), but that heat itself, its essence and quiddity, is motion and nothing else..... Heat is a motion, expansive, restrained, and acting in its strife upon the smaller particles of bodies[1].' Locke, also, shortly afterwards, expressed himself in much the same terms. He said:—'Heat is a very brisk agitation of the insensible parts of the object, which produces in us that sensation from whence we denominate the subject hot; so that what in our sensation is *heat*, in the object is nothing but *motion*.' But it was not till quite the close of the last century, in 1798, that Benjamin Thompson, afterwards Count Rumford, announced to the Royal Society his conviction, based upon real experimental evidence, that heat was a mode of motion. Whilst superintending the boring of cannon in the military arsenal at Munich, Count Rumford was much struck with the heat acquired by the brass after it had been bored for a time, and also with the intense heat of the metallic chips which were separated by the borer[2]. He then instituted the most careful experiments to ascertain the source of this heat, and in his memoir, after having detailed the nature and results of these experiments, he made the following remarks in opposition to the then prevalent notion that heat was a material substance, a kind of igneous fluid named 'caloric:'—'We have

---

[1] Bacon's Works, vol. iv. Spedding's Translation.
[2] See Tyndall's 'Heat Considered as a Mode of Motion.' 1863. p. 53.

seen that a very considerable quantity of heat may be excited by the friction of two metallic surfaces, and given off in a constant stream or flux *in all directions*, without interruption or intermission, and without any signs of *diminution* or *exhaustion*. In reasoning on this subject we must not forget *that most remarkable circumstance*, that the source of the heat generated by friction in these experiments appeared evidently to be *inexhaustible*. It is hardly necessary to add, that anything which any *insulated* body or system of bodies can continue to furnish *without limitation* cannot possibly be a *material substance;* and it appears to me to be extremely difficult, if not quite impossible, to form any distinct idea of anything capable of being excited and communicated in those experiments, except it be Motion.' In 1812 also, Sir Humphrey Davy in his first Memoir[1] brought forward most valuable scientific evidence to show that no such thing as 'caloric' existed, that heat was not an elastic fluid, and that the 'laws of the communication of heat are precisely the same as those of the communication of motion.' One of his experiments was of the most conclusive nature. 'He succeeded in melting two pieces of ice by rubbing them together in vacuo, at the same time preventing the access of external heat. The water produced in this experiment has a much higher relative heat than the ice; hence the potential heat which caused the ice to melt must have been obtained by the conversion of

[1] Sir Humphrey Davy's Works, vol. ii.

the mechanical force employed for the friction[1].' For, as Sir Humphrey Davy reasoned, a motion or vibration of the corpuscles of bodies must be necessarily generated by friction and percussion, and so, he adds, 'we may reasonably conclude that this motion or vibration is heat, or the repulsive power.' Then, in 1827, Lardner Vanuxem published in Philadelphia an essay[2] in which he speaks of caloric, light, electricity, and magnetism as being mutually convertible. His utterances are, however, somewhat dubious, since he at first treats of them as 'four different states' of 'one kind of repulsive matter', though, further on, he acknowledges that the existence of these as 'four distinct fluids, or kinds of æthereal matter, is inadmissible; for this conversion or change of characters is analogous to what are called the *properties* of bodies and not to the bodies themselves.' Again, in 1839, Séguin, in a work entitled 'De l'Influence des Chemins de Fer,' called attention to the mutual convertibility of heat and mechanical force, and he gave a calculation of their equivalent relation not differing materially from that afterwards published by Mayer and Joule. In January, 1842, in a lecture delivered before the Royal Institution, Professor Grove declared that 'light, heat, electricity, magnetism, motion, and chemical affinity are all convertible material *affections*;' and in

[1] Orme's 'Science of Heat,' 1869, p. 163.
[2] 'On the Ultimate Principles of Chemistry, Natural Philosophy, and Physiology.'

the recently published third edition of his 'Correlation of the Physical Forces,' he says, 'As far as I am now aware, the theory that the so-called imponderables are affections of ordinary matter, that they are resolvable into motion, that they are to be regarded in their action on matter as *forces*, and not as *specific entities*, and that they are capable of mutual reaction, thence alternately acting as cause and effect, had not at that time been publicly advanced.' But it was also in the year 1842, though in its latter part, that Dr. Mayer[1], a physician of Heilbronn, announced independently a doctrine substantially similar, to the effect that the imponderables were forces at once indestructible and convertible. He actually calculated the mechanical equivalent of heat out of data derived from the velocity of sound in air—an intellectual feat only possible to a man of rare originality. Professor Tyndall says[2] of him, 'When we consider the circumstances of Mayer's life, and the period at which he wrote, we cannot fail to be struck with astonishment at what he has accomplished. Here was a man of genius working in silence, animated solely by a love of his subject, and arriving at the most important results some time in advance of those whose lives were entirely devoted to Natural Philosophy. It was the accident of bleeding a feverish patient at Java, in 1840, that led Mayer to

---

[1] 'Bemerkungen über die Kräfte der unbeleten Natur,' Liebig's Annalen, 1842, vol. xlii.
[2] Loc. cit. p. 445.

speculate on these subjects. He noticed that the venous blood of the tropics was of a much brighter red than in colder latitudes, and his reasoning on this fact led him into the laboratory of natural forces, where he has worked with such signal ability and success.' But in the following year, 1843, Mr. Joule of Manchester published his first paper on the 'Mechanical Value of Heat,' in which he detailed the most valuable results of a series of experiments, conducted whilst he was in ignorance of the labours of Séguin and of the reasonings of Mayer. It is to him that we are principally indebted for the actual experimental determination of the mechanical equivalent of heat. A paddle-wheel was made to revolve in a copper vessel containing a weighed quantity of water at a known temperature. The mechanical force, derived from falling weights, which was employed in turning the wheel was known; so that when, after the wheel had revolved for a certain time, the temperature of the water was estimated, and the distance through which the weights had fallen in the same time was computed, it became easy to estimate the quantity of heat which corresponded to the fall of a known weight through a given distance. Of course, corrections had to be made, allowing for the heating of the copper vessel, and of the wheel itself, as well as for the loss of heat by radiation. Similar experiments were conducted with oil and with mercury, though under somewhat different conditions; and in all cases the amount of heat evolved by the friction of the vanes of the wheel against the various fluids was ascertained with the greatest care. The uniform results obtained in these experiments enabled Mr. Joule most satisfactorily to establish the mechanical equivalent of what has been termed the unit of heat. He found that the energy of a body weighing one pound which had fallen from a height of 772 feet was exactly equal to the quantity of molecular motion or heat which suffices to raise the temperature of one pound of water by one degree of the Fahrenheit scale[1].

It is needless for us to follow further the ultimate developments of this doctrine with which the names of Clausius, Rankine, Thomson, and Helmholtz are associated. We have called attention to the experiments and reasonings by which it has been shown that an exact relation of equivalence exists between the motion of masses produced by mechanical force, and the motion of the particles of bodies manifesting itself as heat produced by friction. Heat, therefore, has been indubitably established to be a 'mode of motion;' and there is the very best reason for believing that all the other forces or affections of matter are similarly related to motion, whilst they are also mutually convertible. Each alike may arise from, or may give origin to motion either directly or indirectly.

---

[1] The 'unit of heat' therefore, or that amount of heat which will raise a pound of water 1° Fahr., is equal to 772 'foot-pounds,' if we call the actual energy of a body weighing one pound which has fallen one foot, a *foot-pound*.

By the rubbing of substances of a different nature together electricity is produced, as in the ordinary electrical machine. Magnetism, again, may result from motion; either immediately, in a bar of soft iron, through a repetition of percussions, which, producing motion amongst the particles of the bar, facilitate their assumption of the magnetic mode of collocation; or mediately through the intervention of electricity which has itself been generated by motion. And, as Mr. Herbert Spencer says [1], 'The transformations of electricity into other modes of force are still more clearly demonstrable. Produced by the motions of heterogeneous bodies in contact, electricity, through attractions and repulsions, will immediately reproduce motion in neighbouring bodies. Now a current of electricity generates magnetism in a bar of soft iron; and now the rotation of a permanent magnet generates currents of electricity. Here we have a battery in which, from the play of chemical affinities, an electric current results; and there, in the adjacent cell, we have an electric current effecting chemical decomposition. In the conducting wire we witness the transformation of electricity into heat; while in the electric sparks and in the voltaic arc we see light produced..... That magnetism produces motion is the ordinary evidence we have of its existence. In the magneto-electric machine we see a rotating magnet evolving electricity. And

---

[1] 'First Principles,' p. 254.

the electricity so evolved may immediately after exhibit itself as heat, light, or chemical affinity. Faraday's discovery of the effect of magnetism on polarized light, as well as the discovery that change of magnetic state is accompanied by heat, point to further like connections. Lastly, various experiments show that the magnetization of a body alters its internal structure; and that, conversely, the alteration of its internal structure, as by mechanical strain, alters its magnetic condition.' We need allude to all these possibilities of change no further; those who wish for additional information may find it in Mr. Grove's work.

The most attentive consideration of the facts forces us to the conclusion—even to an irresistible belief—that though continually varying in its modes, Force itself is indestructible or persistent. As Mr. Herbert Spencer says, such an allegation really amounts to this, that *à priori* possibilities and experimental evidence alike warrant us in the belief 'that there cannot be an isolated force beginning and ending in nothing; but that any force manifested implies an equal antecedent force from which it is derived, and against which it is a reaction. Further, that the force so originating cannot disappear without result; but must expend itself in some other manifestation of force, which, in being produced, becomes its reaction; and so on continually.'

If forces are nothing but the inseparable qualities, attributes, or affections of matter, and if matter is itself indestructible, then, of course, it must follow as an *à priori* necessity that forces, or the attributes of matter, are also indestructible [1]. As Professor Faraday expresses it [2], 'a particle of oxygen is ever a particle of oxygen—nothing can in the least wear it. If it enter into combination and disappear as oxygen—if it pass through a thousand combinations, animal, vegetable, and mineral—if it lie hid for a thousand years, and then be evolved, it is oxygen with its first qualities. Neither more nor less. It has all its original force, and only that; the amount of force which it disengaged when hiding itself has again to be employed in a reverse direction when it is set at liberty..... Just as the chemist owes all the perfection of his experiments to his dependence on the certainty of gravitation applied by the balance, so may the physical philosopher expect to find the greatest security and the utmost aid in the principle of the conservation of force.

[1] Those who wish to follow this subject further, and to understand what are its ultimate implications, cannot do better than read chapters vi.-ix. of Mr. Herbert Spencer's 'First Principles.' They will then see that '*persistence of force*' is really the most ultimate notion, on which the doctrine of the 'indestructibility of matter' as well as that of the 'continuity of motion' are alike dependent. He says:—' By the Persistence of Force, we really mean the persistence of some power which transcends our knowledge and conception. The manifestations either as occurring in ourselves or outside of us do not persist; but that which persists is the Unknown Cause of these manifestations. In other words, asserting the persistence of force is but another mode of asserting an Unconditional Reality, without beginning or end.'—p. 255, 1st edit.

[2] 'Researches in Chemistry,' pp. 454, 459.

All that we have that is good and safe, as the steam-engine, the electric telegraph, &c., witness to that principle. It would require a perpetual motion, a fire without heat, heat without a source, action without reaction, cause without effect, or effect without a cause, to displace it from its rank as a law of nature.' The time, therefore, must come when the really fundamental doctrine of the persistence or indestructibility of Force will be recognized by all educated persons to have an equal validity with the secondary, though more familiar, doctrine of the indestructibility of Matter. The two doctrines are correlatives, and the admission of one implies the truth of the other as a necessary consequence.

Having come to an understanding as to what views we are to take of Force and of the mutual relations of the several physical forces, we now have to enquire as to the relation in which these stand to the so-called 'vital forces' manifested by Living Organisms.

The first real[1] step in explanation was taken in

[1] In an 'Inaugural Address,' delivered in 1868 at the Jeafferson Medical College, U.S., by Dr. J. Aitken Meigs, he claims the credit for Dr. Metcalfe of having initiated this part of the doctrine. These claims, and also others concerning Lardner Vanuxem, have been considered in the 'British Medical Journal,' January 16, 1869, p. 50. Dr. Metcalfe's work, published two years earlier, in 1843, was entitled, 'On Caloric; its Mechanical, Chemical, and Vital Agencies in the Phenomena of Nature.' Dr. Metcalfe seems to have been a man of much power and originality, though he still looked upon heat as a material substance, an elastic fluid named *caloric*. This view, of course, vitiates his treatment of the subject, though it seems clear, from the passage

1845 by Mayer of Heilbronn, in a memoir on 'Organic Movement in its Relation to Material Changes,' in which he showed that the processes taking place in living organisms, animal or vegetable, were produced by forces acting upon them from without, and that the changes in their composition brought about by these external agencies were the immediate sources of those modes of force apparently generated in the organisms themselves. In the same year also Mr. Newport was led by a consideration of the relations which had been shown to exist between light and electricity by Faraday, and between electricity and nervous power by Matteucci[1], as well as ' by the known dependence of most of the functions of the body on the latter, to consider *light* as the primary source of all vital and constructive power, the degrees and variations of which may, perhaps, be referred to modifications of this influence on the special organization of each animal body[2].' In the following

which we subjoin, that his notions otherwise were verging in the right direction. 'All the chemical changes,' he says, 'that mark the course of nature, are attended with changes of temperature, from the slowest process of fermentation to the most rapid combustion; that is, all the decompositions and recombinations of matter are attended with the addition or subtraction of caloric. Without the continual agency of the solar beams, the vital air, the ocean, and the solid ground would become a motionless mass of inert and chaotic matter. Without the reception of caloric from the atmosphere by respiration, the wonderful mechanism of animal motion, sensation, and life, could not go on.'

[1] Physical Phenomena of living beings.
[2] This passage is to be found only in the 'Athenæum' for Dec. 6.

year Mr. Grove published his now well-known work on the 'Correlation of the Physical Forces,' and in this, after having spoken of the relations existing between the several physical forces, he said, 'I believe that the same principles and mode of reasoning might be applied to the organic, as well as to the inorganic world; and that muscular force, animal and vegetable heat, &c., might, and at some time will, be shown to have similar definite correlations.' This view was taken up by Dr. Carpenter, and was much more fully elaborated by him. In an article contributed to the 'British and Foreign Medico-Chirurgical Review' for January, 1848, Dr. Carpenter maintained 'that the *vital* forces, of various kinds, bear the same relation to the several *physical* forces of the inorganic world that they bear to each other; the great essential modification or transformation being effected by their passage, so to speak, through the germ of the organic structure, somewhat after the same fashion that heat becomes electricity when passed through certain mixtures of metals.' Then, in 1850, a memoir was read before the Royal Society, and afterwards published in the 'Philosophical Transactions,' entitled, 'On the Mutual Relations of the Vital and Physical Forces,' in which the whole doctrine was much

---

1845. Though it originally formed part of a paper which afterwards appeared in the 20th vol. of the 'Transactions of the Linnæan Society,' but from which this particular passage was omitted by desire of the officers of the Society.

more fully discussed, and Dr. Carpenter laboured most successfully to show 'that so close a mutual relationship exists between all the vital forces, that they may be legitimately regarded as modes of one and the same force[1].' And he also maintained that these so-called vital forces were evolved within the living bodies of plants and of the lower animals by the transformation of the light, heat, and chemical action obtained from without, which were given back to the external world again, either during the life of the living beings, or after their death, in terms of motion and heat, and also, to a slight extent, in the form of light and electricity. These doctrines are thus definitely expressed by him[2]:—'The vital force which causes the primordial cell of the germ first to multiply itself, and then to develope itself into a complex and extensive organism, was not either originally locked up in that single cell, nor was it latent in the materials which are progressively assimilated by itself and its descendants[3]; but it is directly and immediately supplied by

[1] In unicellular organisms, all the vital functions, so far as they are differentiated, are carried on in the single cell; and in the higher animals which proceed from the growth and development of some single, equally minute germ, specialization of function goes hand and hand with specialization of structure.

[2] Loc. cit. pp. 752-756.

[3] This holds good for plants, the lowest animals, and the initial changes in the higher animals, though all the later vital manifestations of the latter are dependent almost entirely upon the redistribution of the forces pertaining to the organic substances which constitute their food, and to the various chemical changes taking place within their own

the heat which is constantly operating upon it, and *which is transformed into vital force by its passage through the organized fabric which manifests it.* .... All the *forces* which are operating in producing the phenomena of life are in the first place derived from the inorganic universe, and are finally restored to it again. .... And there is strong reason to believe that the entire amount of force of all kinds received by an animal during a given period is given back by it during that period, his condition at the end of the time being the same as at the beginning. And all that has been expended in the building up of the organism is given back by its decay after death.'

In plants and in the lower tribes of animals we are able to trace a most undoubted relationship between the vital activity of each individual and the amount of heat which it receives from external sources. Even

---

bodies. Mr. Herbert Spencer says:—' We have next to note, as having here a meaning for us, the chemical contrasts between those organisms which carry on their functions by the help of external forces, and those which carry on their functions by forces evolved from within. If we compare animals and plants, we see that whereas plants, characterised as a class by containing but little nitrogen, are dependent upon the solar rays for their vital activities; animals, the vital activities of which are not thus dependent, mainly consist of nitrogenous substances. There is one marked exception to this broad distinction, however; and this exception is specially instructive. Among plants there is a considerable group—the Fungi—many members of which, if not all, can live and grow in the dark; and it is their peculiarity that they are very much more nitrogenous than other plants.' (Principles of Biology, 1864, vol. i. p. 37.)

in 1837, M. Boussingault, after contrasting the meteorological circumstances in which wheat, barley, Indian corn, and the potato are developed at the equator and in the temperate zones, with their different rates of growth in these situations, came to the conclusion 'that the same annual plant everywhere receives the same quantity of heat in the course of its existence.' And in one of his more recent works, speaking of the Foraminifera, Dr. Carpenter says[1], 'We have found strong reason for regarding *temperature* as exerting a most important influence in favouring, not merely increase in size, but specialization of development: all the most complicated and specialized forms at present known being denizens either of tropical or sub-tropical seas, and many of these being represented in the seas of colder regions by comparatively insignificant examples which there seems adequate reason for regarding as of the same specific types with the tropical forms, even though deficient in some of their apparently most important features.' That the rate of growth in plants depends most notably upon the amount of light and heat to which they are subjected is a fact familiar to most of us. The stimulation of the vital processes by heat is, indeed, most easy of demonstration in some cases. It is now perfectly well known that in *Valisneria*, *Chara*, *Anacharis*, and other plants in the cells of which there is a well-marked *cyclosis*, the rate of revolution of the

[1] 'Introduction to the Study of the Foraminifera' (Ray Soc.), 1862, p. 9.

particles of protoplasm is, within certain limits, directly dependent upon temperature. By variations of this, the rapidity of movement of the particles in the cell may be seen to be increased or diminished at pleasure. The amœboid activity of a white blood corpuscle or of a pus corpuscle is similarly stimulated, within certain limits, by the influence of heat. We know also that the hatching of eggs and the germination of seeds may be likewise hastened or retarded by access or deprivation of heat. Considerations such as these at first suggested the doctrine of the Correlation of the Vital and the Physical Forces, —a doctrine which has been slowly, though surely, gaining ground since the date of its first announcement. More and more evidence is gradually being accumulated in its favour, so that we now find Professor Frankland alluding to it in these terms:—'No one possessing any knowledge of physical science would now venture to hold that vital force[1] is the source of muscular power. An animal, however high its organization, can no more generate an amount of force capable of moving a grain of sand, than a stone can fall upwards, or a locomotive drive a train without fuel.' Mr. Herbert Spencer, also, speaking of the same doctrine, says[2], 'It is a corollary from that primordial truth which, as we have seen, underlies all other truths, that

---

[1] That is, any peculiar force existing of and by itself, independently of all the physical forces. See Proceed. of Royal Institution, June 8, 1866.
[2] 'Principles of Biology,' vol. i. p. 57.

whatever amount of power an organism expends in any shape, is the correlate and equivalent of a power that was taken into it from without. On the one hand, it follows from the persistence of force, that each portion of mechanical or other energy which an organism exerts, implies the transformation of as much organic matter as contained this energy in a latent state. And on the other hand, it follows from the persistence of force that no such transformation of organic matter containing this latent energy can take place without the energy being in one shape or other manifested.'

We shall find it worth our while, however, to follow up a little more fully the details of this most important doctrine, as it will aid us so much in forming a true conception as to the nature of Life.

As pointed out by M. Gavarret [1], most of the physical force which, in the form of light and heat, impinges upon a plant, is consumed therein (*travail intérieur*). It is stored up as potential force in the complex organic substances entering into the composition of the plant; these being produced therein (under the influence of the already existing living tissues) by the action of physical forces upon the not-living constituents of the earth, air, and water by which the plant was surrounded. The animal, on the contrary, liberating and using these forces which have been stored up by the plant—after assimilating its substance in the form of food—expends them in the production of that *travail extérieur* which

[1] 'Phénomènes Physiques de la Vie,' 1869, Paris, p. 73.

the animal's nature and the necessities of its existence compel it to manifest. Animals display, in varying proportions, three principal modes of *vital* activity which testify to the continual liberation of force within them:—(1) they appear to produce heat; (2) they move, by reason of the contractility of certain tissues; and (3) they display certain nervous phenomena.

1. Very many animals constantly maintain themselves at a temperature above that of the medium in which they live; this being more especially the case with the so-called *warm-blooded* animals—amongst which birds are most remarkable for the very great difference existing between their temperature and that of the air. The cause of this difference in temperature between the animal and its medium has been variously explained at different times. It was believed by Galen that heat was actually produced *de novo* in the left ventricle of the heart; and even John Hunter thought that the production of animal heat depended upon a special vital force or principle, which was able not only to produce but actually to destroy heat. Others—and that even in comparatively recent times—have striven to prove that some principle resident in the nervous system was capable of giving rise to animal heat. The true theories on this subject, however, may be said to date as far back as the close of the eighteenth century, and to have commenced with the brilliant discoveries of Lavoisier. Speaking of his researches, M. Gavarret says[1]:—

---

[1] Loc cit. p. 99.

'The alimentary substances introduced into the stomach, after being digested and liquified, are absorbed and sent into the vessels, where they mix with the blood; on the other hand, the air introduced at each inspiration into the pulmonary cavity yields to the blood a part of its oxygen. Struck with this double centripetal movement, Lavoisier asked himself what happened to these substances brought into relation with one another within the blood-vessels. Proceeding in this research with all the rigour of a chemical analysis, he showed that the oxygen introduced by the respiratory passages attacks the organic substances furnished by digestion, burns them, combining with their carbon and their hydrogen to form carbonic acid and water. He showed that this slow combustion of the organic materials of the blood is an incessant source of heat[1].' Lavoisier then instituted experiments to determine the quantity of heat abstracted from the animal by radiation, by contact with air, and by evaporation of fluids from the surface of the body. On the other hand, he measured the quantity of oxygen consumed, calculated the proportions of carbonic acid and of water produced by the combination of this oxygen with the materials of the blood, and then estimated the quantity of heat disengaged during these reactions. From a comparison of the results thus obtained in these two series of observations, he came to the conclusion that the chemical reactions carried on within the body would furnish

---

[1] 'Mém. de l'Acad. des Sciences,' 1789.

enough heat to maintain the animal at its proper temperature. This conclusion was afterwards confirmed by many other experiments and observations. The researches of Lavoisier still left us in doubt, however, as to whether the combustion of the materials of the blood took place in the capillaries of the body generally, or in those of the pulmonary circulation. This doubt was removed by Spallanzani; and the subsequent experiments of Magnus and of Claude-Bernard only tended to confirm his conclusion, that the heat-producing chemical changes were carried on in the capillaries of the body generally. Thus the heat evolved in animals is some of that solar heat which had previously impinged upon plants, and which was gradually locked up in the form of potential force, during the growth of the plant-tissue subsequently taken as food by animals.

2. Turning now to the next dynamic manifestation of animals—to their power of movement—we may, for the sake of brevity, consider this as it presents itself in the higher animals only—in those in which the movements depend upon the contractility of definite structures known as 'muscles.' *Contractility* is the essential attribute of the muscle, and, being one of the peculiarly vital endowments, we may now enquire how far this vital property is one which is correlatable with ordinary physical forces, or whether it can display itself independently of these[1]. In the first place, it is important

[1] For a full and admirable treatment of this question we must refer the reader to pp. 120-194 of the work of Gavarret, already quoted.

to state that this contractility of the muscle can be excited, for a time, after the death of the animal of which it formed part: the length of time during which the property persists being, generally, longer in proportion as the animal is lower in the scale of organization. During winter the muscles of certain fish and reptiles have been known to contract for a *week* after death, though in mammals and birds this property of the voluntary muscles disappears after a few hours. From the researches of Nysten upon the bodies of decapitated criminals, it appears that in man, as in the lower animals, a certain order is observed amongst the different muscles of the body in the loss of this vital property. Contractions, from electrical stimuli, ceased in the left ventricle of the heart after forty-five minutes; in the muscles of the extremities after seven hours; and, last of all, in the right auricle of the heart, which, on this account, had been previously spoken of by Galen as 'ultimum moriens.' In one instance, Nysten found that this portion of the human heart could be made to contract $16\frac{1}{2}$ hours after the death of the individual. Contractility of the muscle cannot, therefore, be due to any peculiar 'vital principle' which leaves the body when the organism dies.

Although the muscle is usually excited to contract by a stimulus sent through a nerve, we have now learned—principally through the phenomena observable in animals poisoned by woorara—that the contractility of the muscle may be called into play through the direct action of a stimulus, and without any intervention of the nervous system. The contractility is, however, closely related, and more or less proportionate in degree, to the supply of arterial blood circulating in the capillary vessels with which it is furnished. The experiments of Longet[1] on this subject are most instructive. He found, as a result of experimentation upon many animals, that all traces of contractility after the direct application of a stimulus disappeared from muscles which had received no arterial blood for a space of two hours; but that almost as soon as the afflux of arterial blood to the muscle was again permitted—even in the space of a few minutes—the contractility of the muscles again manifested itself upon the application of a stimulus, either direct or indirect. But those heat-liberating chemical reactions—the processes of combustion necessary for the continuance of the nutritive changes—are carried on in the capillaries of the muscle as well as in the capillaries of other parts of the body; and it would seem that the disappearance of the property of contractility from the muscle is dependent upon that stoppage of the heat-evolution therein which the arrest of the circulation entails. In support of this view, on the one hand, it has been shown by M. Becquerel[2] that the temperature of a muscle becomes sensibly lowered when the artery supplying it is compressed; and, on the other,

[1] 'Traité de Physiologie,' 3me éd. 1869, t. ii. p. 613.
[2] 'Ann. de Chimie de Physique,' 1835, t. lix. p. 135.

we learn, from the experiments of Matteucci[1], that the activity of the processes of combustion within the muscle increase during its contraction[2].

Many separate sets of investigations do indeed tend to show that an excess of heat is developed during muscular activity, though, on the other hand, there is evidence to prove, from the highly interesting experiments of M. Béclard[3], whose results have been confirmed and extended by M. Heidenhain, the increase in the activity of the chemical changes which undoubtedly exists during muscular exercise, is much greater than can be accounted for by the actual increase of sensible heat in the body. After alluding to these various investigations, M. Gavarret generalizes their results as follows[4]:—

---

[1] 'Letture sul l' elettro-physiologia,' Milano, 1867, p. 36.

[2] During a state of rest, or moderate exercise, combustion and elimination of its products are duly regulated in the muscle. So long as this balance is maintained the muscle preserves its physiological properties, and the chemical reaction of its juice remains *neutral* or *alkaline*. But when excessive activity of the muscle is maintained, then the processes of elimination can no longer keep pace with those of combustion: lactic acid accumulates within the muscle, and the reaction of its juice becomes decidedly *acid*. The contractility is gradually enfeebled by the increasing accumulation of these effete products within the muscle, and the feeling of *fatigue* is induced. There is good reason for believing that this feeling of fatigue is rather dependent upon the accumulation of these products of combustion within the muscle than upon an actual molecular wasting of the muscle-substance. There is, however, a more general feeling of fatigue which is dependent rather upon state of nervous system than state of muscle.

[3] 'De la Contraction musculaire dans ses rapports avec la température animale,' Paris, 1861.

[4] Loc. cit. p. 135.

'All these experiments agree in showing that in the muscular system of an animal which accomplishes *actual work* (such as raising a weight, dragging a load, &c.) everything goes on as in an ordinary steam-engine. Whilst the muscle *performs work*, the heat produced by the internal combustions becomes divided into two complementary portions; the one part appears as *sensible* heat, and determines the temperature of the muscle, the other *disappears*, so far as its existence in the form of heat is concerned, and, by the intervention of the muscular contraction, *becomes transformed into mechanical work*. The muscle is an *animated machine*, which, like the steam-engine, utilizes the heat in order to produce work: in both cases there is necessarily an *equivalence* between the heat which disappears, or is consumed, and the external work achieved.' In consideration of its origin, the energy manifested during the contraction of the muscle is directly comparable with the energy due to the elasticity of vapour when this is the motor power at work, as in a steam-engine. Chemical change—combustion, in fact—in each case, in muscle and steam-engine alike, causes the liberation of heat; and in each case part of this liberated force is capable of manifesting itself anew in the form of mechanical energy. It matters not whence the heat is derived—whether it comes from the decomposition of the recently assimilated food-products in the blood which circulates through the muscle, or whether it proceeds from the liberated energy or sun-force that may have been locked up for ages in the bowels of the earth, but which is now set free by a process of combustion in the engine fire—the result is the same, and in the muscle, as much as in the steam-engine, we have to do with a machine in which the transference of heat into mechanical energy is capable of being effected. The muscle, it is true, is a much more subtle kind of machine, and the precise mode of its action is as yet hidden from us; we know not *how* it is—through what precise molecular changes taking place in the substance of the muscle—that the heat which disappears as heat, is, through the property of *contractility*, enabled to reappear in the form of mechanical energy whilst the animal performs its manifold muscular movements. That this is so, however, we know; and we know, moreover, that as a mere machine for the conversion of heat into mechanical energy, the muscle far excels the best steam-engine which has ever been constructed. The merits of such a machine must of course be judged, other things equal, according to the greater or less proportion of the total heat liberated therein which is capable of being converted into mechanical energy available[1] for the execution of actual work. Now, the investigations of Helmholtz and

---

[1] *Available* muscular energy must be distinguished from total muscular energy, some of which—whilst a man is performing work—is expended in balancing the body or in other ways not directly effective. It is the amount of loss of effective or available energy in this and in other ways (such as from friction, radiation, &c.) which regulates the value of muscular and all other machines.

Hirn have gone to show that a man is capable of utilizing, for the production of available muscular energy, *one-fifth* of the total amount of heat developed in his body; whilst the admirable labours of the latter investigator have also shown that even the most perfect steam-engine that has yet been constructed is only capable of utilizing about *one-eighth* [1] of the total amount of heat liberated therein [2]. We now know also, in op-

---

[1] This estimate is much more in favour of the steam-engine than that of other investigators. According to Rankine, only from $\frac{1}{7}$ to $\frac{1}{8}$ of the heat of the fuel is capable of manifesting itself as mechanical energy; Sir William Armstrong, again, considers $\frac{1}{10}$ as the maximum, though he thinks the average conversion to be about $\frac{1}{12}$ of the total potential force of the fuel.

[2] In continuation of this subject M. Gavarret says (loc. cit. p. 146):—
'Mais pour se faire une juste idée du haut degré de perfection qui peut atteindre le moteur animé, il faut fixer son attention, sur la rapidité des mouvements exécutés d'une manière continue par certains oiseaux et les insectes ali's, pendant les heures et même des journées entières.—En quatre ou cinq minutes l'aigle s'élève à 6 ou 7000 mètres et disparaît, dans les airs: d'après Pictio de Lavalle, le pigeon messager de l'erse fait en un jour plus de chemin qu'un homme de pied en six.—Les hirondelles volent pendant des journées entières décrivant mille et mille sinuosités dans les airs pour atteindre les petites insectes dont elles font leur nourriture; leur vol est si rapide et si soutenu que sept à huit jours leur suffisent pour se transporter de nos climats sous la ligne; Adanson en a vu arriver au Sénégal trois ou quatre jours après leur départ d'Europe.—Le faucon de Henri II s'étant emporté après une canardière à Fontainebleau, fut pris le lendemain à Malte et reconnu à l'anneau qu'il portait; un faucon des Canaries, envoyé au duc de Lerme revint d'Andalousie à l'Ile de Ténériffe en seize heures, ce qui fait un trajet de 250 lieues exécuté avec un vitesse moyenne de 16 lieues à l'heure.—Hans Sloane assure qu'à la Barbade les mouettes vont se promener en troupes à plus de 60 lieues de distance en mer, et que le même jour elles regagnent leur point de départ.—Certains insectes,

position to the doctrines of Liebig, that the heat which is transformed into mechanical energy is by no means necessarily derived from the combustion of nitrogenous substances; and, least of all, from an oxidation of the substance of the muscle itself. This doctrine of Liebig, which was for a long time accepted by many physiologists, was from the commencement rejected by a few, and notably so by Mayer, in his celebrated memoir before alluded to [1]. In this memoir he insisted that—'A muscle is only an apparatus by means of which the transformation of force is brought about, but it is not the substance by the chemical change of which the mechanical effect is produced.' The recent admirable researches of MM. Fick and Wislicenus [2] are entirely in favour of this notion. They found, in making a mountain ascent, that the total combustion of nitrogenous materials would only suffice to produce about one-half of the total effective energy which must have been expended during the excursion. This and other considerations render it almost certain that the heat which is converted into mechanical energy during

comme les taons peuvent suivre pendant de longues heures un cheval lancé au grand trot. Par une belle journée de mai ou de juin l'abeille vole d'une manière continue du matin au soir, pour aller cueillir dans les corolles des fleurs et rapporter à la ruche les matériaux nécessaires aux travaux et à la nourriture de la communauté.'

[1] 'Organic Movement in its Relation to Material Changes,' Heilbronn, 1845.

[2] 'Philosophical Magazine,' vol. xxxi. p. 485. For most important additional facts and explanations, see a paper by Prof. Parkes in 'Proceedings of the Royal Society,' 1867. pp. 53-59.

muscular action is derived from no peculiar source. We know that heat is set free by nutritive chemical changes taking place in the blood which circulates through the capillaries of the muscular system, and that the substances which undergo these changes are dissolved non-nitrogenous, as well as nitrogenous products of assimilation. We know, in fact, that the muscle acts only as a machine for the purpose of converting a portion of the heat thence derived into mechanical energy[1], and that the substance of the muscle itself—not yielding the force which is to be transformed—undergoes merely a molecular wasting by virtue of its own functional activity as a transformative apparatus, just as the parts of a steam-engine are subject to a gradual wear and tear produced by the friction occasioned during its activity[2].

[1] The machine being called into action, merely, by the nerve, and the stimulus coming through this being partly, though not wholly, to the contraction of the muscle as the spark is to exploding gunpowder. The experiments of Matteucci ('Letture sul l' elettro-physiologia,' Milan, 1867, p. 35) go to show that the mechanical work effected by a muscle during its contraction may be 30,000 times greater than the work expended in the excitation of the nerve. On the other hand, there is abundant evidence to show that the strength and vigour of the muscular contraction varies with the amount or intensity of the nerve-change which calls it into play. The same muscle which, in certain states of the nervous system, may be almost powerless, may in others be made to contract with far more than ordinary energy.

[2] The molecular restitution of muscle, of brain, and of the nitrogenous tissues generally, which are in continual need of repair, make it essential that nitrogenous substances should to a certain extent be consumed as food. But so far as muscular action is concerned the nitrogenous substances are needed for the repair of the machine, and not, as formerly supposed, as a source of the energy which is to be transformed through the intervention of the machine.

3. Turning now to the third mode of vital activity—to that which manifests itself in the display of nervous phenomena—we shall find that these manifestations are also closely dependent upon the integrity of certain material structures, and that their appearance coincides with an increase in the quantity of heat appreciable in, or in the neighbourhood of these structures.

The Nervous System is made up of nerve-cells and nerve-fibres in various states of aggregation. The nerve-cells are elements in which great molecular changes are supposed to take place, attended by the liberation of molecular motion, whilst the nerve-fibres are, for the most part, mere channels of communication along which this molecular motion is conducted. The matter of which the nervous system is composed was originally almost uniform in structure and property; but, little by little, developmental differentiations take place in the embryo, with which are associated correlated differences in function. As Mr. Herbert Spencer says, all direct and indirect evidence 'justify us in concluding that the nervous system consists of *one* kind of matter under different forms and conditions. In the grey tissue this matter exists in masses containing *corpuscles*, which are soft and have granules dispersed through them, and which, besides being thus unstably composed, are placed so as to be liable to disturbance in the greatest degree. In the white tissue this matter is collected together in extremely slender *threads* that are denser, that are uniform in texture, and that are shielded in an unusual manner from disturbing forces, except at their two extremities[1].' On the one hand, these fibres connect peripheral parts with the nerve-centres, whereby such parts are rendered *sensitive*; whilst, on the other hand, the nerve-centres are also in connection with other sets of nerve-fibres which are accustomed to transmit stimuli outwardly towards the muscles in which they are distributed, so as to call them into activity. The experiments of Phillipeaux and Vulpian have abundantly confirmed the reasonings of Mr. G. H. Lewes[2], which went to show that there was no real difference in property between the so-called sensory and motor nerves. The fundamental property of each alike is the capability of transmitting a stimulus, and for this property Mr. Lewes proposed the name *neurility*. Neurility, therefore, is the characteristic property of a nerve, just as contractility is the characteristic property of a muscle; and the different results produced, when a sensory and a motor nerve respectively are stimulated, is due to the different nature of the organs to which the stimulus is directed. When the stimulus traverses the nerve in an *afferent* direction, this, impinging upon a nerve-centre, liberates a larger or smaller quantity of energy, and may produce what is called a sensation; but when, on the other hand, a stimulus originating in a nerve-centre is propagated in an *efferent* direction, then this

---

[1] 'Principles of Psychology,' 1869, No. 20, p. 14.
[2] 'Physiology of Common Life,' 1859.

stimulus calls into play the contractility of a muscle, and so gives rise to a motor act.

As we have already seen in respect to the muscle, that its contractility lasts for a varying period after the death of the animal, so is it in the case of the nerve. This, after the death of the animal, is still capable of transmitting a stimulus—a fact which is shown by its power (when stimulated) of calling into action the muscle to which it is distributed. The precise length of time during which the property survives increases also in proportion as the animal is low in the scale of organization. Again, there are many experiments of the most striking kind on record which show the complete dependence of the nervous system upon a due supply of arterial blood. Without this all nerve-functions soon cease in parts thus cut off from their stores of potential energy. The experiments of many observers have shown that, when the posterior part of the body of a mammalian animal has been cut off from its blood supply by ligature of the abdominal aorta, the complete insensibility and disappearance of all reflex[1] excitability which soon supervenes, may be made to cease in the course of a few minutes by the removal of the ligature from the main artery. The renewal of the circulation of the blood through the grey matter of the spinal cord restores to this and to the paralysed parts generally their

[1] That is to say, the ability to give rise to movements, in response to external stimuli, through the intervention of lower nerve-centres, independently of the action of Will or volition.

temporarily-abolished functions. Non-sensitive parts again become sensitive, and the paralysis of motor power disappears. Even when the posterior part of the body of such an animal has been completely severed from the anterior, and when all signs of reflex excitability have disappeared, M. Brown-Séquard has, nevertheless, found that the injection for a time of oxygenated and defibrinated blood seems to restore to the spinal cord all its properties—so that irritation of the skin again gives rise to reflex movements. The functions of the brain are similarly dependent upon, and modifiable by, the nature of the blood supply. Sir Astley Cooper having tied the two carotid arteries of a rabbit, completely cut off the afflux of blood to the brain by compressing the two vertebral arteries; when the animal very shortly lapsed into a state of complete stupor or coma, which continued until the compression was removed from the two latter vessels. As soon as this was done, however, the animal again exhibited signs of life. The experiments of M. Vulpian upon frogs have yielded even still more striking results. He stopped the circulation of blood throughout the body generally, by tying the heart at the origin of the great vessels. This occasioned a gradual cessation of all vital manifestations. In such animals, however, these manifestations are slow to disappear, so that it was not till after the expiration of *two* or *three hours* that all signs of life had gone. After this period no trace of any excitability could be detected in the spinal cord, and the animal was practically dead¹ but for the fact that the heart still exhibited feeble contractions², although the presence of the ligature still prevented the egress of blood from its cavities. In this condition the frog might be allowed to remain for even *three* or *four hours*; and yet, when the ligature was removed, the heart still continuing to beat, the circulation soon became completely re-established. The other vital functions reappeared much more slowly. After about half-an-hour the first signs of respiratory movements showed themselves—at first at irregular and distant intervals, and then, gradually, with their accustomed rhythm. But it was not till after about two hours more that the spinal cord, as a whole, regained its excitability, and that reflex movements were producible by irritation of the skin. Later still, the power of voluntary movement was resumed, and the previously dead animal was seen to have recovered all its vital powers³.

[1] The animal, as a whole, was certainly dead, although it retained within itself the potentiality of living. Life might be renewed, if its tissues and organs were again exposed to fitting conditions, but not otherwise.

[2] We have seen, already, how long even in the human subject signs of vitality remain in the right auricle of the heart. All this is much more manifest in the Amphibia, and, from what has been stated above, we can only conclude that the cardiac ganglia, in these creatures as well as in others, are capable of retaining their vital properties longer than the spinal centres.

[3] M. Gavarret calls attention to the Memoir of Legallois published in 1812, 'Sur le Principe de la Vie,' in which he showed a rare insight and prescience. Legallois said (*Œuvres*, t. i. p. 131):—' Si l'on pouvait suppléer au cœur par une sorte d'injection et si en même temps on avait,

It has been ascertained very definitely by the experiments of Helmholtz and of M. Schiff, that the transmission of a stimulus through a nerve is marked by a rise of temperature therein; whilst the extremely interesting experiments of Dr. Lombard seem to show that a similar rise of temperature takes place in the brain itself[1], when it is in a state of activity. Liebreich

pour fournir à l'injection d'une manière continue, une provision de sang artériel, on parviendrait sans peine à entretenir la vie indéfinement dans quelque tronçon que ce soit ; et par cons'quent, après la décapitation, on l'entretiendrait dans la tête elle-même avec toutes les fonctions qui sont propres au cerveau. Non seulement on pourrait entretenir la vie de cette manière, soit dans la tête, soit dans toute autre partie isolée du corps d'un animal, mais on pourrait l'y rappeler après son entière extinction.' These predictions of Legallois have received a most remarkable verification by the experiments of Brown-Séquard, which are thus referred to by M. Gavarret :—' Sur un chien, M. Brown-Séquard sépare la tête du tronc; Il attend *huit* ou *dix* minutes jusqu'à ce que, depuis quelques instants, le bulbe rachidien et le reste de l'encéphale aient bien évidemment perdu toute trace appréciable d'excitabilité ; puis il, pratique des injections réitérées de sang défibriné et oxygéné à la fois dans les artères carotides et dans les vertébrales. Quelques mouvements désordonnés apparaissent au bout de *deux* ou *trois* minutes, puis les muscles des yeux et de la face exécutent des mouvements coordonnés véritables manifestations de la vie, qui tendent à faire admettre que les fonctions cérébrales se sont rétablies dans cette tête complètement separée du tronc.' (Loc. cit. p. 237.)

[1] See 'Journal de Physiologie,' t. i. 670. Intellectual and emotional activity alike produced a rise of temperature, which was always most appreciable over the posterior part rather than the frontal region of the head. We must suppose that the heat detectable in these cases is some surplus portion of that set free in the blood of the part—a portion which has escaped modification into nerve-force. The muscle, as we have seen, is only capable of utilizing a portion of the heat actually liberated. But if the analogy between the mode of action of the muscle and the nerve-centre does not hold—and there is still much room for

and M. Byasson think that such evolution of heat is produced by an increased amount of chemical change in the active parts; though the investigations of Dr. L. H. Wood[1] go to show that (as was the case in the activity of muscle) the liberated energy is not derived from the oxidation of the nerve-substance itself, but rather from an oxidation of the pabulum supplied by the blood to the functionally active parts. It is quite reasonable to suppose, however, that nerve-organs, by virtue of their activity, should undergo a certain amount of waste[2]; and, probably, it is this of which we get evidence in the observations of Liebreich as to the diminution of *protagon* in parts of the nervous system which had long been in a state of uninterrupted activity.

doubt on this subject—then the local increase of heat may be due to mere increased afflux of blood, either alone or supplemented by heat which is liberated during the molecular changes taking place in the nerve-tissue itself.

[1] 'On the Influence of Mental Activity on the Excretion of Phosphoric Acid by the Kidneys.' ('Proceedings of Connecticut Medical Society,' 1869, p. 197.)

[2] The researches of Professor Haughton ('Dublin Quarterly Journal of Medical Science,' 1860) and also of M. Byasson ('Thèse de Paris,' 1868, No. 161) have shown that the same individual during periods in which he has undergone much intellectual labour and a minimum of muscular exercise, passes as much or even more urea than during other similar periods when there has been much muscular exertion and a minimum of intellectual labour. The analyses of M. Byasson go to show that the same individual, under the influence of the same diet, passed in 24 hours the following quantities of urea:—

During a period of rest . . . . 20·46 grms.
During a period of muscular labour . . . . 22·90 ,,
During a period of cerebral activity . . . . 23·88 ,,

The molecular motion or energy, set free in the nervous system, subserves very different purposes. Upon evidence which cannot now be gone into, it could be shown (a) that the nervous system plays an important part in regulating the various secretions and in influencing the nutrition of the body generally. It is nerve-force again (b) which initiates or calls into play the activity of the various muscles by which the countless movements within the bodies of animals are produced, and also those by which locomotion and external visible movements generally are effected. But nerve-changes also (c) give rise to other manifestations—manifestations altogether peculiar in kind and peculiar to the individual in whom they occur. Feeling is the basis of *Consciousness*, and this is a property *sui generis*, which is believed to be called into existence by the action or occurrence of molecular changes within certain parts of the brain[1].

Whilst the manifestation of mental phenomena, in

---

[1] 'Feeling of whatever kind is directly known by each person in no other place than his own consciousness. That feelings exist in the world beyond consciousness is a belief reached only through an involved combination of inferences. That, alike in human and inferior beings, feelings are accompaniments of changes in the peculiar structure known as the nervous system, is also an indirectly established belief. And that the feelings alone cognizable by any individual are products of the action of his own nervous system, which he has never seen, and on which he can try no experiments, is a belief only to be arrived at through a further chain of reasoning. Nevertheless, the evidence, though so indirect, is so extensive, so varied, and so congruous, that we may accept the conclusion without hesitation.'—Herbert Spencer, 'Principles of Psychology,' 1869, p. 128.

the ordinary sense of the term, therefore, corresponds only to a fractional part of nerve-activities in general, there is, again, the very best reason for believing that Consciousness, so far from being co-extensive with Mind, or mental phenomena, is in reality limited to a comparatively small portion of what may be rightly ranged under this category. Many truly mental phenomena never reveal themselves in consciousness at all, and the roots of these strike far and wide; so that, instead of accepting the popular view, that the Brain is *the* organ of Mind, I believe it would be nearer the truth to look upon the whole Nervous System as the organ of Mind—a doctrine which has already been taught by Mr. G. H. Lewes and others. The Brain, it is true, is its principal organ, whilst Consciousness or Feeling[1] is probably only attendant upon the activity of quite a limited portion of this[2]. And,

---

[1] Not using these words, however, in the sense in which they are employed by Mr. Lewes, as has been explained in an article on 'Sensation and Perception' in *Nature*, vol. i. Nos. 8 and 12.

[2] On this subject we have said elsewhere (article on 'Consciousness,' 'Journal of Mental Science,' January 1870, p. 522):—'Mind is generally supposed to be constituted by our conscious states or nerve-actions only; but as these conscious states are themselves only the last terms of a series of molecular actions taking place in ganglionic and other nerve-tissue, we now simply maintain that the components and not the resultant alone ought to be considered as elements entering into the composition of mind. And, similarly, we would make the sum total of the seats of these molecular changes—the whole Nervous System—rather than the seats of the resulting conscious states alone, constitute the organ of Mind as now understood.' And again, in *Nature* (vol. i. No. 12, p. 311):—'Cognition or intellectual action may take

as Mr. Herbert Spencer has so clearly pointed out [1], in the evolution of Mind we each one of us experience the constant transitions whereby a state or act (the recurrence of which was at first always attended by consciousness) at last, when thoroughly familiar, may take place quite unconsciously, or without in the least arousing our attention. The more fully such phenomena, therefore, are recognized as parts of an orderly succession, by which alone greater and greater complexities of thought and feeling are rendered possible, the more will it become evident that the sphere of Mind cannot at any time be circumscribed by the then present or possible states of Consciousness—the more it is obvious that in our conception of Mind we should also include all past stages of Consciousness, the representatives of which, now in the form of unconscious nerve-actions, are from moment to moment manifesting themselves potentially, if not actually, in all our present Thoughts, Feelings, and Volitions.

But though on the question whether Consciousness or Feeling is to be regarded as a possible accompani-

place under the form of a mere *organic* or *unconscious discrimination* without the intervention of consciousness. Thus, in the individual, consciousness or feeling comes to be superadded as an additional accompaniment to certain mere organic discriminations; so that consciousness, without which sensation cannot exist, is secondary, whilst cognition, in the form of unconscious discrimination, is primary. Out of this primary undifferentiated organic discrimination, *such as alone pertains to the lowest forms of animal life*, there has been gradually evolved that which we know as Feeling and Consciousness.'

[1] 'Principles of Psychology,' 1855, pp. 563 and 616.

ment only of certain nerve-changes, or whether it is to be regarded as the invariable and principal result of the activity of the elements of a part which is to be looked upon as the organ of Consciousness, there is still room for doubt; there is, on the other hand, a certainty that the various modes of Consciousness which may be called into activity by any sets of nerve-changes are not to be considered as correlatable with such nerve-changes as a whole. 'We have good reason to conclude,' as Mr. Spencer says, 'that at the particular place in a superior nerve-centre where, in some mysterious way, an objective change or nervous action causes a subjective change or feeling, there exists a quantitative equivalence between the two: the amount of sensation is proportionate to the amount of molecular transformation that takes place in the vesicular substance affected. But there is no fixed or even approximate quantitative relation between this amount of molecular transformation in the sentient centre and the peripheral disturbance originally causing it.' So that, as the same writer also says [1]:—' Between the outer force and the inner feeling it excites, there is no such correlation as that which the physicist calls equivalence—nay, the two do not even maintain an unvarying proportion. Equal amounts of the same force arouse different amounts of the same feeling, if the circumstances differ. Only while all the conditions remain constant

---

[1] 'Principles of Psychology,' 1869, No. 22, p. 194.

is there something like a constant ratio between the physical antecedent and the psychical consequent.'

From all this it may be imagined how hopeless the attempt would be to establish anything like a quantitative estimate of the amount of force answering to these different results of the activity of the Nervous System. In considering the question of muscular activity and its correlation with physical force, we have to do with a measurable effect under the form of mechanical energy. But the manifestations of the activity of the nervous system are much more subtle and eluding. How is it possible for us to estimate the value of the energy expended in regulating the nutrition of the body? How, in a motor act, shall we separate what is due to the nerve and what to the muscle?—nay, where Feeling is aroused, where Consciousness appears, how shall we estimate the equivalent value of this, which each one knows in himself alone, and which seems to differ so absolutely from everything else in the universe? However probable it may be that what we know as *Sensation* and *Thought* are as truly the direct results of the molecular activity[1] of certain nerve-centres, as mechanical energy is the direct result of a muscle, this cannot be proved. MM. Béclard and Heidenhain have shown us how, when a muscle contracts, an amount of heat disappears which holds a

[1] For some most admirable and suggestive remarks as to the probable *unit of Consciousness*, we would refer the reader to Mr. Spencer's 'Principles of Psychology,' No. 21, pp. 148-158.

definite relation to the amount of work done; and so it may well be that when the nerve-centre is in action—when *pains* and *pleasures* are felt, when *thoughts* are rife—this is possible only by reason of a disappearance or metamorphosis of a certain amount of potential energy which had previously been locked up in some of the organic constituents of the body. We cannot, however, prove that it is so, because we have not yet been able to show that there is evolved, during brain action, an amount of heat, or other mode of physical energy, less than there would have been had not the Sensations been felt and the Thoughts thought; and because we have no means of ascertaining what amount of sensation or of thought corresponds to a unit of heat—because it is even impossible for us to gauge the strength of a sensation, or the force of a thought—we are cut off from all means of comparison.

Knowing, however, what we now do concerning the evolution of heat in the animal body and concerning the contractility of muscle; knowing that respiration is, in the main, a process of oxidation; that digestion is an essentially chemical process; it can no longer be said—as of old it was said—that the manifestations of Life in organic beings take place independently of physico-chemical laws, and are regulated solely by occult influences. This error has been fast disappearing since Lavoisier sought to demonstrate the real nature of the phenomena taking place in living things, and since he first taught that many of them were essentially chemical in the ordinary acceptation of the word. What has already been accomplished may well lead us to believe that, as time goes on, the torch of Science will enable us to penetrate still further and to throw light upon some of the remaining mysteries of vital phenomena.

All that we know already, however, concerning the higher animals points strongly to the truth of the conclusion which is thus expressed by Gavarret:—' The action of oxygen upon the material of the blood is then the sole source [1] of force of which the animal can avail itself. In order to accomplish all the internal and external work necessary for the nutrition and for the development of the individual, for the propagation of its kind, and for its action upon the surrounding world, the animal makes use of the force set at liberty during the conflict of oxygen borrowed from the air with the elements of its food. But these alimentary substances in again taking on, under the influence of the burning action of oxygen, their primitive mineral forms, can only set at liberty, and place at the disposal of the animal, their own potential energy—that is to say, that quantity of force which was borrowed by the plant from the solar radiations in order to convert mineral matter into organic matter.'

Matter and force are inseparable—neither can exist alone; and just as the substances which enter into the

---

[1] Either immediate, or mediate.

composition of the plant or of the animal—however high or however low it may be in the scale of organization—have been ultimately derived from the mineral world, so have the forces at work therein been derived from this source and from the Sun—our great centre of light and heat.

CHAPTER II.

THE 'VITAL PRINCIPLE'—NATURE OF LIFE.

Artificial production of Organic compounds. Genesis of living Forms. Influence of modern researches upon conception of Life. Theories concerning Life. Views of Atomists. Pantheistic conception of Anaxagoras. The 'Archæus' of Paracelsus. 'Vitalistic' theories. Difficulties of. Based on misconceptions. Illustrations. Genesis of Living Things. Life a result of molecular organization. Definitions of 'Life.' Why unsatisfactory. Correspondence between Organisms and their Environment. Views of Coleridge. 'Life' an abstract name for the 'qualities' of certain material aggregates. Mere arbitrary nature of distinction into Living and not-living. Gradual passage of the not-living into the Living.

BUT whilst the labours of one set of enquirers have, as we have seen, been directed towards the elucidation of the real nature of the phenomena taking place in living things, with the result of showing them to be much less obscure than had been previously supposed, those of another set have been concentrated upon attempts to build up artificially in the chemical laboratory some of those organic compounds which had hitherto been regarded as the peculiar products of the living organism. The labours of Wöhler, Pelouze, Kolbe, Wurtz, Berthelot, and other celebrated chemists have been especially successful in this direction; and we now can name a goodly array of compounds, previously known only as constituents of animal or vegetable organisms, and previously supposed to be incapable of coming into existence save under the influence of vital forces and vital structures, which are, nevertheless, continually being built up in the chemical laboratory, out of more elementary substances, by processes of synthesis [1].

While thus much has been done to throw light upon some of the phenomena exhibited by living beings, and to diminish the mystery hitherto supposed to enshroud the origin of organic compounds, other efforts, by no means unsuccessful, have been made to account for the production of organic forms, and to reveal how such shapes as are met with amongst the structural units of an organ, as well as those of entire organisms, are the resultants of physical forces acting upon plastic and modifiable tissues. Mr. Rainey[2] has sought to show

[1] Speaking on this subject, Gavarret says ('Phénomènes Physiques de la Vie,' 1869, p. 269), 'De nombreuses et importantes synthèses ont été réalis'es. Les Carbures d'hydrogène peuvent être considérés comme formant la transition entre l'état minéral et l'état organique; beaucoup de ces composés binaires ont été reproduits directement: l'acétylène, l'éthylène et ses homologues, la benzine et ses homologues, la naphtaline, l'anthracine, etc. Les chimistes ont aussi opéré la synthèse d'une quantité considérables de composés oxygénés ternaires: des alcools, des aldéhydes, des acides, des éthers, des corps gras, le phénol et plusieurs de ses homologues, etc. Quelques substances azotées ont été aussi reproduites par synthèse: le cyanogène et ses dérivés, l'urée, la taurine, le glycocolle et ses homologues,' etc.

[2] 'On the Mode of Formation of Shells, of Animals, of Bone,' &c. 1858.

that the mode of formation of the shells of animals, of bone, and of other structures, may be explained by a process of 'molecular coalescence,' and that more or less similar structures may be artificially prepared; and Dr. Montgomery[1] has shown how myeline, a peculiar organic substance, under various physical conditions can be made to assume almost all the different forms of cells at present known; whilst in the second volume of his 'Principles of Biology,' Mr. Herbert Spencer has handled the subject of morphological development, in all its details, with that fulness and philosophic grasp for which he is so distinguished. The shapes of plants—of their branches, leaves, flowers, and cells—are considered on the one hand, and those of animals and of their several parts on the other; and it has been shown that very many of the peculiarities actually met with can be fully accounted for by a consideration of the nature of the incident forces or physical conditions to which they have been subjected during the progress of their growth. Indeed, he goes so far as to say that 'it is an inevitable deduction from the persistence of force, that organic forms which have been progressively evolved must present just those fundamental traits of form which we find them present. It cannot but be that, during the intercourse between an organism and its environment, equal forces, acting under equal conditions, must pro-

---

[1] 'Proceedings of Royal Society,' 1867.

duce equal effects; for to say otherwise is, by implication, to say that some force can present more or less than its equivalent effect, which is to deny the persistence of force. Hence those parts of an organism which are by its habits of life exposed to like amounts and like combinations of actions and reactions, must develope alike; while unlikeness of development must as unavoidably follow unlikeness among these agencies. And, this being so, all the specialities of symmetry, and unsymmetry, and asymmetry which we have traced, are necessary consequences.'

It is impossible to ignore the general direction and bearing which the results of all the researches hitherto referred to must have upon our modern conception of 'Life.' We have seen that in the minds of all scientific men, the doctrine of the Persistence of Force, or of the Conservation of Energy, as it is also termed, now rests upon just as sure a basis as the really equivalent doctrine of the persistence or Indestructibility of Matter[1]. And if matter and force are absolutely inseparable, if the one cannot exist without the other, it will be seen that, even independently of the experimental support which the doctrine has received, the reality of the Persistence of Force must have followed as a logical

[1] As we have previously intimated, the popular doctrine concerning the Indestructibility of Matter resolves itself philosophically into the really fundamental notion of the Persistence of Force. Force and Matter are two aspects of a something one and indivisible; only the idea of Matter is a conception mentally superadded to the various Force-attributes which are alone correlatable with consciousness.

necessity from the Persistence of Matter, which was denied by none. We have seen also how firmly the doctrine has gradually been gaining possession of the minds of the best scientific workers of all kinds, that the so-called 'vital' forces—about the very name of which there was formerly such a ring of mystery—are, after all, nothing more than incident physical forces which have been transformed and conditioned by their 'passage through an organism,' or, as we prefer to express it, are physical forces which have undergone change and have ceased to exist as such in giving birth to those material combinations, which constitute the very matter of the organism itself. As Dr. Frankland has said, 'An animal, however high its organization, can no more generate [that is, actually create] an amount of force capable of moving a grain of sand, than a stone can fall upwards, or a locomotive drive a train without fuel.' The force manifested during the contraction of muscles is the result of the setting free of an equivalent amount of potential energy by the tissue disturbances and chemical changes, of various kinds, which immediately precede and accompany the motor act. And, moreover, if it can be shown that the processes taking place in living beings are in great part amenable to and governed by ordinary physico-chemical laws, instead of being processes altogether occult and peculiar; if it can be shown that products hitherto believed to be producible only under the influence of vital actions taking place within living beings, are capable of being built up artificially by the chemist in his laboratory; and if it can be shown that the shapes and forms assumed by such organic structures are the natural resultants of incident forces acting upon the plastic and modifiable tissues of which they are composed—then may we indeed say that much of the mystery which formerly obscured vital phenomena is being gradually removed. But let it not be supposed that we go further than this, that we suppose *all* mystery has vanished. No, enough still remains to fill our minds with the deepest awe and reverence. The most intimate processes and phenomena of Life remain utterly inexplicable. We have removed the thick husks, but the kernel of the nut as yet lies hidden, enveloped in an impenetrable shell. What do we know concerning the actual phenomena of nutrition? They are still inscrutable mysteries. By what molecular or other laws does an organic unit assimilate to itself matter of a particular kind out of a complex mixture, convert it into its own substance, and endow it with its own properties of doing likewise? Believing, as we may, that sensation and thought are the products of molecular changes taking place in nerve organs, does this belief assist us one iota in explaining the deeper facts? Can we at present frame to ourselves any possible or conceivable way in which mere molecular motion can result in the manifestation of such phenomena as sensations, thoughts, and all the various modes of self-consciousness? Whilst such problems, and many others just as difficult, remain for our solution, it could never be supposed that we believed the problems of Life to be solved. We have cleared some of the approaches, but there is still an impenetrable temple of mystery. Fully to appreciate the extent of our ignorance, however, is the best and surest preparation for widening the sphere of our knowledge.

Glancing now, for a moment, at the conceptions of Life which have been hitherto entertained, let us see how far they are in accordance with modern scientific notions concerning Force.

Two fundamentally opposite doctrines have been maintained again and again as to the nature of Life, under one or the other of which all the views ever promulgated, on this subject, may be ranged. According to the one school, Life is to be regarded as the principle or cause of organization; and according to the other, Life is the product or effect of organization. Democritus and the other Atomists accounted for the whole phenomenal universe on the supposition that the different kinds of matter are made up of the most variously arranged ultimate particles or *atoms*. These atoms differing from one another in size, shape, and weight, were nevertheless thought to be indivisible. They were supposed by Democritus to be able to group and arrange themselves and so to form the various material substances which exist by virtue of these inherent tendencies. Nothing but predestination or 'blind necessity' could, therefore, be assigned by Democritus as the active cause of the continual mutations taking place in the material world. Such a spiritless conception of the Universe was, however, resisted by Anaxagoras. He too, like his predecessors, believed that in the ordinary course of things nothing was created and nothing was destroyed—there was only a continual flux and mutation. But the necessity of a moving force, hitherto almost neglected, was fully realized by him. 'The mythical powers of love and hate, the blind necessity of the mechanical theory, explained nothing; or at least, whatever they explained, they certainly explained not the existence of design in the process of nature. It was consequently seen to be necessary that this notion of design should be identified with that of the moving power. This Anaxagoras accomplished by his idea of a world-forming intelligence (νοῦς) that was absolutely separated and free from matter and that acted on design[1].' Although the function of the νοῦς was, therefore, essentially that of a mere mover or re-arranger of the infinitely minute particles of things into definite shapes and forms, which were thus abstracted from an original chaotic intermixture, still Anaxagoras did endow it with the attribute of thinking—with the power of acting in accordance with design. 'In the case of organized beings more especially, we have the presence

[1] Schwegler's 'Handbook of the History of Philosophy,' translated by Stirling, p. 28.

of the matter-moving νοῦς, which as animating soul, is immanent in all living beings (plants, animals, men), but in different degrees of amount and power. In this way we see that it is the business of the νοῦς to dispose all things, each in accordance with its own nature, into a universe that shall comprehend within it the most manifold forms of existence, and to enter into, and identify itself with, this universe as the power of individual vitality.' Thus was initiated the ancient pantheistic notion of a general soul or Spirit pervading all things—a notion which, with more or less of modification, not unfrequently appears in our own times, and which was exquisitely expressed by our poet Wordsworth in his 'Excursion,' when he said:—

> 'To every form of being is assigned
> An *active* principle: howe'er removed
> From sense and observation, it subsists
> In all things, in all nature, in the stars
> Of azure heaven, the unenduring clouds;
> In flower and tree, in every pebbly stone
> That paves the brooks.'

Whilst therefore the ancients looked upon the spirit or the 'animating principle' of any living thing as an integral part of the general 'Soul of Nature,'

> 'Divinae particulam aurae,'

Paracelsus and his followers, on the contrary, in the sixteenth century, regarded the 'vital principle' as an entity or self-existent something, altogether independent and peculiar. This distinct vital principle was presumed to preside over the processes of nutrition and was known by the name *Archæus*. The doctrines of Paracelsus were more especially developed by his disciple Van Helmont, who sought to explain all the phenomena of Life by the occurrence of chemical changes in the organism taking place under the guidance of this distinct spiritual entity or 'Archæus,' whose place of abode was the cardiac orifice of the stomach. The 'Archæus' of Van Helmont, however, was only one, though the chief, of many 'vital spirits,' which were allotted severally to each organ of the body. In health there was supposed to be a harmonious action of these various 'vital spirits,' whilst disease was a result of their discord. But whether the 'vital principle' was looked upon as a something altogether peculiar and independent, or as an integral part of the general 'Soul of Nature,' in either case the organism as an organism was supposed to have owed its nature and peculiarities to the influence and active working of the 'vital principle.'

Then, in all but modern times, Life was by the greater number of physiologists looked upon as a consequence rather than as a cause of organization; whilst 'vital' actions, or the phenomena presented by living beings, were supposed to be altogether special in kind— to be the peculiar manifestations of the inherent activity of the organized body, and to have no necessary relationship with the physical forces of the inorganic world. Later still, as we have seen, this view gradually underwent a most important modification: 'vital' phenomena, instead of being looked upon as altogether peculiar, were gradually more and more recognized as the results of physical forces which, as Dr. Carpenter expressed it, had been transformed or conditioned in various ways by their 'passage through the organism.' And now amongst nearly all advanced physiologists the same kind of Correlation is implicitly believed to exist between the Vital and the Physical Forces, and between the several vital forces, as we know exists between the physical forces *inter se*. Some there are, however, who still contend that there is such a thing as a peculiar 'vital force,' a something which finds no place amongst this circle of correlated energies[1]. It is argued, that in order to bring about this metamorphosis of the physical forces, which is to give rise to the various manifestations of vegetable and animal life, there must be needed some force inherent in the organism as a whole, and in every part of its structure. That this force or power, altogether independent of the correlated series, is *the* vital force—that which conditions or transforms the physical forces, in order that they may give rise to the most varied vital phenomena. But if the vital or

---

[1] Dr. Lionel Beale, for instance, says in his new work on 'Protoplasm,'—' In order to account for the facts, I conceive that some directing agency of a kind *peculiar to the living world* exists in association with every particle of living matter, which, in some hitherto unexplained manner, affects temporarily its elements, and determines the precise changes which are to take place when the living matter again comes der the influence of certain external conditions.' (2nd ed. p. 119.)

directive power resident in each particle of a living being be other than a transformed physical force, it must be one which—in spite of the well-known formula '*ex nihilo nihil fit*'—is capable of indefinite self-multiplication. Either such force must be continually springing into being without a cause—originating itself, or growing out of nothing—which is an absurdity; or else within the human ovum, or within that of any other animal, there must be *locked up, in this one tiny microscopic cell, the whole of the peculiar vital power* which is afterwards to diffuse itself throughout the body, and which, later still, is to serve as the guiding principle of the whole man. How could the tiny cell retain all this priceless energy? What hydraulic press would be adequate to bring about such concentration, even were it destined to be locked up within walls of adamant, rather than of tender protoplasm? Then, too, we come back to the further difficulty, as to how this original ovum acquired its marvellously concentrated quotum of vital force. The ovum is but a differentiated product, an individual cell, arising from the almost infinite subdivision and growth of a pre-existing ovum, and, therefore, it can only have received an infinitesimal share of the original vital force with which its parent germ was endowed. This parent germ was similarly related to its progenitor, and so we might run back through the races and through the ages, did not the very idea carry absurdity in its face. A force independent of the correlated series of physical forces, and yet capable of perpetual existence, with apparently undiminished powers in spite of an almost infinite number of divisions and subdivisions, surely there are few who will believe that such a force can exist. The doctrine is absolutely inconceivable, it cannot be realized in thought. Dr. Bence Jones has well said[1], 'We know now that in all living things no separate or peculiar matter is present. The stuff which takes part in the living actions and the forces which are inherent in that stuff are there, and indestructible and inseparable. Inorganic matter and inorganic force always exist together in living things; so that if a separable living force be also present, then we must admit that two totally different laws of force must be in action at the same time in the same matter. The unity of nature will at least be preserved by our hesitation to admit the assumption of a force capable of creation and annihilation, until some very conclusive evidence be obtained that there actually is in living things such a force or forces capable of being separated entirely from the matter of which they are made.' And in addition to this kind of argument, we may well ask whether there is the need (such as the advocates for the existence of a peculiar and independent 'vital principle' suppose) for a special force to effect the transformation of physical forces within organized structures? The phenomena presented by living

[1] Croonian Lectures 'On Matter and Force' at Royal College of Physicians ('British Medical Journal,' May 16, 1868, p. 471).

beings are now presumed by almost all physiologists to be dependent upon the agency of transformed physical forces? And, if this be the case, we may well ask (seeing that they are all members of a correlated series) why a special force should be needed to effect the transformation of physical forces into those modes of energy which are active in the manifestations of living beings, whilst no peculiar force is deemed necessary to effect the transformation of one mode of physical force into any other mode of physical force? The mere advancement of such a supposition would seem to show that the promulgators of it had not seized the very essence of the doctrine of the Persistence of Force. Matter and force, it says, are inseparable; the latter manifests itself as the attributes or qualities of the former, and necessarily, if, under the influence of communicated Motion or Force, the particles of matter assume different relationships to one another, this matter will be changed in its qualities, and will display the same to us under the guise of different attributes or force-manifestations[1]. When mechanical energy is converted into

---

[1] 'Redistributions of matter,' Mr. Spencer says, 'imply concomitant redistributions of motion. That which under one of its aspects we contemplate as an alteration of arrangement among the parts of a body is, under a correlative aspect, an alteration of arrangement among certain momenta whereby these parts are impelled to their new positions. . . . Inseparably connected as they are, these two orders of phenomena are liable to be confounded together.' ('Principles of Biology,' vol. i. p. 43.) And again, he points out that the ' transformation of ethereal undulations

heat, the motion in mass, or *molar* motion, of one body expends itself as the body is arrested in producing an equivalent *molecular* motion, or motion of the particles, in its own substance and in those of the body by which it has been arrested. But here there is a simple transference of the motion of the mass into the more diffuse motion of the particles of the masses. The motion ceases to exist in the mass as what we ordinarily call motion, though it persists for a time in the atoms or molecules of the masses, and manifests itself in the form of heat. And, similarly, when the expansive motions of the particles of bodies are checked (and mechanical work is done), the heat diminishes in quantity in proportion as a motion of the resisting mass is produced. When heat gives rise to electricity in a thermo-electric pile, a certain quantity of the incident heat ceases to exist as heat. By acting upon the related metals, it has been able to bring about certain molecular re-arrangements of the particles of these, and owing to this new arrangement, the attributes of the metals or their force-manifestations are altered. The newly-arranged particles cease to manifest heat, though they show an equivalent amount of electrical properties. Now, in these cases, we do not postulate the existence of a peculiar force in the molecules of the bodies by the influence of which the incident physical

---

Into certain molecular rearrangements of an unstable kind, on the overthrow of which the stored-up forces are liberated in new forms, is a process that underlies all organic phenomena.' (Loc. cit. p. 29.)

forces are modified, so as to give rise to new electrical manifestations. Such a view might have been admissible if forces were considered as independent entities, capable of manifesting themselves in different ways, but with an inherent obstinacy of their own—an inborn reluctance to change their mode of action—which could only be overcome by the superior energy of some independent, autocratic demon situated in each particle of a body. We will not speak of the waste of energy which would result, on such a supposition, from the everlasting conflict of these powers, because such doctrines are now effete. Forces are not separable entities. They are merely modes, affections, properties—call it what you will—of matter; and, therefore, necessarily vary with the molecular states of matter. When heat gives rise to electricity, a certain amount of heat vanishes, and an equivalent amount of electricity appears, because the heat, under certain conditions of proximity of other metals, has arranged the metallic molecules in a different way. This heat or force expends itself in producing the molecular change, and the result of the new molecular arrangement is, that electrical properties are manifested instead of heat, because electricity is the property of this particular molecular arrangement, just as heat was the property of the particles when in their immediately antecedent condition. This is just parallel with what we have previously alluded to as characterising the transformation of the motion of masses into heat, or the motion of particles. If we suppose a wooden ball to be allowed to drop from a moderate height from the raised hand of an experimenter into a basin of water, we have no difficulty in imagining what the result would be. A great splashing of the water would occur, and a visible motion of the contents of the basin would remain for a considerable time—though gradually diminishing in extent, and therefore in the ease with which it could be perceived. Here the motion of one mass becomes arrested, but communicates itself in a more diffused manner to a mass of water, the visible motion of which is seen to diminish most gradually. But if the ball had been allowed to fall from a height of three hundred feet, instead of from a height of six feet, and if it had fallen upon a solid floor instead of into a basin of water, then (with the exception of the motion of the rebound) all the force existing as visible motion would have been much more immediately expended in the production of molecular motion in the ball and in the floor, and this would have given rise to heat, recognizable by the aid of a thermoscope. Now the motion of a mass is only the motion of an aggregate of molecules—the molecules being numerous in direct proportion to the size of the mass. So that in this case also, when the mechanical energy resulting from molar motion is converted into heat, the energy (or motion) which the mass displays ceases to manifest itself to us as motion as soon as it has become expended in the production of vibrations in the particles of the bodies which may reveal themselves in the form of heat. The pre-existing force is itself the cause of the change of constitution which results in the new manifestations.

And, similarly, we have the most perfect right to expect that, when a physical force gives rise to any one of the modes of vital force, what takes place is not so much a direct conversion or transmutation of the force itself, but rather that the physical force expends itself in bringing about new collocations of matter—either in converting non-living into living matter, or in altering the molecular constitution of matter which is already alive. The properties of this matter being what we call 'vital' properties, it may be said that the physical force has been transmuted into vital force. Only when understood in this sense, are the words 'conversion' or 'transmutation' suitable for the expression of what really occurs. The almost necessary use of these terms has, we think, nevertheless tended to foster an erroneous impression, which has exercised its misleading influence by causing certain physiologists to suppose that a special 'vital force' is needed to effect the transmutation of incident physical forces within the bodies of living organisms. In reality, no special force is in the least needed to do the work of conversion. Any pre-existing physical force, acting upon an organism, expends itself in producing those molecular re-arrangements which, with others, contribute to enable the organism to carry on its so-called 'vital' processes. If the doctrine of the Correlation of the Vital and of the Physical forces is admitted to be true, it can, we think, be believed only in this form, and the vitalists must give up their last stronghold—we cannot even grant them a right to assume the existence of a special 'vital force' whose peculiar office it is to effect the transformation of physical forces. The notion that such a force does exist, is based upon no evidence; it is a mere postulate. The assumption of its existence carries with it nothing but confusion and contradiction, because the very supposition that it exists and that it does so act, is totally adverse to the general doctrine of the Correlation of the Forces. Need we say more? Does it not follow, if living organisms of the simplest kind are ever now evolved in solutions containing organic matter, that such rudimentary forms of life are to be regarded as resulting from the collocations of organic molecules in peculiar modes, brought about by the expenditure of incident physical forces—whilst the dynamic manifestations of these peculiar aggregates would constitute those phenomena which we term vital, and which are designated in their generality by the word 'Life?'

To speak then of Life as a result of organization is obviously as much in accordance with the general doctrine which we have been unfolding, as the other view—that Life is a cause of organization—is opposed to it. The last doctrine is an appanage of obsolete views; it accords only with the notion that Force is a something separate, or at least separable, from matter—a kind of entity or self-existent principle. But whilst we say that Life is a result of organization, we do not necessarily mean of an organization which is capable of being discovered by means of our microscopes—rather, of a molecular organization, in the sense of a peculiarly complex and unstable collocation of the component atoms of the matter displaying Life, which may exist to perfection after its own fashion, even in what appears to be the perfectly structureless jelly-mass constituting one of the *Protamaba* of Professor Haeckel. And it is important to keep this difference in view—to remember that the only organization necessary for the display of Life is a molecular organization which, in the common acceptation of the term, has often been regarded as no organization at all. Mr. Lewes says, 'Although the question whether Life precedes Organization has been often asked, it is a question *mal posée*. If by organization we are to understand not simply organic substance, but a more or less complex arrangement of that substance into separate organs, the question is tantamount to asking whether the simplest animals and plants have life? And to ask the question whether Life precedes organic substance, is tantamount to asking whether the convex surface of a curve precedes the concave, or whether the motions of a body precede the body[1].' If the word 'organization' is comprehended in its wider

---

[1] 'Fortnightly Review,' July, 1868, p. 73.

sense, however, we may in answer to the oft-put question reply that Life *is* a result of organization. Providing only that the 'molecular organization' is of the right kind, it is true enough, as Mr. Lewes intimates, that the two are inseparable. The word 'Life' is only a generalized expression signifying the sum-total of the properties of matter possessing such an organization. And matter is, as we have before agreed, inseparable from its properties.

This brings us at last to the question of the definition of Life. We will say only a very few words on this subject before alluding to some of the numerous attempts that have been made in this direction, and to the degree of success with which they have been attended.

The word 'Life' is merely an abstract name for those sets of attributes or force-manifestations of living beings which are usually spoken of as 'vital phenomena.' The word itself, however, corresponds only with a mere mental conception : we have observed that a number of things (by common consent looked upon as living beings, whether animal or vegetable) always present a certain set of phenomena or qualities, and in order to express our conception of these in their generality we employ the word 'Life.' Just as, to take a more simple case, after having seen a certain number of things all of which present a black colour, we make use of the word 'blackness' as our name or symbol for the common attribute of all black things. Since, however, this word 'blackness' represents nothing but a mere impression made upon our mind, since it corresponds to no external reality which, in the common acceptation of the phrase, exists of and by itself, and is moreover the name of a simple attribute, it admits of no useful definition[1]. The word 'Life,' however, is not a simple abstract name, it is rather a general abstract name, connoting certain fundamental properties of living things. Such a general abstract name may therefore be defined by distinguishing the nature of the qualities which it implies. This has been attempted by many, but has, we think, been achieved by none so successfully as by Mr. Herbert Spencer. He defines 'Life' as 'The continuous adjustment of internal relations to external relations,' and this phrase is, perhaps, the most generalized statement (being at the same time distinctive) which can be made concerning the phenomena presented by living things. As such, also, it doubtless is a formula of much philosophical interest, though as a mere definition of Life, that is as an explanatory phrase which is likely to make an ordinary reader's notions on the subject any the clearer, we question whether it will be of much service. This, however, is owing to the inherent difficulty of giving any intelligible account in a

[1] It certainly would answer no useful purpose—would explain nothing—if we defined 'blackness' to be the property or power of exciting the sensation of black; and yet this is about the only possible definition of the word.

definition of the meaning of such a general abstract term. The time is, moreover, well-nigh passed when much importance can be attached to attempts to define 'Life.' Such an end might have had more attractions for those who looked upon Life as the manifestation of an independent 'principle' or entity, but it is certainly far less important for those who look upon the word 'Life' as a mere name connoting a set of attributes which belong to all living things. Believing this to be true, believing that anything which can be called Life, or the 'principle' of Life, has no more a separate and independent existence in the world than that 'blackness' has any real existence apart from a thing possessing this quality, it would seem that the reader would be likely to derive clearer notions of the nature of Life, if in place of the definition of this abstract name, we were to substitute the definition of a Living Thing[1]. This should be done in such general terms that—although the definition may be in itself distinctive and only applicable to the objects in question—all things manifesting this set of properties connoted by the word 'Life' may, nevertheless, be included under it. Such a definition of a Living Thing might stand as follows :—

[1] Every abstract name must, in fact, include in its signification the existence of some object to which the quality, of which it is the name, belongs. And inasmuch as no Life can exist without an organism, of which it is the phenomenal manifestation, so it seems comparatively useless to attempt to define this phenomenal manifestation alone—and what is worse, such attempts may tend to keep up the idea that Life is an independent entity.

It is an unstable collocation of Matter, capable of growing by selection and interstitial appropriation of new matter which then assumes similar qualities, of continually varying in composition in response to variations in its Medium, and which is capable of self-multiplication by the separation of portions of its own substance [1].

It is one of the properties of living bodies, one of the consequences of the peculiar collocation of their molecules, that they are only slightly amenable to the influence of some of the physical forces which tend to disintegrate and destroy many forms of not-living matter. It was under the influence of this consideration principally, that Bichat was led to define life as

---

[1] M. Nicolet, in his 'Mémoire sur les Amibes à Corps Nu,' speaking of these creatures, which have been subsequently named *Protamœba* by Professor Haeckel, and which are about the simplest of known living things, says:—'La substance qui en forme le corps peut être considérée comme l'expression d'un premier degré d'animalité de la matière organique. Ici point d'appareils spéciaux affectés aux fonctions de la vie; point d'organe, même rudimentaire, indiquant une similitude plutôt animale que végétale; point de muscles, point de fibres, point de cellules, rien de ce qui manifestent la vie dans ces deux règnes: et cependant elle vit, elle remplit des fonctions qui nécessitent des organes particuliers dans tous les autres êtres; elle se meut, elle se nourrit, elle se reproduit, elle digère, mais la locomotion s'opère par la protension et la rétraction alternative ou simultanées des différentes parties de sa masse. . . . L'Amibe n'a donc aucune organisation appréciable; et lorsque, dépouillée des matières étrangères qu'elle renferme presque toujours dans sa propre substance, elle glisse sur la surface d'un lame de verre immergée, elle se présente toujours comme une *gelée vivante*, finement granulée, dépourvue de téguments, et d'un diaphanéité souvent telle, que sa présence ne se manifeste que par un simple différence de réfraction.'—'Arcana Naturæ,' J. Thompson, 1859, p. 23.

'L'ensemble des fonctions qui résistent à la mort.' Here the notion of a certain antagonism between the organism and its Medium is principally apparent; whilst, on the other hand, in the definition of Mr. Herbert Spencer, already alluded to, we have one of the most general and inclusive statements possible concerning the phenomena of living things: Life is rather represented as the harmonious reaction in living matter to the influence exerted by surrounding matter and force. Stated more fully, his conception of life becomes—'The definite combination of heterogeneous changes, both simultaneous and successive, *in correspondence with external coexistences and sequences.*' And how extremely important this notion of reciprocal action is, has been most happily dwelt upon by Mr. Spencer[1] in the following sentences. 'We habitually distinguish between a live object and a dead one by observing whether a change which we make in surrounding conditions, or one which nature makes in them, is or is not followed by some perceptible change in the object. By discovering that certain things shrink when touched, or fly away when approached, or start when a noise is made, the child first roughly discriminates between the living and the not-living; and the man, when in doubt whether an animal he is looking at is dead or not, stirs it with his stick; or if it be at a distance, shouts or throws a stone at it. Vegetal and animal life are alike pri-

[1] 'Principles of Biology,' vol. I. p. 72.

marily recognized by this process. The tree that puts out leaves when the spring brings change of temperature, the flower which opens and closes with the rising and setting of the sun, the plant that droops when the soil is dry and re-erects itself when watered, are considered alive because of these induced changes; in common with the zoophyte which contracts on the passing of a cloud over the sun, the worm that comes to the surface when the ground is continuously shaken, and the hedgehog which rolls itself up when attacked.' And, not only do we expect some response when a living organism is acted upon by a stimulus, but there is a sort of fitness in the response, different from the reaction of mere dead matter under certain changes of condition. In the latter 'the changes have no apparent relation to future external events which are sure or likely to take place,' whilst in the former the vital changes manifestly have such relations. Then too, as Mr. Spencer says, familiarity with the fact must not allow us to overlook the significance of the consideration, 'that there is invariably, and necessarily, a conformity between the vital functions of any organism, and the conditions in which it is placed —between the processes going on inside of it, and the processes going on outside of it. We know that a fish cannot live in air, or a man in water. An oak growing in the ocean, and a sea-weed on the top of a hill, are incredible combinations of ideas. We find that every animal is limited to a certain range of climate; every plant to certain zones of latitude and elevation. Of the marine flora and fauna, each species is found exclusively between such and such depths. Some blind creatures flourish only in dark caves; the limpet only where it is alternately covered and uncovered by the tide; the red-snow alga rarely elsewhere than in the arctic regions or among alpine peaks.' But having once recognized the importance of this action and reaction continually taking place between the organism and its environment, we become the more alive to the shortcomings of those definitions which do not include this fundamental notion. Though unsatisfactory for other reasons also, the definition of De Blainville will be seen to be eminently defective in this respect. He says, 'Life is the twofold internal movement of composition and decomposition, at once general and continuous.' Almost the same objection may also be alleged against the definition of Richerand, that 'Life is a collection of phenomena which succeed each other during a limited time in an organized body,' even if it had not been useless as a definition of Life, because the same words would be applicable to the process of decay taking place after death in a previously living body.

Life, says Schelling[1], is the '*principle of individuation*, or the power which unites a given *all* into a *whole*.'

[1] As given in an unacknowledged translation by Coleridge entitled 'Hints towards the Formation of a more Comprehensive Theory of Life,' 1848, p. 42.

But Schelling, in reality, in spite of the actual wording of his definition[1], looked upon the words 'life' and 'quality' as conveying to the mind almost identically the same ideas. All things, therefore, possessing qualities—that is everything in the universe—has a Life of its own[2], varying though it may in rank and supremacy, in the case of things ordinarily spoken of as non-living or living respectively[3]. And this brings us to what we consider to be the true conception of Life —to the meaning which ought to be attached to the word. All bodies in Nature have properties or qualities—they are in fact known to us only as aggregates of such and such properties. Bodies are, however, divided into two great classes—the living and the not-living—according as they do or do not possess certain qualities or properties. These differentiating qualities are those which are generalized and included

---

[1] However unsatisfactory Schelling's formula may be as a definition of Life, we cannot fail to recognize that it is an expression of one of the most notable *tendencies* of life in all its higher manifestations.

[2] Burdach ('Traité de Physiologie,' Trad. par Jourdan, 1837, t. Iv. p. 149) says, 'Effectivement nous rencontrons des traces de vie dans toute existence quelconque.'

[3] Thus are we again brought face to face with the old philosophic conception that there exists a 'soul' in all things, or, as Wordsworth tells us, an all-pervading Power :—

> 'Whose dwelling is the light of setting suns,
> And the round ocean and the living air,
> And the blue sky, and in the mind of man:
> A motion and a spirit that impels
> All thinking things, all objects of all thought,
> And rolls through all things.'

under the abstract name 'Life.' We must not be blinded, however, by the use of such a word; we must not fall into the old error of supposing that because by a process of generalization we have conceived a mere abstract notion which we name 'Life,' that, therefore, there is anything existing, of and by itself, answering to this term. No, each material body has properties of its own—properties which are due to its molecular constitution—and which make it what we know it to be. These properties are, however, often classed together in a definite way; certain of the objects around us, for instance, have a power of growing, of developing, and of reproducing their kind. Bodies possessing such properties have been *arbitrarily* named 'Living' bodies, and the word 'Life' has been used as a mental symbol connoting the sum total of the properties which distinguish such an aggregate from the member of the other great class whose representatives do not present such properties. These properties may be looked upon as of a higher and more subtle nature, but it should be distinctly understood that they are as much dependent upon the mere qualities and nature of the material aggregate which displays them, as the properties of a metal or the properties of a crystal are the results of the nature and mode of collocation of the atoms of which these bodies are composed. Hence in using the phrase 'Genesis of Life,' it must not be supposed that we should, in so doing, refer to the actual origination of any 'principle' or 'force' that did not pre-exist;

rather, we should wish to convey the idea, that a particular aggregation of matter had been brought about, of such a kind as to enable it to manifest the properties of a Living Thing, properties which are expressed in their generality by the word 'Life.' Philosophically speaking, therefore, there can be no abrupt line of demarcation between the living and the not-living. Living things are peculiar aggregates of ordinary matter and of ordinary force which in their separate states do not possess the aggregate of qualities known as 'Life.' The transition must be most gradual, therefore, between some of the ordinary not-living states of these and the formation of those particular collocations which constitute them living things. 'Construed in terms of evolution,' as Mr. Spencer says[1], 'every kind of being is conceived as a product of modifications wrought by insensible gradations on a preexisting kind of being:' to which we will only add, that the physical forces expending themselves in bringing about any particular collocation manifest themselves anew in the properties which this displays. *Omnia mutantur: nibil interit.* As Dumas[2] has said, there is an 'eternal round in which death is quickened and Life appears, but in which matter merely changes its place and form.'

[1] Appendix to 'Principles of Biology.'
[2] 'Chemical and Physiological Balance of Organic Nature,' 1844 (Translation), p 48.

CHAPTER III.

NATURE OF ORGANIZABLE MATERIALS AND OF LOWEST LIVING THINGS.

No real distinction between Organic and Inorganic matter. Artificial Production of Organic Compounds. *Organizable* matter. Its constitution and Properties. Belongs to colloidal division of matter. Professor Graham's views on *colloids*. Original Evolution of Organic Matter on our Globe. Primordial Evolution of Living Things. Probable nature of these. The factors being a plastic material and ethereal undulations. Conversion of insensible into sensible motion. Mr. Herbert Spencer's explanations. Important nature of these. Constructive functions of Plants. Continual conversion of non-living into Living Matter in processes of Growth.
Views of Life to be tested by nature of simplest living things. Illustrations of physical theory. Death in higher Animals. Different degrees of 'Individuation.' Death in lower Organisms.
Lowest present Living Things. A third Organic Kingdom, *Protista*, intermediate between Plants and Animals. Nature of its simplest Forms. The Protoplasm Theory. No Absolute Commencement of Life.

BEFORE Wöhler announced to the scientific world that he had succeeded in building up an organic compound in his laboratory with the aid of no more mysterious agencies than usually lie at the chemist's disposal, and before the labours of other distinguished chemists had been crowned with a like success, there was more reason than there is at present for the belief that the forces in living things are altogether peculiar, because it appeared that certain compounds of carbon with other elements, known as *organic* substances, were capable of being produced only within these laboratories of nature. A department of Inorganic chemistry has hitherto existed, separated quite definitely from another known as that of Organic chemistry. In the former were included all those elements and their compounds which were naturally met with amongst, and which made up the not-living constituents of our globe, whilst under the latter department were ranged those compounds and their derivatives which were supposed to exist only in plants and animals. The so-called organic compounds were for a long time regarded as altogether peculiar; not as regards composition—for they were known to be composed of precisely the same elements as were most abundant in the inorganic world—but rather in point of origin. *They* were the products only of living things: had been produced under the influence of 'vital' forces. The action of physical forces in the world without was deemed inadequate to give rise to such combinations, and therefore they were separated by a hard and fast line from all other compounds with which the chemist manipulated. Thus the popular belief of the time concerning Life was fostered; and an argument for the special and peculiar nature of the 'vital forces,' could, at least, be based on the supposed fact that living things did produce substances—were in fact almost entirely built up of material combinations—which could not be evolved by the agency of mere physical forces, either in the grand laboratory of nature, or under the hands of the chemist. But now all this has changed. Chemists have already succeeded in building up some hundreds of such compounds, and, as each month passes by, the list is swelled by fresh conquests. The speciality then of these compounds has passed away; the difference between Organic and Inorganic chemistry is fast vanishing—has, in fact, well-nigh vanished. At all events, these names can no longer be retained as definite marks; they have lost their significance, and if it be desirable still to partition off the great department of chemical compounds formerly represented by the word 'organic,' it must be done by fixing upon some really common and distinguishing characteristic of the members of the group, and embodying this in some new class name or phrase under which they can be ranged. Numerous suggestions have been made, but none of them seems so good as that of Kekulé. All the compounds named 'organic' invariably contained carbon as a constituent, and with the exception of at most three or four, *all* the compounds of carbon were formerly placed under this category, so that when Kekulé not long since brought out a work [1], 'On the Chemistry of Carbon Compounds,' its

[1] 'Lehrbuch der Organischen Chemie, oder der Chemie den Kohlenstoffverbindungen,' 1861, in which this subject is discussed at pp. 8–11.

scope was found to be as nearly as possible what it would have been had it appeared solely under the old name of 'Organic Chemistry.'

Thus the Matter of living things, the combinations which they are capable of producing, have no distinguishing peculiarity—they can be built up by the chemist in his laboratory—the mysterious agency of Life is now no longer all essential. This knowledge is a great gain to science, and it harmonizes well with our conclusion in the last chapter, that there is no evidence whatever for a belief in the existence of a peculiar 'vital force'—a something independent of matter, and not convertible with the ordinary physical forces.

It will now be necessary for us to furnish some explanations as to the nature and composition of organizable matter in general—of those substances in fact which enter into the composition of living things —and in so doing we shall avail ourselves freely of the writings of those who are best entitled to speak on the subject.

Organizable matter always contains, as principal and fundamental ingredients, carbon, oxygen, hydrogen, and nitrogen, and to these are often added traces of sulphur and phosphorus. The first four elements are, however, all-essential, and it is especially worthy of remark that no less than three of them are gaseous. Mr. Herbert Spencer says [1]:—'When we remember

[1] 'Principles of Biology,' vol. i. chap. i., 'Organic Matter.' This and

how these re-distributions of Matter and Motion which constitute Evolution, structural and functional, imply motions in the units that are redistributed; we shall see a probable meaning in the fact that organic bodies which exhibit the phenomena of Evolution in so high a degree, are mainly composed of ultimate units having extreme mobility.' When such mobile units enter into various combinations, this initial property though masked is still potentially present, and must have its influence upon the molecular mobility of the compounds into which they enter. Hence Mr. Spencer adds, 'We may infer some relation between the gaseous form of three out of the four chief organic elements, and that comparative readiness to undergo those changes in the arrangement of parts which we call development, and those transformations of motion which we call function. . . . . One more fact that is here of great interest for us must be set down. These four elements of which organisms are almost wholly composed, present us with certain extreme antitheses. While between two of them we have an unsurpassed contrast in chemical activity; between one of them and the other three we have an unsurpassed contrast in molecular mobility. While carbon by successfully resisting fusion and volatilization at the highest temperatures that can be produced, shows us a degree of atomic cohesion greater than that of any other known element,

the succeeding chapters of Mr. Spencer's work should be read by all who wish fully to understand this part of the subject.

hydrogen, oxygen, and nitrogen show the least atomic cohesion of all elements. And while oxygen displays, alike in the range and intensity of its affinities, a chemical energy exceeding that of any other substance (unless fluorine be considered an exception), nitrogen displays the greatest chemical inactivity [1]. Now on calling to mind one of the general truths arrived at when analyzing the process of Evolution in general, the probable significance of this double difference will be seen. It was shown ("First Principles," § 123) that, other things equal, unlike units are more easily separated by incident forces than like units are—that an incident force falling on units that are but little

[1] Hence its compounds are generally most unstable. 'Here it will be well to note, as having a bearing on what is to follow, how characteristic of most nitrogenous compounds is this special instability. In all the familiar cases of sudden and violent decomposition, the change is due to the presence of nitrogen. The explosion of gunpowder results from the readiness with which nitrogen contained in the nitrate of potash yields up the oxygen combined with it. The explosion of gun-cotton, which also contains nitric acid, is a substantially parallel phenomenon. The various fulminating salts are all formed by the union with metals of a certain nitrogenous acid called fulminic acid; which is so unstable that it cannot be obtained in a separate state. Explosiveness is a property of nitro-mannite, and also of nitro-glycerine. Iodide of nitrogen detonates on the slightest touch, and often without any assignable cause. Percussion produces detonation in sulphide of nitrogen. And the body which explodes with the most tremendous violence of any that is known, is the chloride of nitrogen. Thus these easy and rapid decompositions, due to the chemical indifference of nitrogen, are characteristic. When we come hereafter to observe the part which nitrogen plays in organic actions, we shall see the significance of this extreme readiness shown by its compounds to undergo change.'—Spencer, loc. cit. p. 8.

dissimilar does not readily segregate them, but that it readily segregates them if they are widely dissimilar. Thus, these two extreme contrasts, the one between physical mobilities, and the other between chemical activities, fulfil in the highest degree a certain further condition to facility of differentiation and integration.'

Thus, then, the very fact that organizable matter is, in the main, compounded of elements with such dissimilar properties, affords a strong *à priori* presumption that such organizable matter would be most unstable, and most prone to undergo metamorphic changes under the influence of even slight changes of condition—such as might operate without appreciable result upon the majority of inorganic substances. The properties of the various *protein* substances which form the all-essential constituents of living tissues, are found to correspond entirely with these *à priori* requirements. This can scarcely be better shown than it has been by Mr. Spencer when he wrote [1] :—'It is, however, the nitrogenous constituents of living tissues that display most markedly those characteristics of which we have been tracing the growth. Albumen, fibrin, casein, and their allies are bodies in which that molecular mobility exhibited by three of their components in so high a degree is reduced to a minimum. These substances are known only in the solid state : that is to say, when deprived of the water

[1] Loc. cit. p. 12.

usually mixed with them, they do not admit of fusion, much less of volatilization. To which add, that they have not even that molecular mobility which solution in water implies; since though they form viscid mixtures with water, they do not dissolve in the same perfect way as do inorganic compounds. The chemical characteristics of these substances are instability and inertness carried to the extreme. .... It should be noted, too, of these bodies, that though they exhibit in the lowest degree that kind of molecular mobility which implies facile vibrations of the atoms as wholes, they exhibit in a high degree that kind of molecular mobility resulting in isomerism, which implies permanent changes in the positions of adjacent atoms with respect to each other. Each of them has a soluble and insoluble form. In some cases there are indications of more than two such forms. And it appears that their metamorphoses take place under very slight changes of conditions. .... In these most unstable and inert organic compounds, we find that the atomic complexity reaches a maximum: not only since the four chief organic elements are here united with small proportions of sulphur and phosphorus, but also since they are united in high multiples. The peculiarity which we found characterized even binary compounds of the organic elements, that their atoms are formed not of single equivalents of each component, but of two, three, four, and more equivalents, is carried to the greatest extreme in these compounds that take the leading part in organic actions. According to Mulder, the formula of albumen is 10 $(C_{4}, H_{31}, N_{5}, O_{12}) + S, P$. That is to say, with the sulphur and phosphorus there are united ten equivalents of a compound atom—containing forty atoms of carbon, thirty-one of hydrogen, five of nitrogen, and twelve of oxygen: the atom being thus made up of nearly nine hundred ultimate atoms.'

These complex nitrogenous compounds, to the properties of which we have just been alluding, belong to the class of bodies named *colloids* by Professor Graham. They all have an extremely low diffusive power when in solution, and on this account they have been separated from the *crystalloids*, or kinds of matter which tend to crystallize, and also undergo diffusion much more rapidly. Gelatine may be taken as the type of this *colloidal condition of matter*. A most radical distinction is presumed to exist between crystalloids and colloids, in regard to their intimate molecular constitution. Professor Graham says[1]:—' Every physical and chemical property is characteristically modified in each class. They appear like different worlds of matter, and give occasion to a corresponding division of chemical science. The distinction between these kinds of matter is that subsisting between the material of a mineral, and the material of an organized mass.' Referring to the colloidal class of substances, Professor Graham also

[1] 'Phil. Trans.' 1861, p. 220.

says [1]:—'Among the latter are hydrated silicic acid, hydrated alumina, and other metallic peroxides of the aluminous class, when they exist in the soluble form; with starch, dextrine and the gums, caramel, taurin, albumen, gelatine, vegetable and animal extractive matter. Low diffusibility is not the only property which the bodies last enumerated possess in common. They are distinguished by the gelatinous character of their hydrates. Although often largely soluble in water, they are held in solution by a most feeble force. They appear singularly inert in the character of acids and bases, and in all the ordinary chemical relations. But, on the other hand, their peculiar physical aggregation, with the chemical indifference referred to, appears to be required in substances that can intervene in the organic processes of life. The plastic elements of the animal body are found in this class.' These compounds are so all-important in living organisms, both from a structural and from a functional point of view, that it is most desirable to learn as much as we can concerning their properties as mere material aggregates —i.e. when they exist alone and not as constituents of living bodies. We find that they themselves exhibit a constant tendency to change in response to the most delicate impressions, after a fashion which is suggestive, at least, of the more complex though still comparatively simple action and interaction taking place between one of the lowest kinds of Amœbæ and its environment.

[1] 'Phil. Trans.' 1861. p. 183.

This tendency we must attribute to the large size and complexity of the colloidal molecules [1]. Professor Graham says on this subject:—'Another and eminently characteristic quality of colloids is their mutability. Their existence is a continued metastasis. A colloid may be compared in this respect to water while existing liquid at a temperature under its usual freezing point, or to a supersaturated saline solution..... The solution of hydrated silicic acid, for instance, is easily obtained in a state of purity, but it cannot be preserved. It may remain fluid for days or weeks in a sealed tube, but it is sure to gelatinize and become insoluble at last. Nor does the change of this colloid appear to stop at that point. For the mineral forms of silicic acid deposited from water, such as flint, are

---

[1] 'Applying to atoms the mechanical law which holds of masses, that since inertia and gravity increase as the cubes of dimensions, while cohesion increases as their squares, the self-sustaining power of a body becomes relatively smaller as its bulk becomes greater; it might be argued that these large aggregate atoms which constitute organic substance, are mechanically weak—are less able than simpler atoms to bear, without alteration, the forces falling on them. That very massiveness which renders them less mobile, enables the physical forces acting on them more readily to change the relative positions of their component atoms; and so to produce what we know as rearrangements and decompositions.' (Spencer, loc. cit. p. 14.) Professor Graham also says:—' It is difficult to avoid associating the inertness of colloids with their high equivalents, particularly where the high number appears to be attained by the repetition of a smaller number. The inquiry suggests itself whether the colloid molecule may not be constituted by the grouping together of a number of smaller crystalloid molecules, and whether the basis of colloidality may not really be this composite character of the molecule.' (Loc. cit. p. 221.)

often found to have passed, during the geological ages of their existence, from the vitreous or colloidal into the crystalline condition¹. The colloidal is, in fact, a dynamical state of matter; the crystalloid being the statical condition. The colloid possesses ENERGIA. *It may be looked upon as the probable primary source of the force appearing in the phenomena of vitality.* To the gradual manner in which colloidal changes take place (for they always demand time as an element), may the characteristic protraction of chemico-organic changes also be referred.' Thus, then, we seem to have found materials which are modifiable and plastic enough to enter into the composition of living things².

But, let us now glance at the theories and requirements of those who seek to account for the first appearance of Organisms.

To all those who are firm believers in the Evolution

[1] Even a 'colloid holding so high a place in its class as albumen' may be met with in the opposite or crystalline condition. Professor Graham says:—' In the so-called blood-crystals of Funke, a soft and gelatinous albumenoid body is seen to assume a crystalline contour.' Can any facts more strikingly illustrate the maxim that in nature there are no abrupt transitions, and that distinctions of class are never absolute?'

[2] 'While the composite atoms of which organic tissues are built up possess that molecular mobility fitting them for plastic purposes, it results from the extreme molecular mobilities of their ultimate constituents, that the waste products of vital activity escape as fast as they are formed.' (Spencer, loc. cit. p. 24.) Vital actions entail decompositions, in which comparatively stable and simple combinations result from the breaking up of the more complex and highly unstable protein compounds. It is necessary that these effete products should be got rid of.

hypothesis, it will, as Dr. Child has already said [1], seem 'an almost irresistible conclusion that there must have been a stage in the development of the universe when the earliest forms of organic life were evolved from some special collocation of inorganic elements by the continued operation of the laws already in action.' Professor Haeckel, indeed, tells us that the occurrence of an original evolution of Life on our globe 'has at present become a *logical postulate of scientific natural history;*' and, similarly, Mr. Herbert Spencer, though 'granting that the formation of organic matter, and the evolution of life in its lowest forms, may go on under existing cosmical conditions,' believes it 'more likely that the formation of such matter and such forms took place at a time when the heat of the earth's surface was falling through those ranges of temperature at which the higher organic compounds are unstable.' 'Exposed to those innumerable modifications of conditions,' he adds, 'which the earth's surface afforded, here in amount of light, there in amount of heat, and elsewhere in the mineral quality of its aqueous medicine, this extremely changeable substance must have undergone now one, now another of its countless metamorphoses.'

The exponents of the Evolution hypothesis, in fact, lead us to believe, that, prior to the evolution of Life and the appearance of living things on our globe, there must have gone on a long series of changes in

[1] 'Essays on Physiological Subjects,' 2nd edition, 1869, p. 144.

the combinations and re-combinations of matter on its surface, leading to the formation of different kinds of aggregates, the molecules of which were large and complex. Such molecules, then, existing in a state of solution, are supposed to have been as prone to undergo changes under the modifying influence of incident forces, as are those of the more or less similar compounds named 'organic' in our own day. Before the lowest forms of Life could have been evolved, it is presumed that there must have been gradually going on the progressive elaboration of an 'organizable' material, resulting, perchance, in the production of states of matter more or less resembling those named *protein*, states which, under the influence of incident forces, may have been thrown into phases of unstable equilibrium, slowly and gradually resulting in new combinations presenting such lowest modes of vital manifestation as present themselves in the minute and simple jelly-specks constituting the *Protamœbæ* of Professor Haeckel.

Modes of action and reaction between such unstable bodies and their environment, not wholly different from those which a colloid presents, may at last have led, through the most insensible gradations, to those altogether indefinite, though successive, changes which constitute the vital phenomena of the lowest known forms of Life. 'Construed in terms of evolution,' says Mr. Spencer, 'every kind of being is conceived as a product of modifications wrought by insensible gradations on a pre-existing kind of being; and this holds as fully of the supposed "commencement of organic life" as of all subsequent developments of organic life. It is no more needful to suppose an "absolute commencement of organic life," or a "first organism," than it is needful to suppose an absolute commencement of social life and a first social organism.'

It is of the utmost importance to keep this last consideration clearly in view in discussing the problem of the origin of Life.

The labours of the chemists who have succeeded in building up organic compounds in their laboratories now come to our aid. They throw even more than a faint glimmer of light upon the possibilities to which we have just been alluding, since, as Mr. Spencer says, 'Organic matters are produced in the laboratory by what we may literally call *artificial evolution*.' This opinion he explains in the following passage, which we cannot forbear quoting, notwithstanding its apparent technicality. 'Chemists find themselves unable to form,' he says, 'these complex combinations directly from their elements; but they succeed in forming them indirectly, by successive modifications of simpler combinations. In some binary compound, one element of which is present in several equivalents, a change is made by substituting for one of these equivalents an equivalent of some other element; so producing a ternary compound. Then another of the equivalents is replaced, and so on. For instance, beginning with ammonia, NH_3, a higher form is obtained by replacing one of the atoms of hydrogen by an atom of methyl, so producing methyl-amine, $N(CH_3)H_2$; and then under the further action of methyl, ending in a further substitution, there is reached the still more compound substance dimethyl-amine, $N(CH_3)(CH_3)H$. And in this manner highly complex substances are eventually built up. Another characteristic of their method is no less significant. Two complex compounds are employed to generate, by their action upon one another, a compound of still greater complexity; different heterogeneous molecules of one stage, become parents of a molecule a stage higher in heterogeneity. Thus having built up acetic acid out of its elements, and having by the process of substitution described above changed the acetic acid into propionic acid, and propionic into butyric, of which the formula is $\left\{\begin{array}{c} C(CH_3)(CH_3)H \\ CO(HO) \end{array}\right\}$; this complex compound by operating upon another complex compound, such as the dimethyl-amine named above, generates one of still greater complexity, butyrate of dimethyl-amine $\left\{\begin{array}{c} C(CH_3)(CH_3)H \\ CO(HO) \end{array}\right\} N(CH_3)(CH_3)H$. See then the remarkable parallelism. The progress towards higher types of organic molecules is effected by modifications upon modifications; as throughout Evolution in general. Each of these modifications is a change of the molecule into equilibrium with its environment—an adaptation, as it were, to new surrounding conditions to which it is subjected; as throughout Evolution in general. Larger, or more integrated, aggregates (for compound molecules are such) are successively generated; as throughout Evolution in general. More complex or heterogeneous aggregates are so made to arise, one out of another; as throughout Evolution in general. . . . And it is by the action of the successively higher forms on one another, joined with the action of environing conditions, that the highest forms are reached; as throughout Evolution in general [1].

If, however, we may suppose that by a process of Evolution, under the influence of natural forces, any such complex and unstable bodies as those to which we have been referring could have come into being in remote periods of the Earth's history, then scarcely any conceivable limit could be placed upon the variations which might still result under the continued play of incident physical forces. In the first place, most of these compounds whose molecules are very complex, are found to be capable of existing under many different isomeric modifications. *Protein*, for instance, according to Prof. Frankland, is capable of existing under probably at least a thousand isomeric forms; and this is the substance which, in one state or another, enters so largely into the fabric of living things, as to be, above all else, *the* organizable material. But even this is not all; there are chemical possibilities more favourable still for the origination and developmental variation of living things. 'There are facts,' Mr.

---

[1] Appendix to 'Principles of Biology' (published separately), p. 482.

Herbert Spencer says[1], 'warranting the belief that though these multitudinous isomeric forms of protein will not unite directly with one another, yet they admit of being linked together with other elements with which they combine. And it is very significant that there are habitually present two other elements, sulphur and phosphorus, which have quite special powers of holding together many equivalents—the one being pentatomic and the other hexatomic. So that it is a legitimate supposition (justified by analogy), that an atom of sulphur may be a bond of union among half-a-dozen isomeric forms of protein; and similarly with phosphorus.'

These then are the materials, or such as these, from the nascent action and interaction of which and their environment there may have sprung up those modes of change and growth which may gradually win for themselves the title of 'vital' phenomena, and which, becoming more pronounced, may at last suffice to stamp the most infinitesimal and variable forms which present them as Living Things.

But, for these changes and actions to take place, the continued action of Forces upon the matter is needed —even though this be of the most unstable description, and therefore the most prone to assume new molecular re-arrangements. There must also be *causes* of change acting from without. Have we not seen that the phenomena taking place in living things, all essentially

[1] Loc. cit. p. 486.

vital characteristics, may be described as '*the continuous adaptation of internal to external relations?*' This is the essence of Life in its dynamical aspect. The causes of change are, however, omnipresent; and the most potent of them seem to be those rays of *Heat* and *Light* which are transmitted to us from our great central luminary in the form of molecular motions—by means of subtle impacts and wave-like undulations in the intervening realms of ether-space. These are the best known, and possibly the most influential of the forces which, emanating from the centre of our solar system, spirit-like, work their vivifying influence by producing such material combinations as are capable of manifesting the phenomena of Life.

The question how such ethereal undulations are capable of bringing about the gradually more complex molecular re-arrangements by which an organizable material has been supposed to be producible; and how in the already existing living thing they exert their influence in those processes of assimilation and growth, *whereby not-living materials are continually being converted into living tissue*, is one of the deepest interest—towards the solution of which Mr. Spencer has contributed some most valuable suggestions.

'The elements of the problem,' as Mr. Spencer says, 'are these:—The atoms of several ponderable matters exist in combination: those that are combined having strong affinities, but having also affinities less strong for some of the surrounding atoms that are otherwise combined. The atoms thus united, and thus mixed among others with which they are capable of uniting, are exposed to the undulations of a medium that is relatively so rare as to seem imponderable. These undulations are of numerous kinds: they differ greatly in their lengths, or in the frequency with which they recur at any given point. And under the influence of undulations of a certain frequency, some of these atoms are transferred from atoms for which they have a stronger affinity, to atoms for which they have a weaker affinity. That is to say, particular orders of waves of a relatively imponderable matter, remove particular atoms of ponderable matter from their attachments, and carry them within reach of other attachments. . . . . Now the discoveries of Bunsen and Kirchoff respecting the absorption of particular luminiferous undulations by the vapours of particular substances, joined with Professor Tyndall's discoveries respecting the absorption of heat by gases, show very clearly that the atoms of each substance have a rate of vibration in harmony with ethereal waves of a certain length, or rapidity of recurrence. Every special kind of atom can be made to oscillate by a special order of ethereal waves, which are absorbed in producing its oscillations; and can by its oscillations generate this same order of ethereal waves. Whence it appears that immense as is the difference in density between ether and ponderable matter, the waves of the one can set the atoms of the other in motion, when the successive impacts of the waves are so timed as to correspond with the atoms. The effects of the waves are, in such case, cumulative; and each atom gradually acquires a momentum made up of countless infinitesimal momenta.' Mr. Spencer then points out that the elements of a chemically-compounded atom (or 'molecule,' as it is usually termed by chemists), being still free to move within certain limits, we must suppose them to remain severally capable of vibrating in unison with the same kinds of ethereal waves, as were capable of moving them when they were in their uncombined condition. The component atoms, therefore, retain their original rates of oscillation, modified only as they may be by their mutual influence upon one another; whilst the compound atom or molecule will have a capacity of oscillating determined by the attributes of its constituent atoms. Taking the case of binary molecules as an example, it becomes evident that if the members of such molecules differ from one another considerably, they are almost sure to be thrown into different rates of vibration, and 'it is manifest that there must arise a tendency towards the dislocation of the two—a tendency which may or may not take effect, according to the weakness or strength of their union, and *according to the presence or absence of collateral affinities.*' This inference is perfectly in harmony with certain known facts. The metallic compounds which are most decomposable under the influence of the chemical rays of light are silver, gold, mercury, and lead, all of which have high atomic weights, whilst others, such as sodium and potassium, the atomic weights of which are low, are much less changeable. In binary compounds of these several metals having high atomic weights there would be a greater difference between the weights of the component elements, than if we had to do with compounds of the small-atomed metals, and so also, it has been found that it is precisely those compounds which consist of the most dissimilar elements that are the most decomposable. But there is also another most interesting aspect of the question. Mr. Spencer says:—'Strong confirmation of this view may be drawn from the decomposing actions of those longer ethereal waves which we perceive as heat. On contemplating the whole series of binary compounds, we see that the elements which are most remote in their atomic weights, as hydrogen and the noble metals, will not combine at all: their vibrations are so unlike that they cannot keep together under any conditions of temperature. If again we look at a smaller group, as the metallic oxides, we see that whereas those metals that have atoms nearest in weight to the atoms of oxygen, cannot be separated from oxygen by heat, even when it is joined by a powerful collateral affinity; those metals which differ more widely from oxygen in their atomic weights, can be de-oxidized by carbon at high temperatures; and those which differ from it most widely, combine with it very reluctantly, and yield it up if exposed to thermal undulations of moderate intensity. And here indeed, remembering the relations between the atomic weights in the two cases, may we not suspect a close analogy between the de-oxidation of a metallic oxide by carbon under the influence of the longer ethereal waves, and the decarbonization of carbonic acid[1] by hydrogen under the influence of the shorter ethereal waves?'

These discoveries and suggestions are, we think, of the deepest interest and importance. They open up possibilities of explaining problems which had hitherto seemed well-nigh insoluble, and that, too, in the simplest way, and by the application of strictly physical principles. Having to deal with such mutable materials as the unstable and big-atomed colloids, and being aware of the above-mentioned explanations as to the way in which vibrations communicated to an imponderable ether may bring about motions amongst the atoms of ponderable matter, much of the seemingly impenetrable mystery which has hitherto enshrouded the nature of the changes taking place in living tissues, appears to be notably lessened. No subject seemed more hopelessly difficult, and yet we can now only agree with Mr. Spencer when he says:—'These conceptions help us to some dim notion of the mode in which changes are wrought by

---

[1] The decomposition of carbonic acid and the fixation of carbon as one of the component elements of living tissue is continually taking place in the leaves of plants under the stimulus of solar light and its actinic rays.

light in the leaves of plants. Among the several elements concerned there are wide differences in molecular mobility, and probably in the rates of molecular vibration. Each is combined with many of the others, but is capable of forming various combinations with the rest. And they are severally in presence of a complex compound into which they all enter, and which is ready to assimilate to itself the new compound atoms that they form. Certain of the ethereal waves falling on them when thus arranged, there results a detachment of some of the combined atoms and a union of the rest. And the conclusion suggested is, that *the induced vibrations among the various atoms as at first arranged, are so incongruous as to produce instability; and to give collateral affinities the power to work a re-arrangement which, though less stable under other conditions, is more stable in the presence of these particular undulations.'* Thus the way seems opening for us to comprehend how, under the mere influence of physical forces, not-living combinations may be broken up so as to give place to those more subtle combinations of matter which are only possible where much incident force is retained. We know that the food of plants consists of not-living or so-called mineral ingredients, we know also that the plant grows, and therefore that these non-living ingredients must be decomposed in order to give place to the new living matter which is continually being produced. Physical forces and natural affinities are, therefore, supposed to be the only factors necessary for bringing about this marvellous transformation, for enabling Living Matter to originate in the tissues of plants by means of a complex rearrangement of pre-existing not-living elements.

To some these views concerning the nature of Life and vital manifestations may seem to be sadly insufficient, reducing it, as the theory does, to a mere interplay between a material aggregate of a particular kind and its environment. But, it must not be forgotten that the only fair way, in judging of the adequacy of such an hypothesis, is to consider how far it is applicable as an explanation of the phenomena exhibited by the *lowest Living Things*. The more we look to the higher forms of Life, the more apt are we to be blinded to the real and essential nature of the phenomena taking place, owing to the greater complexity which has arisen in their various functions step by step with the structural differentiation of the organism itself. Nevertheless, even from phenomena presented by some of these higher organisms, evidence may be obtained which is certainly more reconcilable with the conceptions of Life to which we have just been alluding than with any other.

When seeds of wheat, produced by living plants in times antecedent to the Pharaohs, can remain in the Egyptian catacombs, through century after century—displaying of course no vital manifestations, but nevertheless retaining the potentiality of growing into perfect plants[1] whenever they may happen to be brought into contact with suitable external conditions, we must presume that, either (1) during this long lapse of centuries the 'vital principle' of the plant has been imprisoned in the most dreary and impenetrable of dungeons, whither no sister effluences from the general 'soul of nature' could affect it, and whence escape was impossible; or else (2) that the germ of the future possible living plant is there only in the form of an inherited structure whose molecular complexities are of such a kind that, after moisture has restored mobility to its atoms, its potential life may pass into actual life, because the ever-recurring ethereal pulses of motion, and other changes in its environment, are capable of giving rise to a definite series of simultaneous and successive changes in its own structure. This series of actions and re-actions—most variously complex though they may be—constitute the essential phenomena of Life, and the structure of the organism or living thing manifesting them is but the material embodiment resulting from such actions.

[1] In connection with periods of rest in Plant life, Alex. Braun (*Rejuvenescence in Nature*, Syd. Soc. 1853, p. 200, et seq.) makes some very interesting remarks. We will extract the following sentences only:—
'The formation of fixed oil is intimately connected with that of starch in the economy of cell-life; its appearance, in like manner, announces the repose of age in cell-life, its disappearance the beginning of Rejuvenescence. We meet with fixed oil in the cells, either mixed with starch, substituted for it, or gradually displacing it; its occurrence is perhaps still more general than that of starch, since it exists even in the Fungi and Phycochromiferous Algæ.'

But such things are not only true concerning the germs of plants; somewhat parallel phenomena are presented even by adult organisms in the animal series. The 'Sloths' of Spallanzani, the Rotifers, and the Free Nematoids or Anguillules, certainly should be taken into account by those who would wish to arrive at correct conceptions as to Life. These animals, having comparatively definite and complex organizations, are now

Fig. 1. Animals found in tufts of Moss and Lichen.
a. *Plectus paristinus*, a Free Nematoid.
b. *Rotifer vulgaris*, the common Wheel Animalcule.
c. *Emydium testudo*, one of the 'Sloths' of Spallanzani.

notorious for their tenacity of Life, their power of resisting the most adverse external conditions, and, above all, for their power of resuming active vital manifestations, after these have been completely in abeyance for five, ten, fifteen, or even more than twenty years[1].

[1] More complete details concerning these properties may be found in a memoir on 'The Anatomy and Physiology of the Nematoids, Parasitic

Living together, as they generally do, tenanting the same tufts of moss or the same patches of lichen, they eke out their existence by instalments, instead of enjoying a more or less definite and continuous span of life. And, during their most extreme degrees of desiccation they certainly can have no more title to be looked upon as living things than can the seeds in the catacombs of Egypt. Though not living, they also retain the potentiality of manifesting Life: and, for each alike, in order that this potentiality may pass into an actuality, the first requisite is water, with which to restore to them that possibility of molecular re-arrangements under the influence of incident forces, of which the absence of water had deprived them, and without which Life, in any real sense, is impossible [1].

and Free.' Philosophical Transactions, 1866, p. 613-620. With regard to Nematoids I have there said that 'the remarkable tenacity of Life of which we have been speaking is met with only amongst the representatives of four land and freshwater genera, *Tylenchus*, *Plectus*, *Aphelenchus*, and *Cephalobus*; whilst those of all the other genera, excepting *Rhabditis*, marine as well as land and freshwater, are rather remarkable for the very opposite characteristic, they being incapable of recovery even after the shortest periods of desiccation.' It was formerly supposed that all the Free Nematoids exhibited this tenacity of Life.

[1] Professor Owen says (Monthly Microscopical Journal, May 1, 1869, p. 294), 'There are organisms (*Vibrio*, *Rotifer*, *Macrobiotus*, &c.) which we can devitalize and revitalize—devive and revive—many times. As the dried animalcule manifests no phenomenon suggesting any idea contributing to form the complex one of "life" in my mind, I regard it to be as completely lifeless as is the drowned man whose breath and heat have gone and whose blood has ceased to circulate. . . . . . The change of work consequent on drying or drowning forthwith begins to alter relations or "composition," and, in time, to a degree

But the Death of organisms is even capable of teaching us something as to their life: their mode of dying is typical of their mode of living. The more highly developed an organism has become, the more has specialization been brought about in the functions of its several parts, and (in almost the same proportion) the more has the *all* become welded into a *whole*. The greater the degree of interdependence existing between the actions of its several parts, the more is the well-being of the entire organism interfered with by damage occurring to any one of these principal parts. Through the intervention, for the most part, of the nervous system and the vascular system, this individuality of the entire organism is carried to the most marked extent in the highest vertebrata, so that the Life of one of these creatures—regarded as a whole, or sum total of phenomena—differs almost as widely as it is possible from that of some of the lowest animals on the one hand, and from that of plants on the other. Their mode of death also is quite different. And as with Life, so is it with Death, we are perhaps too apt to form our notions concerning each from what we see taking place in man himself and in the higher living things—many people apparently never reflect upon the striking differences which are presented, in this respect, by the lowest animals as well as by the members of the

---

adverse to resumption of the vital form of force, a longer period being needed for this effect in the Rotifer, a shorter one in the Man, still shorter, it may be, in the Amœba.'

vegetable kingdom. In man we find a fully developed and almost inconceivably complex organism; in the working of which, as in that of any ordinary but extremely complex piece of machinery, there is seen to be the closest interdependence between the actions of the several parts. Destined as a whole to perform a certain work, we may constantly see, for instance, in the wool-factories of our manufacturing districts a piece of machinery in which the sum total of work to be done is parcelled out amongst different related and interdependent parts—wheels of every description, large and small, plain and toothed; combs of various kinds; rhythmically acting knives, reels and thread twisters, all combine simultaneously or successively to elaborate the woof out of which our garments are woven. The action of some parts are more essential, that of others less essential to the action of the machine as a whole. An interference with the revolution of some central wheel may suffice instantly to interrupt the working of the entire mechanism, just as the functional workings in the body of a highly organized vertebrate animal may be as suddenly arrested by a puncture in a particular part of its nervous system. In both instances the first result is a simple cessation in the action of a complex machine; and, in the case of the animal—seeing that its body has been gradually built up in a given manner under the influence of certain definite actions or functions, the continuance of which is absolutely necessary—it follows that when such actions are arrested irretrievably, the organism as an individual whole must die, although its separate parts and anatomical elements may and do perish much more slowly, after different intervals. These perish simply by default—because the conditions suitable for the continuance of their life are no longer forthcoming; and not because they themselves as vital units had received any damage at the time that the organism as a whole ceased to live—when the action of the vital machine was stopped. Every anatomical element of even the highest animal may fairly be said to possess Life and a specific mode of action, each after its own kind; only, the vital manifestations of the whole of these units are subordinated to the Life—and, in health, work towards the well-being—of the higher organism of which they form part. The death of the Organism as a whole, results from the stoppage of its machinery; but the death of its component parts subsequently follows as a consequence of the cessation of those more general actions—under whose influence they were produced, and without whose existence *they* can no longer live. If the medulla oblongata has been punctured and the heart has ceased to beat, there is a permanent stoppage of this function, without which Life, in such a being as a mammalian vertebrate, is impossible. It consequently dies. If the blood no longer circulates, the anatomical elements, which are absolutely dependent upon this fluid for their pabulum, must also, after a time, necessarily die. The individual muscular and nervous elements may and do still live for a time—the nerve will conduct a stimulus under which the muscle will contract; and so is it, even more markedly, with the epithelial cells—those possessing cilia display their characteristic vital actions long after the organism considered as a complex whole has ceased to live.

Now the lower we descend in the scale of living things, the less marked does the life of the organism as a whole become, in contradistinction to the life of its several parts. The 'tendency to individuation' becomes less and less manifest in proportion as the structural differentiation diminishes. The more the several parts of an organism resemble one another, the less difference is there between the functions discharged by these several parts, and therefore the importance is proportionately less to the whole organism when one of these functions is interfered with. This is but saying, in other words, that the machinery of Life grows less and less complex, and that we are gradually approximating more and more to a state of things in which, to employ the same simile, we have a mere aggregate of wheels, a mere repetition of more or less similar parts, with progressively less of mutual interdependence between their several actions. Who has not noticed the slowness with which a serpent dies, how the toad clings to Life? Look at the writhing segment of the worm whose body has been cut by the gardener's spade, or at the green *Nereis* of the rock-pool whose body has been accidentally torn, and let us think of the powers of repair possessed by each— it is not killed, and an attempt will be made more or less effectually to reproduce the lost parts, just as a crystal, in its own proper medium would, after injury, tend to reproduce its original symmetry of form. Look again at the little polyp of our lakes and ponds—the *Hydra*, whose individual Life is so dwarfed in com-

Fig. 2. *Hydra viridis* in different stages of extension and contraction, reproducing gemmiparously—attached to roots of Duckweed. (Rösel.)

parison with the Life of its several parts that you may cut it or injure it to almost any extent, and yet the separate parts will still live [1]. It can, in fact, scarcely

---

[1] It has, moreover, been recently revealed by the experiments of Haeckel that a similar power of reproduction, previously unsuspected, is possessed by *Medusæ*. Haeckel says: 'My experiments proved that it prevails to an amazing extent in many medusæ, especially in those be-

be said to constitute a living whole, for the one animal may be divided into two, and the two into four, and each part will grow into an organism like that of which it is a segment—the parts grow into wholes, and in the place of the one individual organism we get four others similar in kind. By mechanical injury or compression we may destroy any single part so compressed, but we do not affect the total organism, except for a time: the lost part is reproduced.

These also are the kinds of phenomena and modes of Life with which we are familiar throughout the Vegetable Kingdom—nowhere do we meet with anything like that same amount of integration or individuation which is characteristic of the higher animals. Mere fragments of plants in the form of buds, 'cuttings,' or portions of the root, separated from the parent organism, are capable of reproducing plants similar to those from which they have been derived. The 'tendency to individuation' exists here also, but even in the most perfect plant the accomplished result is small indeed, when compared with what we encounter amongst animals. The absence of a nervous system

---

longing to the family *Thaumantiadæ* of Gegenbauer (*Laodicea* of Agassiz). In several species of this family I could divide the umbrella into more than a hundred species; and from each, provided it only contained a portion of the margin of the umbrella, grew in a few days (from two to four) a complete small medusa. Merely a loosened shred of the fringe on which the base (the adjoining piece of the edge of the umbrella) remained, formed a medusa in a few days.'—' Monograph of Monera.' Transl. in 'Quart. Journal of Micros. Science,' April, 1869, p. 117.

however, combined with the less perfect condition of the vascular system, are sufficient to account for this want of integration in the plant, and the great amount of independence shown by its individual parts.

Such are some of the principal differences in the nature of the Life, or aggregate vital manifestations of the members of the Animal and of the Vegetable Kingdoms: and great as are the differences between the phenomena of the higher and of the lower forms of these, we may look for even still lower manifestations of Life in a group of organisms whose characteristics, whether structural or functional, are so little marked as to make the most philosophic naturalists unable to assign them a place amongst either the one or the other of these Organic Kingdoms.

It might have been expected, in accordance with the doctrines of Evolution, that the lowest living things would present characters of the most general description. They ought to be simply living things, without visible organization, and should as yet present no special characters by virtue of which a place might be assigned to them either in the vegetable or in the animal kingdom. The older naturalists thought that every living thing must be either an animal or a plant, and they accordingly ranged all organic forms under one or other of these categories. But there were certain of them whose characteristics were so indefinite that they could really claim for themselves no place in either of these kingdoms, and they were consequently placed in the one or in the other alternately as the state of knowledge at the time varied, or almost according to the whim of successive writers. But now, at last, after this unseemly bandying to and fro, their proper position is being generally recognized. The merit of taking a definite step as regards the classification of these animals rests with Professor Haeckel, who says[1]:—'I have made the attempt in my "General Morphology" to throw some light upon this systematic chaos, by placing, as a special division between true animals and true plants, all those doubtful organisms of the lowest rank which display no decided affinities nearer to one side than to the other, or which possess animal and vegetable characters united and mixed in such a manner that, since their discovery, an interminable controversy about their position in the animal or in the vegetable kingdom has continued. Manifestly this controversy becomes reduced to the smallest compass if the disputable and doubtful intermediate forms are separated for the present (though only provisionally) both from the true animals and from the true plants, and united in a special organic "kingdom." Thereby we obtain the advantage of being able to distinguish both true animals and true plants by a clear and sharp definition, and, on the other hand, a special proportion of attention is attracted

[1] 'Monograph of Monera.' Translation in 'Quarterly Journal of Microscopical Science,' July, 1869, p. 230.

to the very low organisms hitherto so much neglected, and yet so extremely important. I have called this boundary kingdom intermediate between the animal and the vegetable kingdoms, and connecting both, the PROTISTA [1].' All the members of this kingdom multiply by an exclusively non-sexual method of reproduction. It should be understood, however, that in proposing such a classification Prof. Haeckel by no means wishes to establish an absolute wall of separation between these three organic kingdoms. He is much more disposed to believe that animals as well as plants have gradually arisen out of modifications which have taken place in the simplest Protista. This primordial organic kingdom he divides into ten groups, in the lowest of which, named Monera [2], are included such mere naked, non-nucleated jelly-specks as those belonging to the genera

---

[1] τὸ πρώτιστον, the first of all, primordial. 'Gen. Morph.' vol. i. p. 203, and vol. ii. p. xx. and p. 403. Elsewhere he says:—' The question which has been so often debated during the last twenty years as to a boundary between the animal and the vegetable kingdoms will be decided by the Monera, or, more correctly, they will prove that a perfect separation of both kingdoms, in the manner in which it is usually attempted, is impossible. The Monera are apparently such peculiar organisms that they can be classed with equal propriety, or rather with equal arbitrariness, as primitive animals or as primitive plants. They may just as well be regarded as the first beginnings of animal as of vegetable organization. But as no one mark of distinction inclines them more to one side than to the other, it seems most correct at present to class them as intermediate between true animals and true plants.' ('Journal of Micros. Science,' Jan. 1869, p. 29.)

[2] Name from μόνηρης, simple.

Protamœba and *Protogenes*, to which we shall have occasion again to allude. The other members of this primitive kingdom being comprised under one or other of the following groups:—Flagellata, Labyrinthulea, Diatomea, Phycochromaceæ, Fungi[1], Myxomycetes, Protoplasta[2], Noctilucæ, and Rhizopoda.

The homogeneous and shapeless masses of plasma constituting the group Monera are supposed by Prof. Haeckel to have come into being by a process of equivocal or 'spontaneous' generation, and these are regarded by him as *the* primordial living things[3]. We think, however—for reasons which will subsequently appear—that, side by side with these, should stand *Bacteria, Torula*, and other equally primordial forms not alluded to by Prof. Haeckel. We merely mention this conclusion at which we have arrived, but will not enlarge upon it at present.

It will be useful for us to see, however, what Prof. Haeckel has to say concerning the members of his group Monera, including as it does the two genera above mentioned, as well as others (such as *Protomyxa* and *Vampyrella*) the species of which are no longer naked,

---

[1] In justification of the removal of these from the Vegetable Kingdom Haeckel says:—' The whole method of nourishment and assimilation of the fungi, in connection with many other characters (especially the total absence of chlorophyll), remove them so far from the true plants that the earlier botanists long since wished to establish for the fungi a special organic kingdom.'

[2] In this group are included all the higher nucleated *Amœba*.

[3] Loc. cit. p. 330.

but are bounded by an outer membrane[1]. He says[2]:
—'I have called those forms of life standing at the lowest grade of organization Monera. Their whole body, in a fully developed and freely moving condition, consists of an entirely homogeneous and structureless substance, a living particle of albumen[3], capable of nourishment and reproduction. These simplest and most imperfect of all organisms are, in many respects, of the highest interest. *For the albumen-like organic matter meets us here as the material substratum of all life phenomena,* apparently not only under the simplest form as yet actually observed, but also under the simplest form which can well be imagined. Simpler and more incomplete organisms than the Monera cannot be conceived. . . . Indeed, the whole body of the Monera, however strange this may sound, represents nothing more than a single, thoroughly homogeneous particle of albumen, in a firmly adhesive

[1] Professor Haeckel proposes that the word 'Sarcode,' introduced by Dujardin, should be applied to the free protoplasm which exists without a covering or limiting membrane, only with the distinct understanding that such free protoplasm differs in no essential respect from that which is encapsuled, whether it is marked off from surrounding things by a mere limiting membrane, or whether it is enclosed within a definite cell-wall.

[2] Translation in 'Journal of Micros. Science,' Jan. 1869, p. 28.

[3] 'In all chemical and physical respects,' Prof. Haeckel writes elsewhere, 'this substance shows the qualities of a consistent carbonaceous compound of the group of albuminous substances (Proteine). It is identical with the substance which as Plasma or Protoplasm forms the contractile living substance of all organic Plastides, of all cells, and cytodes of animals, protista, and plants.'

THE BEGINNINGS OF LIFE.

condition. The external form is quite irregular, continually changing, globularly contracted when at rest. Our sharpest discrimination can detect no trace of an internal structure, or of a formation from dissimilar parts. As the homogeneous albuminous mass of the body of the Moner does not even exhibit a differentiation into an inner nucleus and an outer plasma, and as, moreover, the whole body consists of a homo-

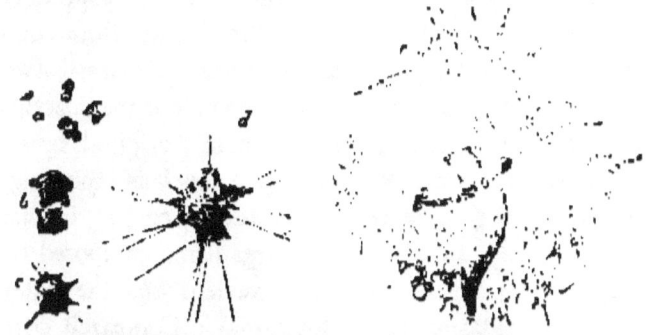

FIG. 3. Representatives of Haeckel's group *Monera*.

a. Most minute specks of protoplasm from fine surface mud of fresh-water ponds, Hendon. (× 800.)
b. *Protamœba primitiva* (Haeckel). Two individuals resulting from a recent fission.
c. *Vampyrella pendula* (Cienkowski).
d. *Amœba porrecta* (Max Schultze). This is really a Protamœba.
e. *Protomyxa aurantiaca* (Haeckel) developed into a 'plasmodium,' either from the simple increase of a single amœba-like germ or by the union of several originally distinct individuals. A devoured *Iulmia* and a *Navicula* are visible in the homogeneous parenchyma of the sarcode; also numerous vacuoles. (b, c, d, and e × 220.)

geneous plasma, or protoplasma, the organic matter here does not even reach the importance of the simplest cell. It remains in the lowest imaginable grade of organic individuality.' Professor Haeckel afterwards says:—'The Monera are indeed Protista. They are neither animals nor plants. They are organisms of the most primitive kind: among which the distinction between animals and plants does not yet exist. But the term "organism" itself seems scarcely applicable to these simplest forms of life; for in the whole conception of the "organism" is especially implied the construction of the whole from dissimilar parts,—from organs or limbs. At least, two separate parts must be united to complete the description of a body as an organism in this original sense. Every true Amœba, every true (i. e. nucleus-including) animal and vegetable cell, every animal-egg, is, in this sense, already an elementary organism, composed of two different organs, the inner nucleus and the outer cell-matter (Plasma or Protoplasma). Compared with these last the Monera are strictly "organisms without organs." Only in a physiological sense can we still call them organisms; as individual portions of organic matter, which fulfil the essential life-functions of all organisms, nourishment, growth, and reproduction. But all these different functions are not yet limited to different parts. They are all, still, executed equally by every part of the body [1].'

---

[1] Prof. Haeckel then continues:—'If the natural history of the Monera is already, on these grounds, of the highest interest as well for morphology as for physiology, this interest will be still more increased

One of the most rudimentary, and at the same time the first member of this group observed by Prof. Haeckel, he named *Protamœba primitiva*. 'I observed it,' he says, 'for the first time at Jena, in the summer of 1863, in water which I had brought from a small pond in the Tautenburg forest (opposite Dornburg, on the right bank of the Saal). The bottom of this shallow little pond is thickly covered with fallen decayed beech-leaves, and in the fine brown mud, among the decayed leaves, I found the little Protamœba.' It was a minute plasma-ball, perfectly homogeneous, rather more than $\frac{1}{1000}$ of an inch in diameter, which moved with extreme slowness, and also changed its form as slowly, by means of alternate protrusions and retractions of bluntly rounded portions of its body-mass. The whole substance of *Protamœba primitiva* is absolutely structureless and homogeneous. At one time it will multiply itself by a process of fission, whilst, at another time, individuals

by the extraordinary importance which these very simple organisms possess for the important doctrine of spontaneous generation or archegony. I have shown in my "General Morphology" that the acceptation of a genuine archegony (once or repeated) has at present become a *logical postulate of scientific natural history*. Most naturalists who have discussed this question rationally believed that they must designate simple cells as the simplest organism produced thereby, from which all others developed themselves. But every true cell already shows a division into two different parts, i.e. nucleus and plasma. The immediate production of such an object from spontaneous generation is obviously only conceivable with difficulty; but it is much easier to conceive of the production of an entirely homogeneous, organic substance, such as the structureless albumen body of the Monera.'

originally separate coming into contact accidentally, unite or fuse together into a single individual. The blunt projections of its body-mass, by means of which it is continually varying in form, contrast notably with the fine thread-like prolongations, occasionally interlacing, which are thrown out from Max Schultze's nearly allied *Amœba porrecta*. These latter projections, or *pseudopodia*, as they have been termed, closely resemble those met with in the shelled-amœbæ or *Foraminifera*[1].

But even in 1857 an organism was procured from great depths in the Atlantic Ocean by Captain Dayman, which ought, apparently, to be placed in this same group *Monera*. This and other products of Captain Dayman's expedition were examined by Professor Huxley, and since the publication of Haeckel's Memoir, he has proposed to look upon this organism as a 'Moner,' placing it in a new genus *Bathybius*. Recent expeditions and fresh investigations have tended

---

[1] Speaking of this animal, the *Amœba porrecta*, Max Schultze says:—
'It sends out from its colourless body, on all sides, numerous fibrous processes, short and broad on their first extrusion, but which gradually elongate until they exceed the diameter of the body eight or ten times, and taper to such fine extremities that a magnifying power of 400 diameters is needed to distinguish them. The figure and extension of the body change every moment, according to the side in which the ramifications are extended. If two or more of the filiform processes touch, a coalescence takes place, and broader plates or net-like interlacements are produced, which, in the continual changes of figure, are either taken up again into the general mass, or otherwise are further increased by a fresh influx of matter, until finally the entire body is transposed to their place.'

to throw a great additional interest over this oceanic Moner, which, it is now believed, must have existed far back in geologic time, and must have played a most important part, by the accumulation of its inorganic remains, in the formation of ancient chalk strata, just as it is now being instrumental in the deposition of another chalk stratum in the bottom of our great Atlantic Ocean[1]. Captain Dayman was much

[1] Referring to this subject in an interesting lecture 'On a Piece of Chalk' ('Macmillan's Mag.' Sep. 1868, p. 399), Prof. Huxley says:— 'The result of all these operations is that we know the contours and nature of the surface-soil covered by the North Atlantic for a distance of 1,700 miles from east to west, as well as we know that of any part of the dry land.... It is a prodigious plain—one of the widest and most even plains in the world. If the sea were drained off, you might drive a waggon all the way from Valentia, on the west coast of Ireland, to Trinity Bay in Newfoundland.... From Valentia the road would lie down hill for about 200 miles to the point at which the bottom is now covered by 1,700 fathoms of sea water. Then would come the central plain more than a thousand miles wide, the inequalities of the surface of which would be hardly perceptible, though the depth of water upon it now varies from 10,000 to 15,000 feet; and there are places in which Mont Blanc might be sunk without showing its peak above water. Beyond this, the ascent on the American side commences, and gradually leads, for about 300 miles, to the Newfoundland shore.... Almost the whole of the bottom of this central plain (which extends for many hundred miles in a north and south direction) is covered by a fine mud, which, when brought to the surface, dries into a greyish-white, friable substance. You can write with this on a black board, if you are so inclined, and to the eye it is quite like very soft, greyish chalk. Examined chemically, it proves to be composed almost wholly of carbonate of lime; and if you make a section of it in the same way as that of the piece of chalk was made, and view it with the microscope, it presents innumerable *Globigerinæ*, embedded in a granular matrix.... Thus this deep sea mud is substantially chalk. I say substantially, because there are

struck with the sticky, viscid character of the mud from great depths, and thus speaks of it in his Report[1]:—
'Between the 15th and 45th degrees of west longitude lies the deepest part of the ocean, the bottom of which is almost wholly composed of the same kind of soft mealy substance, which, for want of a better name, I have called ooze. This substance is remarkably sticky, having been found to adhere to the sounding-rod and line (as has been stated above), through its passage from the bottom to the surface, in some instances from a depth of more than 2000 fathoms.' This is the character of the mud in the warm area of the ocean, though the more recent expeditions of Dr. Carpenter and Professor Wyville Thompson have shown that the character of the bottom is totally different in the cold portion of the strait between the Faröe and the Shetland Islands—in that part over which flows the down-current from the Arctic basin. Referring to Captain Dayman's description, Professor Huxley says[2]:—'This stickiness of the deep sea mud arises, I suppose, from the circumstance that, in addition to the *Globigerinæ* of all sizes which are its chief constituents, it contains innumerable lumps of a transparent, gelatinous substance. These lumps are of all sizes, from patches

a good many minor differences.' For further information on this most interesting subject we must refer the reader to the Lecture itself.

[1] 'Deep-Sea Soundings in the North Atlantic Ocean,' 1858.
[2] On some Organisms living at great Depths in the North Atlantic Ocean. 'Quarterly Journal of Microscopical Science,' October, 1868, p. 105.

visible with the naked eye to excessively minute particles. When one of these is submitted to microscopical analysis it exhibits—imbedded in a transparent, colourless, and structureless matrix—granules, cocoliths, and foreign particles [1].'

But those who wish to make themselves acquainted with the *Protamœba*, need not seek for them only in comparatively inaccessible regions. They are in reality common in the fine surface mud of many of our freshwater ponds, and may easily be detected by the skilled microscopist when once he has familiarized himself with their appearance. We have lately detected, in material taken from such situations, organisms similar in kind though much more minute than the *Protamœba*

---

[1] One of the most interesting subjects attaching to these lower organisms of the Protistic kingdom, is the enquiry as to how they are nourished—whether, like plants, they live upon inorganic elements abstracted from their environment, or, like animals, upon organic substances already elaborated. Dr. Wallich has strongly maintained the former view in opposition to Dr. Carpenter's opinions that the *Foraminifera* are nourished after the fashion of animals. In these and in similar low oceanic organisms he has frequently expressed his belief that 'nutrition is affected by a *vital act* which enables the organism to extract hydrogen, oxygen, carbon, nitrogen, and lime from the surrounding medium, and to convert these ingredients into sarcode and shell material.' ('Monthly Microscopical Journal,' January 1, 1869.) This elimination of inorganic elements, and their conversion into protoplasm, Dr. Wallich believes to be dependent upon 'a special vital force inherent in the protoplasmic mass itself, and diffused, in all probability, throughout its substance.' In view of this hypothesis, or of certain modifications thereof, concerning Protistic life, it is most interesting for us to learn, from the analyses of Dr. Frankland, that a large quantity of nitrogen, both free and combined, exists in the water of the Atlantic Ocean.

primitiva of Prof. Haeckel. These have presented themselves in the form of minute irregularly-shaped, almost transparent specks of homogeneous jelly, about $\frac{1}{10000}''$ in diameter. They seldom showed even a vacuole in their interior. They underwent slow, though obvious changes in form; and they exhibited slight to-and-fro, or somewhat jerkingly-progressive movements. Essentially similar organisms will, in all probability, hereafter be found to be most widely distributed. They are, in almost every respect, similar to the minute jelly-specks, which we shall afterwards find making their appearance in previously homogeneous organic solutions; and they are, we believe, thoroughly primordial organisms, capable of originating *de novo* in organic solutions. Concerning this part of our subject, however, we shall have more to say hereafter.

This then is the material which was spoken of by Professor Huxley[1] as 'The Physical Basis of Life;' and the upholders of the Protoplasm or Sarcode theory maintain that this substance has an essential unity of nature. So that, in spite of minute specific and isomeric differences, we have in reality to do with one and the same generic substance, whether existing as the 'contents' of animal and vegetable cells, or as naked masses of protoplasm—whether as parts of higher organisms, or as single independent beings such as we have just been describing. The belief that all these various forms are but

[1] 'Fortnightly Review,' 1869.

trifling alterations of a single genus of primitive organizable material, and that in all cases this 'albuminous material is the original active substratum of all vital phenomena, may,' says Professor Haeckel, 'perhaps be considered one of the greatest achievements of modern biology, and one of the richest in results.'

Protoplasm then, in its most general and undifferentiated condition, in the form of a naked contractile mass of seemingly homogeneous jelly, is the substratum for all the life-movements of the lowest living things, even in their adult condition. A structureless mass of jelly suffices for the display of all the vital phenomena of the lowest organisms. Here, without the aid of organs of any kind, are carried on the vital phenomena of 'growth' and 'reproduction;' here do we see the first germs of that organic irritability and contractility which attain their highest development in the conscious sensibility and power of movement possessed by those living things which stand at the head rather than at the foot of organic nature. Here does that which has what we call Life approximate most closely to that which has no Life: and who will venture to draw a rigid line which is to separate these two categories from one another? As we have said before, the theory of evolution knows nothing of 'absolute commencements;' rather, as Mr. Herbert Spencer puts it, 'every kind of being is conceived as a product of modifications wrought by insensible gradations on a pre-existing kind of being.' We must not, therefore, look for an absolute barrier between the Living and the not-living. We know nothing of an absolute commencement of Life; we may know some of the lowest living things, as mere specks of almost inconceivable smallness, barely perceptible even by our highest microscopic powers—but these are even then living organic units. We cannot, however, penetrate further—who can describe the primordial collocations? However much we may wish it, we cannot be present at the genesis of Life—the veil is still there. The gradual transition from the not-living to the Living is still hidden from our view, and so, perhaps, it may ever remain.

CHAPTER IV.

RELATIONS OF ANIMAL, VEGETABLE, AND MINERAL KINGDOMS. THEORIES OF ORGANIZATION.

The two higher Organic Kingdoms. Relations of Plants and Animals to one another, and to Air, Earth, and Water. Plants produce and Animals consume organic matter. Plants derive Carbon from the air. Illustrations from past succession of Life on our globe. Nature's Cycle. Plants continually producing *Living Matter* from inorganic materials.

Theories of Organization. Cells. Doctrines of Schleiden and Schwann. Views of Goodsir. Virchow's Cellular doctrines. Modifications of views concerning the Cell and its powers. These necessitated by our knowledge of the *Protista*. Cells and Plastides. Dr. Beale's views concerning Germinal matter and 'Formed material.' Prof. Huxley's opposition to Cellular Theories. Dr. Hughes Bennett's 'Molecular Theory of Organization.' Doctrine now maintained by very many Physiologists. This in harmony with Evolution Hypothesis. Reason why Cells are so common as morphological units. Do they arise *de novo* in blastemata?

LEAVING now for a time the consideration of the nature of the lowest known forms of Life, and all speculations as to the mode of evolution of those combinations of matter and motion out of which, by the most insensible gradations, they have gradually arisen, it will be desirable to turn our attention to the mutual relation of Plants and Animals to one another, and to those great storehouses of inorganic elements—earth, air, and water.

Whatever be the nature of the functions of the lowest living things, and their relations with the environment, or aqueous medium in which they alone exist, we find, on coming to those more definite organisms which can, without room for doubt, be ranged under either the Animal or the Vegetable Kingdom, that the members of each great class have functions definitely related to one another and to the world of unorganized matter.

Bearing in mind that *the* fundamental constituents of living things are carbon, nitrogen, hydrogen, and oxygen, we must also remember that the degree in which other constituents (such as sulphur and phosphorus with various saline materials) enter into the composition of organic matter, is altogether trifling when compared with the immense bulk of living tissue that is almost solely built up of these four elements in their diverse modes of combination.

We shall then be the better able to appreciate the doctrine so eloquently expounded by the eminent French chemist, M. Dumas, in a work by himself and M. Boussingault, on 'The Chemical and Physiological Balance of Organic Nature.' He calls attention again and again, in the most forcible language, to the all-important complemental relation existing between the functions of plants and animals. Plants in their natural and healthy state decompose carbonic acid incessantly, fixing its carbon and setting free its oxygen: similarly they decompose water, seizing upon its hydrogen and releasing its oxygen; whilst, lastly, they abstract nitrogen either directly from the atmosphere, or indirectly from the nitrate of ammonia which, under particular conditions, has been formed therein. Plants, therefore, are marvellous apparatuses of reduction, working with the aid of the heat and light derived from the Sun. But this is not all. The carbonic acid, the water, and the nitrate of ammonia are decompounded, because the carbon, the hydrogen, and the nitrogen entering into their composition, unite with oxygen to produce the various organic substances entering into the fabric of plants. Reduction takes place, but only that combinations of a higher order may arise. Animals, on the contrary, are true apparatuses of combustion: in their bodies carbonaceous matters are burnt incessantly during the performance of animal functions, and are returned to the atmosphere in the shape of carbonic acid; hydrogen burnt incessantly is returned as water; whilst nitrogen is ceaselessly exhaled in the breath and thrown off in the different excretions[1]. 'From the animal

[1] This continual process of combustion is dependent upon the conjoint and reciprocal action of the respiratory and nutritive functions. Through the process of respiration the animal is supplied with an all-important element, needed for the production of such changes. Mr. Spencer says:—'The inorganic substance, however, on which mainly depend these metamorphoses in organic matter, is not swallowed along with the solid and liquid food, but is absorbed from the surrounding medium—air or water, as the case may be. Whether the oxygen taken in, either, as by the lowest animals, through the general surface, or, as by the higher animals, through respiratory organs, is the immediate cause

kingdom, therefore, as a whole,' M. Dumas says, 'carbonic acid, watery vapour, and azote or oxide of ammonium are continually escaping—simple substances and few in number, the formation of which is intimately connected with the history of the atmosphere itself:' substances, too, which plants are continually needing, and are as continually abstracting from the air. M. Dumas also says:—'It is in plants, consequently, that the true laboratory of organic nature resides; carbon, hydrogen, ammonium, and water are the elements they work upon; and woody fibre, starch, gums, and sugars, on the one hand, fibrine, albumen, caseum, and gluten, on the other, are the products that present themselves as fundamental in either organic kingdom of nature— products, however, which are *formed in plants, and in*

of those molecular changes that are ever going on throughout the living tissues; or whether the oxygen, playing the part of scavenger, merely aids these changes by carrying away the products of decomposition otherwise caused; it remains equally true that these changes are maintained by its instrumentality. Whether the oxygen absorbed and diffused through the system effects a direct oxidation of the organic colloid which it permeates; or whether it first leads to the formation of simpler and more oxidized compounds, that are afterwards further oxidized and reduced to still simpler forms; matters not in so far as the general result is concerned. In any case it holds good, that the substances of which the animal body is built up enter it in a but slightly oxidized and highly unstable state; while the great mass of them leave it in a fully oxidized and stable state. It follows, therefore, that whatever the special changes gone through, the general process is a falling from a state of unstable equilibrium, to a state of stable chemical equilibrium. Whether this process be direct or indirect, the total molecular rearrangement and the total motion given out in effecting it must be the same.' ('Principles of Biology,' vol. i. p. 34.)

plants only, and merely transferred by digestion to the bodies of animals.'

Thus we find that the vegetable world is the great originator and source of that pabulum which is necessary for the existence of animals. Plants are the active agents ever ministering to the wants of animals. They, in fashioning their own structures, are continually giving birth to organic substances which are to constitute the materials necessary for the maintenance of animal life. Animals, as a rule, are powerless for the creation of organic matter [1]; they can assimilate and modify the organic substances which have been built up for them in the tissues of plants; but they cannot abstract from earth, air, and water the elementary constituents of organic matter, and force them to enter into such and such combinations. They use the materials which have been elaborated for them by plants, since they all feed either directly upon members of the vegetable kingdom, or else indirectly by living upon animals which have been so nourished. Plants, then, are the great factors of organic matter—the vegetable

---

[1] 'Animals assimilate or absorb the organic substances which plants have formed. They alter them by degrees; they destroy or decompound them. New organic substances may arise in their tissues, in their vessels; but these are always substances of greater simplicity, more akin to the elementary state than those they had received. They decompose, then, by degrees the organic matters created by plants. They bring them back by degrees towards the state of carbonic acid, water, azote, and ammonia, a state which admits of their ready restoration to the air.' Dumas, loc. cit. p. 48.

kingdom is nature's laboratory, within whose sacred precincts dead brute matter is coerced into more elevated and complex modes of being, and is made to display those more subtle characteristics which we find in living tissues. Using only the great forces of nature —availing themselves only of the subtle motions emanating from the Sun under the names of heat, light, and actinism—plants compel carbonic acid to yield up its carbon, water its hydrogen, and nitrate of ammonia its nitrogen; and, at the same time, these separated elements, with some of the retained oxygen[1], are still further forced by an accumulation of these mysterious impacts to enter into combinations of a higher order.

M. Dumas, speaking of the sources whence are derived the ammonia and the nitric acid used as food by plants, says:—' They are, in fact, produced upon the grand scale by the action of those magnificent electric sparks which dart from the storm-cloud, and furrowing vast fields of air, engender in their course the nitrate of ammonia, which analysis discovers in the thunder shower. . . . As it is from the mouths of volcanoes, then, whose convulsions so often make the crust of our globe to tremble, that the principal food of plants, carbonic acid, is incessantly poured out; so is it from the

---

[1] Dumas says ('Lec. de Philosophie Chimique,' p. 100, Paris, 1837): 'These are the four bodies, in fact, which, becoming animated at the fire of the sun, the true torch of Prometheus, approve themselves upon the earth, the eternal agents of organization, of sensation, of motion, and of thought.'

atmosphere on fire with lightnings, from the bosom of the tempest, that the second and scarcely less indispensable aliment of plants, nitrate of ammonia, is showered down for their behoof.' Thus the air is the great storehouse for the pabulum of plants, so that, looking at the subject, as M. Dumas says, 'from the loftiest point of view, and in connection with the physics of the globe, it would be imperative on us to say that, in so far as their truly organic elements are concerned, plants and animals are the *offspring of the air.*'

It might be thought that plants derive the principal part of the ingredients with which they build up their own structures from the soil; but the experiments of M. Boussingault have long since disproved this formerly favoured assumption. He found that peas sown in pure sand, moistened with distilled water, and fed by the air alone, nevertheless found in this air all the carbon necessary for their development, flowering, and fructification. Carbon is the most fundamental ingredient of the vegetable kingdom; all plants fix this substance, and all obtain it from carbonic acid—either abstracting it directly from the air by their leaves, or obtaining it through their rootlets. In the latter case they may obtain it from rains which have fallen to the earth impregnated with the carbonic acid of the atmosphere, or else they procure it from that which is liberated by the gradual decomposition of organic particles in the soil. But that the air is the great storehouse whence, either mediately or immediately, plants procure their carbon, is rendered more and more obvious to us by the consideration of such facts as those to which Schleiden refers when he says [1]:—'From forests maintained in good condition we annually obtain about 4000 lbs. of dry wood per acre, which contains about 1000 lbs. of carbon. But we do not manure the soil of the forests, and its supply of humus, far from being exhausted, increases considerably from year to year, owing to the breakage by wind and the fall of the leaf. The haymaker of Switzerland and the Tyrol mows his definite amount of grass every year on the Alps, inaccessible to cattle, and gives not back the smallest quantity of organic substance to the soil. Whence comes this hay if not from the atmosphere? The plant requires carbon and nitrogen, and in the woods and on the wild Alps there is no possibility of its acquiring these matters save from the ammonia and carbonic acid of the atmosphere.'

How important such facts as these are in throwing light upon the past history of our globe, when we attempt to study it with the aid of those relics, preserved as fossil plants and animals, and distributed through the various successive strata of its crust, the palæontologists are best entitled to inform us. M. Ad. Brongniart, one of the most able and eloquent of these, even so long ago as the year 1828 announced, before the Academy of Sciences, the fol-

---

[1] 'Biography of a Plant.'

lowing broad views concerning the succession of Life on the earth[1]:—

'We know, in fact, that in the strata of older date than, or of the same epoch as, the coal formations, there are no remains of any terrestrial animal, whilst at this epoch vegetation had already made great progress, and was composed of plants as remarkable for their forms as for their gigantic stature. At a later period terrestrial vegetation loses in a great measure the signal vigour which it formerly possessed, and cold-blooded vertebrate animals become extremely numerous: this is what is observed during the third period.

'Subsequently, plants become more varied, more perfect; but the analogues of those that existed originally are reduced to a vastly smaller stature: this is the epoch of the appearance of the most perfect animals, of animals breathing air, of mammalia, and birds.

'Is there no means of discovering some cause adequate to explain in a natural way this vast development, this vigorous growth of plants breathing air, even from the most remote epochs in the formation of the globe? And, on the other hand, of the appearance of warm-blooded animals, that is to say, of animals whose aerial respiration is most active in the last periods of its formation only? May not this difference in the epoch of the appearance of these two classes of beings depend on the difference in their mode of respiration, and

[1] Quoted in Dumas and Boussingault's 'Chemical and Physiological Balance of Organic Nature.'

of the circumstances in the state of the atmosphere calculated to favour the development of one and to oppose that of the other?

'Under what form at the epoch of the creation of organized beings did the whole of the carbon exist which these beings subsequently absorbed, and which is now buried with their spoils in the bosom of the earth, or which is still met with distributed among the infinite multitude of organized beings that actually cover the face of our globe?

'It is obvious that animals derive carbon neither from the atmosphere nor the soil, but exclusively from their food.

'We cannot conceive how plants could have assimilated this carbon had it been in the solid state; and, moreover, in the formations older than those that include the first remains of vegetables, we scarcely encounter any traces of carbon.

'This carbon, then, which the vegetables of the primitive world, and those of the subsequent and present world, absorbed, must necessarily have existed in a shape proper to furnish them with nutriment; and we only know of two—humus or vegetable mould, which, resulting itself from the decomposition of other vegetables, would lead us into a vicious circle, and carbonic acid, which, decomposed by the leafage of vegetables under the influence of solar light, deposits its carbon, and so serves for their growth.

'It appears to me impossible, therefore, to suppose

that vegetables can have derived from any other source than the atmosphere, and in the state of carbonic acid, the carbon which is found in all existing species of plants and animals, as well as that which, after having served the vast primeval forests for sustenance, has been deposited, under the form of coal, lignite, and bitumen, in the different sedimentary strata of the earth. If we suppose, then, that the whole of this carbon was diffused through the atmosphere in the shape of carbonic acid prior to the creation of organized beings, we shall see that the atmosphere, instead of containing less than the one-thousandth part of its bulk of carbonic acid as at present, must have contained a quantity which it is not easy to estimate exactly, but which was perhaps in the proportion of 3, 4, 5, 6, and even 8 per cent.'

But the experiments of M. Saussure have shown that such a super-abundance of carbonic acid in the atmosphere, far from being detrimental, is positively favourable to the life of plants when they are at the same time exposed to the influence of the solar light and heat. So that, as M. Brongniart says,—'This highly probable difference in the constitution of the atmosphere may, therefore, be regarded as one of the causes influencing most powerfully the more active and very remarkable vegetation of the first organic period of our globe[1].

[1] 'But this same circumstance must, on the contrary, have interfered materially with the decomposition of the remains of dead vegetables

'On the other hand, this difference in the composition of the atmosphere, so favourable to the development, growth, and preservation of vegetable matter, must have proved a bar to the existence of animals, particularly of warm-blooded animals, whose respiration, as it is more active, also requires a purer air: during this first period, consequently, not a single animal breathing air appears to have existed.

'During this period the atmosphere must have been purged of some portion of the excess of carbonic acid which it contained, by the vegetables which then existed; these assimilated it first, and subsequently buried it in the state of coal in the bowels of the earth. It is after this first period, in the course of our second and third periods, that this immense variety of monstrous reptiles makes its appearance, animals which, by the nature of their respiration, are capable of living in an atmosphere of much less purity than that which warm-blooded animals require, and were the heralds and precursors of these.

'Vegetables continued incessantly to abstract a portion of the carbon of the air, and thus rendered

and their transformation into soil; for this kind of decomposition is owing essentially to the abstraction of a portion of the carbon of the wood by the oxygen of the air: and if the atmosphere contained less oxygen and more carbonic acid, the decomposition in question must have been without doubt both more difficult and slower. Hence the accumulation of vegetable *débris* in extensive beds, even in circumstances and from vegetables which, in the actual state of the atmosphere, would give rise to no such layers of combustible material.'

it every day more pure; but it was not till the appearance of a vegetation altogether new, abounding in mighty trees, the source and origin of numerous deposits of lignite, a vegetation which seems to have covered the surface of the earth with vast forests, that a great number of mammiferous animals, analogous in all the essential features of their organization to those that still exist in the world, appeared for the first time upon its surface.

'Would it not be fair to suppose from this, that our atmosphere had now arrived at that degree of purity which could alone comport with the active respiration of warm-blooded animals, and prove alike favourable to the development of plants and animals, whilst the simultaneous existence of these two orders of beings, and the inverse influence of their respiratory actions, conduce to maintain our atmosphere in the state of stability which is one of the remarkable characters of the present period?'

Such, then, is the mighty round of things, such are the interchanges ever taking place on the surface of our globe. The inorganic is continually being fashioned into the organic, and this after passing through successive changes, and after having displayed the manifestations of Life, is ever passing again into the inorganic, ever again giving up its fashioning forces. 'The crude and formless mass of the air gradually organized in vegetables, passes without change into animals, and becomes the instrument of sensation and thought; then vanquished by this effort, and, as it were, broken, it returns as crude matter to the source whence it had come.' 'Thus,' Dumas also says, 'is the mysterious circle of organic life upon the surface of the globe completed and maintained! The air contains or engenders the oxidized substances required — carbonic acid, water, nitric acid, and ammonia. Vegetables, true reducing apparatus, seize upon the radicals of these, carbon, hydrogen, azote, ammonium; and with them they fashion all the variety of organic or organizable matters which they supply to animals. Animals, again, true apparatuses of combustion, reproduce from them carbonic acid, water, oxide of ammonium, and azotic or nitric acid, which return to the air to reproduce the same phenomena to the end of time.'

Thus we see that throughout vast epochs, and even in the present day, the Vegetable Kingdom has been, and now constitutes, the great laboratory in which the combination of dead inorganic or mineral materials into living *matter* is continually taking place. We have also seen that animals have no such direct power of elevating matter taken immediately from its inorganic sources, that they, on the contrary, avail themselves of the previously constructive energies of plants, and use for the building up of their own tissues complex substances which have been obtained, more or less directly, from the members of the vegetable kingdom. We have next to enquire briefly into what has been called the 'Theory of Organization,' in order to learn how far—

within the tissues of plants and animals—there is at present, and has been taking place, a corresponding evolution of living *forms*, or morphological units. This enquiry will involve a consideration of the present aspect of the 'Cellular theory' of organization, and a sketch of the principal modifications which, of late years, that doctrine has undergone.

Facts are still multiplying day by day which tend to show that the elements of the tissues in man and in the higher animals are possessed of an inherent power and activity of their own—of a separate individuality in fact, though one which is subordinate to the higher and more complex individuality of the organism to which they belong, and as parts of which they have been evolved. Tissue elements, such as epithelial cells, are to a certain extent like distinct organisms. They have a definite Life of their own — longer or shorter according to the situation in which they occur, and which is therefore very variously related to that of the whole organism. Their individuality of character or function is, moreover, further shown by the power which they possess of selecting their own peculiar nutritive elements out of a complex fluid, or nutritive blastema—the blood—common to all parts of the organism. But, granting all this, the question then comes for consideration as to whether we are to look upon 'Cells' as the invariable and ultimate morphological units—whether they alone can exhibit those subordinate vital activities upon which the vital manifestations of the organism as a whole depend. On this subject much difference of opinion exists. Though we cannot go into detail, we will briefly consider the doctrines which have been principally advocated.

An enormous impulse was given to such enquiries by the publication, in the year 1839, of the researches of Schleiden and Schwann[1], who endeavoured to prove that all the tissues of both plants and animals were entirely built up of morphological units called 'cells.' They believed that cells were continually being produced *de novo* in the bodies of plants and animals. Speaking on this subject Schwann said[2]:—'The following admits of universal application to the formation of cells; there is in the first instance a structureless substance present, which is sometimes quite fluid, at others more or less gelatinous. This substance possesses within itself, in a greater or less measure, according to its chemical qualities and the degree of its vitality, a capacity to occasion the production of cells. When this takes place the nucleus usually appears to be formed first, and then the cell around it. *The formation of cells bears the same relation to organic nature that crystallization does to inorganic.* The cell when once formed continues to grow by its own individual powers, but is at the same time directed by the influence of the entire organism, in such

---

[1] 'Microsc. Researches into the Accordance in the Structure and Growth of Animals and Plants.' Translation (Sydenham Society), 1847.
[2] Loc. cit. p. 39.

manner, as the design of the whole requires. This is the fundamental phenomenon of all animal and vegetable vegetation. *It is alike equally consistent with those instances in which young cells are formed within parent cells, as with*

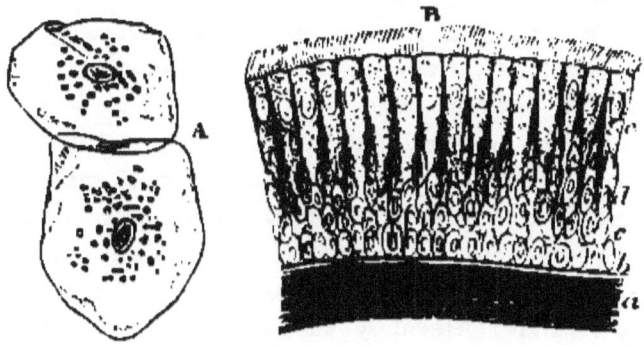

Fig. 4.

Animal Cells.

A. Flattened Epithelium cells from the inside of the mouth. (× 260.)
B. Ciliated Epithelium from the human Trachea; magnified 350 diameters. *a.* Innermost part of the elastic longitudinal fibres. *b.* Homogeneous innermost layer of the mucous membrane. *c.* Deepest round cells. *d.* Middle elongated cells. *e.* Much larger superficial cells, bearing cilia, and containing nucleolated nuclei. (Kölliker.)

those in which the formation goes on outside of them. The generation of the cells takes place in a fluid or in a structureless substance in both cases[1]. We will name

[1] There are most important differences between these two modes of cell-formation dependent upon the nature of the material in the midst of which the new units arise. This will be pointed out further on.

this substance in which the cells are formed, cell-germinating material (Zellenkeimstoff), or cytoblastema. It may be figuratively, but only figuratively, compared to the mother-lye from which crystals are deposited.'

The cells thus formed might remain isolated, or, by the subsequent development and coalescence of their walls in different ways, they might tend to produce the various textures of the plant or animal. All the tissues being thus either made up of cells variously aggregated or derived by a metamorphic process from cells, they maintained that 'the cause of nutrition and growth resides, not in the organism as a whole, but in the separate elementary parts—the cells.' Schwann believed that the 'same process of development and transformation of cells within a structureless substance is repeated in the formation of all the organs of an organism, as well as in the formation of new organisms;' and he thought that the fundamental phenomenon attending the exertion of productive power in organic nature was always of this kind.

Shortly afterwards Professor Goodsir[1] advanced the doctrine that it was not so much the cells as the *nuclei of the textures* which are the potential elementary parts of the organism, and which therefore may be called 'centres of nutrition.' In a communication on this subject he said:—'The centre of nutrition with which we are most familiar is that from which the whole

[1] 'Anatomical and Pathological Observations,' 1845.

organism derives its origin—the germinal spot of the ovum. From this all the other centres are derived, either mediately or immediately, and in directions, numbers, and arrangements, which induce the configuration and structure of the being. . . . As the entire organism is formed at first, not by simultaneous formation of its parts, but by the successive development of these from one centre, so the various parts arise each from its own centre, this being the original source of all the centres with which the part is ultimately supplied. . . . From this it follows, not only that the entire organism, as has been stated by the authors of the cellular theory, consists of simple or developed cells, each having a peculiar independent vitality, but that there is, in addition, a division of the whole into departments, each containing a certain number of simple or developed cells, all of which hold certain relations to one central or capital cell, around which they are grouped[1]. It would appear that from this central cell all the other cells of its department derive their origin.' And then he adds:—' Centres of nutrition are of two kinds—those which are peculiar to the textures, and those which belong to the organs. The nutritive centres of the textures are in general permanent. Those of the organs are in most instances peculiar to their embryonic stage, and either disappear ultimately or break up into the various centres of the

[1] This doctrine of 'departments,' doubtless, suggested to Virchow his modification of a similar conception, concerning 'cell territories.'

textures of which the organs are composed. . . . A nutritive centre, anatomically considered, is merely a cell, the nucleus of which is the permanent source of successive broods of young cells.'

But later still, Virchow announced [1] views which have had an immense influence on pathological doctrines throughout all the schools of medicine, and wherever biological studies have been cultivated. He, too, maintains that 'the cell is really the ultimate morphological unit in which there is any manifestation of life, and that we must not transfer the seat of real action to any point beyond the cell [2].' But then he denies altogether the origin of cells *de novo* in blastemata taking place after the fashion described by Schleiden. He holds that cells can be produced only from or by pre-existing cells. And, moreover, he does not attempt to prove that the whole bulk of the tissues is made up exclusively of cells; he admits the existence of a large amount of intercellular material in many tissues, and so, in order to reconcile this fact with his previous doctrine, he is compelled to put forward the hypothesis that such intercellular material may be broken up into imaginary 'cell territories,' each of which 'is ruled [3] over by the cell which lies in the

[1] 'Cellular Pathologie,' 1858.
[2] Translation by Chance, 1859, p. 3.
[3] This is like a degradation of the old 'archæus' or vital principle. Instead of one monarch holding his court in the stomach, this doctrine would give us an incalculable number of potentates holding their sway in cells over 'cell territories.'

middle of it.' He also is disposed to attach much importance to the nucleus, and believes that 'as long as cells behave as elements still endowed with vital power, the nucleus maintains a very constant form.' Thus, according to Virchow, '*every animal presents itself as a sum of vital unities*,' or as a large kingdom made up of an enormous aggregate of minute dependencies, each of which is endowed with more or less power of self-government—these dependencies being invariably constituted by definite morphological units known as cells, though there may or may not be included under the sway of each a certain outlying 'cell territory.' Such is the essence of Virchow's doctrine.

Before proceeding further, however, it will be well to point out that important modifications had been growing up, even before the publication of Virchow's theories, as to the true conception of the nature of a cell. So far the cell has been spoken of as an altogether definite structure—as a body with a distinct wall or bounding membrane and also certain contents, which include amongst other things one of the most fundamental parts of the cell, the nucleus—which again may contain a nucleolus. But it was maintained by Naegeli [1], and also by Alexander Braun [2], and then more

[1] 'Zeltschrift für Wissen. Botanik,' 1846 (Transln. Ray Soc. 1849, p. 95).
[2] 'The Phenomena of Rejuvenescence in Nature,' 1851 (Transln. Ray Soc. 1853).

emphatically declared by Max Schultze [1], that a distinct investing membrane or cell-wall was not an essential character: afterwards the typical cell was still further shorn of its characteristics when it was shown (if this had not been already done by Naegeli and Braun) by Brücke [2], Kühne [3], and others, that even the nucleus was a non-essential constituent of that body, which was formerly thought to represent not only *the* morphological, but also *the* vital unit. So that, in place of the old 'cell' with its definite characters, this would reduce us to a mere naked, non-nucleated bit of protoplasm as the simplest material substratum adequate to display all those vital manifestations which were previously considered as the essential attributes of certain formed elements known as 'cells.' The power of displaying vital manifestations was, in fact, trans-

---

[1] 'Reichert und Du Bois Reymond's Archiv,' 1861. A mere mass of protoplasm with a nucleus was sufficient to constitute a 'cell;' and at the same time it was maintained that the substance of the cell (or that within the wall, where this existed) was *protoplasm*, a contractile substance answering to what Dujardin had named *sarcode*. These later modifications are, however, by no means antagonistic to the notions of Schwann as may be gathered from the following passages:—'There is no contradiction involved in the supposition that a nucleus may be contained in a solid globule as well as in a cell. . . . A given object may really be a cell when even the common characteristics of that structure, namely the perceptibility of the cell membrane, and the flowing out of the cell contents, cannot be brought under observation. . . . The most important and abundant proof as to the existence of a cell is the presence or absence of the nucleus.'—Loc. cit. p. 37.

[2] 'Wiener Sitzungsberichte,' 1861, pp. 18–22.

[3] 'Protoplasma und die Contractilität.' Leipzig, 1864.

ferred from definitely formed morphological units to utterly indefinite and formless masses of what is called protoplasm. Instead therefore of an obvious *form* of Life, we are reduced to a *matter* of Life, presenting no appreciable morphological characters. It becomes evident, moreover, that if the old term 'cell' is now applied to these bits of living stuff or protoplasm (simply because biologists have been compelled to transfer the power of manifesting vital properties to such masses, instead of restricting this power to definitely formed morphological units) the term must, nevertheless, have entirely lost its old signification, and can be regarded in no other way than as a mere courtesy title when so employed. Vital power has obviously been transferred from a morphological unit (the cell) to mere formless living matter, and if some persist in calling a portion of such mere matter by the name of the morphological unit, simply because this was of old also *assumed* to be the ultimate vital unit, we must not allow our minds to be confused by such use of the word [1].

In order to prevent this, a new term must be introduced, and the old term must lose something of its definiteness: it must, at the same time, renounce for ever one of the characteristics with which many have credited it. In accordance with the views above expressed, the 'cell,' even in its modern sense—the mass of protoplasm containing a nucleus—cannot be regarded as the ultimate vital unit. It is also less

[1] See Hutchison Stirling's 'As regards Protoplasm,' &c., 1869, p. 16.

definite in its morphological characters, since it is now acknowledged that the cell may or may not be enclosed by a membrane or cell-wall. For the structureless mass of protoplasm—the mere bit of plasma, or living matter—in which no inner differentiation has yet taken place, we cannot do better than adopt Haeckel's[1] term *'plastide.'* The plastide, like the cell, may vary much in size: it, also, may be either naked or bounded by a membrane.

The old doctrine as to the fundamental properties of the 'cell' as a vital unit, did well enough in those days when the lowest known living things—the lowest plants and the lowest animals—were thought to be 'unicellular

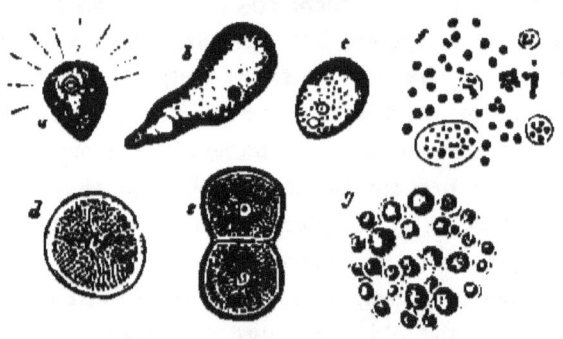

FIG. 5.

'Unicellular Organisms.'

a, b, c. Three of the higher Amœbæ.
  a. *Nuclearia simplex.*
  b. *Amœba Limax.*
  c. *Amœba guttula.*
d and e. *Gregarina Sipunculi.*

f. One of the most minute and simple of the unicellular Algæ—*Hematococcus æruginosus.*
g. The 'red snow' Alga—*Protococcus nivalis.*

[1] 'Journal of Microsc. Science,' 1869, vol. ix. p. 332.

organisms,' closely approximating in their characters to the morphological units of which the higher plants and animals were compounded. But, since our knowledge has increased, since we have become more familiar with the various living things which now constitute the lowest groups of the third organic kingdom—*PROTISTA*—the maintenance of such doctrines (leaving aside all other reasons) has become impossible. Have we not seen that although the *Protoplasta* are amœboid animals, possessing the old cell characters—that is, having a distinct nucleus and a definite bounding membrane — there are, nevertheless, adult animals entering into the composition of the lowest group *Monera*, some of which have no bounding membrane though they have a nucleus, whilst others, simpler still, are mere bits of protoplasm, naked, non-nucleated, structureless? Yet, such minute, homogeneous, and altogether indefinite bits of protoplasm, are as capable of displaying the fundamental characteristics of Life as are the more definite unicellular organisms, to which such attributes were previously supposed to be restricted. Without visible structure they nevertheless assimilate materials from their environment, and grow. They constantly vary their form, and are capable of executing slow movements. Though possessing no nucleus, they, nevertheless, are able to divide and reproduce their kind.

Dr. Lionel Beale, whilst admitting the existence of a morphological unit answering to the cell of other observers, which is found to enter largely into the composition of many of the tissues of the body, denies that anything to which *the ordinary definition of a cell* would be applicable can be said to constitute the elementary part of many tissues. He says[1]:—'We may, however, use this term, which is very short and convenient, if we give it a more general meaning. I would venture to describe the cell or elementary part as a structure always consisting of matter in two states, *forming* and *formed*, or *germinal matter* and *formed material*. The first or active substance is surrounded and protected by the outer passive matter, through which all the pabulum to be converted into germinal matter must pass.' Looking therefore upon the central portion (corresponding to nucleus and part of cell contents) as the *living* part or germinal matter, in which the active powers of growth reside, and by the division of which new germinal centres are produced; he regards the peripheral portion (corresponding to the outer part of cell contents, the cell-wall and the intercellular substance of most other writers) as *dead* matter, incapable of undergoing any further changes that may be called vital. The outermost layers of germinal matter are supposed to be continually losing their peculiar powers, and passing into formed material; whilst the new materials of growth penetrate to the very centre of the germinal mass, where all the

[1] 'Structure and Growth of Tissues.' 'Journal of Microscopical Science,' 1861, p. 62.

vital processes are thought to be in their greatest activity. Further changes in the *formed* (or dead) material, result, in some cases, in the formation of the various secretions, and in others, in the production of the characteristic parts of such tissues as muscle and nerve.

We now know, however, that the simplest living things present no such distinction of parts as those to which Dr. Beale alludes; and it has always appeared to me to be a very fundamental objection to his theory that so many of the most characteristically vital phenomena of the higher animals should take place through the agency of tissues—muscle and nerve for instance—by far the greater part of the bulk of which would, in accordance with Dr. Beale's view, have to be considered as *dead*, and inert. Dr. Beale has quite recently said [1]:—'The contractile material of muscle may be shown to be continuous with the germinal matter, and oftentimes a thin filament of the transversely striated tissue may be detached with the oval mass of germinal matter still connected with it, showing that, as in tendon, the germinal matter passes uninterruptedly into the formed material. This contractile tissue is not, like the germinal matter which produced it, in a *living* state. In the formation of the contractile tissue the germinal matter seems to move onwards, and at its posterior part gradually undergoes conversion into the tissue. At the same time it absorbs nutrient material, and thus, although a vast amount

[1] 'Protoplasm,' 2nd edition, 1870, p. 54.

of contractile tissue may have been produced, the germinal matter which formed it may not have altered in bulk.' Then, concerning the nature and mode of formation of nerve fibres, Dr. Beale says:—'The nerve fibre is composed of formed material, which is structurally continuous with the formed material of the nerve cells of the nerve centres. A nerve fibre at an early period of development consists of a number of oval masses of germinal matter linearly arranged. As development proceeds, these become separated farther and farther from one another, and the non-living *tissue* which is thus spun off as they become separated, is the nerve.'

Dr. Beale's dictum that the matter which he calls 'formed material' is dead, we regard as a singularly foundationless hypothesis, the maintenance of which is beset with difficulties. If muscles and nerves perform work, such functional activity must be attended by tissue changes in their very substance. How then is repair to be effected? Not after the fashion in which living tissues are renovated, for these, according to Dr. Beale, are dead, and therefore cannot be amenable to the laws which govern the repair of living structures. I have no faith, however, in the ability of carmine to discriminate the not-living from the Living, and can only state my total inability to accept the opinion of Dr. Beale when he says:—'The difference between germinal or living matter and the pabulum which nourishes it, on the one hand, and the formed material which is produced by it, on the other, is, I believe, absolute. The pabulum does not shade by imperceptible gradations into the living matter, and this latter into the formed material, but the passage from one state into the other is sudden and abrupt, although there may be much living matter mixed with little lifeless matter, or *vice versa*. The ultimate particles of matter pass from the lifeless into the living state, and from the latter into the dead state, suddenly. Matter cannot be said to *half-live* or *half-die*. It is either *dead* or *living, animate* or *inanimate* ; and formed matter has ceased to live.' We do not wonder that any one who could hold such a doctrine as this should exhibit so much antagonism towards the Evolution Hypothesis. But how such marvellously abrupt transitions are brought about we are not told; and Dr. Beale, moreover, forgets to mention upon what evidence he feels himself entitled to make such positive and startling assertions.

To a certain extent, however, we find there is an agreement between Dr. Beale's doctrine and that of other excellent observers. He says [1]:—'However much organisms and tissues in their fully formed state may vary as regards the character, properties, and composition of the formed material, all were first in the condition of *clear, transparent, structureless, formless* living matter.' Surely, however, he is uttering something quite contradictory when he says, in effect

[1] Loc. cit. p. 48.

previously, and also subsequently[1] in actual words:—'All that is essential to the cell or elementary part is *matter that is in the living state—germinal matter*, and matter that *has been in the living state—formed material*.' Such 'formed material' as Dr. Beale here speaks of may be necessary in order to support certain theories, but it does not actually exist in the simplest living things or elemental living parts—these are, as he has himself frequently stated, perfectly structureless[2].

But even so far back as 1853, before the doctrine as to the constitution of the 'cell' had undergone these modifications—or rather, as we should more strictly say, before it had been generally acknowledged that vital manifestations could be displayed by mere bits of protoplasm lacking this form hitherto supposed necessary—Professor Huxley had put forth[3] a powerful remonstrance against the then all-prevalent 'cellular theory' of organization. His opinions were announced even five years before Virchow, the last great champion of the old doctrine, issued his celebrated 'Cellular Pathologie.' Following in the main the doctrines of Wolff and Von Baer, Professor Huxley contended that the primitive organic substance is a homogeneous plasma

---

[1] Idem, p. 55.

[2] If the reader chooses to consult Dr. Beale's work on 'Protoplasm,' it will be found—in accordance with fact rather than theory—that the figures of living things and elementary parts there given in Pl. II, especially figs. 3, 5, and 6, represent only homogeneous living matter, with no trace of formed material externally. Dr. Beale's accuracy as an observer is thoroughly well known.

[3] See 'British and Foreign Medical Chirurgical Review,' 1853, p. 306.

in which a certain differentiation takes place, but that there is no evidence whatever to show that the *molecular forces* of this living matter (the 'vital forces' of most modern writers) are by this differentiation localized in any one part more than in any other part— be it cell or be it intercellular tissue. 'Neither is there any evidence,' he says, 'that any attraction or other influence is exercised by the one over the other; the changes which each subsequently undergoes, though they are in harmony, having no causal connection with one another, but each proceeding, as it would seem, in accordance with the general determining laws of the organism.' Whilst believing that the *periplast*— corresponding with the cell-wall and intercellular tissue of other writers—is the seat of all the most important metamorphic processes, out of which the various tissues are produced, he also believes that this differentiation is not brought about by any mysterious action on the part of the cell or nucleus—that it is rather a result of intimate *molecular* changes taking place in the plastic matter itself after a definitely successive, though inexplicable fashion. The fundamental position of Professor Huxley is, in fact, that the 'primary differentiation is not a *necessary* preliminary to further organization—that the cells are not machines by which alone further development can take place,' they are rather mere indications of accustomed modes of evolution. This view he has further illustrated as follows:— 'We have tried to show,' he says, 'that they are not instruments but indications—that they are no more the producers of the vital phenomena, than the shells scattered *in orderly lines* along the sea-beach are the instruments by which the gravitative force of the moon acts upon the ocean. Like these, the cell marks only where the vital tides have been, and how they have acted.'

Professor Huxley's doctrine must be distinguished from another put forward by Dr. Hughes Bennett shortly afterwards[1], and then more fully in the 'Proceedings of the Royal Society of Edinburgh,' in 1861. This is more especially known as 'The Molecular Theory of Organization.' 'The first step,' Professor Bennett says, ' in the process of organic formation, is the production of an organic fluid; the second, the precipitation in it of organic molecules, from which, according to the molecular law of growth, all other textures are derived either directly or indirectly.' So that 'the ultimate parts of the organism are not cells nor nuclei, but the minute molecules from which these are formed. They possess independent physical and vital properties, which enable them to unite and arrange themselves so as to produce higher forms. Among these are nuclei, cells, fibres, and membranes, all of which may be produced directly from molecules. The development and growth of organic tissues is owing to the successive formation of histogenetic and histolytic molecules. The breaking

---

[1] 'Report of the British Association,' 1855, p. 119.

down of one substance is often the necessary step to the formation of another: so that the histolytic or disintegrative molecules of one period become the histogenetic or formative molecules of another[1].' The theory of organization advocated by Prof. Huxley and others is 'molecular' from a functional point of view, whilst this of Dr. Hughes Bennett bears principally upon the developmental and structural aspects of the doctrine[2], although he also distinctly teaches that the vital forces are dependent upon molecules and not upon cells. Speaking of his general doctrine, Dr. Bennett says:—
'The molecular, therefore, is in no way opposed to a true cell theory of growth, but constitutes a wider generalization, and a broader basis for its operations. Neither does it give any countenance to the doctrine of equivocal or spontaneous generation[3].' It can scarcely be said that Dr. Bennett has succeeded in convincing

---

[1] Lectures 'On Molecular Physiology,' &c., 'Lancet,' 1863 (vol. i.). p. 56.

[2] A doctrine of this kind had been previously hinted at by Pineau in 1848 ('Annal. des Sciences Naturelles'), when he expressed his belief that the primary phenomenon in the development not only of cells, animal and vegetable, but also of Infusoria, consisted 'essentiellement en une agglomération des granules.' He described observations by which he had satisfied himself that such a mode of formation occurred in the origin of certain Infusoria, and also in the formation of the spores of certain Lichens. According to Virchow (loc. cit. p. 26), Baumgärtner and Arnold had also expressed their belief in a similar mode of origin of tissue elements.

[3] Lectures in 'Lancet,' 1863, p. 4. Lately, however ('Pop. Science Review,' Jan., 1869), Dr. Hughes Bennett has proclaimed his firm belief in the doctrine of 'Spontaneous Generation.'

physiologists as to the truth of his doctrines so far as they bear upon structure and development, although they are undoubtedly true in several important respects.

Now the essence of the doctrine propounded by Prof. Huxley, and in this respect also by Dr. Hughes Bennett, is that the vital forces are 'molecular forces,' that they are not dependent upon morphological forms or 'cells,' and therefore, that essentially vital manifestations may take place in mere formless living matter[1]. But, as we have just seen, this is precisely the doctrine to which so many other distinguished biologists have now given in their adhesion. They too —Max Schultze, Haeckel, Kühne, and others—have gradually recognized that a something of definite form is no longer necessary—that there are independent living things even lower in the scale than the old unicellular organisms, and that whether to constitute one of these or to constitute a functional unit of a higher organism, all that is needed is mere indefinite formless protoplasm—a mere 'shred' of the matter of Life[2].

This then being the theory to which our most accomplished microscopists and physiologists have arrived, it will be interesting for us to see how such a conclusion harmonizes with the hypothesis of Evolu-

---

[1] This is the logical outcome also of the doctrine of Schwann, since he so distinctly maintained that, 'The formation of cells bears the same relation to organic nature, that crystallization does to inorganic.'

[2] See Mr. Stirling's pamphlet, 'As regards Protoplasm in relation to Professor Huxley's Essay on the Physical Basis of Life,' 1869, p. 16.

tion. We cannot do better than quote what Mr. Herbert Spencer writes on this subject in his 'Principles of Biology.' 'We set out with molecules[1],' he says, 'one degree higher in complexity than those molecules of nitrogenous colloidal substance into which organic matter is resolvable; and we regard these somewhat more complex molecules as having the implied greater instability, greater sensitiveness to surrounding influences, and consequent greater mobility of form. Such being the primitive physiological units, organic evolution must begin with the formation of a minute aggregation of them—*an aggregate showing vitality only by a higher degree of that readiness to change its form of aggregation which colloidal matter in general displays*; and by its ability to unite the nitrogenous molecules it meets with, into complex molecules like those of which it is composed. Obviously the earliest forms must have been minute; since in the absence of any but diffused organic matter, no form but a minute one could find nutriment. Obviously, too, it must have been structureless; since as differentiations are producible only by the unlike actions of incident forces, there could have been no differentiations before such forces had had time to work. Hence distinctions of parts like those required to constitute a cell were necessarily

---

[1] Mr. Spencer here refers to chemical molecules of a very complex nature, and not to minute visible granules. For an account of these complex molecules or 'physiological units' see 'Prin. of Biol.' vol. i. p. 182.

absent at first. And we need not therefore be surprised to find, as we do find, specks of protoplasm manifesting life and yet showing no signs of organization[1].'

But if, then, mere 'cellular' form is so non-essential for the display of vital manifestations, how, it may be asked, is its frequent recurrence throughout the tissues of plants and animals to be explained[2]? We can only make more or less probable surmises in reply to this question. We must imagine, in the first place, that the telluric conditions acting upon plastic organizable matter are such as to be especially favourable for the evolution of this particular organic form. The very interesting experiments of Mr. Rainey, as well as those of Dr. Montgomery, have indeed already shown that non-living semi-fluid matter, under certain conditions, is especially prone to assume such shapes. Thus the action of environing conditions, combined

---

[1] Loc. cit. vol. ii. p. 11.

[2] It must not be supposed that a cellular structure is more prevalent than is really the case. Nothing of the kind exists, as we have seen, in many Amœbæ, and likewise in the Foraminifera. No true cells can be said to be present in Diatoms or Desmids, and from what the Rev. M. J. Berkeley tells us there are what may be considered non-cellular Algæ and Fungi. Speaking of these plants, he says (' Introduction to Crypt. Botany,' p. 248) :—' The cellular tissue varies in almost every conceivable way, both as regards form and composition. Cells occur perfectly globose, and almost extremely elongated and attenuated; and in some instances, as in *Vaucheria* (Fig. 22), not a single dissepiment is formed (Fig. 23) from the first germination of the spore till impregnation; so that the whole plant is a single ramified cell whose apices fall off and reproduce the species.' Many other Algæ agree with *Vaucheria* in presenting no trace of a cellular structure.

with the inherent tendencies of the lowest living things, would predispose towards their evolution into unicellular organisms — both animal and vegetable. And similar determining causes might be presumed to be in part operative in the production of those higher organisms which are composed of variously arranged aggregates of such morphological units. But we must not forget, as Mr. Spencer reminds us, that from the *Law of Heredity*, considered as extending to the entire succession of large groups of living things on the surface of our globe, during its whole past history, 'it follows that since the formation of these small simple organisms must have preceded the formation of larger and more complex organisms, the larger and more complex organisms must inherit their essential characters. We may anticipate,' Mr. Spencer continues, 'that the multiplication and combination of these minute aggregates or cells will be conspicuous in the early developmental stages of plants and animals; and that throughout all subsequent stages, cell-production and cell-differentiation will be dominant characteristics. The physiological units peculiar to each higher species will, speaking generally, pass through this form of aggregation on their way towards the final arrangement they are to assume; because those primordial physiological units from which they are remotely descended, aggregated into this form. And yet, just as in other cases we found reason for inferring (§ 131) that the traits of ancestral organization may, under certain conditions, be partially or wholly obliterated, and the ultimate structure assumed without passing through them, so here it is to be inferred that the process of cell formation may, in some cases, be passed over. Thus the hypothesis of evolution prepares us for these two radical modifications of the cell doctrine which the facts oblige us to make. It leads us to expect, that as structureless portions of protoplasm must have preceded cells in the process of general evolution, so in the special evolution of each higher organism there will be an habitual production of cells out of structureless blastema. And it leads us to expect, that though generally the physiological units composing a structureless blastema will display their inherited proclivities by cell development and metamorphosis; there will nevertheless occur cases in which the tissue to be formed is formed by direct transformation of the blastema [1].'

Fully admitting, therefore, that the 'cell' is a most important structure, that it is a kind of *whole* having in complex organisms a subordinate individuality of its own, that cells do frequently multiply by division of pre-existing cells, that they are in fact morphological units, which by their uniformity of structure and wide-spread diffusion throughout the tissues of both plants and animals may well claim to be *the* morphological units—still, we must not, on this account, endow them with an undue importance. We have

[1] Loc. cit. vol. ii. p. 12.

seen how strongly many of our leading physiologists and zoologists are in favour of the view that such a definite *form* is no longer necessary for the display of vital manifestations—nay, it is a view which they cannot do other than hold, now it has become a matter of absolute knowledge that the lowest living things—far from being unicellular organisms—are mere bits of protoplasm, devoid of nucleus, devoid of cell-wall, Proteus-like, changing in outline from moment to moment. Whilst, therefore, fully alive to the great service which Virchow has done to the cause of pathology, by calling attention so forcibly to the importance of a consideration of the inherent activities of the tissue elements as factors in the nutritive processes, whether healthy or morbid, we believe, nevertheless, that he has pushed his doctrines to a perilous and erroneous extreme. We feel it impossible—and perchance he would now do the same—to admit that 'the cell is really the ultimate morphological unit in which there is any manifestation of life, and that we must not transfer the seat of real action to any point beyond the cell.' Then, too, the accumulated weight of other evidence, of various kinds, makes it impossible for us to agree with him in regard to the doctrine that cells can only originate from division or endogenous multiplication of pre-existing cells, that they can never be evolved *de novo* out of homogeneous blastemata[1]. Virchow's doctrine on this subject is—

[1] 'Cellular Pathology.' p. 27.

'Where a cell arises, there a cell must have previously existed (*omnis cellula e cellula*), just as an animal can spring only from an animal, a plant only from a plant.' To what extent this is true we have now to enquire.

CHAPTER V.

MODES OF ORIGIN OF REPRODUCTIVE UNITS AND OF CELLS.

Modes of origin of reproductive units. Development of 'zoospores' in *Conferva area*. Evolution of ciliated spore in *Vaucheria*. Formation of 'resting spore' in *Œdogonium*. Development of spores in *Achlya prolifera*; rapidity of process. Similar mode of formation in other Fungi, and in Lichens. Mode of origin of Nuclei. Formation of Cells within the internodes of *Chararea*. Development of ovule, and of endosperm cells, in Flowering Plants. Mode of origin of germs in *Protomyxa*, and in higher Amœbæ. Formation of ova in lower Animals. No doubt about mode of formation of yelk-mass and vitelline membrane in Nematoids. Mode of origin of ova in higher Animals. Origin of Spermatozoa, antherozoids, and pollen grains.

Above evidence shows that independent Living Units are at first formless. The Cell a product of Evolution. Non-essential nature of nucleus and cell-wall. Virchow's hypothesis untenable. Most necessary to consider properties of Living Matter.

Origin of Living Units, as specks of protoplasm, in blastemata. Experiments of Onimus. Observations on mode of origin of white blood corpuscles. Another mode in which Cells originate. Five fundamental modes by which independent Living Units are produced. Can a fluid live? Comparison between the Growth and Genesis of Living Matter. Theoretical indications not adverse to Archebiosis.

THE mere *form*, therefore, of living things, or of the active elemental parts of higher organisms, has lost its importance. Vital manifestations are now known not to be dependent upon visible organization of any kind; they are the results of peculiar molecular aggregations: visible organization is, in fact, a result rather than a cause of Life and living action. The cell is not the ultimate unit, without which the phenomena of Life are unable to occur. It is itself the product, immediate or remote, of an antecedent evolution. Life is dependent upon *matter* of particular kinds, and results from the aggregated and interdependent play of the molecular forces pertaining to such matter, in an organism. The old and much disputed problem, therefore, as to whether cells can originate, independently of pre-existing cells, in homogeneous fluids or blastemata within the body, may and must be resolved into the still simpler question, Whether mere minute, almost microscopically invisible, specks of protoplasm (plastides), which are able to develope into definite 'cell' forms, can originate in such fluids? With the view of throwing light upon the subject, we may call attention to some facts which, though familiar to very many, do not seem to have been adequately appreciated in their bearing upon this question.

We will first enquire into the mode of origin of the most important of all living units—of those which are destined to perpetuate the species. And, having done so, we must test the facts thus ascertained not by the old notions concerning the 'cell,' but by the new facts and views concerning the powers of mere formless living matter, which the present state of biological science compels us to accept.

The reproductive units of Algæ, which, after escaping

from certain cells or chambers of the parent plant, for a time move about in the water with great activity, before developing into the future plant, are named 'zoospores,' and also 'gonidia.' The nature and mode of origin of these bodies were most carefully studied by M. Thuret[1], and the investigation has since been followed up by many other observers. They seem to be always produced as a result of differentiations taking place in a previously formless protoplasm, and in their free active stage of existence they closely resemble certain infusorial animalcules, though, of course, they differ from these altogether as regards their ultimate fate. As Dr. Lindley pointed out[2]:—'The reproduction of algals by zoospores is a much more common phenomenon than has been supposed. Instead of being confined to the lower forms of the alliance, it occurs in the most completely organized forms, such as Laminarias, which are hardly more remarkable for their gigantic size than for the complexity of their structure.' One mode of formation and liberation of these bodies is well described by Agardh. He says[3]:—'The filaments of *Conferva area* are, as is well known, articulated or divided at equal distances into little compartments (joints), which have no communication among themselves other than what results from the permeability of the dissepiments. The green matter

---

[1] Ann. des Sc. Naturelles. Sér. 3, t. xiv.
[2] 'Vegetable Kingdom,' 3rd edition, p. 11.
[3] 'Ann. des Sc. Naturelles,' 1836, t. xii. p. 194.

contained in these joints appears at first altogether *homogeneous*, as if it were fluid; but in a more advanced state it becomes more and more granular. The granules are, at their formation, found adhering to the inner surface of the membrane; but they soon detach themselves, and the irregular figure which they present at first passes to that of a sphere. These granules congregate by degrees in the middle of the joint into a mass, at first elliptical, but which at length becomes perfectly spherical. All these changes are conformable to the phenomena known in vegetable life; those which are to follow have more analogy with the phenomena of animal life. At this stage an important metamorphosis exhibits itself by a motion of *swarming* (un mouvement de fourmillement) in the green matter. The granules of which it is composed detach themselves from the mass one after another, and having thus become free, they move about in the vacant space of the joint with an extreme rapidity. At the same time the exterior membrane of the joint is observed to swell in one point, till on it there forms a little mammilla, which is to become the point from which the moving granules finally issue. . . At first they issue in a body, but soon those which remain, swimming in a much larger space, have much more difficulty in escaping; and it is only after innumerable knockings against the walls of their prison that they succeed in finding an exit. From the first instant of the motion one observes that the granules or sporules are furnished with a little beak, a kind of anterior process, always distinguishable from the body of the seed by its paler colour. . . . Escaped from their prison they continue their motion for one or two hours, and retiring always towards the darker edge of the vessel, sometimes they prolong their wandering course, sometimes they remain in the same place, causing their beak to vibrate in rapid circles. Finally they collect in dense masses, containing innumerable grains, and attach themselves to some extraneous body at the bottom or on the surface of the water, where they hasten to develope filaments like those of the mother plant.'

The mode of formation of the single ciliated spore [1] of *Vaucheria* is perhaps still more interesting, because the parent organism, which is a fine tufted filamentous Alga, presents not the slightest trace of a cellular structure, and because of the rapidity with which the spore is produced. The ramified tubular structure of the Alga is lined with minute but bright green chlorophyll vesicles or granules. All the phenomena which attend the formation of the spore were frequently observed, and have been carefully described by Dr. A. H. Hassall, from whose work [2] we abstract the following details. When spores are about to form, the extremities of some of the filaments swell up in the form of a club, and the green matter becomes so much condensed at this part as to assume a

[1] About $\frac{1}{500}''$ in diameter.
[2] 'History of the British Fresh Water Algæ,' 1845, p. 16.

blackish tint. Near the base of the enlargement the

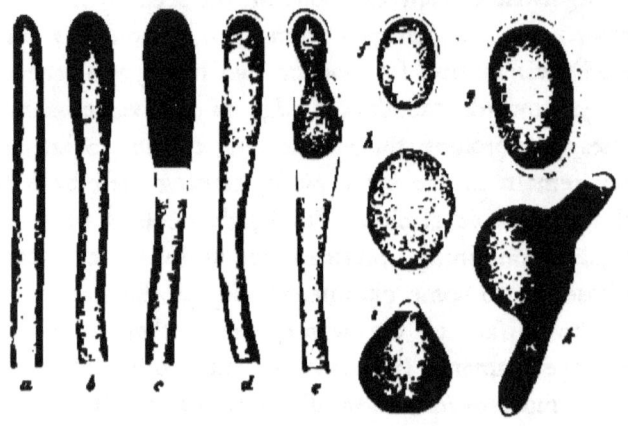

Fig. 6.

Formation of Spore in *Vaucheria*. (Hassall.)

a, b, c, d. Successive changes in one of terminal filaments prior to the separation of the spore.
e. Spore emerging from ruptured extremity of filament.
f. Spore immediately after separation.
g. Spore at later stage, larger and ciliated.
h. Later still, showing changes which precede germination.
i, k. Commencing growth of filaments from the stationary spore.

chlorophyll granules are seen separated from one another, leaving a clear and ultimately well-defined space, in which transparent mucilage only is to be seen, separating the matter of the future spore from that of the filament. All this takes place most rapidly, so that in a few minutes from its commencement the embryo spore assumes an elongated oval form, and the whole of it, with the exception of its proximal or inferior extremity, is almost black from the condensation of chlorophyll that has taken place in its substance. 'It is then,' Dr. Hassall says, 'that the crisis commences: the superior extremity suddenly becomes protruded, the granular fluid empties itself into the protruded portion, which quickly increases in volume, so that the opposite extremity becomes separated from the filament. At the same time the spore commences to turn on its great axis in such a manner as that all the granules which it contains are seen to pass rapidly from right to left, and from left to right, as though they moved in the interior of a transparent cylinder.' The spore soon completely frees itself from the filament[1], and 'springs with rapidity into the surrounding liquid,' where it swims about with its colourless portion always in advance, and may then be seen to be surrounded by a tolerably thick transparent membrane. It continues revolving on its axis, at the same time that it moves about from place to place. 'In general it quickly reaches the edge of the glass as though it tried to escape; sometimes it stops; then in an instant afterwards it resumes its course.' The cilia which cover the whole surface of the transparent membrane are mostly invisible on account of the rapidity of their movement; but when their motion is retarded by putting some opium into the water containing the spore, the individual cilia

---

[1] These remarkable phenomena may occur more than once. Dr. Hassall says, 'I have seen the operation thrice repeated upon the same filament.'

can be easily discriminated. With regard to the first appearance of these Dr. Hassall says:—'I have observed many times the emission of the spore in a coloured infusion, and then noticed that the agitation of the granules[1] by the motion of the cilia is not felt until about a fourth part of the spore has been released.' Prof. Unger saw these spores moving about for more than two hours, but when they were covered by a thin slip of glass, as during the observations of Dr. Hassall, they never continued to move for more than nineteen minutes. Dr. Hassall says:—'The vibration of the cilia continues sometimes after the spore is arrested, only it is not sufficiently strong to displace the corpuscle. When at last they cease to move, the contour of the spore undergoes during some instants a sensible alteration, which announces, perhaps, the decomposition or the absorption of the vibratile organs[2]. The motionless spore delays not to modify itself once again: it becomes spherical; the green matter distributes itself equally, and the episporic membrane, in part reabsorbed, at last escapes the sight; very soon germination commences . . . The elongation of the filaments progresses, one might say by eye-sight; for I have measured more than once an increase of three-twentieths of a millimetre in an hour.' The formation of the spores always takes place during the first hours of the

[1] Of carmine or indigo.
[2] The rapid formation and disappearance of the cilia surrounding these spores are features of extreme interest.

day. Dr. Hassall says:—'The tufts which I have gathered the day before, and which presented no indication of the formation being near at hand, were in general covered with spores the next morning; and after midday these were all gathered on the surface of the water beginning to germinate.'

The mode of origin of the so-called 'resting spore' or 'seed-cell [1]' in *Œdogonium* is also very interesting, and illustrates in an important manner the question we are now considering. In this case, the whole of the protoplasmic contents of one of the cells of the plant goes to produce a single new reproductive element, instead of many as in the case of *Conferva area*. Alexander Braun [2] describes the changes which take place as follows:—' In the formation of the resting seed-cells of Œdogonium we see the thickish cell-contents composed of greenish coloured mucilage, mixed with chlorophyll and starch vesicles, which, in the earlier vegetative period of the cell, form a lining

---

[1] These are reproductive products which do not develope immediately after they have been formed, into the plant which they may ultimately produce. They continue, as Braun says, 'for a long time in a condition of rest, during which, excepting as regards imperceptible internal processes, they remain wholly unchanged.' The direct germ-cells, or swarming-spores (*gonidia*, or *zoospores*), however, pass on, after their evolution, through a continuous process of growth and development till the perfect plant is reproduced. These latter are the bodies of which we have already spoken in connection with *Conferva area*, and of whose development in *Achlya prolifera* we are shortly about to speak.

[2] 'Rejuvenescence in Nature' (Translation by Henfrey, Ray Society), 1853. p. 164.

of the wall, retreat from this membrane, and present themselves as a new, everywhere free cell, destined for reproduction. The cell-body thus detached from the walls, appearing in a new form, with a new vital direction, presents itself with regular form and boundaries, *before a trace of the cell membrane subsequently clothing it is visible.* It mostly assumes a perfectly globular form, even when the mother-cell is longish; in this first period of formation its surface appears somewhat uneven from the projection of chlorophyll vesicles; the whole internal cavity is filled up, and of deep green colour. Very slowly and gradually there appears, first a simple, afterwards a double, and sometimes even a triple-layered membrane upon the surface, while the chlorophyll and starch formations in the contents progressively vanish, and give place to reddish oil-drops, which at length occupy nearly the whole cavity, and give the seed-cell a brownish-red, sometimes even a red-lead coloured appearance[1]. The seed-cells of the

[1] These metabolic changes of a chemical nature taking place within the cell are of the highest interest. We have already had occasion (note, p. 105) to refer to the properties conferred upon a seed by the presence of much oil and starch in its interior, and we shall subsequently (p. 212) have occasion to refer to the metabolic capacities of fatty products. One of the best instances of the conversion of chlorophyll and protoplasm into *colourless* fatty and other materials, and of the subsequent reconversion of these into coloured protoplasm, is to be met with in the life-history of *Palmoglœa*. The reproduction of this plant is brought about by the union of two green vegetative cells, the contents of which are converted into a single seed-cell. Braun says:— 'During the gradual growing together and fusion of the two combining cells, we may trace the formation of fixed oil step by step. Before the

Zygnemaceæ originate in the same way as those of *Œdogonium*, with the single distinction that in the former the contents of two chambers become united to form one seed-cell.'

A mode of production of zoospores different from that already described by Agardh, and resembling more closely that by which the seed-spore of *Œdogonium* is produced, is now known to take place in *Achlya prolifera*—a curious little plant first discovered by Prof. Goodsir, on the gills of certain gold fish which were in an unhealthy condition. It was formerly thought to be a species of Conferva, but it is now regarded by the Rev. M. J. Berkeley and others as merely a submerged or aquatic form of a Mucor. This, as one of the simplest kinds of Fungi, has been made the subject of a most careful investigation by Prof. Unger[1]. When in the

beginning of the combination, the cells are filled with finely granular contents, in which we see arise, during the progress of the union, shining drops, at first very small and distant, gradually growing larger, coming in contact and coalescing, so that the intermediate contents almost entirely disappear, and the complete spore appears filled merely with a mixture of oil drops of the most varied size. During this process the colour of the cells changes from green to a light yellowish brown. Vegetative cells with homogeneous green contents originate subsequently through transformation and division of the contents of these oleaginous seed-cells.' (Loc. cit. p. 202, and Pl. I, II.) In connection with this subject, also, we may call attention to the fact elsewhere (Linn. Soc. Trans. xxv. 1865, p. 84) mentioned, of the large amount of free fat frequently existing within the intestinal canal of many of the Free Nematoids, which appears to result from the more or less direct transformation of the cellulose taken as food.

[1] 'Einiges zur Lebensgeschichte der Achlya prolifera,' in 'Linnæa,' 1843. t. iv.

perfect state, it consists of transparent threads of extreme fineness packed together as closely as the pile of velvet. Dr. Lindley says [1]:—'These threads are terminated by an extremity about $\frac{1}{1500}$" in diameter, consisting of a long single cell, within which is collected some green mucilage intermixed with granules. . . . The contents

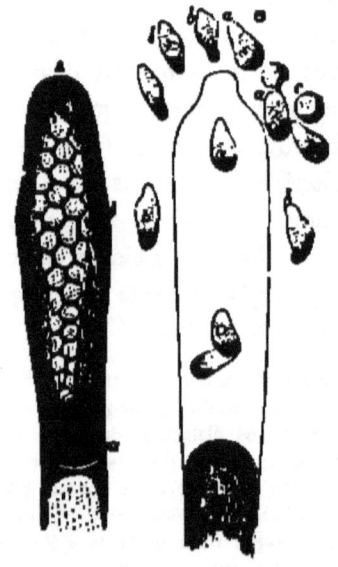

Fig. 7.
Development of Zoospores in *Achlya prolifera*.
A. Dilated extremity of a filament, *b.* separated from the other portion by a partition, *a.* and containing young zoospores in process of formation.
B. Club-head after most of the active zoospores have been set free. (Unger.)

[1] 'Vegetable Kingdom,' 3rd edition, p. 17.

of the cell are seen to be in constant motion. . . . While this is going on the end of the cell continues to grow, and at the same time the contents collect at the extremity, and distend it into a small head, in form resembling a club, immediately after which a chamber is formed and then the first stage of fructification is established. The next change is observed to take place in the granular matter of the club-head, which itself enlarges, whilst the contents gain opaqueness, and by degrees arrange themselves in five or six-sided meshes, which are in reality the sides of angular bodies that are rapidly forming at the expense of the mucilage above mentioned, which has disappeared. It is not the least surprising part of this history that all the changes above mentioned take place *in the course of an hour or an hour and a half*, so that a patient observer may actually witness the creation of this singular plant. At this time all the vital energy seems directed towards changing the angular bodies in the inside of the club-head into propagating germs or spores. Meanwhile the club-head grows, and gives them a little room, and they in their turn alter their form and become oval. Then it is that is witnessed the surprising phenomenon of spontaneous motion in the spores, which, notwithstanding the narrow space in which they are born, act with such vigour that at last they force a way through the end of the club-head. At first one spore gets out into the water, then another and another, till at last the club-head is emptied. All this takes place with such rapidity that a minute or two suffices for the complete evacuation of the club-head or spore-chamber. The spores when they find their way into the water are generally egg-shaped, and swim with the small end foremost. . . . They are extremely small, their breadth not exceeding the $\frac{1}{1800}$" of an inch [1].'

But such a mode of formation of reproductive spores is by no means a method peculiar, amongst Fungi, to

[1] The formation of spores in *Leptomitus lacteus* is said by Braun ('Rejuvenescence in Nature,' translation by Henfrey, Ray Society, 1853, p. 270), to take place after precisely the same fashion. The two plants are, in fact, closely allied. In both, according to Braun, the dichotomous filaments are not articulated, they are merely divided into sections by regular strictures, though these sections have been taken for closed cells. He says:—' It is only in the fruit that isolated, mostly terminal sections are actually shut off, swell up to some extent, and become spore cases.' And yet the gonidia of *Leptomitus* differ from those of *Achlya* by being *motionless*. In one of the white rusts (*Cystopus candidus*), moreover, the gonidia, produced in the same fashion, are motionless when discharged, but in a very short time become quite active. (Cooke's 'Microscopic Fungi,' 2nd Edit., 1870, pp. 127, 132, and 141.) The presence or absence of motility in the gonidia probably depends upon minute differences in molecular constitution. We are quite unable to give any precise reason, however, why such a difference should exist between the reproductive spores of nearly allied species as is found in these and other cases. In connection with this subject it may be mentioned that I have frequently seen the chlorophyll vesicles within portions of the filament of a *Vaucheria* which were about to die, exhibiting slow oscillating movements; though in the healthy plant they are always quite motionless. And similarly, in the examination of specimens of human blood with the microscope, I have very frequently seen certain of the red corpuscles in a 'crenated' state oscillating most distinctly, whilst other normally shaped red corpuscles, which may have been by their side, similarly isolated, and apparently equally free to move, were nevertheless quite motionless.

the somewhat anomalous species of which we have just been speaking. A similar mode of origin of spores is, in fact, very common even in highly organized Fungi, and also in very many Lichens. Thus it prevails universally throughout the family of ascomycetous

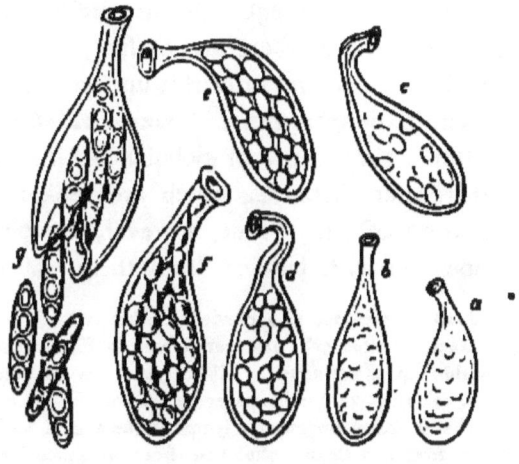

Fig. 8.

Development of Spores in one of the Ascomycetous Fungi
(*Perisporium vulgare*). (Corda.)

a, b, c. Commencing differentiation of homogeneous matter within asci.
d, e, f. Apparent resolution of this into distinct rounded spores.
g. Rupture of ascus, and exit not of separate spores, but of sets of four, each contained within a delicate theca.

Fungi [1], and also amongst all the ascigerous Lichens:

[1] The Rev. M. J. Berkeley, our leading cryptogamic botanist, says:—
'There is another point of immense importance, which the cryptogamic observer has in a peculiar degree the power of studying successfully. Questions often arise as to the point whether cellular structure can

and in these cases the process differs only in matters of minor detail from that which takes place in *Achlya*. In the genus *Peziza*, according to Corda[1], the following phenomena may be observed. The contents of the mother-cells, or spore-cases, consist originally of a mucus-like substance through which are diffused a number of granules—though there are, at first, no traces of cells or nuclei. In the midst of this uniformly granular material, within the spore-case of *Peziza acetabulum*, there appears, after a time, a row of globular-looking bodies, ranged at regular distances, which are spoken of by Corda as drops of oil. These, however, are probably mucilaginous nuclei[2], judging from their relation to

originate without the presence of a previous mother cell. It is a question, for instance, whether cells are ever formed in Phænogams from mere organizable sap, as presumed by Mirbel (Ann. des Sc. Naturelles, Second Séries, vol. xi. p. 321) in his paper on the Date Palm; or again, whether, in what is called organizable lymph in the animal world, cells can originate freely, without pullulation from neighbouring tissue with which the lymph is in contact.... Now in those fungi in which, as in *Sphæria* and *Peziza*, the reproductive bodies are generated by the endochrome of the fructifying cells, the Cryptogamist has the power of watching the development of the *spores* from the very moment when the endochrome commences to be organised, and he can with confidence assert that they *are not the creatures of previously existing cells, but the produce of the endochrome itself.* He will be able to compare with this what takes place in the embryo sac of Phænogams, and will be better prepared to appreciate all the arguments which bear upon the Schleidenian Theory of the formation of the Embryo.'—('Introduction to Cryptogamic Botany,' Lond. 1857, p. 25).

[1] 'Icones Fungorum.'

[2] The nuclei seem to be produced in this case after a fashion similar to that by which the nuclei of the common water-net (*Hydrodictyon*) originate. The process is a most important one, and we are inclined to

the spores which ultimately appear. Lighter coloured areas are then produced around these nuclei—

believe that the nuclei of many cells in the human body, and in animals generally, are not unfrequently produced after this fashion. The appearances in *Hydrodictyon* are thus described by Braun (loc. cit. p. 261). 'At the time when *gonidia* are about to form, the mucilaginous contents of the cells change altogether in appearance. The fresh transparent green becomes more opaque, and the entire mucilaginous layer acquires, even before the solution of the starch granules is completed, a peculiar regular appearance, closely beset with *lighter spots*, which appearance, however, is only distinctly perceptible when the focus is adjusted to the bottom of the mucilaginous layer. These spots are not the starch grains undergoing solution, as might be conjectured, for their number is much larger than that of the latter.... The little green granules of the contents, which, for the sake of brevity, I shall call chlorophyll granules, do not disappear with the starch grains, but separate from each other as the period of the formation of the spots, and become accumulated as dark boundary lines between the brighter spots.... The spots themselves are *roundish spaces free from granules* existing in the thickness of the mucilaginous layer.' A little further on (p. 266) Braun says:— 'Seeking, in the first place, the import of the light spots which characterize the first stage of the new cell-formation of the water-net, it is beyond doubt that they represent the centres of so many new cells, consequently are either actual nuclei, or, since we cannot detect any defined outlines, accumulations of albuminous substance analogous to nuclei.' This mode of formation of nuclei was also fully recognised by Nægeli. He summed up his researches on the subject in the following manner:— 'The nucleus originates in two ways; either free in the contents of the cell or by division of a parent nucleus' (Henfrey's Translations, Ray Society Pub. 1849, p. 168). The nucleus is described as appearing in the embryo-sacs of *Scilla cernua* and other flowering plants in the form of 'globular drops of perfectly homogeneous mucilage.' The nuclei in the large ventral glands of some of the Free Nematoids, and in the glandular substance lining the longitudinal muscles of others, present precisely similar characters, and may be seen represented elsewhere (Phil. Trans. 1866, Pl. 27, fig. 8, and Pl. 28, fig. 32 c.), in a memoir on the anatomy of these animals. Whilst still unaware of the views above mentioned concerning the origin of the nucleus I had come to owing apparently to the darker granules accumulating in the form of zones between them—as in the formation of the spores of *Hydrodictyon*. Later still, a redispersion of these granules takes place, leaving light streaks, instead of dark granular boundary lines, between what are to be the future spores. Then a solution of continuity is gradually effected, between the several spores, in the situation of these light streaks, and also between them and the membrane of the spore case, till the whole of the contained protoplasmic matter has thus been broken up into moving reproductive bodies.

The phenomena taking place within the spore-cases of Lichens are essentially similar. It is stated by Pineau[1] that the process can be best watched in *Physcia ciliaris*, on account of the large and transparent nature of the spore cases in this species. The first step in the formation of the spore in this plant is said to be the formation of aggregations amongst the granules which had been previously dispersed throughout the mucilaginous contents of the spore-case. These

the conclusion that such was the mode of origin of the nucleus in the white blood corpuscle. (See p. 227.) Here, as in other cases, the definite bounding-wall of the nucleus is, like the cell-wall itself, an after production.

In certain cases the nucleus makes its appearance before the complete individuation of the embryo cell has taken place, but, just as frequently (as is the case with white blood corpuscles), the nucleus appears, after the fashion above indicated, in an already isolated non-nucleated embryo cell, or plastide.

[1] 'Ann. des Sc. Naturelles,' 1848, p. 59.

constitute so many foci, and as a result of changes subsequently occurring around these granule-heaps the separate spores result.

Another most striking instance of the new origination of cells within the tissues of plants, has been revealed by the researches of Mr. H. J. Carter on changes taking place within the internodes of different members of the family *Characeæ*[1]. He principally examined specimens belonging to the genus *Nitella*,

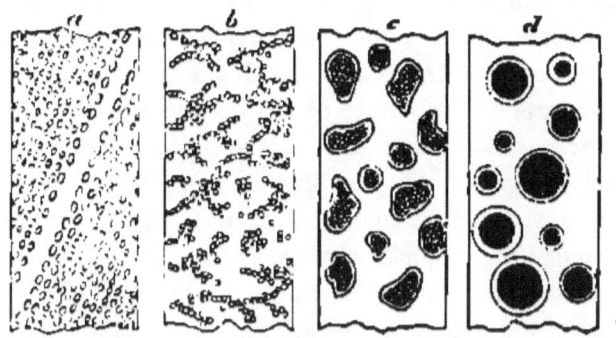

FIG. 9.

Development of new cells in internodes of *Chara*. (Carter.)
 a. Natural arrangement of chlorophyll vesicles.
 b. Commencing rearrangement of these.
 c. Aggregation into distinct masses.
 d. Assumption of cell form.

which were to be found in the ponds at Bombay. In order to make his description clear, the reader

[1] 'Observations on the Development of Gonidia from the Cell-contents of the *Characeæ*,' by H. J. Carter, F.R.S., 'Annals of Nat. Hist.' July 1855.

should understand that the branches of this plant are made up of elongated, cylindrical, and transparent cells, or internodes, of a greenish colour. On microscopical examination it has been ascertained that the colour is due to the presence, immediately beneath the cell-wall, of a layer of green chlorophyll disks or vesicles, each of which is about $\frac{1}{7300}$" in diameter. These are uniformly distributed, except along a spirally disposed line—which is therefore colourless—on each side of the cell. In the situation of this line (along which the green disks are absent), the 'mucus' or protoplasmic layer has also less depth than it has over other parts of the surface of the internode. The layer of green disks lies, in fact, in the outermost or superficial portion of the protoplasmic layer, whilst within this is situated a colourless axial fluid. The inner surface of the protoplasmic layer is irregular and undergoes constant changes of form. It is these contractions of the mucus or protoplasmic layer, taking place in a regular manner, which communicate their motion to the contained fluid, and thus produce the so-called 'cyclosis' of the cell-contents. With these explanations the reader will readily understand Mr. Carter's description. He says:—'All are aware that in the fresh-water Algæ commonly called Confervæ, the formation of the spore is preceded by a breaking up or displacement of the cell contents, after which a condensation and rearrangement of them takes place, and they are then invested with a capsule which remains entire, until the time arrives for the spore thus formed to germinate. Now, under certain circumstances, which appear to be *the approaching dissolution or death of the cell-wall*, a similar process takes place in the cells of the Characeæ; and following this from the beginning, we find, that it first commences with a cessation of the circulation, after which the lines of green disks forming the green layer become displaced, and, as if obeying a still continued but inappreciable movement of the mucus-layer, they roll themselves up into lines which assume a more or less irregular arrangement *across* the internode, or into groups of different sizes, more or less connected by narrow lines of mucus and single disks, so as to present an areolar structure in contact with the inner surface of the cell-wall. The next stage is the separation of the disks into still more distinct groups, which, having become more circumscribed and circular, leave the cell-wall and evince a certain amount of polymorphism and locomotion. The cavity of the internode hitherto rendered turbid by the breaking up of the green layer, now clears off and becomes transparent, save where the circular masses, which have changed from their original green into a brownish-green or yellow colour, intercept the light. After a day or two,—but the time seems to vary,— the green disks become entirely brown, and the group assuming a more circumscribed and circular form, shows that it is surrounded by a transparent globular cell[-wall]; this we shall henceforth call the gonidial cell.' I have also, of late, since having become acquainted with these observations of Mr. Carter, repeatedly watched the formation of independent cells of this kind within the filaments of *Vaucheria*—resulting from modifications taking place in what were at first irregular masses of protoplasm containing chlorophyll granules. A definite cell-wall is soon formed around these variously-sized masses, whilst the most striking changes also take place in the substance of the newly constituted cell. These changes, however, will be more fully described in a later chapter.

Hitherto we have been speaking of Cryptogamic plants, but through the admirable researches of Hofmeister[1] we know that just as good instances of 'free' cell formation are to be met with amongst the Phanerogamia, or ordinary flowering plants. The investigation of the subject here, is however much more difficult for the observer. There is this difference also, with these more complicated plants, that the embryo-sac, or mother-cell, itself persists for a time, instead of being destroyed by the reproductive process. We will quote the description given by Braun[2] of the phenomena taking place during the formation of the seed in one of the flowering plants. He says:—'The embryo-sac, or germ-sac, as it is termed, is the last cell of the mother plant, the uppermost in the axial row of cells of the ovule, destined to become the focus of re-

[1] 'Der Enstehung des Embryos der Phanerogamen,' 1849.
[2] Loc. cit. p. 276.

production, the mother-cell of new individuals; the germinal vesicles forming in it are the real rudiments of the new individuals, the unicellular germs of new plants. They are formed already before the period of the scattering of the pollen, as *free nuclei* originating in the upper part of the embryo-sac (the end turned to the apex of the nucleus and the micropyle), in which the protoplasm is principally accumulated. Around these nuclei soon appear sharply defined masses of contents, which are, as it were, "cut out" of the general mass of contents of the embyro-sac. The number of germinal vesicles is mostly three, rarely more.... Ordinarily only one of them becomes developed into an embryo, this outstripping the others in growth even before fertilization—or the latter even die away and dissolve about that epoch.' After mentioning the mode in which it comes into contact with the pollen tube, Braun says:—'In other respects the germinal vesicle remains wholly free during its development into suspensor (vorkeim) and embryo; becoming developed without any connection with the other phenomena of cell formation in the embryo-sac ... so that it affords us, not merely in its present formation, but also in its further behaviour, the example of the freest and most independent cell-formation which the plant exhibits.' During the process of formation of the germinal vesicles and certain transitory cells at the other end of the embryo-sac, this latter as a whole seems to retain its vitality; its primary nucleus usually survives and may even increase in size after the formation of the germinal vesicles. According to Braun, 'The nucleus of the embyro-sac is only dissolved during or shortly before the period of fertilization, and then a profound reconstruction commences in the interior of the embyro-sac, expressed in the production of daughter cells likewise free, but so numerous that they soon exhaust the independent life of the former, and the entire cavity becomes filled up by the cohering newly-formed cells. The tissue produced in this way is the endosperm, or, as it is called, the albumen of the seed, in which the developing embryo of the new plant then becomes imbedded. The endosperm cells, like the germinal vesicles, originate as free nuclei in the fluid of the embryo-sac, which subsequently becomes surrounded by masses of contents and clothed with membranes. The cells thus formed very soon combine into a continuous parenchyma, in which there is no longer evidence of the origin from free cells.' Such is the mode of origin and development of the seeds of most of the flowering plants.

If we now turn our attention to some of the methods by which reproductive germs, or ova, are produced in the members of the Protistic and Animal Kingdoms, we shall find these strikingly analogous to the modes of origin of reproductive units, such as we have just been citing, amongst the various members of the Vegetable Kingdom.

The first example to which we shall refer will be the

process of reproduction recently described by Professor Haeckel as occurring in *Protomyxa aurantiaca*, one of the lowest amœboid creatures, belonging to the group *Monera*, found by him on a shell dredged from deep water near the Canary Isles. It existed in the form of a mass of jelly-like substance of a reddish-yellow colour, visible even to the naked eye, the peripheral portions of whose body-mass were prolonged into moving, branch-like appendages. These very frequently became more or less united and interlaced amongst one another, whilst the homogeneous body-substance displayed in its interior only a number of small granules, interspersed with larger, highly refractive, and more or less spherical particles, and also a variable number of merely temporary spaces, or vacuoles, containing fluid. The granules, particles, and vacuoles were invariably found to increase in direct proportion to the amount of food which the *Protomyxa* had previously taken. After a time some of the highly-fed individuals were seen to undergo a process of encystment. They began to retract their various branch-like *pseudopodia*, and to eject all *débris* of food that might still remain within their body-substance, whilst the vacuoles in their interior diminished in number. After some days, instead of the previously branched plasmodium, little orange-red spherical balls were to be seen. The external layers of these gradually became more and more defined, and afterwards the contracted body-mass was found to be enclosed within a thick colourless envelope or cyst. The vacuoles and large particles gradually disappeared until nothing but

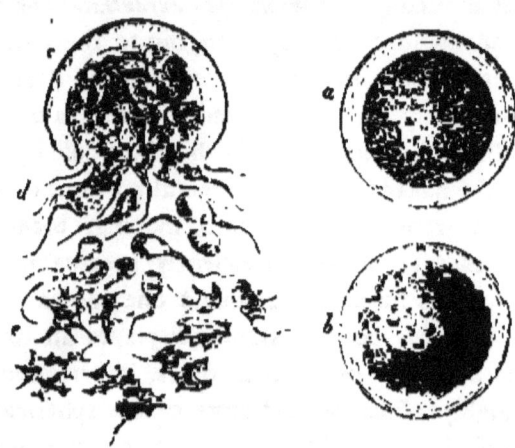

FIG. 10.

Reproduction of Protomyxa. (Haeckel.)

a. *Protomyxa aurantiaca* encysted; a homogeneous ball of protoplasm, surrounded by a structureless, gelatinous covering. × 300.
b. The same in later stage of development. The plasma ball completely divided into small globular bodies. × 300.
c. Cyst ruptured, showing exit of active spores, having long tail-like prolongations. After a time these become stationary; they retract their tails, and protrude instead a number of pointed irregular processes. In this condition, they are true amœboid creatures, still without vacuoles or nucleus in their homogeneous body substance.

a few fine granules were left scattered through the otherwise perfectly homogeneous protoplasm mass. Then, in the course of a day or two, and after it had retracted somewhat from the hyaline capsular wall, traces of segmentation revealed themselves in this enclosed mass of protoplasm; whilst by a continuance of the process it eventually became broken up into a number of small reddish balls about $\frac{1}{1500}''$ in diameter. After the lapse of about a week Professor Haeckel noticed that a slow movement of the naked protoplasm masses had commenced within the cyst. He says:—'The motion consisted in no regular rotation of the balls, but in a slow change of place among them, in which they crowded in all directions among each other without any fixed order. . . . Some hours afterwards the motion had become livelier; and the red balls had assumed a pear-shaped form, in which one end was produced into a fine point. In their confused motions within the cyst they changed the shape of their soft pear-shaped bodies many times, becoming sometimes drawn out into a longer, sometimes into a shorter club-shaped body, and sometimes they became twisted. . . . Next day I found one of the cysts burst; the empty collapsed wall lay shrivelled at the bottom of the watch glass, and a great number of small club- or pear-shaped red bodies moved about freely in the sea-water. It now appeared that the red balls were the sporules of the Protomyxa, and that they danced about after issuing from the cyst like Flagellata, or like the sporules of Algæ.' These germs were quite simple and homogeneous throughout—no nucleus or contractile vacuole was to be seen, no limiting membrane, but only a yellowish-red protoplasmic substance in which were imbedded a few fine granules. The swarming movements of the germs were precisely similar to those of the sporules of the Myxomycetæ[1]. The movement is progressive, accompanied by a rotatory or lash-like action of the cilium, which consists merely of a prolongation of the body-substance of the germ. The swarming time of the Protomyxa spores seems to last at least one day. On the day following that of their exit from the cyst, Professor Haeckel mostly found them lying quiet at the bottom of the watch glass. And then, he says, 'the tail of the spore was drawn in, and the pear-shaped form of the body was exchanged for that of an irregular roundish disc, whose star-shaped circumference was drawn out into several processes. The reddish-yellow plasma bodies now completely resembled in outline the spores of *Myxomycetæ* when they had come to rest; or likewise *Amœba radiosa* of Ehrenberg. . . . Most of the processes were simple, but, at this stage, the largest already began to divide themselves dichotomously, or repeatedly to ramify themselves. The protrusion and retraction of the ever-changing processes was accomplished throughout in the same manner as in the lively moving species of Amœba.' These separate amœboid creatures now began to take food for themselves; they rapidly increased in size, and then also began to throw out more numerous and complex processes from their circumference. Then, too, they first developed large refractive particles in their

[1] These however, even at a similar early stage, *are* provided with a contractile vacuole.

interior, as well as the so-called vacuoles—the latter, which constantly change in size and in situation, being usually filled with fluid contents[1].

Another most interesting mode of development of reproductive germs occurring in the higher nucleated forms of Amœbæ—the *Protoplasta* of Prof. Haeckel—has been described by Nicolet[2]. In these higher Amœbæ, which, though they continually change their form, do not send out complicated processes like those of the *Protomyxa*, multiplication takes place by means of fission and also by germ-formation. The process of germ-formation—closely resembling that by which the spores are produced in *Conferva area*—only takes place towards the close of the life of the parent Amœba, whose existence is terminated by the setting free of its numerous progeny. At a certain stage in the life of one of these individuals—such as would have been named *Amœba princeps* by Ehrenberg—the granules contained in the

---

[1] Although a *Protomyxa* is capable of increasing much in size and complexity by the ordinary processes of growth, there is also another process by means of which the larger individuals are produced. Professor Haeckel says, 'I could many times immediately follow in the swarms of Protomyxa under my eyes the formation of a plasmodium by the growing together (concrescence) of two or more Amœbæ.' Sometimes it happened that two Amœbæ, attaching themselves to a single Navicula, would, by drawing themselves over it, meet in the middle and then become united to one another. After the process of digestion, the united plasma-mass would free itself from the silicious diatom shell, but would remain as a single individual. To such fusions of originally distinct living things we shall have again to refer.

[2] Thompson's *Arcana Naturæ*, 1859 (Paris), p. 27.

midst of its body-substance are said to come together

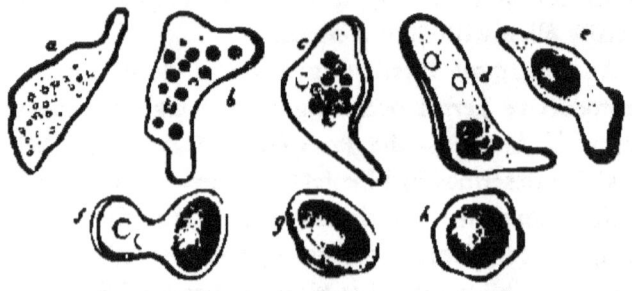

Fig. 11.

Formation of reproductive units in *Amœba*. (Nicolet.)

a. *Amœba princeps* (Ehr.) containing refractive granules and particles in its interior.
b, c, d. Different stages in aggregation of granules.
e, f, g, h. Showing gradual concentration and increase in size of reproductive mass, with corresponding diminution and contraction of surrounding substance.

here and there so as to form much larger refractive particles. These latter unite again to form still larger masses, and ultimately, after several steps of this kind, only to be followed by prolonged observation, the different granule heaps collect into a single mass which, at first, is irregular and mamillated, but gradually becomes smooth and assumes an ovoid or spherical form. According to Nicolet, the contractile body-substance of the animal diminishes and becomes more transparent in direct proportion to the increase in size of this central aggregation of granules. The movements of the Amœba, also, become slower; it remains for a longer time stationary in the same situation. It devours no more food, and sends out only short projections. When the central mass has attained its maximum size, and when no further trace of granules remains in its glutinous body-substance, the Amœba contracts and becomes rounded, by collecting its outlying portions around the enclosed and altered granular mass. Then, after a time, suddenly and with the rapidity of lightning, the germ-mass breaks up and disappears, shooting out around the space which it had previously occupied myriads of oblong particles, each furnished with a thread-like flagellum [1]. These dart about in the water and closely resemble very minute *Astasiæ*.

In the great majority of animals *ova* are produced from germs arising either (*a*) in the upper part or blind extremity of an ovarian tube, or else (*b*) in the midst of the stroma of a more or less solid organ, called an ovary, where each is invariably lodged within an 'ovisac' or so-called Graafian follicle. The best examples of the first mode of origin of ova are to be met with amongst Nematoids and Insects; whilst in Birds and throughout the Mammalian series, on the

---

[1] In the case of *Conferva area*, however, the granules, instead of separating from one another at once and with such rapidity, are stated by Agardh to detach themselves one by one from the spherical heap of granules similarly formed. Then, however, they also move about with great rapidity. The suddenness of the dispersion reminds one of the phenomena of 'diffluence' which have been observed in certain Amœbæ and Ciliated Infusoria, and to which, indeed, Nicolet calls the attention of his readers.

contrary, we are presented with typical instances of their origination in the midst of the more or less solid tissue of the ovary.

The development of ova has been studied perhaps with the greatest success amongst members of the order *Nematoidea*; for, on account of the simplicity and transparency of the ovarian tubes, the whole process of egg formation can be watched in these animals more readily than in many others. As pointed out by Dr. Nelson[1] and by Prof. Allen Thomson[2], the process of egg development commences in the *Ascarides*, or Round Worms, by the appearance 'of minute cell-germs in the upper part of the ovarian tube, immediately adjoining its cæcal termination.' Leaving aside all theories as to the precise mode of origin of these 'cell-germs,'—since this is a question on which we possess no decisive evidence—it is admitted by Dr. Thomson himself that 'some from the highest part are mere *molecules*,' although others a little further down have already assumed the appearance of minute nucleated cells. These nucleated cells constitute the so-called 'germinal vesicles.' Concerning the remaining steps in the formation of the ovum in these animals there is the greatest unanimity of opinion amongst anatomists; so that, although we avail ourselves of the description given by Dr. Allen Thomson, it must

[1] 'Reproduction of the Ascaris mystax,' in Philosophical Transactions, 1852.
[2] 'Cyclopædia of Anatomy and Physiology,' vol. v. 1859, p. 120.

be understood that his opinions are in accordance with those of other naturalists. The second stage in the formation of the ovum has to do with the deposit of the vitelline or yolk-substance around the germinal vesicle.

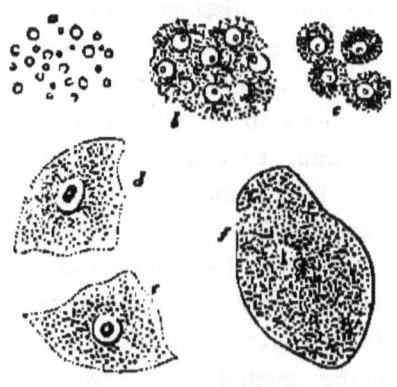

FIG. 12.

Early forms of ova in *Ascaris mystax*. (Thomson.)

a. Molecular condition.
b, c. Germinal vesicles becoming surrounded by yolk granules.
d, e. Irregular forms of ova due to tight packing.
f. Later stage showing first traces of vitelline membrane.

Dr. Thomson says:—'The granules of the yolk-substance very soon collect round the exterior of the germinal vesicles[1]. These granules appear at first to be

---

[1] In some cases, however, the order is different. The germinal vesicle may at first be surrounded by more or less of a clear viscous material in which granules, after a time, make their appearance. Thus Professor Thomson tells us (loc. cit. p. 133) that 'In most animals

suspended in fluid; but a little later, as they come to collect round the germinal vesicles, they are united together in a mass by a firmer but clear basement substance, and when the minute ova have somewhat increased in size, the outline of this clearer basement substance of the yolk is distinguishable. There is not, however, at first any external or vitelline membrane; of this Dr. Nelson and I have convinced ourselves by repeated observations in *Ascaris mystax*. . . . The ova, as they continue to descend in the vitelligenous part of the tube in immense numbers closely pressed together, assume the form of subtriangular flattened bodies. . . . A prodigious number of ova are thus packed together in a very small space.' In many instances it is only after fecundation has taken place that the vitelline membrane seems to become developed. The production of this is usually spoken of as the third stage in the formation of the ovum. In all the simpler kinds of ova it is supposed to result—after the fashion of the cell-wall generally—from 'the consolidation of the superficial part of the basement substance' of the yolk [1].

the yolk-substance, when it first begins to be formed, is scarcely granular, and in some instances quite *clear, consisting of a viscous blastema*. . . . Very soon, however, and in many animals indeed from the first, *fine opaque granules make their appearance, as if by precipitation or deposit in the clearer basement substance*, and thus the primitive yolk-substance of the ovum in all animals is formed.'

[1] This mode of formation of the ovum in *Ascaris* corresponds with the mode of origin of cells described by the upholders of the 'investment theory' (Umhüllungs-theorie).

Referring now, for a time, to the other mode of formation of the ovum, we may state that the question, concerning which there is the most uncertainty (and at the same time one to which a considerable interest attaches) is 'whether the ovisac is to be regarded as the vesicle of evolution of the ovum, or

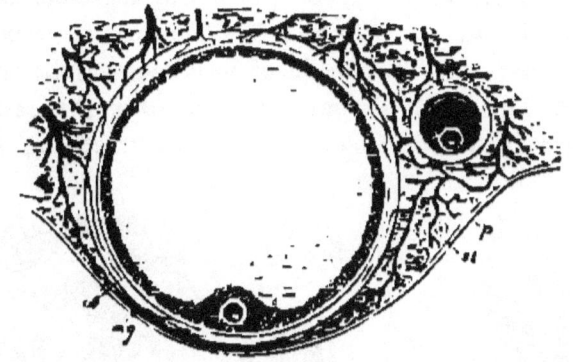

FIG. 13.

Diagrammatic representation of section of two Graafian Follicles or Ovisacs in different stages of advancement in the ovary of a mammifer; enlarged about ten diameters. (Coste.)
p. Peritoneal covering of the ovary.
st. Ovarian stroma.
ov. The two layers of the ovisac.
mg. Membrana granulosa, near which is the discus granulosus, with the ovum embedded.

whether the ovum, or parts of it at least, are previously formed, and the ovisac is afterwards superadded[1]?'

[1] 'Cycloped. of Anat. and Phys.' vol. v. p. 554. In its later stages the ovum of all the higher animals is found to be contained within a most distinct ovisac or Graafian vesicle—that is, within a comparatively large receptacle filled with a granular fluid, in which the

Whether or not the first rudiments of the ovum, the germinal vesicle, is formed first or formed within the ovisac, must therefore still be considered an open question, although the balance of evidence seems, perhaps, rather more favourable than adverse to its secondary formation; and if this were the case, the process would strongly resemble that by which the vegetable ovule arises in all flowering plants. Turning, however, to the question of the mode of formation of the ovum itself, Dr. Allen Thomson tells us that the earliest stages in its development are best traced in such

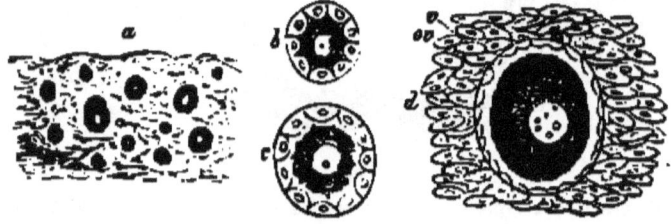

FIG. 14.

Portions of the Ovarian Stroma and Ovisacs of the Thrush. (Thomson.)

a. Earliest state of ova to be perceived in ovarian stroma, consisting, first of minute granular spots; next of clear points within a granular mass; and thirdly, of small germinal vesicles surrounded by the minutely granular dark yolk-substance.

b, c. Different stages of formation of the ovisac round the small ova: epithelium is seen to line the sac, and the germinal vesicle, with occasionally a single macula, is now apparent.

d. The ovisac and ovum in a more advanced stage.

ov. Ovisac with epithelial lining.

v. Minutely granular yolk.

animals as the thrush, the yellow-hammer, or the chaffinch — on account of the transparency of the ovarian tissue in these smaller singing birds. He describes the earliest appearances in the ovarian stroma of the thrush to be as follows: first, the appearance 'of minute granular spots; next, of clear points within a minute granular mass; and third, of small germinal vesicles surrounded with the minutely granular dark yolk-substance.' Afterwards the ovisacs are said to form around the rudimentary ova. Here again, therefore, we meet with mere granules or molecules as the first representatives of the future ova. These molecules, however, appear to belong to the yolk, whereas in the Nematoid ovarian tube those which first appeared were representatives of the future germinal vesicles. Even Dr. Allen Thomson, who is quite indisposed to believe that cell elements can spring up *de novo*, is yet nevertheless compelled to make the following statement concerning the origin of the germinal vesicle, the potential part, as he and others believe, of the egg itself:—'The manner of the *very first origin of the germ of the ovum* is still involved in obscurity, for we only know of the existence of an ovi-germ when the germinal vesicle has attained an appreciable size. *Whence the first germs of the germinal vesicle proceed can as yet be matter only of conjecture*. . . . Here observation fails, and we are lost in the region of speculation.' It is open therefore for us to presume that an aggregation of granules, such as he himself describes and figures as occurring in the thrush, may be the very first rudiments of the egg[1] in these cases. Certain it is, however, as he and almost all other embryologists admit that, even in the higher animals, the yolk is always formed by a mere aggregation of granules and of a mucilaginous substance, subsequently becoming limited by a vitelline membrane. And yet the granular substance of the yolk constitutes, by its segmentation, the initial embryonic mass of the future animal. In certain animals, indeed, the yolk mass is apparently all that exists: the germinal vesicle seems to be absent.

Seeing the undecisive nature of the evidence as to the precise mode of origin of the 'germinal vesicle,' it is desirable to learn whether its subsequent fate bears out the generally prevalent notion of its immense importance as a constituent of the ovum. What follows refers equally to ova produced by either of the two methods above referred to—to those which have a free origin within tubular organs, or to those arising in the midst of a more or less solid organ.

Before the mingling of the contents of the sperm-cells with the granules of the vitelline substance—that is before fecundation[2] has taken place—it seems to be

---

[1] The 'clear point' which next makes its appearance, the rudiment of the future germinal vesicle, may be evolved as a gradually increasing dot of homogeneous mucilage—after the same fashion as the nucleus is now known to appear in so many cells which are in process of evolution.

[2] It may be well to quote here some philosophical remarks of Dr. Allen Thomson bearing upon the phenomena of fecundation. He says: 'The physiologist agrees, for the sake of convenience of expression, to adopt the terms *power, property, force*, &c., to denote the conditions necessary for the occurrence of certain actions or changes. . . . .

the rule for the germinal vesicle to disappear. Dr. Allen Thomson says:—'In some animals, as Mammalia and Birds, it has been observed that shortly before the diffluence of the vesicle its delicate wall undergoes a softening on approaching solution, so as to make it impossible to separate the vesicle entire. After this, when the diffluence is complete, the contents disappear from the situation they have previously occupied, but what becomes of them has not yet been determined.' Thus, at all events, we get rid of the only element of the ovum about whose precise mode of origin there is any doubt or uncertainty. We are now reduced to a mere amorphous mass of granular material dispersed through a homogeneous basement substance. But in the midst of this mass there shortly arises *de novo*, in

---

The fecundating *power* of the semen is an expression used only for convenience to denote the invariable sequence or relation as cause and effect which has been observed to subsist between the contact of spermatic matter with the ovum, and the changes in the latter which follow on the act of fecundation. We might with as much propriety have given a name to a separate power residing in the egg or its germ, which render it susceptible of fecundation, as of a special power belonging to the semen by which that susceptibility of the ovum is acted upon. The efficient cause of the process of fecundation can only be educed, as in all physical as well as vital changes, from a perfect knowledge of all its phenomena, and the statement of the efficient cause of such actions is only the expression of the most general and best known law to which a full acquaintance with the phenomena enables them to be reduced. Fecundation is to be regarded as a purely vital change, seeing that it takes place only in the usual conditions of vitality; but, like all other vital changes, it appears more probable that a variety of conditions of the organic matter, rather than any one known property or condition, are necessary for its occurrence.'—(Loc. cit. p. 138.)

the ova of most animals, a new vesicular element which is called the 'embryo cell.' This does not appear until after the process of fecundation, and just anterior to the

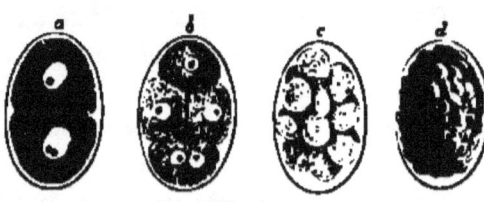

Fig. 15.
Segmentation of the Yolk after Fecundation.
a, b, c. Ovum of *Ascaris nigrovenosa*. (Kölliker.)
d. That of *A. acuminata*, showing later stage. (Bagge.)

commencement of segmentation in the yolk mass. This new cell, that which takes the place of the germinal vesicle after fecundation, is generally tolerably distinct, and nucleated, but Dr. Thomson says[1]:—'In other instances a clear spherule or space only is observed in the place of the embryo-cell, and in a few animals no clear part of this nature has yet been detected.' Here then we certainly have the new evolution of a cell or nucleus in the midst of the granular yolk-substance after a fashion with which we are not unfamiliar[2]. But

[1] Loc. cit. p. 139.
[2] Much interest attaches to these facts. We see now, in respect of the presence or absence of an embryo-cell, how close is the correspondence between these reproductive units of higher animals and the spores of Algæ, Fungi, and Lichens, or the reproductive germs of the lower Amœba. In them also, as we have seen, the presence of a nucleus was by no means invariable; and in some of the cases where it did exist (*Hydrodictyon*, *Praiza*, &c.) it also made its appearance, at first, as a mere 'clear space.' See note, p. 184.

Dr. Thomson says, 'The origin of the embryo-cell is still involved in obscurity;' and when he adds, 'Most ovologists are disposed to connect it *in some way or other* with the previously existing germinal vesicle, or some part of its contents, and more especially the nucleus,' we can only recognize in this statement an evidence of the enormous amount of influence which the old doctrine concerning the potentiality of the nucleus once exercised over the minds of physiologists. As Dr. Thomson frankly admits, there is no direct evidence that can be produced in favour of such an hypothesis: it would probably never have been advanced had it not been for the old doctrines concerning the marvellous powers of the nucleus, which we have now gradually learned to discard. The fact that segmentation does actually commence in certain ova where no nucleus or embryo-cell is present—just as the protoplasmic contents of a spore-case, or of an encysted *Protomyxa*, may break up into separate living units in spite of the absence of a nucleus—should go far to convince us that such a body is not in the least necessary, in order that the phenomena of segmentation and development may be initiated. Although, therefore, it may be present in many cases, and may seem to take the initiative by its early division, we must not on this account suppose that any influence or power emanating from the embryo cell is the *cause* of the segmentation of the yolk-mass: we should rather regard both sets of phenomena as merely associated changes, each alike being referrible to the properties of the matter of which the ovum is composed. This, too, was the view expressed by Professor Huxley when he said [1], 'Neither is there any evidence that any attraction or other influence is exercised by the one over the other; the changes which each subsequently undergoes, though they are in harmony, having no causal connexion with one another, but each proceeding, as it would seem, in accordance with the general determining laws of the organism.' Nevertheless, from the yolk-mass itself (constituted, as we have seen, by a mere aggregation of granules, or by an increasing mass of granular mucilage) there is produced, as a result of this segmentation, the germinal or 'blastodermic' tissue[2], out of which, by a continuous series of changes

---

[1] Essay previously quoted, 'British and Foreign Medico-Chirurgical Review,' October 1853, p. 386.

[2] Dr. Thomson says :—'The last result of the segmentation is the production of the blastoderma or germinal membrane in which, by other changes, the rudiments of the embryo subsequently make their appearance. According to most ovologists, the last globules formed by segmentation are the nucleated organized cells immediately constituting the blastoderma. But a different view of the process, as it occurs in Mammalia, has been taken by Bischoff, and is very decidedly set forth in his two most recent works on the development of the guinea-pig and the deer respectively. In these memoirs he makes the announcement that '*the last resulting spherules formed by segmentation are not true cells, and that previous to the formation of the blastodermic cells the yolk-germ falls completely into an amorphous or homogeneous finely granular substance, out of which, secondarily, the blastodermic cells are produced by a process of cyto-genesis.* It seems probable that, in the different classes of animals, there may be considerable variety in the degree of perfection in organization or advance in cell structure to which the segments of the yelk have attained at the

—occurring with a still more mysterious regularity—there is gradually evolved the future organism, however complex [1].

Hitherto we have considered the mode of origin of spores, germs, and ova, but if we turn our attention

period when the development of the embryo begins to manifest itself. But in the higher animals, at least, the weight of evidence appears to me in favour of the view that the process of segmentation results directly in the formation of blastodermic cells. The facts now established by the observations of Reichert in Entozoa, in 1841, of Ransome in osseous fishes, and more particularly those of Remak in Batrachia, that a delicate membrane is formed over the surface of each of the segments as they appear, and that the last and smallest segments possess a delicate membranous envelope, appear to show that, in these animals, each segment has the structure of an organized cell, and is very similar to, if not identical with, those of the blastodermic lamina.'

We shall find, hereafter, that the mode of production of cells described by Bischoff as occurring during the development of the ovum of the guinea-pig and of the deer, can be almost exactly paralleled by a similar production of cells, in certain areas of the ' pellicle' which forms on organic solutions. In these cases, also, the material that undergoes change is an albuminous basis substance, containing a multitude of newly produced granules (plastide particles and bacteria).

[1] It is interesting to note the very large proportion of fatty compounds which enter into the composition of the yolk of eggs, and also, as previously stated (note, p. 178), in the reproductive cells of many algæ. Many of these fatty products seem to be extremely unstable, and therefore well suited to initiate developmental changes. It is in the ovum especially, and in nerve tissue, that complex phosphuretted fats are met with—and it is here also that developmental and metabolic changes occur to the most notable extent. According to Dr. Allen Thomson, in the egg of the common fowl 'the yolk contains little more than half its weight of water, or 54 per cent. The remaining 46 parts consist of about 17 of albumen, or analogous principles, 28 of oily matter, and 1½ of salts. These last are chiefly alkaline muriates and sulphates, phosphate of lime and magnesia, and traces of iron, sulphur, and phosphorus.'—(Loc. cit. p. 61.)

to the male reproductive elements, both in Animals and in Plants, we shall find them invariably arising out of modifications taking place in the protoplasmic contents of certain cells or vesicles. Thus Wagner and Leuckart, after pointing out that spermatozoa in the various kinds of animals are produced separately in the interior of vesicular elements, as was first made known to us by Kölliker, say [1]:—'It is difficult to trace the intimate development of the spermatozoa in the interior of these vesicles; but *it appears probable that it is brought about by the junction of molecular corpuscles*, which join each other linearly, and which have been deposited from the contents of the vesicles.' With regard to the precise nature of the 'vesicles' of development, however, there is some uncertainty. In very many cases they are undoubtedly, as Kölliker supposed, nuclei; and referring to this view Wagner and Leuckart say:—'The unity in the mode of development of the spermatozoa which would thus be established is certainly very attractive; but we dare not conceal it from ourselves that this inference from analogy is the less to be depended upon, since the genesis of the spermatozoa in the Decapoda furnishes us with a proof that the formation of these elements may also take place immediately in the interior of cells, without the nuclei at all participating in it.' All the known modes of origin of these spermatic bodies may, however,

---

[1] Art. 'Semen,' 'Cyclop. of Anat. and Physiol.' vol. iv. p. 499.

be ranged under three principal heads, which are thus spoken of by the authors above cited:—'1st. The cell membrane and nucleus of the formative vesicles convert themselves immediately into the spermatozoon. 2nd. The nucleus of the formative vesicles alone metamorphoses itself into the spermatozoon. 3rd. A new formation, which takes place in the interior of the nucleus (or immediately in the cell cavity), performs the functions of a spermatozoon.' But it appears that of those produced by these different methods, 'the spermatozoa resulting from endogenous formation are most highly developed; they are the produce of a perfectly new generative process;' and it should be remarked also that this mode of origination is far more frequently met with than either of the others.

We will not bring forward any further details however; we will say nothing concerning the mode and origin of antherozoids[1] in the lower members of the Vegetable Kingdom, or of the pollen grains in flowering plants, since these details would, in essence, be little more than a repetition of modes of origin of independent units, similar to what have been already described. The instances already cited, although scarcely one tithe of those which might have been quoted, are abundantly sufficient for our present purpose. Of themselves they almost force us to come to a conclusion similar to that at which we have already arrived. The

[1] See 'Botanische Zeitung' for March 25 and April 1, 1853; also 'Ann. des Sc. Nat.' 1852, and Lindley's 'Vegetable Kingdom,' p. 19.

history of the development of germs, spores, ova, and spermatic elements, tends to show us most convincingly that independent and even active, newly-formed Living Units, have at first no trace of a cell-wall—this being a product which is subsequently formed. Then, we have ascertained, also, that some of these when first they present themselves exhibit no trace of a nucleus—such being the case with the actively moving progeny of *Protomyxa* and many other organisms. The germs or spores of these are mere masses of living matter—protoplasmic in nature. They present no trace of cell-wall or of bounding membrane, and there is a similar absence of anything like a nucleus or nucleolus. It matters not, therefore, if in certain other cases (as in the formation of spores within the asci of *Peziza* and other fungi) we do find nuclei making their appearance in the midst of the living matter, before this has begun to show any traces of its approaching segmentation. Such primary appearance of nuclei, when it occurs, should not be regarded as a necessary preliminary, or one which is in any way causative of those changes which are about to follow. How could we come to such a conclusion, when, in so many instances, *similar processes of segmentation may be seen taking place in living matter where no such nuclei exist?* This matter itself, therefore, perfectly homogeneous save for the presence of a few minute granules scattered here and there, is the real elementary life-stuff—that which already possesses the properties of a living thing, and which is capable (by virtue of its own inherent tendency to undergo a process of differentiation) of taking on the real cell form. Before a nucleus is evolved, whilst still without a bounding membrane, the simple living unit (*plastide*) is able to assimilate nutritive material and grow; it may be able to move from place to place and continually vary in its form; it is able to divide and reproduce its kind. In course of time a cell-wall may consolidate around it, and a nucleus may arise in its interior. The Cell is, therefore, seen to be only a developed form, a more visibly complex condition, which a simpler but already living and independent Plastide may or may not assume.

Some of the opinions we have just expressed were uttered by Alexander Braun in 1851, when he said [1]:— 'The cell is thus a little organism which forms its covering outside, as the mussel, the snail, or the crab does its shell. The contents enclosed by these envelopes form the essential and original part of the cell, in fact must be regarded as a cell, before the covering is acquired. From the contents issues all the physiological activity of the cell, while the membrane is a product deposited outside, a secreted structure, which only passively shares the life, forming the medium of intercourse between the interior and the external world, at once separating and combining the neighbouring cells, affording protection and solidity to the individual cell in connection with the entire tissue. Hence the development of the

[1] Loc. cit. p. 155.

cell-coat, as a product of cellular activity, always stands in inverse proportion to the physiological activity of the cell. In youth, thin, soft, and extensible, the cell coat allows abundant nutrition and advancing growth; subsequently, thickened and therewith hardened by the deposit of lamellæ[1], it compresses the contents within continually narrower boundaries, more and more excludes intercourse with the external world, and puts a term to growth.'

Taking that view of the case, therefore, which would alone seem tenable in our present state of knowledge, it could not be imagined that any changes occurring in a simple living unit, or plastide, would be essentially altered in character because its external layers had become condensed into a so-called cell-membrane. It is useless, also, to resort to the nucleus as an element possessing a mysterious power of its own, and to attribute, as was formerly the case, all the important phenomena occurring within a Cell to the effects of its influence. We are told by Nägeli[2] that whole families of plants are devoid of anything like a nucleus, and

[1] This more especially refers to the thickening and condensation of the wall which takes place in many vegetable cells.

[2] Speaking of the occurrence of this previously supposed necessary element of the cell, Braun says (loc. cit. p. 174):—'Nägeli's extensive researches have demonstrated its occurrence in all divisions of the vegetable kingdom; only in particular families of the Algæ, as, for example, in the Palmellaceæ, Chlorococcaceæ, Oscilatorineæ, and Nostochineæ, as also in the large-celled *Cladophora*, and the unicellular Algæ with unlimited growth of the cell (*Vaucheria, Codium, Caulerpa*), no trace of a nucleus has yet been discovered.'

yet all the ordinary vegetative and reproductive phenomena go on within the chambers of which they are composed. And if we are still to call these non-nucleated chambers 'cells,' we nevertheless find similar vegetative and reproductive phenomena taking place within structures which certainly have no right to such a name. It appears that *Leptomitus, Saprolegnia, Vaucheria, Codium, Bryopsis, Caulerpa,* and perhaps other Algæ as well as Fungi are branched filiform organisms presenting no trace of a cellular structure, although by a strange perversion of language they have been spoken of as 'branched unicellular organisms' by those who were anxious to interpret all facts so as to make them yield to the requirements of an exclusively 'cellular' Theory of Organization. At a definite stage in the life of such organisms a partition extends across, near the extremity of certain of the filaments, so as to cut off a small terminal chamber. This chamber enlarges rapidly, and its contents undergo changes such as we have described in *Achlya*, speedily leading to the formation of actively moving zoospores. Are such changes due to the properties of the living matter itself, or are they attributable to the mere chamber in which it is enclosed? Has the growth of the partition suddenly given rise to a potentiality previously non-existent? Again, when the *Protomyxa* contracts, when its living matter devoid of a nucleus condenses externally, so as to form a cell-wall or cyst, are the phenomena of segmentation which subsequently occur still to be considered as dependent upon the properties of the living matter itself under the influence of its medium, or are we to suppose that suddenly, with the assumption of this pseudo 'cell' form, there has arisen an entirely new force capable of inducing certain developmental changes not otherwise producible? The answers to these questions cannot, we think, be doubtful; and yet if we were to accept some theories at present in vogue, we should have to believe in the truth of the latter assumption[1].

All the phenomena of so-called 'endogenous cell-formation' are therefore, if rightly interpreted, capable of strengthening our belief in the necessity for the existence of mere *matter* of a particular kind as the physiological basis of all life-phenomena. They equally lead us to reject as preposterous the doctrine of Virchow that the cell is the ultimate vital unit, or, as he expresses it, that 'the cell is really the ultimate morphological unit in which there is any manifestation

[1] It may be well at this stage to call attention to the fact that the views of Dr. Beale are so far quite in accordance with those above expressed. He believes in the formless nature of primitive living matter, and in the absence of any special functions or importance attaching to the nucleus. We have already seen that he regards the cell-wall, when present, as a dead and inert appanage of the living matter within. Thus the only active potential part is the living but structureless germinal matter. He says, moreover, 'it must be borne in mind that at all periods of life, in certain parts of the textures and organs, and in the nutrient fluids, are masses of germinal matter, destitute of any cell-wall, and exactly resembling those of which at an early period the embryo is entirely composed.' See 'Protoplasm,' second ed. pp. 45-47, 48, 59.

of life, and that we must not transfer the seat of real action to any point beyond the cell.' All these instances of endogenous cell-formation which, indeed, are frequently spoken of as examples of 'free cell-formation'—do, in spite of their having taken place in what are called 'cells,' lead us on by insensible gradations to those purest and most unquestionable instances of free cell-formation, in which we may find new living units, or plastides, arising in homogeneous blastemata, and independently altogether of pre-existing cells.

As we have already endeavoured to show, it would be quite unreasonable to expect to get evidence of the genesis of minute though fully formed Cells in blastemata. This was the old point of view—and one which was more justifiable in the days of Schleiden and Schwann. Now, however, knowing as we do that a cell with its cell-wall and nucleus is a product of evolution, we must go back to formless matter, if we wish to trace out the origin of the cell. We must look for the appearance of mere specks—minutest particles of living matter—which, continually growing in size, may ultimately take on the form of cells, after the fashion already described.

We are thus led to enquire into the truth of a doctrine long maintained by Charles Robin, though one which has been as warmly repudiated by Virchow and his school. The former believes that simple living units are produced *de novo* in blastemata, and he maintains that there is a strong anatomical resemblance—a perfect similarity in fact—between the earlier stages of all kinds of pus and mucus corpuscles, and the white corpuscles of the blood [1]. He accordingly uses the word 'leucocyte' as a generic appellation for the various living units of this type which are to be met with either as physiological or pathological tenants of the different fluids of the body. And although it is not denied that such units are capable of undergoing rapid multiplication by processes of fission and gemmation, they are, as Robin maintains, also capable of being evolved *de novo* in the several fluids of the body.

M. Onimus [2] has lately recorded some very carefully conducted experiments made for the purpose of obtaining more satisfactory evidence as to the mode of origin of leucocytes. He found that when serosity was taken as soon as possible from a rapidly formed blister, and then filtered, no leucocytes, and only a very few epithelial scales, were recognizable by the aid of the microscope on the filter; whilst the fluid which had passed through was never found to contain any formed element, leucocytic or epithelial [3]. But, whenever the serosity had been taken from the blister one hour after its effusion, then, almost invariably, a certain number of leucocytes were found on the filter, and at

[1] 'Sur quelques points de l'Anatomie et de la Physiologie des Leucocytes ou Globules Blancs de Sang.' Brown-Séquard's 'Journal de la Physiologie,' tom. ii. 1859. p. 41.

[2] 'Journal de l'Anat. et de la Physiol.' 1867.

[3] The magnifying power employed, is unfortunately not stated.

the same time, M. Onimus says, some of them passed through the filter and were recognizable in the filtered fluid. The recently effused serosity was, therefore, always made use of in his subsequent experiments, after he had satisfied himself that such serosity appeared to be quite homogeneous and to contain no formed elements of any kind[1]. Small portions of this fluid were enclosed in little bags of gold-beater's skin, firmly secured, and these were then inserted beneath the skin of rabbits, in order to ensure the submission of the fluid to the requisite temperature. The contents of the bags were examined after different intervals; and before the bags were opened they were subjected to the action of a full stream of water, in order to wash away every trace of formed element (derived from the wounded tissues of the rabbit) which might have adhered to any part of their surface. When a portion of the fluid was examined after the bag had remained for twelve hours beneath

---

[1] He ascertained, by trial with the older fluids containing leucocytes, that when some of this serosity had been allowed to remain undisturbed for five or six hours in a small conical glass, its upper strata had, by this time, become clear, owing to the leucocytes having gravitated to the narrow lower portion of the vessel. When the recent serosity however was tested in the same way, he invariably found that the last drops of the fluid in the bottom of the glass were quite devoid of leucocytes, and indeed of all trace of solid matter, however minute. He therefore concluded that such a fluid was really a homogeneous blastema. It must be remembered, however, that exceedingly minute particles of living matter less than $\frac{1}{50000}$" in diameter might not sink in the way described, and that such particles easily make their way through an ordinary filter.

the rabbit's skin, it was found to be already slightly opalescent, owing to the presence of myriads of minute particles. After twenty-four hours, the fluid in other bags was found to have become whitish and cloudy—from its containing, in addition to the particles, numerous well-formed leucocytes. When examined after a period of thirty-six hours, the fluid was invariably found to be quite white and milky, owing to the presence of myriads of leucocytes, which exhibited the characteristic amœboid movements, and seemed to differ in no essential respect from ordinary young pus corpuscles or from white corpuscles of the blood [1].

[1] M. Onimus found that the nature of the blastema employed modified the results obtained in a most remarkable manner. He says:—' All the experiments we have hitherto recorded are true only on condition that the fibrine is not coagulated; for neither leucocytes nor any other kind of anatomical elements are produced in the serum of blisters whose fibrine has been coagulated.' These results are most interesting to the physician, and harmonize well with his own experience. He does not expect to meet with pus corpuscles in an effusion into the pleura which has not been caused by inflammation, whilst he is quite prepared to find them in abundance in an inflammatory effusion. In the former case the fluid would not contain both the protein compounds necessary for the production of fibrine, whilst in the latter it would probably contain them in large quantity. Although it is fully granted that the pus corpuscles in an empyematous fluid may be derived in part from wandering white blood corpuscles, and in part from subdivision of any of the nuclear elements of the tissues in contact with the fluid, I fully believe that another, and perhaps a very large section of them, have been evolved *de novo* in the blastema itself. Corpuscles derived in either of these ways may of course multiply indefinitely in the fluid by processes of gemmation. In these various ways may we account for the presence of the untold legions of leucocytes which are met with in inflammatory fluids.

Now by these experiments Onimus seems to have shown quite conclusively that the corpuscles met with in his experimental fluids had not been derived from the fission of any visible pre-existing cells. It seems almost equally certain that they did not even originate from particles which were recognizable by the microscopic powers employed, since the fluids were at first, to all appearance, perfectly homogeneous. Either, therefore, the minute particles which were seen at a later stage must have originated owing to some primitive formative process taking place in a really homogeneous organic solution, or else the fluid, seemingly homogeneous, in reality contained the most minute particles (microscopically invisible), derived in some unknown way from the previously existing protoplasmic elements of the tissues[1]. Further than this we cannot go by direct observation—reason alone must be our guide in the selection of the one or the other alternative. We, however, incline to the former view;

[1] We are quite unable to disprove such a supposition. It is but the germ theory under another form, and being based only upon analogical evidence it belongs to the region of pure hypothesis. Those who would be inclined to believe in the existence of such infinitesimal off-castings from pre-existing cells are, however, no more able to prove that organic units, seemingly originating *de novo*, are in reality derived from such supposed *invisible* germs, than we are to disprove their hypothesis. We must be guided therefore by evidence of an indirect nature, and those who at present still doubt the probability of leucocytes originating *de novo*, may, perhaps, be more inclined to admit that the tendency of the evidence above adduced is strongly in favour of the actuality of such a process, after they have read other portions of this work, relating to the *de novo* origination of wholly independent living things.

and we believe it to be in the highest degree probable that the fully developed leucocytes or plastides which were seen in the later examinations had arisen out of the growth and development of the mere organic specks met with in the earlier stages of the enquiry.

This latter view receives the strongest support from observations that have been made as to the nature and mode of origin of the white corpuscles of the blood. I have obtained some very striking evidence on this subject from the study of specimens of blood taken from two persons suffering from Leucocythæmia, though I had previously been tending towards the same conclusion from a careful study of its condition in other states of disease in which the white corpuscles existed in undue proportion. In these two cases the number of the white was equal to that of the red corpuscles: instead of the two kinds of elements existing in the normal proportion of about one of the former to three hundred of the latter. The other most striking feature in the specimens of blood from these patients was the extreme variability in the size of the white corpuscles—some being nearly twice as big as usual, whilst others were seen of all intermediate sizes between this and a mere protoplasmic speck $\frac{1}{10000}$" in diameter. The corpuscles also presented different aspects, the largest of them appeared to possess a cellular structure—there were slight evidences of a boundary wall, and numerous large protein granules within, more or less completely concealing a faint ovoid nuclear-looking body. This granular appearance seemed to become more and more marked as the corpuscles became larger, and the nucleus also became more and more distinct, though only appearing as a space free from granules. The corpuscles which were about $\frac{1}{2500}$" in diameter, as well as all those that were of smaller size, presented none of these characters. They were, in fact, not cells but plastides—solid homogeneous bits of protoplasm, exhibiting very slow

Fig. 16.

Showing the different stages in the development of white blood corpuscles, as seen in blood from a case of Leucocythæmia. All gradational sizes to be seen from a mere homogeneous speck of protoplasm $\frac{1}{10000}$" in diameter up to that of a corpuscle of the ordinary size. Those under $\frac{1}{4000}$" in diameter are homogeneous bits of protoplasm, showing only a very few granules and no nucleus or distinct bounding wall. × 600.

amœboid variations in shape[1]. There was no break whatever in the continuity of the series; all gradations in size could be and were measured, from the mere plastide particle $\frac{1}{10000}$" in diameter, up to the fully developed corpuscle; and until the size above indicated

[1] The amœboid movements of the white corpuscles, however, are not generally very marked in blood taken from Leucocythæmic patients. They have often seemed to be much less obvious than usual—a large number of the corpuscles remaining for a long time more or less spherical.

was reached we had to do with mere bits of growing protoplasm, or plastides, differing from one another in no other respect except that of size[1]. But in those corpuscles which exceeded $\frac{1}{3300}''$ the protoplasm gradually became granular, and they then began to exhibit changes which appear characteristic of age and approaching degeneration[2]. Then, also, the nucleus seemed to be evolved as a growing spherule of homogeneous matter, without distinct boundary wall—and therefore appearing as a mere circular space gradually increasing in size amongst refractive granules, which also grew larger and larger. It is extremely difficult to recognize in its earlier stages and when it is very minute in size: there can be little doubt, however, that it is evolved after the same fashion as the nucleus in many vegetable cells[3].

Whether the minutest specks of protoplasm seen

---

[1] Since the above was written I find that Dr. Hughes Bennett has alluded (*Lancet*, 1863, vol. ii., p. 378 and fig. 61) to the occurrence of bodies of different sizes in the blood of certain Leucocythæmic patients. Our interpretation of the appearances is, however, quite different, since he regards the smaller particles as 'nuclei' which have been liberated from the white corpuscles.

[2] I have again and again noticed the results of an evolution of this kind (though more marked in degree) which appears to take place in white corpuscles, after the death of the individual. In autopsies made 36 or 48 hours after death, I have frequently found on examination of the pia mater that the white corpuscles had assumed a most distinctly cellular appearance—each cell containing one or perhaps two well-defined ovoidal nuclei and a variable number of protein granules. In these cases the corpuscles have a distinctly vesicular appearance, and the nuclei also seem to be bounded by a distinct wall.

[3] See note, p. 184.

had been evolved out of the fluid plasma of the lymph; whether, as such, they had been introduced into the lymph, from the lymphatic glands and other sources; or whether they had been thrown off by a process of gemmation from the pre-existing white corpuscles themselves, we have no evidence to enable us positively to decide, although it seems that the facts at present in our possession are most favourable to the first mode of explanation. We have, however, in these facts much stronger evidence to show that the fully developed white corpuscles have grown out of the mere specks of living matter[1]; that these, even when they

---

[1] And, therefore, evidence tending to upset the notion generally prevalent amongst physiologists, that the white corpuscles of the blood have been produced by modifications which have taken place in lymphatic corpuscles as starting points—these bodies being not less than $\frac{1}{2500}''$ in diameter.

There are other reasons also against this mode of origin of the white corpuscles which have been advanced by Ch. Robin. He says (loc. cit. p. 49):—' L'existence des leucocytes dans le sang de l'embryon à une époque où les lymphatiques manquent encore, montre qu'il en naît dans les vaisseaux sanguins, et que, chez l'embryon, du moins, ceux du sang ne proviennent pas nécessairement de la lymphe. . . . Leur présence dans le canal thoracique à tous les âges montre qu'il en naît pendant toute la vie dans les lymphatiques, puisque ceux de ces derniers arrivent dans le sang avec la lymphe. Comme on trouve des leucocytes dans les réseaux et les conduits lymphatiques, du pied du testicule etc., avant leur arrivée aux ganglions correspondants il est manifest aussi que ce ne sont pas ces derniers organes qui seraient spécialement chargés de les former, et qu'il naisse dans le liquide même qui les renferme, c'est à dire dans toutes les parties du système lymphatique probablement. . . . D'autre part, c'est après une hypothèse contredite par les faits les plus élémentaires qu'on a pu admettre que produire cette espèce d'élément anatomique était l'usage, le rôle que tel ou tel organe était chargé de remplir.'

have nearly attained their full size, are still (although units exhibiting a distinct vitality of their own) mere structureless bits of protoplasm, without cell-wall and without nucleus—differing, in fact, in no respect from the *Protamœba* of Professor Haeckel, except that they are subordinate parts of a higher organism, and therefore do not lead an entirely independent existence. It seems evident also that such homogeneous masses of matter (plastides), already exhibiting vital characteristics, are afterwards capable of evolving a nucleus, and of assuming that cellular form without which it was formerly supposed no vital manifestations could occur.

Such a mode of origination of living units, together with their subsequent evolution, affords perhaps the best illustration that can be given of the birth of cells *de novo* in blastemata. Other evidence of various kinds can however be adduced tending towards the same conclusion, and to this we will now briefly allude. When working at the anatomy of a diseased spinal cord in the year 1866, before my faith in Virchow's doctrines had been notably shaken, I was much struck by certain appearances met with throughout the degenerated portions of a cord in which the interstitial fibrous tissue had become abnormally increased in quantity. As in such tissue generally, there was a very great increase in the number of nuclei, and although very many of them appeared about $\frac{1}{3000}''$ in diameter, there were others even larger than this, and others still in great abundance representing every intermediate size between these and a mere granular speck or dot about $\frac{1}{10000}$" in diameter. In an account of this case published shortly afterwards[1] there occurs the following passage:—'The large nuclei were apparently unconnected with fibres, and all intermediate sizes could be traced between them and the small dot-like forms. They existed in the greatest abundance, and seemed to represent only different ages of one and the same element. All alike became deeply stained with carmine[2].' I have since repeatedly seen similar appearances in other specimens of diseased nerve tissue. It is impossible to say positively, of course, whether the minute dots, the mere formless specks of living matter, had been given off bodily, as buds, from pre-existing living matter, or whether they had originated *de novo* out of fluid plasma. The probabilities are certainly, to say the least, as much in favour of the one mode of origin as of the other; and even if they had proceeded from previously living matter,

---

[1] 'Medico-Chirurgical Transactions,' 1867, vol. l., 'On a Case of Concussion-Lesion, with extensive Secondary Degenerations of the Spinal Cord.'

[2] At the time I was somewhat puzzled to understand how the large nucleated granulation corpuscles, which were also so numerous, could have originated. Acknowledging the difficulty, it was then suggested that the cells had become developed around some of the originally free 'nuclei,' and had afterwards undergone a rapid process of fatty degeneration. Now, however, I feel much more inclined to believe that some of the original 'nuclei' underwent a rapid process of growth, that each of these subsequently developed a nucleus in its interior, and then underwent a process of degeneration. (See loc. cit. Pl. XI. fig. 10.)

this, though a mode of origin of new organic units which has been long spoken of by Dr. Beale, is not one which has been much mentioned by Virchow and others of the Cellular School of Pathology. They speak principally of cell multiplication taking place by equal division of pre-existing cells or nuclei—a mode of reproduction which, though undoubtedly very common, does not, in my opinion, play such an important and almost exclusive part in tissue growth as has been represented, and which does not, moreover, enable us to account for many appearances that are frequently met with.

Cells may also originate after another fashion in the human body, as I have satisfied myself from a most careful study of the results of inflammation when occurring on the pericardium, or lining membrane of the heart. It appears that small nuclei-like bodies, or plastides, about $\frac{1}{7000}$" in diameter originate by a direct process of differentiation, from the homogeneous and tenacious so-called 'lymph' which is produced on the surface of the serous membrane [1]. This structureless lymph-like matter is capable of being resolved, or of differentiating, more or less rapidly, into an areolar tissue and plastides of the kind above mentioned. I

---

[1] In what precise way this is produced we have still no certain knowledge. I feel convinced that it is no mere 'exudation' from the blood-vessels; neither is it produced by an abundant proliferation and over-growth of the superficial tissue elements. It is at first quite structureless, and, judging from the changes which it subsequently undergoes, it seems to be formless living matter.

will not speak more in detail on this subject now, as the particulars would be somewhat too technical. Such a mode of origin of new organic units is closely allied to the process which gives birth to the zoospores of certain Fungi and Algæ, or to the reproductive gemmules of *Protomyxa*. In each case there exists, at first, formless living matter: only the independent units into which it afterwards divides remain to form a coherent tissue in the one case, whilst they separate and form independent reproductive units in the other instances mentioned.

A careful consideration of all the facts adduced in the present chapter leads us to the conclusion that Living Units, whether reproductive or not, may originate by one or other of five principal methods within the bodies of pre-existing organisms:—

1. In a not-living organizable fluid we have good reason to suppose that a living unit may originate; and this being so we should have in such case a veritable instance of the passage of the not-living into the living. Life would here begin *de novo* owing to the occurrence of certain new molecular combinations. To this process we propose to apply the name **Archebiosis** [1].

2. Where living particles or portions of living matter exist in a fluid or semi-fluid medium some of

---

[1] From ἀρχή, 'beginning,' and βίω, 'to live.'

these may aggregate, as a result of which after certain mysterious changes, or more or less directly, there may originate a new-formed element, reproductive or other. As instances of this process—for which we propose the name **Biocrasis** [1]—we may cite the mode of formation of ova in *Nematoids* and in many other animals, of the spore in *Vaucheria*, and of the so-called 'gonidial cell' in *Nitella*.

3. New units may arise, without obvious differentiation of pre-existing living matter, by the well-known processes of *fission* or *gemmation*. Or again, new units may arise owing to actually existing living matter undergoing a process of differentiation, followed by a simultaneous division into few or many separate living things—by a method, in fact, such as we see occurring in the reproduction of *Protomyxa* or *Achlya* [2]. All such modes of formation of living units we propose to comprise under the term **Biodiæresis** [3].

[1] From βίος, 'life,' and κρᾶσις, 'fusion.' We are at present speaking only of the origin of independent units *in* pre-existing organisms; and therefore we only incidentally call attention to the most typical instance of this process, viz. the fusion of two originally distinct *Amœbæ* into a single individual.

[2] In the process of organization of pericardial lymph, otherwise similar, the new-formed units do not separate from one another, and are therefore somewhat less independent. The mode of origin of the reproductive units in *Achlya* and *Protomyxa* leads us on almost insensibly to the process of *Biocænosis*—the products of the molecular re arrangement are here multiple instead of single.

[3] From βίος, 'life,' and διαίρεσις, 'division.'

4. Living matter being already in existence, it may after a time undergo a thorough molecular rearrangement whereby it acquires fresh powers and an increased vitality, fitting it for independent existence. By this process—for which we propose the name **Biocœnosis**[1]—the spore is produced in *Œdogonium* and other algæ, and also, after 'conjugation,' in *Palmogleæ* and the *Zygnemaceæ*[2].

5. Lastly, in the midst of already existing living matter (in the form of cell or plastide) there may arise a new centre of growth and life, which may subsequently lead an independent existence. Such is the mode of origin of the embryo in all *Phænerogamia*, of the majority of spermatozoa, and possibly of the ova in Birds and Mammals; also of nuclei in many plastides, which may outlive the latter and subsequently lead an independent existence. These processes we propose to include under the name **Bioparadosis**[3].

---

[1] From βίος, 'life,' and καίνωσις, 'renewal.'

[2] These are some of the phenomena spoken of by Alexander Braun under the name 'Rejuvenescence' (Verjüngung).

[3] From βίος, 'life,' and παράδοσις, 'transmission.' The phrase 'free cell formation,' as used by older writers, includes these endogenous processes, and also that which we designate *Archebiosis*. There is, moreover, a certain resemblance between *Archebiosis* and *Bioparadosis*. In the one case a centre of Life is initiated in the midst of mere organizable matter, whilst in the other it is initiated in an equally mysterious way in the midst of already existing living matter. The

Thus we have in all, five principal processes or modes of origin of living units, which in each case may or may not, by virtue of subsequent developmental processes, assume the 'cell' form:—

    Life-origination.........*Archebiosis.*
    Life-fusion...............*Biocrasis.*
    Life-division ....*Biodiæresis.*
    Life-renewal ....*Biocænosis.*
    Life-transmission ......*Bioparadosis.*

Although, however, we have arrived at a very strong presumption that specks of living protoplasm are evolved *de novo* in certain fluids within the body, it will doubtless at first be said by many that such an occurrence affords no instance of a passage of the not-living into the living, because the phenomenon takes place in a fluid which is already endowed with Life. Let us not deceive ourselves, however, by any inconclusive assumption. The organic fluids pertaining to higher animals and plants can be said to live only because they constitute *parts* of living organisms. But is this enough? The several fluids have each peculiarities of their own, and are certainly very different from one another in their degree of elaboration. Thus, when dead organic matter in the shape of food is introduced into the stomach of an

---

mode of origin of the zoospores of *Conferva area*, and of the reproductive units of certain Amœbæ, as described by Nicolet, may perhaps be regarded as instances of *Bioparadosis* with multiple products instead of with the origination of a single reproductive unit.

animal, it is first converted into chyme; then, having been absorbed from the intestinal canal and submitted to the action of certain parts of the lymphatic system, it is converted into fully elaborated chyle, which is afterwards poured into the proper vascular system. Now when, during this process, does the solution of dead organic matter assume the qualities of Life? when, or at what stage, does it become a living fluid? is it, in fact, ever anything else (even in its most elaborated condition of blood-plasma) than a mere organizable solution of organic compounds, capable of acting as pabulum for already existing living matter, and of permitting the *de novo* origination of new centres of growth and Life? Certain it is that at some stage the passage from the not-living to the living must be effected; and the process is probably not more abrupt than that reverse process by which living matter again reverts to not-living materials, such as are cast off in various excreted fluids. Starting with dead organic and inorganic matter, imbibed as food, we pass, in all living animals and plants, through fluids of various degrees of elaboration, till we find these food ingredients becoming converted into actual Living Matter. The animal or plant is nourished, and *grows* by the occurrence of such a process. We contend, however, that the fluids concerned cannot be said to live. The property, or aggregate of properties, designated by the word 'Life' does not pertain to the fluids themselves, though their constitution is such as to favour, under the influence of certain conditions, new modes of collocation amongst the molecules of the matter in solution, whereby the transition may take place from the not-living to the living. When these molecules aggregate so as to form the smallest conceivable specks of protoplasm, then does nascent or potential pass into actual Life. But, it may well be asked, must not the process be essentially similar, whether we have to do with the phenomena of growth or the phenomena of evolution? *In each act of growth not-living matter must be converted into matter which lives;* just as we now suppose such a process to occur when the minutest specks of living matter arise in homogeneous organizable fluids. We are as powerless to explain the one process, of which no one doubts the reality, as we are the other, which—in part, because it is less familiar—so many seem to think an impossible one. That living matter is capable of growing and increasing in bulk is an obvious and undeniable fact. Physiologists and others can, however, if they choose, doubt the reality of the occurrence of that to which we have been alluding, since *Archebiosis*, far from being obvious, is even extremely difficult to establish with certainty. And accordingly, whilst many physiologists readily grant that during the growth of organisms the not-living does continually pass into the living under the influence of physical forces alone [1], they, influenced by old theoretical

[1] It cannot of course be expected that those physiologists who still believe in the existence of a special 'vital principle' should so easily

considerations which they are unable thoroughly to cast aside, cannot bring themselves to believe—think it, in fact, a stupendous step to have to imagine—that the same matter and the same forces, should be able of themselves to collocate into independent centres of growth. Whilst teaching, as they implicitly or explicitly do, that the growth of organisms is a process akin to crystallization (a process which has to do only with ordinary matter of a certain kind acted upon by ordinary forces) they nevertheless persist in believing that—whilst the crystal can and does originate *de novo* by virtue of the action of those molecular affinities which are potential in its growth—the organism is quite unable similarly to originate by the play of those very same affinities which are afterwards alone admitted to be necessary for its increase. Whilst the first particle of a crystal owes its origin to the same causes as those which subsequently determine its growth, the first particle of a living organism, though also substantially similar to those which are subsequently formed, is arbitrarily assumed to be incapable of arising under the influence of the causes which are believed to determine their existence. This assumption is obviously opposed to what we might expect *à priori*. The real point of view, therefore, for the emancipated scientific enquirer of the present day, in looking into the evidence

become converts to a doctrine of evolution by which the not-living is, through a series of successive changes, supposed to be converted into the living.

bearing upon this subject, is rather to see whether it tends to countenance an assumption so contradictory to the present teachings of biological science, or whether it is now altogether and more strongly in favour of the doctrine of Evolution.

PART II.

ARCHEBIOSIS.

CHAPTER VI.

MEANINGS ATTACHED TO TERM 'SPONTANEOUS GENERATION.'

The term should be discarded—being bad and Insufficient. Includes two fundamentally different sets of phenomena. Influence of general views concerning 'Life.' Opinions of Burdach. Meanings of terms *Homogenia* and *Heterogenia*. Burdach, Buffon, Needham, Pouchet, and others, never believed in *Archebiosis*. This, antagonistic to their general views concerning Life. Previous use of term *Heterogenesis* therefore correct and may be retained. May occur during Life of Organism as a whole, or after its death. Modes of origin of living things.
Views of earlier writers concerning 'Spontaneous Generation.' Aristotle, Ovid, and others. Continuance of these views till time of Harvey. Doubt as to his exact doctrine. Experiments and opinions of Redi, Needham, Buffon, Spallanzani, and Bonnet. Views of other writers at close of last and early part of present century. Contrast between doctrines of Lamarck and Burdach. Observations of Pineau. Views of Ehrenberg. Experiments of Schwann and Schultze. Writings of M. Pouchet. Vigorous discussion excited thereby. Labours of M. Pasteur. Modern aspects of discussion to be more fully explained hereafter.

AS human knowledge increases concerning any department of science it almost always becomes necessary to give up some terms or modes of expressions long in use, and which may not have seemed faulty whilst the science was in its infancy. Certain of them, however, may gradually become less and less suitable, because they convey notions absolutely irreconcilable with the later development of knowledge on the subject, or because they are too vague and general. Hence it is that the phrase 'spontaneous generation' should be rejected in the present day. The phenomena hitherto referred to under this name are no more 'spontaneous' than are any others which take place in accordance with natural laws. The phrase is, moreover, utterly inadequate, since under it, if retained, we should have to include two sets of phenomena at least, which, in the present day, ought to be carefully discriminated from one another.

This discrimination has, however, been attempted only by a few writers. Many who have written on the subject of 'spontaneous generation' have failed to appreciate the full extent of the difference which exists between the origin of living things from not-living materials (Archebiosis), and their origin in whatever fashion—whether by modes which are familiar, or by others which are unfamiliar—from the substance of a pre-existing living thing. This difference, which is so little dwelt upon by some, assumes in the minds of others an overwhelming importance—*they* might be open to conviction as to the possibility of living things arising by previously unknown methods from the matter of pre-existing living things, whilst they would regard the origin of living things from not-living materials to be altogether impossible. In the first set of cases, however bizarre the mode of generation might be, there would at least be a continuity of Life—the peculiar powers of living matter would be directly communicated or transmitted, although such living matter might take on new modes of growth and development; but in the occurrence of Archebiosis they would have to imagine the actual new creation of the special and peculiar 'something' which they mentally associate with the word 'Life.'

The general views entertained concerning Life—its nature, or the meaning to be attached to it as a term—exercise no small influence in producing a variation in the point of view of different writers as to the nature of certain phenomena. Thus, statements which appear to many to be consistent only with a belief in Archebiosis, are, when taken in conjunction with the general views of the writers, often found not to warrant such a conclusion. This may be best explained by a reference to the opinions of two or three well-known writers on the subject.

In the first volume of his 'Physiologie,' published in 1826, Burdach introduced the words *Homogenia* and *Heterogenia*, as names for the two principal class distinctions in the mode of origin of living things. *Homogenia* was the class-name applied to the processes by which an individual results from a pre-existing living thing, similar to itself in organization; whilst *Heterogenia* was the class-name for processes by which living things arise from the matter of pre-existing organisms belonging to a totally different species.

Concerning these latter processes Burdach said[1]:—
'On appelle *Hétérogénie* (*generatio heterogenea, primitiva, primigena, originaria, spontanea*) toute production d'être vivant qui, ne se rattachant, ni pour la substance ni pour l'occasion, à des individus de la même espèce, a pour point de départ des corps d'un autre espèce, et depend d'un concours d'autres circonstances. C'est la manifestation d'un être nouveau et dénué de parens, par conséquent une génération primordiale, ou un création.' So far, this would seem to intimate the possibility of the formation (by Heterogeny) of living things only from the matter of pre-existing organisms, but Burdach did not really confine himself to this doctrine, as may be seen from the following quotation taken from the next page. He says:—'Nul doute que notre planète ne soit arrivée par degrés à son état actuel, qu'à une époque très reculée elle n'ait été inhabitable pour les êtres organisés, et que tous ces êtres ne soient formés peu à peu sans parens, conséquemment par la voie de l'hétérogénie. Si l'on juge d'après ce fait et autres semblable, la terre a possédé jadis un exubérance de *force plastique*; cette force ne peut point avoir été transitoire et accidentelle; elle ne peut avoir été qu'essentielle et inséparable de la nature, elle ne saurait donc être éteinte actuellement. Limitée quant à l'étendue de ses manifestations, elle continue toujours d'agir pour la conservation de ce qui a été créé, et,

---

[1] In the second edition of his work, as translated by Jourdan—'Traité de Physiologie,' 1837, t. I. p. 8.

quoiqu'elle ne maintienne les formes organiques supérieures que par la seule propagation, il ne répugne point au bon sens de penser qu'aujourd'hui encore elle a la puissance de produire les formes inférieures avec des éléments hétérogènes, comme elle a créé originairement tout ce qui possède l'organisation.' But, although this passage shows that Burdach believed in the possibility of the origin of living things from what are called not-living materials, nevertheless he did not believe that in such a case there would be a creation of a something altogether new, which we term 'Life.' This divergence arises from the nature of his theoretical views. The whole universe is to him *the* organism of organisms, and endowed with Life. Elsewhere[1] he says:—'Mais si l'univers est l'organisme absolu, chacune de ses parties doit être un tout organique ..... Il y a plus encore: la force du tout doit être inhérente à chaque chose particulière, et effectivement *nous rencontrons des traces de vie dans toute existence quelconque*[2].' Similar considerations have to be taken into account before we can thoroughly comprehend the doctrines of Pouchet, and those of Buffon, Needham, and others who are professed

[1] 'Traité de Physiol.' t. iv. p. 149.
[2] The relation of Force to Life seems to have been clearly seen by Burdach, whose doctrine approximates to that of Schelling. We differ only in restricting the attribute 'living' to its conventional use; though we fully recognize that all things—whether living or not-living—are fundamentally related from the point of view of the origin of their 'properties,' or 'qualities.'

'vitalists.' They all agree that pre-existing 'vital force' of some kind—pre-existing Life, therefore—is necessary, and that without the agency of this no living thing can come into being. M. Pouchet did not believe in what we term 'Archebiosis,' and he quite legitimately called himself a heterogenist; because the molecules of the infused animal or vegetable substances (with which alone he experimented) were supposed by him to be possessed by some special 'vital force,' or 'force plastique,' under whose directive agency the new collocations arose[1]. He says[2]:—'I have always thought that organized beings were animated by forces which are in no way reducible to physical and chemical forces.' And accordingly M. Pouchet has never attempted to show that living things might come into

[1] In this point of view he is indeed supported by the doctrines announced quite recently by a celebrated French chemist, concerning 'corps hémiorganisés.' M. Frémy says ('Compt. Rend.' t. lxvii. p. 1165):—'Ces corps sont les albumines, la fibrine, la caséine, les substances vitéllines, &c. La synthèse chimique ne les reproduit pas. Il est impossible selon moi de les considérer comme des principes immédiats définis : je les désigne, sous le nom général de *corps hémiorganisés*, parce qu'ils tiennent le milieu entre le principe immédiat et le tissu organisé. . . . . Ils ne sont pas encore organisé mais cependant ils sont doués d'une véritable force vitale, car sous l'influence de l'air humide ils entrent en décomposition comme des corps vivants et réellement organisés.' He says also:—'*en raison de la force vitale qu'ils possèdent*, ils éprouvent alors des décompositions successives, donnent naissance à des dérivés nouveaux, et engendrent des ferments dont la production n'est pas due à une *génération spontanée*, mais à une force vital préexistante dans les corps hémiorganisés et qui s'est simplement continuée en se manifestant par les transformations organiques les plus variées.'

[2] 'Hétérogénie,' 1859. p. 418.

being in solutions which had previously contained merely mineral ingredients. This was only possible, he thought, in organic solutions, the matter of which had been previously formed under the influence of Life, and whose properties it still retained[1]. The postulation by Needham of a special 'force vegetative,' and by Buffon of the invariable agency of vital, though immaterial, 'molécules organiques,' suffice to place them in this same category: they are all persons whose theoretical views have been framed in such a way as to exclude the possibility of their belief in the origin of the living from the not-living. The possibility of Archebiosis not being one of the elements of their philosophical creed, they would give a different interpretation to certain facts which, in the minds of others, might seem to testify to the occurrence of such a process.

Seeing that the notion represented by the word 'Archebiosis' is one which—on account of these theoretical views—does not very often occur in previous writings upon 'spontaneous generation,' and seeing how desirable it is to separate this idea from that

[1] Many will, however, rather agree with us in thinking that a mere solution made by infusing animal or vegetable tissues, has—apart from germs of living things which it may contain—no more title to the epithet 'living,' than has any solution of mineral substances a right to such an appellation. For those who hold such opinions, therefore, the appearance of living things in organic solutions (after all pre-existing germs had been destroyed), should it occur, would be as much a case of the origin of the living from the not-living, as if the new forms of life had appeared, in spite of similar precautions, in solutions containing mere mineral or saline constituents.

primarily indicated by *Heterogenia*, it seems to us that all the necessities of the case will be met by the introduction of the one new term 'Archebiosis.' This will permit the limitation of the word '*Heterogenia*' (or 'Heterogenesis'), to the sense originally given to it in Burdach's definition, and, as we have seen, to the sense in which it has almost invariably been employed [1].

It is a matter of altogether secondary importance whether the individualisation of the portion of the matter of an organism (with power of independent development) takes place during the life of the organism or after its death. As we have already seen, an organism is an organic whole made up of a number of partially independent living units. The death of the organism we have compared to the arrest of motion in a complex machine; it does not at once entail the death of the matter entering into its composition. There is a

[1] The word 'Hétérogénèse' was first used by Breschet in the article '*Déviation Organique*,' in the first edition of the 'Dictionnaire de Médecine' (t. vi. 1823). He divided monstrosities into four classes: (1) Agénèses, (2) Hypergénèses, (3) Diplogénèses, and (4) Hétérogénèses; and these he proposed to describe in detail in the article '*Monstruosité*.' This, however, was never done; the latter article being written instead by Andral, without reference to Breschet's classification, which was never accepted. In the second edition of the 'Dictionnaire de Médecine,' the article 'Monstruosité' was written by Ollivier, who, in an unfavourable criticism of Breschet's system, called special attention to the unsatisfactory nature of the division Hétérogénèses, under which were included conditions which had no sort of relationship to one another, such as albinism, extra-uterine fœtation, displacement of viscera, &c. No objection, therefore, can be made, on the score of previous appropriation, to the transition from 'Heterogenia' to 'Heterogenesis,' which has gradually been brought about.

cessation only of the combined action which constitutes the life of the entire organism, though its constituent parts continue to live for a time, and gradually, at different intervals, lapse into the condition of mere dead matter. It is unimportant, therefore, in order that heterogeny may occur, whether a certain portion of the matter of an organism becomes individualised into a distinct and independent living thing during the life of such organism, or after its death, so long as its individual parts continue to live[1]. When death has once fallen upon these—when they have lapsed into the condition of mere not-living organic matter—no further organizing changes are, for a time, possible. The matter must undergo solution, and must give up its solid form;

[1] M. Milne-Edwards, in his 'Leçons de la Physiologie et de l'Anatomie Comparée' (1863, t. 8*e*. p. 251), thinks this difference one of more importance, apparently; for, though he does not believe in the occurrence of either, he proposes that the first process should be spoken of as *nécrogénie*, and the second as *zénogénie*. What we term *Archebiosis*, he spoke of as '*agénétique* mode d'origine' of organisms. We have endeavoured to show that this process has only very rarely been included under the word 'Hétérogénie'—which has almost invariably been used to signify what M. Milne-Edwards needlessly includes under the two words *zénogénie* and *nécrogénie*. His statement, therefore, that in place of the word *zénogénie*, he should have preferred 'le nom d'*hétérogénie* si ce nom n'avait déjà reçu une acceptation différente et beaucoup plus étendue,' refers only to its having been used, as he supposes, as an equivalent to all the processes which have been spoken of under the head of 'spontaneous generation.' This, however, is an erroneous supposition. The surrender of the word 'Hétérogénie' is, therefore, no more necessary than desirable; and it is fortunate that this is the case, because the word is already so deeply stamped into the literature of this and other countries that any change would cause much confusion.

and then, if new living things appear, we have no longer to do with Heterogeny, but rather with Archebiosis.

As to the various modes in which *Heterogeny* may occur, we will say nothing more at present than may be found in the following table. Numerous variations will be subsequently described.

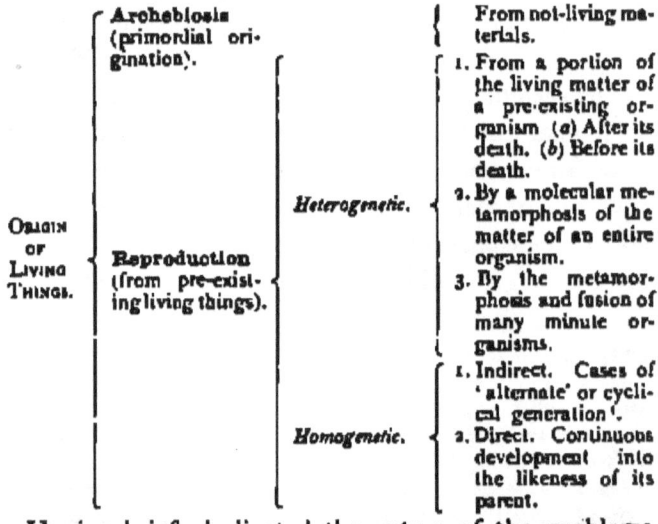

Having briefly indicated the nature of the problems which require to be carefully discriminated from one another, we will now, before enquiring into the possibility of Archebiosis taking place in the present phase of the earth's history, briefly enumerate some of the different opinions which have been expressed by earlier writers on the subject of ' spontaneous generation.'

---

[1] These are the cases for which Mr. Herbert Spencer has appropriated the term 'Heterogenesis' (see 'Principles of Biology,' vol. i. p. 210). The above arrangement would, we think, meet his requirements.

Aristotle believed in the 'spontaneous' origination of eels and other fish out of the slimy mud of rivers and marshes; also that certain insects took origin from the vernal dew on plants; and that lice were spontaneously engendered in the flesh of animals. He believed also that animals might proceed from vegetables—that the caterpillars of certain butterflies, for instance, were actually the products of the plants upon which they feed. Some of these beliefs were echoed by Lucretius[1] and Ovid more than two hundred years later. When the latter of these poets had described the means adopted by Deucalion and Pyrrha for repeopling the world after the deluge—how the backwardly-thrown stones, the bones of mother earth, grew into human beings—he thus accounts for the origin of all the lower living things:—

> 'Cætera diversis tellus animalia formis
> Sponte sua peperit, postquam vetus humor ab igne
> Percaluit Solis, cœnumque udæque paludes
> Intumuere æstu: fecundaque semina rerum
> Vivaci nutrita solo, ceu matris in alvo,
> Creverunt, faciemque aliquam cepere morando.
> Sic, ubi deseruit madidos septemfluus agros
> Nilus, et antiquo sua flumina reddidit alveo,
> Æthereoque recens exarsit sidere limus;
> Plurima cultores versis animalia glebis
> Inveniunt, et in his quædam modo cœpta per ipsum
> Nascendi spatium, quædam imperfecta, suisque
> Trunca vident numeris: et eodem corpore sæpe
> Altera pars vivit, rudis est pars altera tellus[2].'

[1] 'De Rerum Natura,' lib. v. 793.
[2] This passage (Metamorph. bk. i. 416-429) has been thus translated by Dryden:—

Such an origin for various kinds of animals was also referred to by Diodorus Siculus and by Plutarch—the soil of Egypt, and the bed of the Nile in particular, being more especially alluded to as the seat where such marvels had been observed. Ovid, moreover, speaks of bees originating in the putrefying flesh of a bull.

These old and crude notions as to the possibility of the new evolution of complex and highly organized animals out of decaying organic, and even out of inorganic materials, survived till far on into the middle ages. The influence of the teachings of Aristotle was still all-powerful in such subjects. What he had affirmed, multitudes implicitly believed for many centuries.

The transition from the ancient to the modern popular view, was initiated by that illustrious phy-

> 'The rest of animals from teeming earth
> Produc'd, in various forms receiv'd their birth.
> The native moisture, in its close retreat
> Digested by the sun's ætherial heat
> As in a kindly womb, began to breed,
> Then swell'd and quicken'd by the vital seed.
> And some in less, and some in longer space,
> Were ripen'd into form and took a several face.
> Thus when the Nile from Pharian fields is fled,
> And seeks, with ebbing tides, his ancient bed,
> The fat manure with heav'nly fire is warm'd:
> And crusted creatures, as in wombs, are formed;
> These, when they turn the glebe, the peasants find;
> Some rude, and yet unfinished in their kind.
> Short of their limbs, a lame imperfect birth;
> One half alive, and one of lifeless earth.'

sician and biologist, William Harvey, the discoverer of the circulation of the blood. The modern theory of development (Epigenesis) dates from a celebrated treatise by Harvey, entitled *Exercitationes de Generatione Animalium*; and he also is commonly believed to have taught the doctrine of the continuity of Life on our globe, as opposed to views concerning its *de novo* origination. But although, apparently, a disbeliever in the doctrine that living things could take origin from not-living materials (Archebiosis), Harvey was a firm believer in Heterogenesis. On this subject Burdach said[1]:—'The rallying-cry of the adversaries of spontaneous generation is the following sentence, resting upon classical authority: *omne vivum ex ovo*. But they can only quote this sentence in support of their opinion by neglecting the spirit and fixing merely upon the letter of what was said. Valentin has already called attention to the fact that Harvey himself, far from wishing to deny thereby all spontaneous generation, used the word "egg" as a general term to designate a substance capable of germinating—that is to say, for every kind of matter which develops immediately into an organised body—and that, consequently, he extended this denomination even to the substance called "primordial mucus[2]."' It seems quite certain, from many passages in Harvey's writings, that he was

[1] 'Traité de Physiologie,' 2nd edition, 1837, t. i. p. 10.
[2] This is the name given by Burdach to the pellicle which forms on organic infusions.

still a believer in Heterogenesis[1], though it is somewhat doubtful whether he had rejected the old notions as to the direct origin of the living from the not-living. Although grave doubts may be entertained, therefore, as to the propriety of expressing Harvey's doctrine by the phrase *omne vivum ex ovo*, it is not even altogether free from doubt whether the modification suggested by M. Milne-Edwards, *omne vivum ex vivo*, really embodies the notion taught by Harvey. In illustration of this difficulty, we need only quote the following general statement made by Harvey in summing up his doctrines[2]:—' His autem omnibus (sc. animalibus et stirpibus) . . . . sive sponte, sive ex aliis, sive in aliis, vel partibus, vel excrementis eorum putrescentibus, oriantur . . . . . *id commune est, ut ex principio vivente gignantur*, adeo ut omnibus viventibus primordium insit ex quo et a quo proveniant. . . . . Diversa scilicet diversorum viventium primordia; pro quorum vario discrimine alii atque alii sunt generationis animalium modi, qui tamen omnes in hoc uno conveniunt, quod a primordio vegitali, tanquam e materia efficienti virtute dotata, oriantur: differunt autem, quod primordium hoc vel sponte et casu erumpat, vel ab alio præexistente tanquam fructus proveniant.' Whilst every living thing, therefore, is said to derive its immediate origin from a 'living principle,' Harvey also

[1] Attention was again prominently called to this fact in 1865, by M. Pouchet.
[2] Loc. cit. p. 270.

thought that this 'primordium' might arise 'sponte et casu,' so that he can scarcely be said to have been a strict believer in the continuity of Life.

The first adversary who seriously attacked the old and then accepted doctrines was Redi, a Florentine physician, who, in 1638, announced and demonstrated before one of the learned academies, of which he was a member, that the maggots which appear in putrefying flesh are deposited by flies, and are not engendered, as had been generally[1] supposed, in the flesh itself. This demonstration gave rise to much discussion at the time, and undoubtedly shook the faith of many in the truth of the old doctrines. But even Redi himself, it appears, rather attempted to disprove some alleged cases of 'spontaneous generation,' than to disprove the whole doctrine. He inclined to the belief that parasites were produced from a modification of the substance of the

---

[1] The Rev. M. J. Berkeley has lately called attention to the fact that Homer was fully aware of the real origin of the larvæ which appear in putrefying carcases. In Iliad xix. 23-27 there occurs the following passage:—

ἀλλὰ μάλ' αἰνῶς
Δείδω μή μοι τόφρα Μενοιτίου ἄλκιμον υἱὸν
Μυῖαι καδδῦσαι κατὰ χαλκοτύπους ὠτειλὰς
Εὐλὰς ἐγγείνωνται, ἀεικίσσωσι δὲ νεκρόν—
Ἐκ δ' αἰὼν πέφαται—κατὰ δὲ χρόα πάντα σαπήῃ.

Which is thus rendered in the late Lord Derby's translation:—

'Yet fear I for Menœtius' noble son,
Lest in his spear-inflicted wounds the flies
May gender worms, and desecrate the dead,
And, life extinct, corruption reach his flesh.'

animal in which they were found. And, similarly, he believed that the grubs which are to be met with in the galls of plants, are produced by a modification of the living substance of the plant—these galls being, in fact, as he thought, organs destined to produce such animals[1]. In 1745, Needham, who was shortly afterwards elected a Fellow of the Royal Society of London, came forward with much additional evidence in favour of the doctrine of 'spontaneous generation,' and affirmed that, if the mere putrefaction of meat could not of itself engender insects, as Redi had shewn, it could at least give origin to myriads of microscopic animalcules. Four years after the publication of Needham's researches, the great naturalist Buffon expounded his views[2] concerning 'organic molecules,' and the universal origination of the lowest forms of animal life, by a process answering to what was termed 'spontaneous generation.' He said :—'There are, perhaps,

---

[1] 'Esperienze intorno alla Generazione degl' Insetti,' p. 129. Redi was therefore a partial believer in the doctrine which we now name *Heterogenesis*. According to this doctrine, as taught by Burdach and others, strange living things might be generated from the matter of pre-existing living beings, both during their life and after their death. In the opinion of Redi, however, such a process could only take place whilst the parent organism was living (Loc. cit. p. 14). It will afterwards be more fully seen that this is quite an unimportant limitation, because it is one of a purely arbitrary nature, based upon the imperfect knowledge of the time. We now know that the constituent elemental parts of one of the higher organisms may continue to live long after the organism as a whole is dead.

[2] These will be referred to more fully in a subsequent chapter.

as many living things, both animal and vegetable, which are produced by the fortuitous aggregation of "molécules organiques," as there are others which reproduce themselves by a constant succession of generations.' But it was the experiments of Needham, more especially, that aroused one who was for a long time the most celebrated opponent of these doctrines. The renowned Abbé Spallanzani soon took up the question, and entered into a controversy with Needham on the subject. He maintained that the air of our atmosphere bears with it everywhere the germs of infusorial animalcules and of other organic forms, and that Needham had not taken sufficient account of this fact in his experiments. In this view he was supported by the fantastic assumptions of Bonnet, and their doctrine—since known by the name of '*Panspermism*'—has received the most powerful support from Pasteur and others in our own times. The questions in dispute could not be settled by these two champions, and successive advocates were continually springing up in favour of one or other of the adverse doctrines till the commencement of our own century. Two of the most famous of them, Gleichen and Otho F. Muller, were dissentients from the doctrines of Bonnet and Spallanzani. A little later Tréviranus made known an important fact in favour of the doctrine of heterogeny, to the effect that the species of animalcules found in the infusions varied with, and seemed to depend upon, minute differences in the nature of the infusions themselves. In 1809 appeared the 'Philosophie Zoologique' of Lamarck, in which he expressed himself strongly in favour of the spontaneous origination of Life—declaring that matter was continually changing, not only in regard to its states of combination, but also changing in its nature—that it was now passing from the living state into a lifeless one, and now again assuming the forms and properties of living matter under the combined and mystic influence of heat, light, electricity, and moisture. 'These transitions,' he said, 'from life to death and from death to life, evidently form part of an immense circle of all kinds of changes to which, in the course of time, all physical substances are submitted.' But such a mode of origin was only possible, as he thought, for the lowest kinds of living things. This is expressed in the following passage, which he also prints in italics:—'*La nature à l'aide de la chaleur, de la lumière, de l'électricité, et de l'humidité, forme des générations spontanées ou directes à l'extremité de chaque règne des corps vivants, où se trouvent les plus simples de ces corps.*' Soon afterwards, two philosophers, Cabanis and Oken, also declared their belief in the possibility of a new evolution of life out of dead inanimate matter. According to Oken, 'the animal body is only an edifice of monads,' and 'putrefaction is nothing more than the disaggregation of the monads, and a return to the primitive condition of the animal kingdom.' Then followed other distinguished naturalists, amongst whom we may mention Bory St. Vincent, Bremser, Tiedemann,

J. Müller, Dujardin, and Burdach, who were all more or less in favour of the doctrines of heterogeny. These views received their fullest and most complete exposition, however, from the last whom we have mentioned. In his well-known work, Burdach gave a somewhat detailed account of his views on that primordial mode of generation to which he first attached the name 'generatio heterogenia.' But like those of his predecessors and fellow-countrymen, Bremser and Tiedemann, his views were of a retrograde description, when compared with those of Lamarck. He no longer limited the possibility of such a mode of origin to the lowest members of the animal and the vegetable kingdoms, but also contended that certain worms, insects, crustacea, and even fish *might* in this way appear upon the scene without ordinary parentage.

After him, however, came Pineau in 1845, who declared that he had actually watched, step by step, the heterogenetic origin and development of two ciliated infusoria—*Monas lens* and a *Vorticella*—and also of a microscopic fungus—*Penicillium glaucum*. This was the first announcement of a kind of evidence altogether new—based upon actual observation rather than upon experimental inference.

Advocates of the opposite or panspermic doctrine, however, were abundant enough also during the first half of the present century: amongst the most distinguished of these must figure the names of P. Gervais, Schwann, Schultze, and Ehrenberg. The latter, in his remarkable 'Mémoire sur le développement et la durée de la vie des infusoires,' endeavoured to establish the fact that the generation of infusoria takes place normally by means of eggs, and that their multiplication by this process, in combination with that by fission, was sufficient to account for their numbers in organic infusions. Schultze and Schwann, however, sought to undermine the position of the heterogenists by adducing experimental proofs in support of the panspermic doctrine. Schultze alleged that no organisms of any kind were produced in a fermentable solution which had been raised to a temperature of 212° F., provided the air which was allowed access to this fluid had been previously made to traverse concentrated sulphuric acid, so as to free it from all possible germs; and Schwann stated that the experiments were, with certain reservations [1], marked by the same sterility when calcined or highly heated air only was allowed access to the vessel containing the previously boiled solution of organic matter. These assertions, which have been subsequently disproved, had an immense influence at the time against the doctrine of heterogeny.

Though in the intervening years the subject was still worked at from time to time, yet almost a new epoch in the controversy may be said to have commenced

[1] His results were conflicting and contradictory whilst dealing with materials which underwent the alcoholic fermentation. Sometimes organisms were to be met with in such solutions in spite of all his precautions.

about twelve years ago. Since this time, and in France more especially, the truth or falsity of the doctrine of 'spontaneous generation' has formed the subject of a most vigorous discussion. Its renewal was initiated in 1858 by the communication of a paper by M. Pouchet to the Académie des Sciences of Paris, entitled 'Note sur des Proto-organismes végétaux et animaux nés spontanément dans l'air artificiel et dans le gaz oxygène.' The views and experiments of M. Pouchet were warmly repudiated by men so distinguished as MM. Milne-Edwards, de Quatrefages, Claude Bernard, Dumas, Payen, and Lacaze Duthiers. Nevertheless, Professor Mantegazza very shortly afterwards also communicated to the Academy of Sciences the results of his researches upon the generation of infusoria, which he had previously laid before an Italian academy in 1852. The conclusions at which he had arrived agreed almost perfectly with those of M. Pouchet; and in the following year the latter published his treatise on 'Hétérogénie [1],' in which much new matter was added in support of his doctrines. But it would be in vain for us now to attempt to follow out all the intricacies of the discussions which have taken place since this time [2]. Many of the most interesting points will be

[1] To this treatise we must refer those also who desire a more complete historical sketch than we have deemed it necessary to give.

[2] This has been attempted by M. Pennetier, in a work entitled 'L'Origine de la Vie,' which, in addition to a sketch of the later stages of the controversy up to the year 1869, contains a very complete list of works and papers on the whole subject, arranged in chronological order.

alluded to in our succeeding chapters—though others will scarcely be referred to, as we wish to narrow the question in dispute down to its simplest issues. We will, now, only state that early in the following year an accomplished chemist, M. Pasteur, entered the field, and henceforth became the most prominent objector to the doctrines of heterogeny. Although many others have taken part in the contest, still it was, for a long time, in the main carried on between M. Pasteur on the one hand (backed by the immense moral support of the French Academy) and by MM. Pouchet, Joly, and Musset, on the other. Most valuable experimental evidence was, however, adduced in 1862 in support of the possibility of the origin of living things from not-living matter, by Professor Jeffries Wyman of Cambridge, U.S., and in 1868 by Professor Cantoni of Pavia.

CHAPTER VII.

MODE OF ORIGIN OF PRIMORDIAL LIVING THINGS: NATURE OF PROBLEM.

Changes which occur in an Organic Infusion. Evolution of Gas. Plastide-particles and *Bacteria*. Formation of 'Pellicle.' Mode of formation of *Bacteria*. Views as to their nature. Different kinds of *Bacteria* and allied organisms—*Vibriones, Leptothrix*, and *Spirillum*. Composition of 'proligerous pellicle.' Views of Cohn and Pouchet. Sometimes no 'pellicle' forms, only turbidity, flocculi, or deposit. Mode of origin of *Torula*. Views of Hallier. Micrococci, cryptococci, and arthrococci. Their mutual relations to one another and to Fungi. Nature and mode of origin of *Sarcina*. Development of Fungus 'spores.' Doubt as to mode of origin of these forms. Useless to look in Air for germs of *Bacteria*. Mode of appearance of these in thin films of fluid. Only two explanations possible. Origin either germless or from invisible germs. Existence of latter must not be recklessly postulated. Similar problem in case of origin of Crystals. Statical and dynamical aggregates. Solution of problem concerning Crystals. Mr. Rainey's observations. Microscopical evidence similar in both cases. This can neither confirm nor invalidate the supposition as to invisible germs, crystalline or living. The existence of both equally hypothetical.

WHEN a fluid containing an organic substance in solution is allowed to remain in contact with air during moderately warm[1] weather, it soon undergoes

[1] Fermentation usually ceases in an organic solution when the temperature falls to about $45°$ F.; and it is interesting to find that the poetic imagination of Ovid had, by a kind of happy guess, led him to attach

changes of a putrefactive or fermentative character. A slight evolution or liberation of gas generally takes place as the first obvious stage of the process[1], and after a variable time (hours or days, according to the temperature, the nature of the solution, and other modifying conditions) during which the infusion has gradually become more and more turbid, a slight whitish, though semi-translucent, scum or pellicle, that soon thickens into a membrane, makes its appearance on the surface of the fluid. This constitutes the 'primordial mucous layer' of Burdach, or the 'proligerous

the same importance to the influence of solar heat in the evolution of Life which modern science now allots to it. We have already quoted one passage to this effect, but here is another:—

'Ergo ubi diluvio tellus lutulenta recenti
Solibus ætheriis, altoque recanduit æstu,
Edidit innumeras species.'

[1] This may be well seen by adding to the fermentable infusion sufficient isinglass to 'set' the fluid slightly. The bubbles of gas liberated, are for a long time retained in the slightly gelatinous liquid, and may be seen throughout its substance. Very contradictory opinions prevail as to the order of appearance and cause of this gaseous evolution. M. Pasteur believes that the evolution of gas takes place *after* the appearance and on account of the changes induced by the presence of organisms. In his opinion all fermentations are brought about by the presence and development of organisms (derived from the atmosphere) in the fermenting fluids. His opponents, however, maintain that the organisms are *results* of chemical changes brought about by physical conditions in the molecularly mobile and unstable matter of an organic infusion, and that the gaseous evolution is dependent upon some of these antecedent, or formative, chemical changes. The gases most commonly liberated in fermentations and putrefactions are hydrogen, carbonic acid, sulphuretted hydrogen, or ammonia.

pellicle' of Pouchet. On microscopical examination of the fluid by the highest powers, as soon as it begins to grow clouded, it will be found swarming with multitudes of mere moving specks or spherical particles, intermixed with short staff-like bodies, known as *Bacteria*, which also exhibit more or less active movements. The specks, that have hitherto been called 'Monads[1]' or 'microzymes[2],' I shall henceforth term *plastide-particles*. They are primordial particles of living matter, and may be seen, with our present optical powers, to vary between $\frac{1}{100000}''$ and $\frac{1}{10000}''$ in diameter.

An examination of the 'pellicle,' moreover, shows that it is composed of a dense superficial aggregation of such bodies as may previously have been found diffused through the liquid. In addition to plastide-particles and *Bacteria*, however, other low organisms, of

---

[1] Much confusion results from the classifications of the older naturalists, who (following O. F. Müller) arranged under the same genus (*Monas*) the mere moving specks above referred to, and also certain of the most elementary and smaller of the Ciliated Infusoria—of which the so-called *Monas lens* is about the most abundant representative. It will now be better, in order not to clash with modern usage, to follow the example already set by others, and to restrict the word 'Monad' to the ciliated organisms which have lately been so well described by Cienkowski and others.

[2] They were called *Microzyma* by Béchamp, but I do not adopt this designation, because it is too special. All minute living particles, whose nature cannot be distinguished by the microscope, may well be designated by one generally applicable name. Minute off-castings from white blood corpuscles are quite indistinguishable microscopically from the living specks which appear in fermenting solutions, and yet it would not be reasonable to call the former 'small ferments' (microzymæ).

which we shall subsequently speak, are very often found in both situations.

With regard to the mode of origin and nature of *Bacteria*, much difference of opinion still exists. They have been supposed by some persons to result from the coalescence and fusion of plastide-particles; whilst the longer and more developed bodies, called *Vibriones*, have been thought to result from a similar union of *Bacteria*.

This is the view of M. Dumas and of Dr. Hughes Bennett, though it is doubted by Pouchet and most other observers. It seems much more probable that both *Bacteria* and *Vibriones* are only later stages in the growth and development of certain primary plastide-particles. Dr. Bennett[1] states that he has actually seen the union above referred to taking place; but, judging from my own experience, I should say that it is an occurrence of the most extreme rarity. During a very long series of observations I have never perceived such a coalescence.

The most discordant opinions have always existed as to the nature of these *Bacteria*. Naturalists have been in doubt as to whether they should be regarded as independent living things of the lowest grade, having an individuality of their own; or whether, rather, they should be looked upon as developmental forms of some higher organisms — either animal or vegetal. There seem to be four principal views con-

[1] 'Pop. Science Rev.,' Jan. 1869.

cerning them:—(1) that they are animal organisms of the lowest grade, having an individuality of their own, as conjectured by Ehrenberg; (2) that they are, as supposed by Hallier, of the nature of spores, produced from, and destined again to develop into, some of the simplest microscopic fungi¹; (3) that they represent,

¹ This view has been advocated by Dr. Pololebnow of St. Petersburg, in a memoir presented to the Vienna Academy on June 3, 1869. He thinks that *Bacterium*, *Vibrio*, and *Spirillum* are all developmental stages of *Penicillium glaucum*. Prof. Huxley has lately ('Quart. Journal of Microsc. Science,' Oct. 1870, p. 360) expressed opinions having a similar bearing. It will be seen, however, from the words which are placed in italics, that Prof. Huxley's views on this subject are, in part, mere surmises, rather than positive impressions based on a complete research. He says:—' With Torula, then, we find Bacteria in great numbers in this quiescent state. Usually masses are to be seen adhering very closely or tightly to one Torula cell or another, and such masses are very difficult to separate from the cell to which they are fixed. *It seems probable* that the Bacteria proceed in this way from the Torula cells, as the Torula cells do from Conidia. *It is probable* that Bacterium is a similar thing to Torula—a simplest stage in the development of a fungus. By sowing Conidia you also get Bacteria in abundance. You get the Bacteria adhering like this (fig. 6, *d*) to the Conidia, and they are, *I believe*, developed from the protoplasm of the Conidia just as Torulæ are; and we may compare these two forms to the Microgonidia and Macrogonidia of Algæ. They are all terms in the development of Penicillium.' With reference to this theory, my own observations make me certain that *Bacteria* may appear in solutions (thin films) where no *Torula* exists. And more rarely, *Torula* cells may be seen in myriads in infusions, not only without attached *Bacteria*, but even without any discoverable *Bacteria* in the free state. I am quite familiar with this appearance, as of budding *Bacteria*, in connection with *Torula* and certain mycelial filaments. I look upon it, however, as the exception rather than the rule; and even where it exists, it seems by no means clear that the appearance is not due to the mere adhesion of some of the previously free *Bacteria*, which, in such cases, are always to be found co-existing with the *Torula* or *Fungus*-filaments.

as Cohn[1] thinks, the later free-swimming stage in the existence of certain algæ, intermediate between *Palmella* and *Oscillatoria*; or lastly (4) that they are the first and most common developmental phase of newly-evolved specks of living matter, which are capable, either singly or in combination, of developing into many different kinds of living things.

Ehrenberg's is an almost obsolete point of view. *Bacteria* are no more animal than vegetal organisms—they are protists. And few even of the firmest believers in the constancy of specific forms would now be inclined to maintain this doctrine with respect to *Bacteria*. The opinions of Hallier and Cohn will be again referred to in other portions of this chapter.

I have been compelled to take the fourth view, and to look upon plastide-particles as the mere temporary and initial developmental form of many organisms which may afterwards present distinct characteristics of their own[2], though certain of these particles may, through default of the necessary conditions, never actually develop into higher modes of being. But a very large number of them undoubtedly give rise to the bodies known as *Bacteria*, by a direct process of growth and development. These *Bacteria* vary very considerably in size, and also in the quality of their movements. Their size seems to

---

[1] 'Entwickelungs-geschichte der Mikroscop.' Algen und Pilze, 1854.
[2] Many of what may seem to be mere plastide-particles, are only *Bacteria* seen endwise.

differ according to the degree of putrescibility of the solution, the amount of heat to which it has been exposed, and other modifying circumstances. Those which have been produced at the same time are often pretty uniform in size, so that the different dimensions are frequently more marked in different solutions than between *Bacteria* existing in the same solution. They are, in their most common form, straight, rod-like bodies, varying in length from $\frac{1}{15000}''$ to $\frac{1}{1000}''$ of an inch; and they generally present a joint or line in the middle, dividing them into two equal parts. Their movements are frequently of a more or less rapid, oscillating, or irregularly-rotating character; though at other times they may be seen darting from place to place, either directly or in curves of various descriptions. All gradations exist, in fact, between movements which suffice at once to stamp them as living things, and mere slow oscillations, the presence of which alone may make us doubtful as to whether we have to do with living or with dead organisms.

It should be distinctly understood, however, that such *Bacteria* as are above described, with all their differences in size, only constitute one variety of the many lower forms of life met with in organic solutions. The most varied and diverse forms of these simple organisms exist, and the *Bacterium* already alluded to is only to be considered as the most constant and abundantly represented type. Instead of the rigid, simple, or bi-segmented, staff-like bodies, we may see—intermixed with these—other bi-segmented bodies less cylindrical in shape, and which, instead of being perfectly rigid, have a flexible joint, so that the two segments are freely movable. These bodies (about as large as medium-sized, ordinary *Bacteria*) generally exhibit the most active movements—darting about from place to place with rapid eel-like bendings of their body. Other forms are not unfrequently met with in which

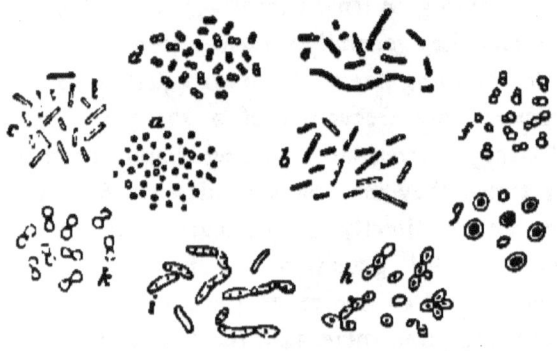

Fig. 17.
Some of the most common Primordial Forms of Life: *Bacteria, Torulæ*, &c. × 800.

the tendency to assume a bicellular shape is more obvious—though their bodies are similarly rigid, and their movements are not more active than those ordinarily displayed by *Bacteria*. Whilst the common *Bacterium* looks like a solid simple or bi-segmented rod, these latter forms seem rather to be made up of two juxtaposed, minute, cell-like elements, and in their early stages present the appearance of mere figure-of-8 particles. We also frequently see straight necklace-like rows composed of from two to fifteen bead-shaped bodies about the size of ordinary plastide-particles, though having a more hollow appearance. These aggregates are either motionless, or they exhibit a slow vibratile movement[1]. Not unfrequently organisms are met with which present an appearance somewhat similar to that of the smaller vegetative cells of the yeast-fungus—commonly known by the name of *Torula*; they are, however, more minute than these, and seem rather solid than cellular—presenting no evidences of a nucleus. One spherule is frequently seen with a much smaller bud-like particle attached, and they may exhibit pretty active oscillations, though never movements of a more extensive nature. In addition, there are to be seen in fermenting fluids more than ordinarily refractive particles, between which and minute though obvious *Fungus*-spores or *Torula* cells all intermediate forms can be detected.

These are the simplest organisms most frequently met

[1] Such chaplet-like combinations are considered by Pasteur to be very minute *Torulaceæ*, but I think they are more closely allied to *Bacteria* than to *Torula*. They are almost invariably to be met with in urine in company with other organisms when this is undergoing change. Indeed Pasteur even says:—' Je suis très porté à croire que cette production constitue un ferment organisé, et qu'il n'y a jamais transformation de l'urée en carbonate d'ammoniaque sans la présence et le developpement de ce petit végétal.' It develops in the body of the liquid and not specially at the surface, where we frequently meet with a pellicle made up of bodies of the kind next to be mentioned. Both these forms, however, may be found in fluids which are altogether different in nature.

274   THE BEGINNINGS OF LIFE.

with, though very many other modifications of form may be encountered, and will soon become familiar to those who work much at this subject.

With respect to the larger organisms known as

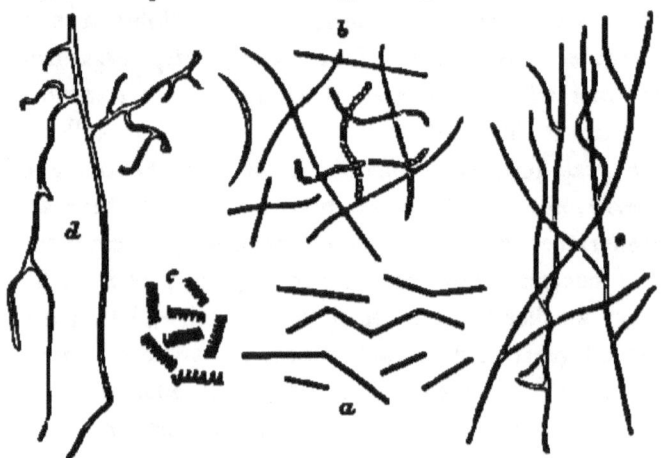

Fig. 18.
Other Early Forms of Life from Organic Infusions.

a. *Vibriones.*
b. Different kinds of simple *Leptothrix.*
c. *Spirilla.*
d. Mycelial filaments of an incipient *Fungus* (Hallier).
e. Branched *Leptothrix* or mycelial filaments (Pasteur).

Vibriones[1], these are two or many-jointed bodies, composed of long rod-like segments bent at various angles, which exhibit certain slow movements—either a mere

[1] These *Vibriones* of organic solutions are totally different organisms from the minute *Nematoid* worms to which the name has also been very improperly applied—the so-called *Vibrio tritici*, for instance.

bending of the body, or else an actual progression of an undulating anguilluloid character. In size they may vary from that of the largest *Bacterium* up to a body $\frac{1}{360}''$ in length by $\frac{1}{17000}''$ in breadth, though there is no definite limit to their dimensions. Notwithstanding the observations of Dumas and Bennett, it cannot be considered that these are ordinarily produced by the aggregation of *Bacteria*. It seems much more consistent with what may be observed, to believe that they arise by the gradual development of simple *Bacteria*, which—from some cause unknown to us—do not undergo such frequent processes of fission, and possess a great inherent power of growth. M. Davaine has also described certain straight or slightly bent, though motionless, bodies, closely resembling *Vibriones* as far as size and general appearance are concerned, to which he has given the name *Bacteridia*[1]. These are the organisms met with in the blood of animals suffering

[1] He looks upon *Bacteria* and *Vibrio* as genera which are closely allied to the *Oscillatoriæ*, and thinks that these *Bacteridia* form a still closer connecting link. Many of them are, in fact, even longer than *Vibriones*, and therefore in point of size they do approach more closely to the *Oscillatoria*. M. Davaine says he has also met with many kinds of *Vibriones* in the intestines of mammals and birds, as well as in salt-water infusions, which have been invariably motionless throughout their whole period of existence. He maintains that when those species which have previously exhibited movements cease to manifest them, we must by no means look upon them as necessarily dead; such organisms may preserve an unchanged appearance for many days or weeks, whilst, when they really die, they undergo disintegration in from twelve to twenty-four hours. (See 'Compt. Rend.' 1864, and 'Gaz. Méd. de Paris,' 1864.)

from a certain pestilential disease[1]; and although they may, as M. Davaine imagines, exhibit close affinities

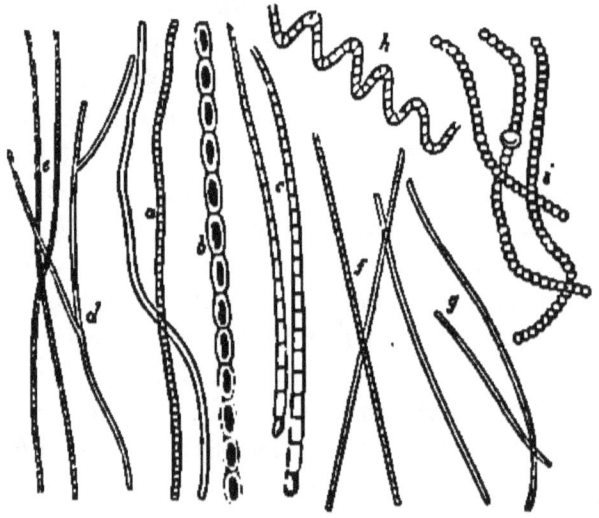

Fig. 19.
Oscillatoria and other simple Fresh-water Algæ (Hassall[2]). These forms are known by the following names:—

a. *Lyngbya prolifica.*
b.   ,, *vermicularis.*
c. *Raphidia viridis.*
d. *Tolypothrix rufescens.*
e. *Microcoleus gracilis.*
f. *Oscillatoria autumnalis.*
g.   ,, *splendida.*
h. *Spirillum Jenneri.*
i. *Nostoc communis.*

to the low algæ known as *Oscillatoriæ*, they, on the

---

[1] The 'Miltzbrand,' 'sang de rate,' or 'the blood,' as it is called in different countries; and from the contagion of which the *Malignant Pustule* of man is produced.

[2] Selected from Hassall's 'British Fresh-Water Algæ,' in order to show the simple structure of the filaments.

other hand, are just as closely related to *Leptothrix*, and through these to the lower kinds of *Fungi* known as 'moulds.' *Leptothrix* filaments are also, for the most part, quite motionless, and are often not much thicker than *Vibriones*. They may be either straight or undulating in outline, and perfectly plain or marked by minute segmentations after the fashion of the larger fungus filaments into which they sometimes develop. In addition to the larger organisms already mentioned, there are other rarer forms, belonging to the genus *Spirillum*, characterized by the most active movements, and in which the body is thread-like though twisted into the form of a helix or spiral.

It will be easily understood that the nature of the pellicle must vary very much in different solutions, according to the varying proportions in which these several kinds of organic units and organisms enter into its composition. All are agreed, however, that plastide specks and the more minute and simpler organisms are the first things to make their appearance in previously homogeneous solutions; and that, later, whilst these increase in number, there may gradually appear *Vibriones*, *Leptothrix* filaments, *Fungus*-spores, or some of the other lower forms of life. A very large proportion of the organisms met with in organic infusions are *Bacteria*, and their life and active movements continue for a longer or a shorter period, the duration of which is altogether uncertain. After a time, at all events, they gradually tend to accumulate at the surface of the solution, and, becoming motionless, to form a very densely aggregated but pretty uniform layer of a more or less granular appearance, constituting the so-called 'proligerous pellicle.' But even the simplest pellicle is not constituted solely by the mere aggregation of these bodies. As pointed out by Cohn[1], the organic particles are surrounded by, and imbedded in, a thin pellucid and almost invisible jelly-like stratum, which is best revealed, in a microscopical specimen, after the addition of a drop of a dilute aqueous solution of iodine. The gelatinous matter is not coloured by this reagent, and is thus rendered apparent.

The pellicle gradually continues to increase in thickness, and owing to the additions being made from below, its under surface frequently becomes very irregular, from the presence of numerous bosselated projections. As fast as the *Bacteria* and plastide-particles accumulate, they appear to become surrounded by the almost invisible gelatinous material above referred to. In this condition they are motionless, and it has been assumed, without sufficient proof, by Pouchet and most of the other heterogenists, that they were also dead. *Bacteria* which are really dead, however, do not become enveloped in such a material. The observations of Cohn, which I have frequently confirmed, show that the *Bacteria* again begin to move as soon as any of them may have been set free from the

---

[1] 'Entwick. Geschichte der Mikros. Algen und Pilze, 1854.'

gelatinous layer in which they had been imbedded[1]. They do not, however, resume their active movements of translation. They merely exhibit more or less rapid oscillations, which, although quite compatible with life, differ in no important respect from the *Brownian* movements which would be displayed by similarly-light not-living particles.

It is the presence of the gelatinous material which gives consistence to the pellicle, and makes the name 'primordial mucus,' bestowed upon it by Burdach, more suitable than it would otherwise have been.

[1] Whilst agreeing with Cohn so far as this observation is concerned, I by no means agree with him in his general estimate of the life-history of the *Bacteria*. On account of their existence in the above-named jelly, more especially, he came to the conclusion that *Bacteria* are most closely allied to certain algæ, composing the genera *Palmella* and *Tetraspora*, which have a similar gelatinous stage of existence. He considers that they have affinities with these on the one hand, and with the *Oscillatoriæ* on the other. The gelatinous condition represents the early stage in the life-history of *Palmellæ* and *Tetrasporæ*. In the later stages the cells previously contained in the jelly loosen themselves, and become independent, free-swimming organisms. Cohn thinks that a similar order is observed in the life-history of *Bacteria*. He believes that these appear first in solutions as small jelly-masses, which gradually increase, unite, and grow into a uniform pellicle, out of which the *Bacteria* ultimately appear as free-swimming organisms. The real order is, as I think, precisely the reverse. At first they are independent bodies, in the form of minute moving organisms scattered through the fluid. After a time they gradually accumulate in the midst of the fluid, or, more commonly, at the surface, and, becoming motionless, are found to be imbedded in a pellucid jelly. What is the mode of origin of this jelly—whether it also merely accumulates at the surface, or whether it is formed around and by the *Bacteria* in this situation—nobody seems to know, although the latter seems to be the more probable supposition. It certainly is a most important constituent of the pellicle.

The pellicle that forms at first is, however, not always persistent: after twenty-four or thirty-six hours it may sink to the bottom, whilst another gradually takes its place which may prove more durable. It is not very plain why some pellicles break up and sink in this way, but it would seem very probable that such an occurrence may be associated with an imperfect secretion or formation of that transparent jelly which, in ordinary cases, so much helps to give it coherency and strength, and whose presence is probably as necessary in order that subsequent evolutional changes may ensue. In some infusions or fermentable solutions, however, no distinct pellicle is ever formed. Flocculi may appear in the clouded liquid, which, after a time, sink to the bottom of the vessel; or, without the formation of flocculi, a deposit gradually accumulates, whilst the previously clouded supernatant liquid becomes more or less clear.

Occasionally it happens that the substance of a pellicle may be almost wholly composed of minute *Torula* cells—*Bacteria* being well-nigh absent. I once saw a very remarkable instance of this in an infusion of turnip. In certain of the cases, also, in which no distinct pellicle forms, the fine sediments or flocculi which gradually collect at the bottom of the vessel— more especially when the infusion has an acid reaction— are found to consist either[1] wholly or largely of vegetating *Torula* cells.

[1] In two or three cases I have failed, after a long search, to find a single *Bacterium* amongst the myriads of *Torula* cells.

Since only a casual allusion has hitherto been made to the mode of origin of *Torula*, it will be necessary to speak more distinctly concerning this subject, and also with reference to the mode of origin of other forms of *Fungus*-spores in solutions in which previously no such incipient organisms could be recognized. They appear, as a general rule, to arise somewhat more slowly than *Bacteria*, and their existence is often significant of a lower or impaired fermentative energy in the solution in which they occur.

As to the origin of ordinary *Torula* cells, their first appearance may be watched in various kinds of solutions, though I have found none more suitable for this purpose than a weak solution of neutral ammonic tartrate in distilled water[1]. During the past summer I found that *Bacteria* and *Torula* cells soon appeared in such a solution when placed in a flat-bottomed watch-glass and merely protected by an inverted glass. After twenty-four hours or more (according to the temperature), if the watch-glass be removed, without shaking, to the stage of a microscope, and if the flattened portion of the surface of the glass be scrutinized by a powerful immersion lens[2], numerous small but quite distinct colonies of *Torula* cells may be seen scattered over this area, the members of which are perfectly motionless[3].

[1] About 10 or 15 grains of the crystalline salt to an ounce of water.

[2] I generally employ a $\frac{1}{12}$" objective, and frequently double its ordinary magnifying power by the use of a long draw-tube, so as to get an amplification of about 1000 diameters.

[3] Other *Torula* cells, however, often exhibit distinct oscillating movements.

In these several patches there may be seen delicate ovoid *Torula* cells of almost any size beneath $\frac{1}{5000}$" in diameter. The larger cells are united in little groups of twos and threes, and budding from them may be seen pullulating projections of different sizes. Separate cells also exist, smaller and smaller in size, till at last they cease to be cellular in form, and we see only peculiarly refractive dots or specks less than $\frac{1}{10000}$" in diameter. In other places a colony of *Torula* cells seems to be about to grow up. Here there may be seen merely one or two of the smallest bodies which distinctly display the cellular form interspersed amongst a variable number of the refractive specks of all sizes down to the *minimum visible* stage. And when such a patch is marked and watched at different intervals a crop of perfect *Torula* cells is soon seen to occupy the same situation. The *Torula* cells do undoubtedly multiply pretty rapidly by a process of gemmation[1], when they have attained their full size, and possibly also they may increase by processes of fission during their earlier stages. Accordingly, their distribution is such as might have been expected amongst such self-multiplying units. Very rapid processes of sub-division cannot be recognized amongst ordinary plastide-particles and *Bacteria*, although many persons assume that such phenomena do take place[2], and, moreover, when

[1] M. Pouchet doubts the occurrence of this mode of multiplication ('Nouvelles Expériences,' &c., 1864, p. 168).

[2] I have actually seen the fissiparous division of a *Bacterium* only on comparatively few occasions.

these first appear in a homogeneous film of fluid, they present a more or less uniform distribution. *Torula* cells, on the other hand, can be seen to pullulate and multiply, and being motionless, are observed to be distributed, not uniformly but in groups or colonies through certain fluids in which they did not previously exist. As to the origin of the minute specks or plastide-particles which subsequently develop into *Torula* cells, two views may be taken: either (1), they are the developed representatives of pre-existing, though not-visible, particles which have been derived from the spores or filaments of pre-existing Fungi, or (2), they are the representatives of previously invisible particles of living matter which have originated *de novo*.

The former is the doctrine advocated by Professor Hallier, of Jena, whose views on this subject we may now briefly epitomise. Such bodies as I have been terming plastide-particles, Professor Hallier names 'micrococci.' He, also, regards them as minute particles of plasma, or naked living matter, though he assigns to such particles a very definite mode of origin. He believes them to be produced by the repeated subdivision of the nuclei of some fungus-spores, or by the breaking up of the protoplasmic contents of certain larger reproductive cells produced by fungi. Although not recognized by other botanists, Hallier regards the production of micrococci, after the manner stated, to be a normal occurrence in the life-history of many of the smaller fungi. Whilst disagreeing with him in this view, my own observations do pretty closely accord with his, as to the future fate of these so-called 'micrococci.' When introduced into a fluid capable of undergoing alcoholic fermentation, they develop, according to Hallier, into bodies resembling ordinary yeast cells or *Torula* (named by him 'cryptococci'), whereas in an acid fluid, or one which becomes acid by the establishment of a new kind of fermentation, they assume an elongated form, and constitute one variety of what are ordinarily termed

FIG. 20.

The 'Micrococci' and 'Cryptococci' of Hallier.

Bacteria (or 'arthrococci' in the nomenclature of Hallier). Micrococci and arthrococci are said to multiply by fission, whilst cryptococci increase by a process of gemmation. By an elongating growth, accompanied by the formation of septa at intervals, arthrococci are said to be capable of developing into distinct fungi of the *Oïdium* type. Thus, according to the nature of the fluids, 'micrococci' develop either at once into *Torula* cells, from which a mycelium and a perfect fungus may result; or else into *Bacteria*, which also may develop into segmented filaments, and thence into distinct *Fungi* of a different type. These various kinds of *Fungi*, thus resulting from the development of mere micrococci (or plastide-particles), are supposed by Hallier to be capable of reproducing micrococci in the manner already indicated by a breaking-up and individualisation of the protoplasmic contents of certain reproductive cells[1]. Thus he claims to have shown that such particles, and *Bacteria*, are merely the ultimate reproductive elements of Fungi; and he also tries to show that they are the active infective agents in the establishment of cholera and many other contagious diseases[2].

[1] See Twelfth Report of the Medical Officer of the Privy Council, 1870, p. 243 (' Introductory Report on the Intimate Pathology of Contagion'). It will be seen on p. 245 of this 'Report' that Dr. Sanderson proposes to include micrococci, arthrococci, other forms of *Bacteria*, and *Bacteridia*, under the single designation '*microzymes*.' This, however, we consider for many reasons undesirable. 'Microzyme' seems to be too theoretical and specific as a name for a simple particle of plasma, which may have nothing to do with fermentation; and we think that such rudimentary particles ought to be distinguished by name from those which have assumed some developed form. For this latter reason, therefore, we consider Nägeli's term, '*Schizomycetes*,' even still more objectionable, since according to De Bary, who adopts it, we are to include under this designation 'forms of extreme minuteness, as yet insufficiently known as regards their organization, which are represented by the generic names, *Vibrio, Bacterium, Zooglæa* (Cohn), *Nosema* (Nägeli), *Sarcina*, &c.' ('Morphologie der Pilze,' Leipzig, 1866, S. 3.)

[2] These claims and views have been carefully considered by Dr. Burdon Sanderson, who says, in the before-mentioned Report, 'If it is true that our common cereals are infected with an endophyte which requires only certain very easily combined conditions of soil and tempe-

In spite of all that has been said upon the subject, however, no success has yet attended the attempt to show that *Bacteria* usually derive their origin from Fungi, although the concurrent testimony of many observers tend to show that they may, after undergoing various developmental phases, grow into Fungi. The actual origin of the plastide-particles or micrococci, therefore, still remains an open question.

What I have said concerning the appearance of *Torula*, and their derivation from minute particles, seems to apply also to *Sarcina*, though my observations on this subject are less complete and satisfactory. I am even doubtful as to whether *Sarcina* is really a living organism[1]. It was originally discovered by Prof. Goodsir[2], in fluid vomited by a patient suffering from disease of the stomach. Subsequently it has been discovered in other situations—in urine by various observers, in the lungs by Prof. Virchow, in fluid from the ven-

---

rature in order to produce nests of microzymes, and if such nests are, as Hallier states, to be found in all contagious liquids, the fact can hardly fail to have a certain significance in its bearing on the etiology of infective diseases;' but then he adds:—'At present there is no ground for stating either the one or the other. The former is denied by all botanists, the latter by all pathologists.'

[1] See *Appendix* A., pp. li—v.
[2] See 'Edinb. Med. and Surg. Journal,' vol. lvii., 1842. The description then given was as follows:—'*Sarcina*, plants coriaceous, transparent, consisting of 16 to 64 four-celled square frustules, arranged parallel to one another in a square transparent matrix. Species 1. *Sarcina ventriculi* (mihi), Frustules 16, colour light brown, transparent matrix very perceptible between the frustules, less so around the edges; size 800 to 1000th inch. Hab., the human stomach.'

tricles of the brain by Sir Wm. Jenner, in a gelatinous stratum on the surface of old bones by Mr. Stephens, and in a few other habitats[1]. It is believed by the Rev. M. J. Berkeley to be some unusual form of one of our common moulds, though great obscurity is acknowledged to prevail on this subject, and nothing is certainly known concerning its subsequent morphological

FIG. 21.

Sarcina, from an Ammonic Tartrate and Sodic Phosphate Solution.

condition, or from what organism it has been derived. Mr. Berkeley says[2], 'Every attempt to make it germinate and produce its proper fruit has at present failed.' I have met with it several times in closed flasks containing ammonic tartrate and sodic phosphate, though not in other saline solutions with which I have experimented. It appears to be always produced in slightly acid fluids, and it seems very probable that

[1] For further particulars on this subject, see Dr. Tilbury Fox's 'Skin Diseases of Parasitic Origin,' pp. 152-163. M. Pasteur ('Ann. de Chim. et de Phys.,' 1862, Pl. 11, fig. 27, e, and p. 80) has figured and alludes to an 'Algue formée de cellules quaternaires, déposée sous forme de précipitate,' upon the walls of a flask which had contained 'l'eau de levûre non sucrée,' and which, if not *Sarcina*, must be very closely allied thereto.

[2] 'British Fungology.' 1860, p. 69.

the presence of phosphates or of phosphoric acid may be also necessary for the development of this product. The specimens found in urine are about half the size of those which occur in the stomach; the latter also have a brownish tint, whilst those found in my saline solutions[1] have been colourless and more sharply defined, though very variable in size.

I have still to refer to another observation throwing light upon the mode of origin of what appeared to be distinct, double-contoured, *Fungus*-cells, of a kind concerning which we shall have more to say hereafter. These again seemed to originate from minute particles, which, a short time previously, had not been visible in the fluid. The observation now to be recorded is interesting also in other respects, and is sufficiently suggestive as to the possible influence of electrical conditions in promoting evolutional, or developmental changes.

Referring to notes made at the time, I extract the following particulars:—About eleven P.M. on the 14th of June a small quantity of ordinary ammonic sesquicarbonate was dissolved in some apparently pure (though not distilled) water, in a watch-glass. After solution, and in about an hour's time, the fluid was carefully examined with different microscopic powers, and lastly

---

[1] They are not to be obtained at will. I have met with them about eight or nine times, but have very frequently failed to produce them. I have, however, never found well marked specimens except in a solution which contained ammonia and a phosphate.

the bottom of the watch-glass was scrutinised in very many situations with an immersion $\frac{1}{18}''$ objective. No living thing of any kind was seen, though scattered over the bottom of the glass were a large number of tiny crystals, some larger and some smaller than $\frac{1}{8000}''$ in diameter. Under the polariscope they gave the most beautiful and varied colour reactions. The watch-glass was then placed on a mantel-piece with a soft surface (covered with velvet), a wine-glass, with its stem broken off, was inverted over it, and this again was covered by a tumbler, in order, as much as possible, to prevent evaporation and keep out dust. After twenty-four hours the bottom of the watch-glass was again carefully examined with the $\frac{1}{12}''$ object-glass, and no change was observable. There were the same minute crystals—perhaps rather more numerous than before—but no recognisable specks of protoplasm or other trace of living things. The watch-glass was then replaced as before. The next day (June 16th) the weather was hot and extremely sultry. The temperature was about 85° F. in the shade, and a thunder-storm, which seemed imminent during the whole of the day, began about 7 P.M., and continued till the early hours of the morning of the following day. At about 11.30 P.M. of this 16th of June, I again examined the solution in the watch-glass—forty-eight hours after it had been prepared. Then, what appeared to be *Fungus*-spores were seen in all stages of development, scattered over the whole of the bottom of the glass, and intermixed with the small crystals. They were quite motionless, and mostly separate, rather than in distinct groups. They varied in size from the minutest visible speck, to a spherical nucleated body $\frac{1}{3300}''$ in diameter. No moving particles or *Bacteria* were seen. Probably

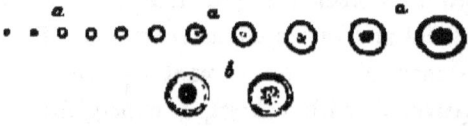

Fig. 22.

Different Developmental Stages of Spores (?) found in an Ammonic Carbonate solution. (× 800.)

more than a thousand of these bodies were developing in the one watch-glass—each growing in its own place, and showing no evidence of multiplication by division or pullulation. In those whose dimensions did not exceed $\frac{1}{10000}''$ in diameter, no nucleus was visible, though the larger of them displayed a distinctly vesicular appearance. As these spores or spore-like bodies increased in size, the thick wall became more and more manifest—though it had a rather rough, granular appearance—and a nucleus gradually showed itself within, which was also granular[1]. The next morning, after

---

[1] This appearance I had not unfrequently seen before, where spores resembling these bodies had been developing in saline solutions, and it had always strongly suggested the notion to me that such spores were formed by an actual coalescence of granules and particles. Here, however, there were no granules or moving particles present; the spore-like bodies were the only possibly living things, and it seemed quite

twelve hours, the spores (?) seemed to be much in the same condition, though numerous small colonies (30 to 50 in each) of motionless *Bacteria* were now visible. During the day the air was clear, and the temperature lower (76° F.); and after twelve hours more (in the evening) the *Bacteria* were found to have considerably increased in number, and several of the spore-like bodies were in a more developed condition—their thick walls being wholly or partially consolidated, and the nucleus also more distinctly defined. In this condition they perfectly resembled the undoubtedly living spores which have been found, either alone or in connection with mycelial filaments to which they have given rise, in many ammoniacal solutions. The great majority of the spore-like bodies in the watch-glass were, however, still in the granular condition—they seemed to have made no advance whatever. On the following day they were not quite so distinct—some of them seemed to be disintegrating, whilst none had undergone any further development. The *Bacteria*, on the contrary, had decidedly increased in quantity. After two days more, minute *Torula* cells began to appear. These did not rapidly multiply, as on other occasions, but soon

certain that they could not have originated after this fashion. They obviously commenced as minute specks, and the granular appearance manifested itself as long as the spore-like bodies were still increasing in size. When growth stopped, consolidation began to take place, and an even, double-contoured wall soon replaced that which was before irregular and granular. (Compare with those in Figs. 29 and 39.)

U 2

began to develop into mycelial filaments, *i.e.* the growth of each was continuous rather than discontinuous.

The thick-walled spores—if such was their real nature—had either developed or come into existence, under the influence of the high temperature and the disturbed electrical condition of the atmosphere[1]. And whatever their nature, they seemed to be so much the creatures of these conditions as to be unable to survive under those which followed.

It seems certain, at all events, that these bodies resembling *Fungus*-spores originated separately in different parts of the solution. And neither have the real spores which they resemble been observed to multiply either by fission or gemmation: they have not even been found aggregated together in a fashion which would suggest the probability of this method of multiplication. The real spores have likewise been seen in gradually diminishing sizes, down to the smallest visible specks.

What, then, is the origin of the plastide-particles which develop into *Bacteria*, *Torulæ*, or other low forms of life that so soon swarm in infusions of animal or vegetable substances, and in certain saline or ammoniacal solutions? Do they owe their origin to the multiplication of germs pre-existing in the air, the

---

[1] We may, perhaps, connect this possibility with the well-known fact that milk, beer, and other fluids are so very prone to turn sour during a thunder-storm, or whilst it is threatening.

water, or the substance infused? or have they been produced *de novo*, and without the agency of germs? These are the questions which most urgently press for solution. Can Archebiosis still take place, or does all Life proceed from pre-existing Life?

I think it will be at once recognised, that it would be altogether useless to search in the *air* for the germs of plastide-particles, or of *Bacteria*. Even M. Pasteur himself admits this. Speaking of the germs of the *Bacterium*, 'which shows itself in all sorts of infusions, and which almost always appears before the other Infusoria,' he says (Annal. de Chimie et de Physique, 1862, p. 56):—' This Infusorium is so small, that one could not distinguish its germ, and still less affirm the presence of such germ, if it were known, amongst the organised corpuscles belonging to the dust in suspension in the atmosphere.'

No investigations as to what the air does or does not contain can, therefore, throw much direct light upon this question as to the mode of origin of *Bacteria*. Seeing that the champion of the Panspermatists admits this, we may for the present completely disregard this aspect of the question, merely pointing out that probably more than nine-tenths of the discussion and experimentation which has taken place upon the question of the existence or non-existence of 'germs' in the air has been almost wholly irrelevant, and without value for the settlement of the main question at issue (see p. 297).

We must, then, have recourse to a microscopical

examination of the *solutions* themselves in which the plastide-particles, and the *Bacteria* or *Torula*, appear. The mode in which they make their appearance was first studied by Mantegazza[1], though others have subsequently made similar observations. I have frequently watched their appearance, during warm weather, in portions of organic solutions hermetically sealed in small glass tubes, or, more advantageously still, in thin films of fluid beneath a covering glass, after it had been cemented[2] to the glass slip, or after the fluid had been otherwise prevented from undergoing rapid evaporation.

If a drop of a very strong infusion of turnip[3] be taken (after it has been filtered five or six times through the finest filtering paper), and mounted in the

---

[1] Professor Mantegazza first watched the appearance of *Bacteria* in a solution containing some fragments of vegetable tissue, enclosed in a hermetically-sealed glass tube. On this occasion he watched the solution assiduously for sixteen consecutive hours. At the expiration of two hours, he saw the first particles appear in the solution, at first simply exhibiting a slow, oscillating movement, but, after a time, darting about with the rapid movements by which active *Bacteria* are characterized. Their number increased imperceptibly, till, at the end of ten hours, the liquid had become quite cloudy. (See 'Giornal. dell. R. Istituto Lombardo,' t. iii. 1851.)

[2] Taking care to employ a cement which has been previously ascertained not to be hurtful to *Bacteria*, and to leave a minute aperture at the circumference of the glass uncovered by the cement. Or a drop of the fluid to be examined may be placed in an ordinary animalcule cage, and the cover then pressed down so as to flatten the drop into a thin film.

[3] This I have found to answer best. The water of the infusion should not at any time be hotter than about $35°$ F. Sometimes the appearance of *Bacteria* has been hastened by neutralizing the natural acidity of the infusion by liquid potassæ.

manner above mentioned, it is not difficult—with the stage of the microscope in a horizontal position—to bring into the field of view a portion of the film, which either contains no visible[1] particles, or only a small number, such as can be easily counted. With the slip resting on one of Stricker's hot-water plates maintained at a temperature of 85°–95° F., it may be found that, in the course of three or four hours, faint and ill-defined whitish specks, less than $\frac{1}{10000}''$ in diameter, make their appearance pretty evenly dispersed throughout the field of view. These are at first almost motionless—exhibiting only the merest vibrations, but no progressive movements. They gradually become more distinct, assume a sharper outline, and after a variable time some of them develop into distinct *Bacteria*[2]. At first they exhibit gentle oscillations and tremblings only, though gradually they display the more characteristic darting movements. The study of the mode of origin of these primordial living forms is, indeed, facilitated and rendered much more certain by the fact that they remain comparatively motionless for a long time after their first appearance, and also continue faint and much less refractive than when in the more mature condition. Hence it becomes a matter of the

---

[1] Working with a magnifying power of 1000 diameters.

[2] The shortest time in which I have seen *Bacteria* develop in such a film has been one hour and a half. More frequently, however, three hours have elapsed, and sometimes longer still, before distinct *Bacteria* have made their appearance in the field of view.

greatest ease to watch their appearance in thin films of fluid, and also to distinguish them from other extraneous particles with which they may coexist.

But if, in a motionless film of fluid, multitudes of living particles subsequently appear, which are themselves almost motionless, how can we account for their origin? Three hypotheses present themselves. It may be said (*a*) that they have arisen through the reproductive multiplication of one or more germs or organisms in the film of fluid which, though *visible*, had escaped observation. The difficulties standing in the way of our acceptance of this explanation are these. The film is motionless, and also those first appearing particles which gradually come into view in portions of it where no such particles had been previously visible. No multiplication by fission or other means can actually be observed to take place by microscopists among the mere particles in question, though this ought to be easily observable if it really occurred at the rate postulated. And lastly, if the subsequent large numbers are to be accounted for by the occurrence of a reproductive process taking place amongst a few visible but unobserved germs, these products of fission, being motionless, ought to be aggregated here and there only[1], whilst as a matter of fact, no such arrangement exists— there is rather a uniform diffusion of the particles. These

---

[1] This does actually take place in the appearance of *Torula* cells in a watch-glass (p. 281), because, being also motionless, they do undergo a rapid process of subdivision, even whilst they are of a very minute size.

various difficulties appearing fatal to this explanation of the mode of origin of the multitudes of plastide-particles and *Bacteria*, we are left with only two other possible modes of origin:—either (*b*) they have been developed from a multitude of pretty evenly disseminated *invisible* germs, or (*c*) they have been produced *de novo* in the fluid by a process of Archebiosis.

Thus the solution of this great problem passes beyond the reach of actual demonstration. Microscopical evidence enables us to bring it to this stage now, and it may perhaps never enable us to do more. It reduces us to a consideration of two rival hypotheses, and to a careful consideration of whatever evidence may be forthcoming to influence us in our choice between these two possible explanations. Nothing that can be said about the abundance of recognisable atmospheric germs can directly affect the solution of this problem. It is one which, if it has to do with germs at all, has to do with *invisible* germs. But invisible germs can have only a hypothetical existence, and even to this they can lay no claim, unless observed phenomena cannot be explained without such postulation. We must not forget the old and well-approved logical rule,—

'Entia non sunt multiplicanda præter necessitatem.'

The 'law of parsimony' may well be quoted for the benefit of those who would ruthlessly people the atmosphere with such countless myriads of 'entities[1].'

[1] Some of those who are so eager to demonstrate the prevalence of 'germs,' are frequently carried away, by their enthusiasm, beyond the

The problem which is now presented, concerning the origin of these low organisms, so precisely resembles that which has had to be settled in the case of some crystals[1], that it may be well to elucidate our subject by this analogy. It will be necessary, however, in comparing the two problems, that the reader should look at the evidence only, with a mind as free as possible from the warping influence of preconceptions.

Crystals are statical aggregations, whilst organisms are dynamical aggregations[2], which, from the evolu-

---

bounds of strict logic. It suffices to show by the agency of the electric light or by some other means, that air and water contain myriads of infinitesimally small particles, some of which are organic in nature, in order that they may at once come to the conclusion that the organic particles are germs. But, seeing the countless forms of life which exist upon the surface of the earth, and how these are from moment to moment, during life as well as after death, undergoing a molecular disintegration, it would be strange indeed if the atmosphere, and water which has been exposed to it, did not contain multitudes of organic particles, both large and small. The great majority of such mere organic particles, however, could have no reasonable title to be called germs.

[1] The analogy between the two problems, as to the possible origin of some crystals and organisms *de novo* in solutions, has been rendered much more obvious since the discovery by the late Professor Graham, that, when dissolved, the saline substance does not remain as such in solution—but that the acid and the base exist separately, and are separable by a process of dialysis. When crystallisation occurs, therefore, we have a combination of molecules taking place similar to, though simpler than, what may be presumed to take place in the genesis of a speck of living matter.

[2] This difference between crystals and organisms, which are in other respects strictly comparable with one another, was clearly pointed out by Burdach. In both cases, he says, " La tendance intérieure à la configuration existe avant sa manifestation. . . . Mais dans le cristal,

tionist's point of view, are supposed to take origin from the recompositions occurring amongst colloidal molecules. Colloids possess so strong an inherent tendency to undergo change, that they were said by Professor Graham to be endowed with properties which form the basis of those manifested by living things. Matter when it passes into the *crystalline* condition exhibits properties of a certain kind; and when it passes into the *living* condition it exhibits properties of another kind, to which we commonly apply the term 'vital.' Now the question in each case is, whether by mere concurrence of certain physical conditions, aiding and abetting the inherent properties of the matter itself, some kinds of matter can fall into modes of combination called *crystalline*, whilst other kinds are capable of falling into modes of combination called *living*; or whether, in each case, a pre-existing 'germ' of the particular kind of matter is necessary, in order to determine, in suitable media, either of these modes of combination. Are we to believe that crystals can appear in no solution whatsoever without the pre-

l'activité s'éteint à moment même où il se produit; il ne conserve ensuite sa forme comme le caillot, que par sa seule cohésion, par l'enchainement chimique de ses éléments, et il ne manifeste plus aucune activité, tant que de nouvelles causes ne viennent point déranger l'équilibre. Le corps organisé au contraire, se maintient par une production incessante, par la continuité des mouvements plastiques, par la permanence de l'antagonisme de forces qui lui a donné naissance. La *pérennité* ou la persistance de l'activité nous apparaît donc comme caractère de la vie."—*Traité de Physiologie*, translated by Jourdan, 1839, t. iv. p. 129.

existence in that solution of certain crystalline germs; and similarly that living things can arise in no solution whatsoever without the pre-existence in such solution of living germs? The very mention of this question in connection with the origin of crystals may seem to some people to be quite absurd, because they have always been in the habit of believing that crystals could, and do, habitually come into being *de novo*, without the agency of pre-existing crystals. But in spite of the fact, that the majority of people are quite content to believe that crystals originate in obedience to purely physical conditions, and independently of pre-existing 'crystalline force;' still, facts somewhat similar to those which are to be met with in connection with the sister problem, have induced some chemists seriously to question the possibility of the *de novo* origination of crystals in some supersaturated solutions. In support of this statement, I need only quote the following passage from Watts's *Dictionary of Chemistry*[1] :—' This sudden crystallisation, if not produced by cold, appears to depend essentially on contact of the solution with small, solid, perhaps crystalline particles; for it is not produced by passing air previously purified by oil of vitriol through the solution, or by agitation with a glass rod previously purified from dust by ignition. *According to Violette and De Gernez, the sudden crystallisation is in all cases induced only by contact with a crystal of the same salt, possessing the same form and degree of hydration as*

[1] Vol. v. p. 349.

the crystals, which separate out; and in the case of those supersaturated solutions which crystallise suddenly on exposure to the air, it is due to the presence of minute particles of that salt floating in the air. From an experiment of De Gernez it appears that microscopic crystals of sodic sulphate may be obtained by passing air, even in the open country, through pure water, and evaporating the water on a glass plate. Jeannel, however, denies the necessity of contact with the salt actually contained in the solution. He finds, indeed, that a supersaturated solution of sodic acetate may be made to crystallise by contact with any solid substance (a piece of paper, for example), and a solution of sodic tartrate by contact with a clean, dry, glass rod.' Here, then, we have a veritable 'germ' controversy referrible to crystals. I have been informed, however, by Prof. Frankland, that even in the case of sodic sulphate it has been shown that, *under certain conditions*, crystallisation can take place where no crystalline germ could possibly have existed.

The 'germ' theory of the origin of crystals in supersaturated solutions has, therefore, not only been in existence, but has been overthrown. This has been possible, however, only because it has been more easy to show that a given set of conditions are inimical to the existence of a crystal, than it has yet been to induce people to believe that any given set of suitable experimental conditions are incompatible with the existence of matter in the living state.

It is worthy of remark, however, that the germ controversy concerning crystals can only be settled in the minds of those who are content to accept the high probability that the properties of any *invisible* portions of crystalline matter would correspond with the properties which similar visible crystalline matter is known to display. And it is this reluctance to admit an equally high probability in the case of living matter, which alone causes the sister controversy to continue. Otherwise, the question as to the possibility of the *de novo* origination of organisms would have been amicably settled long ago.

So far as evidence derived from microscopical examination can be adduced, moreover, it is able to speak no more decisively concerning the *de novo* origin of crystals, than concerning the *de novo* origin of organisms. In the elucidation of this point the valuable, though insufficiently known, observations of Mr. Rainey[1] come most opportunely to our aid. In ordinary cases, it is difficult to watch satisfactorily with the microscope the first stage in the appearance of crystals in solutions containing crystallizable matter, owing to the rapidity with which their growth takes place. This is one point in which crystals are strikingly different from organisms. The slower growth of organisms is, however, as Prof. Graham pointed out, quite in accordance with the general slowness of colloidal changes. But,

[1] 'On the Mode of Formation of the Shell of Animals.' &c. London, 1858.

since Mr. Rainey's discovery that crystals are produced much more slowly, and undergo very important modifications in shape, when they are formed in viscid solutions, the formation of these bodies has, in both respects, become much more obviously comparable with that of organisms. The appearance of these modified crystals may be best watched after mixing solutions of gum and carbonate of potash in the manner which has been carefully described by Mr. Rainey. Owing to the viscid properties of gum, a solution of this substance diffuses with difficulty, and hence, when brought into contact with a solution of carbonate of potash, the malate of lime of the gum only decomposes very slowly. The insoluble carbonate of lime, instead of appearing in its usual crystalline condition, is precipitated in the form of globules resembling calculi. Mr. Rainey thus describes what takes place when portions of the two solutions are mixed under the microscope:—'The appearance which is first visible is a faint nebulosity at the line of union of the two solutions, showing that the particles of carbonate of lime, when they first come into existence, are too minute to admit of being distinguished individually by high microscopic powers[1]. In a few hours exquisitely minute spherules, too small to allow of accurate measurement, can be seen in the nebulous part, a portion of which has disappeared, and is replaced by these spherical particles. Examined at a later period,

[1] Mr. Rainey generally made use of one of Ross's $\frac{1}{4}"$ object-glasses.

dumb-bell-like bodies will have made their appearance, and with them elliptical particles of different degrees of excentricity.' (p. 9.) These modified crystals are, therefore, not produced more rapidly than the lowest living things appear to be in other solutions during hot weather. The shapes of the products in the two cases, judging from Mr. Rainey's figures, are also remarkably similar. (See vol. ii. Fig. 41.)

Thus, then, the problem concerning the primordial formation of crystals and of living things is essentially similar in kind. Any difference in degree between our present knowledge on these two subjects must not blind us as to their similarity in nature. Plastide-particles and *Bacteria* are produced as constantly in solutions of colloidal matter as crystals are produced in solutions containing crystallizable matter. Crystallizable substances are definite in composition, and give rise to definite statical aggregations; whilst colloidal substances, much more complex and unstable, give rise on the contrary to dynamical aggregations. These dynamical aggregations, though they may at first make their appearance in the form of plastide-particles and *Bacteria*, are, by virtue of the properties of their constituent molecules, endowed with the potentiality of undergoing the most various changes in accordance with the different sets of influences to which they are submitted. Respecting the origin of the first visible forms which appear in either kind of solution, the evidence which we possess is precisely similar in nature. If such microscopical evidence does not enable us to get rid of the doubt that the smallest visible specks of living matter may have originated from *invisible* 'germs' of such organisms, neither does it any more enable us to dispense with the supposition that the smallest visible crystals may have originated from pre-existing *invisible* 'germs' of crystals. The very existence of the one set of invisible 'germs' is, in fact, just as hypothetical as the existence of the other. Plastide-particles and *Bacteria* we do know; but concerning the existence of invisible 'germs,' of these we know just as little as we do concerning the existence of invisible 'germs' of crystals.

CHAPTER VIII.

THE LIMITS OF 'VITAL RESISTANCE' TO HEAT.

Conflicting analogies bearing on the question of the Origin of Life. Views on this subject likely to be influenced by wider philosophical beliefs. Physical theories of Life quite harmonious with possibility of *de novo* origin. Both crystalline and living matter may be supposed to originate by same laws as determine their growth. Whether this does occur with living matter has to be determined by experiment. Only one mode of solving the problem. Importance of ascertaining limits of 'vital resistance' to Heat. Previously-existing evidence on this subject. Limits in dry air, and limits in water. General unanimity as to destructive influence of boiling water. Observations of Pouchet, Meunier, Wyman, and Liebig upon the effect of lower temperatures. Brownian and languid vital movements. Their significance and meaning. Occurrence of reproduction the surest test that *Bacteria* are living. New experiments with inoculated ammoniacal solutions. Show that *Bacteria, Torulæ*, and their germs are killed in fluids which have been raised to 140° F. Or by lower temperatures, if exposure last longer. Crucial nature of experiments. Almost similar results with slightly higher organisms. Experiments of Schwann. Value of single, properly-conducted experiment with positive result. These obtained by Schwann himself, and by Pouchet, Mantegazza, Wyman, and others. Also by M. Pasteur. Unfair way in which the latter argues on this subject. Limits of 'vital resistance' said to be higher in neutral or alkaline than in acid solutions. M. Pasteur's conclusions and assumptions.

SCIENTIFIC men are content to believe that crystals may originate without the aid of pre-existing crystalline matter, and it will remain for us, in subsequent chapters, to show how far existing evidence points towards a similar probability in the case of organisms. There is, however, an obvious and fundamental difference between crystals and organisms, which has had an immense and quite natural influence in affecting the opinions entertained as to the mode of origin of each. Crystals do not undergo a process of 'spontaneous division,' and reproduction is unknown amongst them. How else could they arise, then, save by a 'spontaneous' collocation of their atoms? With organisms and with living matter, however, the case is wholly different. These are dynamical aggregates, and the possession of a property of reproduction is their fundamental characteristic. All the higher forms with which we are most familiar do undoubtedly derive their origin from organisms similar to themselves. Why then should the processes with which we are so familiar in the many not be applicable to all? Why should we not implicitly believe that the phrase *omne vivum ex vivo* gives accurate expression to the law of nature? An analogical argument of so striking a nature could not fail to arrest and enchain the attention of those who, for other reasons, might believe or wish that the dogma were true—notwithstanding the fact that another analogical argument speaks almost as strongly in favour of the possibility of the *de novo* origination of some organisms as specks of living matter.

General beliefs will, then, be brought to bear upon the subject, and the views entertained upon this problem, as to the mode of origin of some organisms, will inevitably be influenced by the current doctrines entertained concerning 'Life'—just as these notions, in their turn, are held in subjection to, and are made to harmonize with, higher philosophical or religious beliefs. The influence of such general considerations is immense, and they are only too apt, even unconsciously, to warp the judgments of many of us in our attempts to interpret facts. Then, too, living things manifest such complex properties that the whole notion of Life has been shrouded in mystery. Biologists at first could not bring themselves to believe—some cannot do so now—that the phenomena which living things manifest are absolutely dependent upon the properties of the variously organised matter entering into their composition. They were obliged to have recourse to some metaphysical entity—some 'anima,' 'archæus,' or 'vital principle'—under whose directing influence the living form was supposed to be built up, and upon whose persisting influence many of the phenomena of Life were thought to depend. The aid of no similar metaphysical 'principle' has, however, been deemed necessary in order to account for crystalline structures and properties. It was in the main conceded by most physicists, and the doctrine remained unquestioned by biologists, that matter of certain kinds might, by virtue of its own inherent properties, aided by certain favouring circumstances—and quite independently of all pre-existing germs—fall into such modes of collocation as to give rise to crystals. But, owing to the influence of the theoretical considerations already mentioned concerning the nature of Life, a similar possibility could not easily be granted by many, in reference to the origin of living things. Was it not held that the living thing owed its structure or organization to the active influence of a special and peculiar principle? This 'vital principle' was neither ordinary matter nor ordinary force, neither was it in any way derivable from either of these; how then could it be supposed that the coming together of matter of any kind could give rise to a living thing? The aggregate of properties, which we designate by the word 'Life,' were not supposed to be dependent upon—to be, in fact, properties of the material aggregate which constituted the living thing. Life was presumed to be due to the manifestation of a something altogether peculiar—of a 'vital principle,' which was inseparable from living matter. Doubts, however, as to the truth of this doctrine have gradually multiplied and increased in strength. New means of observation opened up new questions for solution, and the ever-increasing strides of science have wrought the most fundamental changes in our notions concerning Life. Under the influence of the well-established doctrine concerning Persistence of Force—and more especially since the clear recognition of the subordinate doctrine as to the Correlation existing between the Physical and Vital forces—physiologists have now begun to recognise, and most unhesitatingly to proclaim the opinion, that the phenomena manifested by living things are to be ascribed simply to the properties of the matter as it exists in such living things. No one has expressed himself more decidedly on this subject than Prof. Huxley, and he may fairly be taken as an exponent of the modern doctrines on this question. He says [1]: 'Carbon, hydrogen, oxygen, and nitrogen are all lifeless bodies. Of these, carbon and oxygen unite in certain proportions and under certain conditions to give rise to carbonic acid; hydrogen and oxygen produce water; nitrogen and hydrogen give rise to ammonia. These new compounds, like the elementary bodies of which they are composed, are lifeless. But when they are brought together under certain conditions they give rise to the still more complex body, protoplasm; and this protoplasm exhibits the phenomena of life. I see no break in this series of steps in molecular complication, and I am unable to understand why the language which is applicable to any one term of the series may not be used to any of the others. We think fit to call different kinds of matter carbon, oxygen, hydrogen, and nitrogen, and to speak of the various powers and activities of these substances as the properties of the matter of which they are composed. . . . Is the case in any way changed when carbonic acid, water, and ammonia disappear, and in their place, *under the influence of pre-existing protoplasm*, an equivalent weight of the matter of life makes its appearance? . . .

[1] Article on 'Protoplasm,' in the 'Fortnightly Review' for February 1869.

What justification is there, then, for the assumption of the existence in the living matter of a something which has no representative or correlative in the not living matter which gave rise to it?'

The reader's attention must, therefore, again be called to the fact that our precise object is to ascertain whether it is possible for the first particles of future living matter to come together *de novo*, and in obedience to the same physical influences which are deemed adequate to bring about its growth or increase; or, whether we are to suppose that the first particles of an organism cannot be initiated apart from pre-existing protoplasm, even though this protoplasm is believed by a very large section of the physiological world to contain no special and peculiar 'force,' but to owe its qualities entirely to the ordinary physical properties of the elements entering into its composition.

The actuality of the process of Archebiosis, as against the hypothesis of the derivation of some organisms from pre-existing though invisible germs, can only be established if it can be shown that living things are to be met with in the fluids from hermetically-sealed flasks which have previously been exposed to a degree of heat adequate to destroy all pre-existing Life. This is the kind of test which was proposed by Needham and Spallanzani, and which has been accepted by all subsequent workers, including Pasteur, as the only one which was capable of throwing light upon the problem[1]. Much

[1] Though no one would suppose this to be the case from the mere

discussion has taken place as to the means of closing the flasks, concerning the degree of heat which it is necessary to employ, and also as to whether the organisms that have been found in such experiments have been living or dead; but, amidst all varieties of opinion with regard to the several details, there has been a general agreement that the question was only to be settled in some such manner.

The question as to the limits of what M. Pouchet terms 'vital resistance' to heat is that which has excited the greatest share of attention, and is the one which is of most fundamental importance in this enquiry [1].

In spite of the very definite results, however, of experiments carried on with the view of throwing light upon the subject, it is one upon which the opponents of 'spontaneous generation' are most reluctant to come to any decision. They seem ever ready to repudiate the validity of the results at which they had previously arrived, as soon as experiments are published tending to show that—these results being correct—organisms are undoubtedly capable of arising *de novo*.

---

perusal of Prof. Huxley's Inaugural Address before the British Association in 1870, which was destined to enlighten the public on this question.

[1] One of the latest writers on this subject, Professor Wyman, of Cambridge, U. S., says:—'The issue between the advocates and the opponents of the doctrine in question, clearly turns on the extent to which it can be proved that living beings resist the action of water at a high temperature.'—*American Journal of Science and Art*, Sept. 1867.

The positive evidence now existing on this subject, however, which may be considered all the more reliable because it has been partly built up and confirmed by the panspermatists themselves, is of the following nature.

It has been established by most careful observation that in *dry air* or in a vacuum, organisms are capable of withstanding a notably higher temperature than when they are immersed in fluid. According to the direct observations of M. Pasteur, the spores of certain fungi belonging to the family *Mucedineæ* seem to possess this tenacity of life to a very great extent; but even these, he says, though they still remain capable of germinating after having been raised for a few minutes in dry air or *in vacuo* to a temperature of 120° to 125°C (248°—257°F), lose this power absolutely and entirely after an exposure for half an hour, under similar conditions, to a temperature varying from 127° to 130°C (260°—266°F). And the labours of the commission appointed in 1860 by the Société de Biologie (consisting of the following members—MM. Balbiani, Berthelot, Broca, Brown-Séquard, Dareste, Guillemin, and Ch. Robin) to enquire into the subject, led them to the conclusion that the lower animals which were the most tenacious[1] of life—the rotifers, the 'sloths,' and the anguillules of tufts of moss or lichen—succumbed at even a much

[1] This extreme tenacity of life is perhaps due in part to the chitinous integument with which all these animals are provided. It is certain that very many of the lower forms, not so protected, are destroyed more easily by the influence of heat both in the presence and in the absence of moisture.

lower temperature than this. In dry air or *in vacuo*, therefore, we may look upon the temperature of 130°C for thirty minutes, as marking the extreme limit, so far as it has been hitherto possible to fix it, of vital endurance under such conditions—even for animals which are covered by a tough chitinous integument. There is, at present, no evidence forthcoming to shake the validity of this conclusion.

When immersed in *fluids*, however, the power possessed by the inferior organisms of resisting the destructive influence of heat is not nearly so great. Comparatively few, whether animal or vegetable, are believed to be capable of resisting a temperature of 75° C (167° F); and with regard to that of 100° C (212° F), it has been admitted, by MM. Claude Bernard and Milne-Edwards, by M. Pasteur, and by all the other most influential opponents of the doctrines of archebiosis and heterogeny, that such a temperature, even for one minute, has invariably proved destructive to all the lower organisms met with in infusions [1]—so far as

[1] It is quite fair to make this limitation, since we are only concerned with the origin of such organisms. Seeds of higher plants, provided with a hard coat, may—especially after prolonged periods of desiccation—germinate even after they have been boiled for a long time in water. This was ascertained by M. Pouchet to be the case with an American species of *Medicago*. Some of the seeds were completely disorganised by the boiling temperature, whilst a few remained intact, and it was these latter which were afterwards found to germinate. They had been protected from the influence of the hot water by their very dry and hardened coats. On this subject Prof. Jeffries Wyman says:—' Water penetrates the seeds of many plants, and especially of some of the *Legu-*

these had been made the subjects of special and direct experimentation. And, amongst all the diversity of form presented by the lowest living things, there is so much of uniformity in property—living matter, as we know it, agrees in so many of its fundamental characters —that biologists and chemists alike may feel a reasonable assurance as to the probable universality of any such rule which has been proved to hold good for a very large number of organisms, more especially when, amongst this large number of cases, no exceptions have been encountered.

Practically, however, it will be found that, in order to appreciate the bearings of the experiments which we shall have to relate, it will be necessary for us more especially to know what are the limits of vital resistance to high temperatures possessed by *spores* of

minosa, very slowly; in the case of those of *Gleditchia* and *Laburnum*, we have found several days and even weeks necessary for the complete penetration of cold water, though when the water is hot it penetrates much more readily. If, therefore, the seeds are dry when immersed, and are boiled for a few minutes only, they may still germinate. If they are moistened beforehand, the action of boiling water has been found uniformly fatal. In one of our experiments, twenty-eight seeds of *Gleditchia* were soaked until their coverings became soft and swollen; one-half were planted at once, and the others after having been boiled five minutes. None of the boiled ones germinated, while the others did. Similar experiments with beans and with several other kinds of seeds ended in a similar manner.' (*Amer. Journal of Science and Art*, Sept. 1867.) All the organisms in which we are interested, at present, however, have no such protection. These are mere specks or masses of protoplasm, which are either naked, or provided only with thin coverings.

Fungi on the one hand, and by *Bacteria* and *Vibriones* on the other.

I am not aware of any experiments tending to show that *spores* of Fungi can survive after exposure for even a few seconds in fluids raised to the temperature of boiling water (100° C); whilst, on the other hand, there is the concurrent testimony of many observers to the fact that, after such exposure, germination would never take place because the spores were no longer living[1]. This was the result obtained in many experiments made by Bulliard, and related in his 'Histoire des Champignons.' Mere contact with boiling water was found sufficient to prevent germination; and M. Hoffmann[2] similarly ascertained that an exposure for from four to ten seconds to the influence of boiling water sufficed to prevent the germination of all the *Fungus* spores with which he experimented. The experience of other observers has been similar to that above quoted, and amongst these we may cite M. Pasteur himself. Speaking of his experiments with boiled milk in Schwann's apparatus, M. Pasteur says[3]:—'Je n'ai jamais vu se former, dans le lait ainsi traité autre chose que des Vibrions et des Bacteriums, *aucune Mucédinée, aucune*

---

[1] I have lately been informed, however, by Mr Lowne, that he has seen a minute fungus continue to grow, notwithstanding an immersion in boiling water for two or three minutes. So far as I know, this is an altogether unique observation which stands in need of confirmation.

[2] 'Bullet. de la Soc. Bot.' t. viii. p. 803.

[3] 'Annal. de Chim. et de Physique,' 1861, p. 60.

Torulacée, aucun ferment vegetal. Il n'ya pas de doute que cela tient à ce que les germes de ces dernières productions, ne peuvent résister à 100°C au sein de l'eau, ce que j'ai d'ailleurs constaté par des expériences directes.' Professor Wyman says[1]:—' We have tried many experiments upon different kinds of moulds and yeast plants, and have found, as nearly all observers have, that they perish at 212° F.' The observations of Baron Liebig tend to show that they are killed in fluids at a temperature even much below this; he says[2]:—' A temperature of 60° C (140° F) kills the yeast cells; after exposure to this temperature in water they no longer undergo fermentation, and do not cause fermentation in a sugar solution. . . . In like manner, active fermentation in a saccharine liquid is stopped when the liquid is heated to 60°C, and it does not recommence again on cooling the liquid.'

The evidence which we at present possess concerning the tenacity of Life displayed by *Bacteria* and *Vibriones* in fluids whose temperature has been raised, is just as decisive as that concerning the spores of fungi. M. Pouchet's observations led him to believe that *Vibriones*, in common with all the varieties of ciliated infusoria, are killed by raising the temperature of the fluid which contains them to 55°C; M. Victor Meunier also

---

[1] 'Observations and Experiments on Living Organisms in Heated Water,' loc. cit.

[2] Translation of a paper on 'Alcoholic Fermentation,' in 'Pharmaceutical Journal,' July 30, 1870, p. 81.

believed that none of these organisms survived after they had been similarly subjected to a temperature of 60°C; whilst Prof. Wyman, as a result of many experiments, always found that their movements entirely ceased after an exposure for a few minutes in fluids raised to a temperature of 54°–56°C (130°–134°F). There is also every reason to believe, as I shall presently attempt to show, that an exposure to similar conditions kills *Bacteria* as well as their less developed representatives—the primordial plastide-particles.

With reference to *Bacteria*, however, one caution is necessary to be borne in mind by the experimenter. Their movements which they display may be, and very frequently are, of two kinds. The one variety differs in no appreciable manner from the mere molecular or Brownian movement, which may be witnessed in similarly minute not-living particles immersed in fluids; whilst the other seems to be purely vital—dependent that is upon their properties as living things. These vital movements are altogether different from the mere dancing oscillations which not-living particles display: as may be seen when even the most minute *Bacterium* darts about over comparatively large areas, so as frequently to disappear from the field of the microscope. After an infusion which contains organisms exhibiting these unmistakeably vital movements has been boiled for a second or two, I have invariably found that such movements no longer occur, though almost all the plastide-particles and *Bacteria* may be seen to display the Brownian movement in a well-marked degree. They seem to be reduced by the shortest exposure to a temperature of 212°F to the condition of mere not-living particles, and then they become subjected to the unimpaired influence of the physical conditions which occasion these molecular movements[1].

In many cases, however, organisms that are truly

[1] This statement concerning the two kinds of movements of *Bacteria* and the power of boiling water to arrest only one of them, is almost word for word what appeared in 'Nature' (No. 35, p. 171), for June, 1870. I thought at the time that the statement was new in certain respects—at least I cannot refer to any similar statement in the writings of others previous to that time. I was somewhat surprised, therefore, on reading the quotation which is subjoined, to find that Prof. Huxley, on Sept. 13, 1870, mentioned such distinctions as though they were quite novel, and with the tacit suggestion that I was unaware of them. Speaking of Bacteria, he says,—' They have *two distinct kinds* of movements. The very smallest have merely a trembling movement: those which are elongated oscillate on a central point in their long axis rotating whilst in an oblique position. This is one kind of movement. The other kind of movement is a darting across the stage of the microscope, sometimes in a straight line, sometimes accompanied by oscillations, which gives a serpentine appearance to the moving Bacterium or chain of Bacteria, whence the name Vibrio. These two kinds of movement are not to be confounded. They must be explained as due to very different causes; and it seems to me that it is a confusion of these two which is at the bottom of the mistakes made in the assertions as to the survival of Bacteria, &c. after the application of very high temperatures.' Prof. Huxley goes on to say that the temperature of boiling water and other reagents which certainly destroy their life and abolish the last kind of movement, does not put an end to the former; and then adds—
' Do what you will, however, they retain their *tumbling* movement; and this is a very misleading phenomenon.' (*Quart. Jrnl. of Micros. Science*, October, 1870.) What follows is certainly a suggestion that I had been misled by these phenomena, apparently because I was unaware of the distinction then pointed out by Prof. Huxley.

living exhibit only very languid movements, which, as movements, are quite indistinguishable from those that the same *Bacteria* may display when they are really dead[1]. Because the movements, therefore, are of this doubtful character, some are apt, unfairly, to argue that the *Bacteria* which present them are not more living than are the minute particles of carbon obtained from the flame of a lamp when they exhibit similar movements. This, however, is a point of view which becomes obviously misleading if too much stress is laid upon it; and it is more especially so in this case, when it can be shown that *Bacteria* which display the most characteristic sign of vitality—viz. 'spontaneous' division or reproduction—at this time, almost always exhibit such mere languid movements. It should always be borne in mind, in fact, that mobility is not an essential characteristic of living *Bacteria*, whilst *the occurrence of the act of reproduction is the most indubitable sign of their life*; so that any *Bacteria* which are almost motionless, or which exhibit mere Brownian movements, *may* be living, whilst those which spontaneously divide and reproduce are certainly alive—whatever be the kind of movement which they present.

[1] Speaking of the organisms above mentioned, Prof. Wyman says:—'Under certain circumstances, all *signs* of life may cease, but the infusoria may still be alive. If, for example, they are developed in a sealed flask, as soon as the organic matter convertible into infusoria is exhausted, their activity ceases, and they remain dormant for many months; we have kept them in this way for a year; but if fresh material is supplied to them they at once resume their activity.' Loc. cit.

It may naturally be asked if there are any means of deciding whether *Bacteria*, that have been submitted to a given temperature, and which exhibit movements resembling those known as Brownian, are really dead or living. If the movements are primary, or dependent upon the inherent molecular activity of the organisms themselves, they ought, it might be argued, to continue when the molecules of the fluid are at rest; if, on the other hand, they are mere secondary or communicated movements, impressed upon the organisms as they would be upon any other similarly minute particles, by the molecular oscillations of the fluid in which they are contained, then the movements ought to grow less, and gradually cease, as the fluid approaches a state of molecular rest—if this be attainable. Following out this idea, some months ago, I first tested the correctness of the assumption by experimenting with fluids containing various kinds of not-living particles; such as carbon-particles from the flame of a lamp, or freshly precipitated baric sulphate. However perfect may have been the Brownian movements when portions of these fluids were first examined beneath a covering-glass, they always gradually diminished after the specimen had been mounted by surrounding the covering-glass with some cement or varnish. Thus prepared, no evaporation could take place from the thin film of fluid, and after one, three, four, or more hours—the slide remaining undisturbed—most of the particles had subsided, and were found to have come to a state of rest.

In order still further to test these views, I took an infusion of turnip, containing a multitude of *Bacteria*, whose movements were of the languid description, and divided it into two portions. One of these portions was boiled for about one minute, whilst the other was not interfered with. After the boiled solution had been cooled, a drop was taken from each and these were placed at some little distance from one another on the same glass-slip; covering-glasses half an inch in diameter were laid on, and the superfluous fluid from beneath each of them was removed by blotting-paper. When only the thinnest film of fluid was left, the covering-glasses were surrounded by a thick, quickly-drying cement [1]. Examined with the microscope immediately afterwards, it was generally found that the *Bacteria* which had been boiled presented a shrunken and shrivelled aspect—whilst some of them were more or less disintegrated—though, as far as movement was concerned, there was little to distinguish that which they manifested from the slight oscillations of their unboiled and plumper-looking relatives.

If the specimens were examined again after twenty-four or more hours, there was still very little difference perceptible between them as regards their movements. And the same was the case when the specimens were examined after a lapse of some days or weeks. One

---

[1] I always employ a solution of gum mastic and bismuth in chloroform. If a different varnish be employed, it is of course necessary to ascertain that its application is not injurious to the enclosed *Bacteria*.

important difference does, however, soon become obvious. The *Bacteria* which have not been boiled, undergo a most unmistakeable increase within their imprisoned habitat; whilst those which have been boiled, do not increase. The two films may be almost colourless at first (if the *Bacteria* are not very abundant), but after a few days, that composed of unboiled fluid begins to show an obvious and increasing cloudiness, which is never manifested by the other. Microscopical examination shows that this cloudiness is due to a proportionate increase in the number of *Bacteria*.

Is the continuance of the movements of the organisms which had been boiled attributable to their extreme lightness, and to the slight difference between their specific gravity and that of the fluid in which they are immersed? I soon became convinced that this was one, if not the chief reason, when I found that *Bacteria* which had been submitted to very much higher temperatures, behaved in precisely the same manner as those which had been merely boiled; and that other indubitably dead particles which chanced to have a similar specific lightness, also continued to exhibit their Brownian movements for days and weeks. This was the case more especially with the minute fat particles in a mounted specimen of boiled milk[1], and

[1] If an unboiled specimen of milk be mounted, a multiplication of living particles (spherical) takes place here and there amongst the fat globules, just as the multiplication of *Bacteria* occurs in a vegetable infusion. In a boiled specimen, however, no trace of such multiplication can be detected.

also with very minute particles which were gradually precipitated from a hay infusion that had been heated to 302°F for four hours[1]. Trials with many different substances, indeed, after a time convinced me that the most rapid cessation of Brownian movements in stationary films, occurred where the particles were relatively heavy or large; and that the duration of the movement was more and more prolonged, as the particles experimented with were lighter or more minute[2]. So that, when we have to do with *Bacteria*, the minute oil globules of milk, or with other similarly light particles, the movements continue for an indefinite time, and are, in part, mere exponents of the molecular unrest of the fluid. They are always capable of being increased or renewed by the incidence of heat or other disturbing agencies.

In respect of the movements which they may exhibit, therefore, really living, though languid, *Bacteria* cannot always be discriminated from dead *Bacteria*. Both may only display mere Brownian movements[3].

[1] Those of the light particles which come to rest, in such cases, are always in contact with one or other of the contiguous surfaces of glass.

[2] The specific gravity of the fluid being constant. Where this is dense or viscid, as with glycerine, Brownian movements do not occur at all.

[3] That absence of even customary movements is no certain indication of the non-existence of 'Life,' is admitted by most biologists. The Rev. M. J. Berkeley (*Cryptogamic Botany*, 1857, p. 92) says:—'It is curious in two such closely-allied algæ as *Vaucheria sessilis* and *V. clavata*, to find the fruit so very different. The spore of the former is perfectly inactive, while that of the latter revolves by means of delicate cilia covering its whole surface. It is clear, then, that we must not, in these lower cryptogams, attach too much importance to motion.'

Although the movements of *Bacteria* are, therefore, frequently of so extensive a nature as to render it not at all doubtful whether the organisms which display them are living, it becomes obvious that we ought not to rely too strongly upon the mere vibratory character of their movements, as evidence of the death of *Bacteria*. In the experiments which I am about to relate, we shall be able to pronounce that the *Bacteria* are living or dead, by reference to the continuance or cessation of a much more essentially vital characteristic. If *Bacteria* fail to multiply in a suitable fluid, and under suitable conditions, we have the best proof that can be obtained of their death.

Having made many experiments with solutions of ammonic tartrate and sodic phosphate, I have almost invariably observed that such solutions—when exposed to the air without having been boiled—become turbid in the course of a few days owing to the presence of myriads of *Bacteria* and *Vibriones*, with some *Torulæ*. These organisms seem to appear and multiply in such a solution almost as readily as they do in an organic infusion. On the other hand, having frequently boiled similar solutions, and closed the flasks during ebullition, I have invariably found, on subsequent examination of these fluids, that whatever else may have been met with, *Bacteria* and *Vibriones* were always absent. The difference was most notable, and it seemed only intelligible on the supposition that any living *Bacteria* or dead ferments which may have pre-existed in the solution, were deprived of their virtues by the preliminary boiling. These experiments also seemed to show that such solutions, after having been boiled, and shut up in hermetically-sealed flasks from which all air had been expelled, were quite incapable of giving birth to *Bacteria*. The unboiled fluid, exposed to the air, must have become turbid, either merely because it was capable of nourishing living *Bacteria* which it contained, or else because it was capable of evolving these *de novo*, under the influence of fermentative particles whose activity had not been destroyed by heat. Hence, in such a solution we have a fluid which is eminently suitable for testing the vital resistance of *Bacteria*,—one which, although quite capable of nourishing and favouring their reproduction, does not appear capable of evolving them, when, after previous ebullition, it is enclosed in airless and hermetically-sealed flasks.

Three flasks were, therefore, half filled with this solution[1]. The neck of the first (*a*) was allowed to remain open, and no addition was made to the fluid. To the second (*b*), after it had been boiled and had become cool, was added half a minim of a similar saline solution, which had been previously exposed to the air, and which was quite turbid with *Bacteria*, *Vibriones*, and *Torula*. From this flask—after its inoculation with the living organisms—the air was exhausted

[1] In the proportion of ten grains of neutral ammonic tartrate, with three grains of neutral sodic phosphate, to an ounce of distilled water.

by means of an air-pump, and its neck was hermetically sealed during the ebullition of the fluid, without the flask and its contents having been exposed to a heat of more than 90°F. The third flask (*c*) was similarly inoculated with living *Bacteria*, though its contents were boiled for ten minutes (at 212°F), and its neck was hermetically sealed during ebullition. The results were as follows:—the solution in the first flask (*a*), became turbid in four or five days; the solution in the second (*b*), became turbid after thirty-six hours; whilst that in the third flask (*c*), remained perfectly clear. This latter flask was opened on the twelfth day, whilst its contents were still clear, and on microscopical examination of the fluid no living *Bacteria* were to be found. This particular experiment was repeated three times, with similarly negative results, although on two occasions the fluid was only boiled for one instead of ten minutes.

It seemed, moreover, that by having recourse to experiments of the same kind, the exact degree of heat which is fatal to *Bacteria* and *Torulæ* might be ascertained. I accordingly endeavoured to determine this point. Portions of the same saline solution, after having been boiled [1] and then cooled, were similarly inoculated

[1] It was necessary to boil the solution first, in order to destroy any living things or dead ferments which it might contain. As before stated, it must contain one or the other of these, because an unboiled solution of this kind, in a corked bottle about half full, will always become turbid; whilst, after it has been boiled, it may be kept indefinitely under similar conditions without becoming turbid.

with a drop[1] of very turbid fluid, containing hundreds of living *Bacteria, Vibriones,* and *Torulæ*. A drying apparatus was fixed to an air-pump, and the flask containing the inoculated fluid was securely connected with the former by means of a piece of tight india-rubber tubing[2], after its neck had been drawn out and narrowed, at about two inches from the extremity. The flask containing the inoculated fluid was then allowed to dip into a beaker holding water at 122°F, in which a thermometer was immersed. The temperature of the fluid was maintained at this point for fifteen minutes[3], by means of a spirit-lamp beneath the beaker. The air was then exhausted from the flask by means of the pump, till the fluid began to boil; ebullition was allowed to continue for a minute or two, so as to expel as much air as possible from the flask, and then, during its continuance, the narrowed neck of the flask was hermetically sealed by means of a spirit-lamp flame and a blow-pipe. Other flasks were similarly prepared, except that they were exposed to successively higher degrees of heat—the fluid being boiled off, in different cases, at temperatures of 131°, 140°, 149°, 158°, and 167°F. All the flasks being similarly inoculated with living

---

[1] The proportion was one drop of the fluid, opaque with organisms, to an ounce of the clear solution.

[2] Into which a piece of glass tube had been slipped to prevent collapse.

[3] Allowing even five minutes for the temperature of the 1 oz. of fluid to become equal to that of the bath, it would have remained exposed to this amount of heat for about ten minutes.

Bacteria, *Vibriones*, and *Torulæ*, and similarly scaled during ebullition, they differed from one another only in respect to the degree of heat to which they had been submitted. Their bulbs were subsequently placed in a water bath, which during both day and night was maintained at a temperature of from 85° to 95°F. The results have been as follows:—The flasks whose contents had been heated to 122° and 131°F respectively, began to exhibit a bluish tinge in the contained fluid after the first or second day; and after two or three more days, the fluid in each became quite turbid and opaque, owing to the presence and multiplication of myriads of *Bacteria*, *Vibriones*, and *Torulæ*; the fluids in the flasks, however, which had been exposed to the higher temperature of 140°, 149°, 158°, and 167°F, showed not the slightest trace of turbidity, and no diminution in the clearness of the fluid while they were kept under observation—that is, for a period of twelve or fourteen days.

The conditions under which these experiments were made being in every way similar, except as regards the degree of heat to which the inoculated fluids were subjected, and the organisms being immersed in a fluid, which had been proved to be eminently suitable for their growth and multiplication, it seems only possible to suppose that the difference in the results had to do with the difference in the degree of heat. If such inoculated fluids after having been raised to 122° and 131°F for ten minutes, are found in the course of a few days to become turbid, then, obviously, the organisms cannot have been killed by this degree of heat; whilst, if similar fluids, similarly inoculated, which have been raised to temperatures of 140°, 149°, 158°, and 167°F, remain sterile, such sterility can only be explained by the supposition that the inoculated organisms had been killed by exposure to these temperatures[1].

Some of these experiments have been repeated several times with the same results. On three occasions, I have found the fluid speedily become turbid which had only been exposed to 131°F for ten minutes, whilst on three other occasions I have found the inoculated fluid remain clear after it had been exposed to a heat of 140°F for ten minutes[2].

Wishing to ascertain what difference would be manifested if the inoculated fluids were exposed for a very long time, instead of for ten minutes only, to certain temperatures, I prepared three flasks in the same manner—each containing some of the previously boiled solution, which, when cold, had been inoculated

[1] More especially since the fluids which had remained sterile would always, in the course of thirty-six or forty-eight hours after inoculation with living *Bacteria*, show signs of an increasing turbidity.

[2] That the organisms in question—being minute portions of naked living matter—should be killed by exposure to the influence of a fluid at these temperatures, will perhaps not seem very improbable to those who have experienced its effects by attempting to keep their fingers for any length of time in water heated to a similar extent. With watch in hand I immersed my fingers in one of the experimental beakers containing water at 131°F. and found that in spite of my desires they were hastily withdrawn, after an exposure of less than *five-and-twenty seconds*.

with living *Bacteria, Vibriones,* and *Torulæ.* These flasks and their contents were then submitted to the influence of the following conditions:—One of them was heated for a few minutes in a beaker containing water at 113°F, and then by means of the air-pump a partial vacuum was procured, till the fluid began to boil. After the remainder of the air had been expelled by the ebullition of the fluid, the neck of the flask was hermetically sealed, and the flask itself was subsequently immersed in the water of the beaker, which was kept for four hours at a temperature between 113° and 118½°F [1]. The two other flasks similarly prepared were kept at a temperature of 118½°–127½°F for four hours. In two days, the fluid in the first flask became slightly turbid, whilst in two days more the turbidity was most marked. The fluids in the two other flasks, which had been exposed to the temperature of 118½°–127½°F for four hours, remained quite clear and unaltered during the twelve days in which they were kept in the warm bath under observation. These experiments seem to show, therefore, that the prolongation of the period of exposure from ten minutes to four hours suffices to lower the vital resistance to heat of *Bacteria* and *Torulæ* by 12½°–18°F.

Such experiments would seem to be most important and crucial in their nature. They may be considered to settle the question as to the vital resistance of these

---

[1] During nearly the whole of the time the temperature was kept at 113°F. It only rose to the higher temperature for about ten minutes.

particular *Bacteria*, whilst other evidence points conclusively in the direction that all *Bacteria*, whencesoever they have been derived, possess essentially similar vital endowments [1]. Seeing also that the solutions have been inoculated with a drop of a fluid in which *Bacteria*, *Vibriones*, and *Torulæ* are multiplying rapidly, we must suppose that they are multiplying in their accustomed manner—as much by the known method of fission as by any unknown and assumed method of reproduction. In such a fluid, at all events, there would be all the kinds of reproductive elements common to *Bacteria*, whether visible or invisible, and these would have been alike subjected to the influence of the same temperature. These experiments seem to show, therefore, that even if *Bacteria* do multiply by means of invisible gemmules as well as by the known process of fission,

[1] The *Bacteria* and *Vibriones* with which Prof. Wyman experimented were derived from different sources; and so far as I, also, have been able to ascertain, the *Bacteria* of different fluids are similarly affected by exposure to similar degrees of heat. Thus, if on the same slip, though under different covering glasses, specimens of a hay infusion, turbid with *Bacteria*, are mounted, (a) without being heated, (b) after the fluid has been raised to $122°$ F for ten minutes, and (c) after the fluid has been heated to $140°$ F for ten minutes, it will be found that, in the course of a few days, the *Bacteria* under a and b have notably increased in quantity, whilst those under c do not become more numerous, however long the slide is kept. Facts of the same kind are observable if a turnip infusion, containing living *Bacteria*, is experimented with; and the phenomena are in no way different if a solution of ammonic tartrate and sodic phosphate (containing *Bacteria*) be employed instead of one of these vegetable infusions. The multiplication of the *Bacteria* beneath the covering-glass, when it occurs, is soon rendered obvious, even to the naked eye, by the increasing cloudiness of the film.

such invisible particles possess no higher power of resisting the destructive influence of heat than the parent *Bacteria* themselves possess—a result which is by no means surprising when we consider that these gemmules, however minute, could only be portions of a similar homogeneous living matter, and ought therefore to be endowed with like properties.

The results just recorded seem all the more trustworthy also, because they are confirmed by the experiments of M. Pouchet[1], myself, and others, upon the degree of 'vital resistance' to heat manifested by rather higher organisms, which, on account of their very much greater size and other peculiarities, easily enable the microscopist to decide whether they are living or dead. My observations accord very closely with those of M. Pouchet; and I have found that an exposure to a temperature of 131°F for five minutes always suffices to destroy all reliable signs of life in Amœbæ, Monads, Chlamydomonads, Euglenæ, Desmids, Vorticellæ, and all other Ciliated Infusoria which were observed, as well as in free Nematoids, Rotifers, and other organisms contained in the fluids which had been heated[2].

---

[1] 'Nouvelles Expériences,' &c. 1864, p. 38.

[2] In opposition to all this concurrent testimony as to the influence of comparatively low temperatures upon the lower forms of life, Mr. Samuelson (*Quarterly Journal of Science*, Oct. 1870, p. 490) desires to impress us with the idea that they are capable of resisting a very high degree of heat. The evidence which he adduces, however, is quite inadequate to establish the truth of such a conclusion. Having heated

Such is the evidence concerning the power of resisting the destructive influence of heat, manifested by the organisms about which we are at present most

some 'dry dust in an open tube to 480°C' (the mode of estimating the heat not being stated), after it had cooled distilled water was added and the mixture was boiled for a few minutes. The tube containing this was closed with a stopper of cotton wool, and then, on the same evening, again opened to the air, whilst some of the fluid was poured into another tube which was afterwards plugged with cotton wool. The effect of the high temperature was thus cancelled by the subsequent addition of distilled water; and the effects of the boiling of this mixture 'for a few minutes' was subsequently rendered nugatory, so far as all strict experimentation is concerned, by its exposure to the air whilst it was poured into the new vessel. Such evidence is wholly inconclusive and even inadmissible. What has lately been honoured by admission, in detail, into a recent number of the 'Proceedings of the Royal Society' (vol. xix. No. 128), is not much more cogent in its nature. In a paper on the 'Action of Heat on Protoplasmic Life,' Dr. Crace-Calvert asserts that certain 'black Vibrios,' not commonly known to naturalists, and other ordinary Vibrios, are capable of resisting the influence of fluids heated to 300° F for half an hour. The conclusion that the organisms were living or dead in the several experiments, was based apparently upon the mere presence or absence of slight movements of a non-progressive nature, whilst no details are given as to the conditions of observation. In opposition to the statements and experiments of Dr. Crace-Calvert, it may be well to call his attention to the fact (of which he is apparently unaware) that MM. Milne-Edwards, Claude Bernard, Pasteur, Professor Huxley, and many others who cannot be ranged in the category of 'investigators of germ-life who favour the theory of spontaneous generation,' have most deliberately given their assent, based upon experiment and observation, to the view that the lowest forms of life are killed by contact for a very short period with boiling water. The truth of this conclusion has been again, of late, ratified by Dr. Burdon Sanderson—as I ascertain from a revise (with which he has kindly furnished me) of a paper entitled 'Further Report of Researches concerning Contagion,' shortly to appear in the Thirteenth Report of the Medical Officer of the Privy Council.

interested. It will be found quite harmonious with our ordinary every-day experience, and should, therefore, not be very difficult for us to believe [1]. An embryo of one of

[1] It is, moreover, not in the least at variance, as some seem to suppose, with the facts at present known concerning the power which some individuals have displayed of braving the influence of hot *dry air* for very short periods, either for the purposes of experiment or in Turkish baths. When such comparisons are made, two points—frequently lost sight of—should always be borne in mind. In the first place, there is a very great difference between the destructive influence of hot *dry air* and hot *water*; and in the second place, highly organized warm-blooded vertebrate animals are protected, as it were, from the destructive influence of hot *dry air*, for short periods, by certain counteracting phenomena produced by the heat itself. On this subject, in one of our recent and most valuable text-books on Physiology, Prof. Marshall says:—'The chief means of maintaining the normal temperature of the body, in hot climates, consists in a large increase in the amount of the water exhaled from the surface of the lungs and of the skin, especially, however, from the latter. The skin becomes bathed with fluid, the evaporation of which at the high temperature of the surface and of the surrounding air, occasions a loss of heat and a reduction in the temperature of the evaporating surface. The effect in reducing the temperature of the body is greater if the atmosphere be dry as well as warm, and then also if it be in motion: these conditions favour cutaneous exhalation and evaporation. . . . The increased perspiration excited by the great heat of the skin, furnishes, for a certain time, sufficient material for evaporation. There is a limit, however, to the amount of this excretion, and also to its rapidity of evaporation; for, when the surrounding air becomes moist, a check being put to the evaporation, the body is no longer thus defended, and its temperature begins to rise. Thus in a room, the temperature of which was 260° F, and the air dry, it was found possible to remain for eight minutes, by which time the body was not much altered in temperature, although the clothes and other articles in the room became very hot (Blagden and Banks). A case is on record of a person remaining ten minutes in a dry hot-air bath at 284°; whilst Chabert, the so-called fire-king, went into ovens heated from 400° to 600°; but, of course, for a much

the higher animals whilst still contained within its egg may fairly enough be compared with the lower organisms of which we have been speaking, in respect to the quality of the matter of which they are composed; and knowing the profoundly modifying influence of water at a temperature of 212°F upon the comparatively undifferentiated matter of the embryo in the egg—and also, we may add, even upon the differentiated tissues of the parent fish or fowl—need we wonder much that the same temperature should have been hitherto found to be destructive to the simple and naked living matter entering into the composition of *Bacteria* and *Vibriones*, and to the almost naked living matter of *Fungus*-spores? If any other result had been ascertained, would there

shorter period. Many workmen employed in foundries and glass-works also withstand very high temperatures, the skin being profusely bathed with perspiration; these men of necessity drink large quantities of fluid. When, however, the air is moist as well as hot, the temperature that can be endured is much less; for, in a vapour bath, at a temperature of only 120°, the body rapidly gains heat, as much as 70° in ten minutes, and a feeling of great and insupportable discomfort is experienced (Berger and De la Roche). It is said, however, that from habit the Finns can withstand, for upwards of half an hour, moist air or vapour baths gradually raised to 158°, or even to 167°.' (*Outlines of Physiology, Human and Comparative*, 1867, vol. ii. p. 511.) As soon, indeed, as the temperature of the warm-blooded animal, as a whole, is raised to 110°–112°F, it speedily dies; the length of time, therefore, which it can bear exposure to higher temperatures is almost wholly dependent upon the freedom and rapidity with which evaporation of its fluids takes place. Minute particles or specks of naked living matter cannot avail themselves of such antagonising influences, and even if they had any self-protecting resources of this kind, they would be of little or no service in an atmosphere saturated with hot vapour, and of still less avail when the living particles were immersed in heated fluids.

not have been much more reason for surprise? We ought therefore to be very cautious how we attempt to set aside the conclusions which have been arrived at on this subject—founded as they have been upon direct evidence of a most positive character.

From this basis we may now proceed to enquire into the nature and results of the experiments which have been instituted with the view of throwing light upon the origin of *Bacteria* and other similarly low organisms.

The method of experimentation principally relied upon since 1837 has been that introduced by Schwann[1]. His experiments have been occasionally repeated with some slight modification, whilst at other times he has been exactly followed. In the latter case the solution of organic matter is boiled in a flask, the neck of which is securely connected with a tube closely packed with portions of red-hot pumice-stone, or other incombustible substance; and after the solution has been boiled for some time, so that all the air of the flask has been expelled, the flask itself is allowed to cool—whilst the tube containing the closely-packed red-hot materials is still maintained at the same temperature, in order that whatever air enters into the flask may be subjected to a calcining heat as it passes through the tube. When the flask has become cool, its neck is hermetically sealed by the blow-pipe flame, so that it will then contain only the previously boiled solution in contact with air (at ordinary atmospheric pressure) which has been calcined.

---

[1] 'Annales de Poggendorf,' 1837, p. 184. 'Isis,' 1837, p. 523.

Since it has been thoroughly settled that all the lower organisms which may be contained in the organic solutions are killed when the fluids are raised to a temperature of 212°F, and that no organisms have been known to survive after having remained for thirty minutes in air raised to a temperature of 266°F (130°C), the boiling of the fluid for a time and the calcination of the air has generally been supposed to be a sufficient precaution to ensure the destruction of all organisms in the experimental media[1]. Experiments conducted in this way have yielded negative results to some investigators, though many others have always maintained that in spite of such precautions—calculated to destroy all pre-existing living things—they have, after a time, seen multitudes of low organisms in their experimental fluids immediately after the flasks have been broken.

Negative results in these experiments can of course prove little or nothing; they may be explained equally well by either side: either no organisms have been found, because they or all the germs which could give rise to them have been killed; or, as it is just as fair for the evolutionists to say, the absence of organisms can be explained on the supposition, that the fluids employed have not yielded them because of the severely destruc-

[1] The sides of the vessel itself, above the level of the fluid, would, during the whole time, be bathed by the steam given off from the boiling fluid, even if they did not come in contact with it during the process of ebullition, so that any adherent germs would in this way be destroyed.

tive influences to which the particular organic matter had been subjected by the previous boiling of the fluids. When organisms *are* found, however, in solutions which have been legitimately subjected to the conditions involved in Schwann's experiments, then one of two things is proven: either the amount of heat which was hitherto deemed adequate to destroy all pre-existing organisms is in reality not sufficient, or else the organisms found must have been evolved *de novo*, as the evolutionists suppose. Unless, therefore, the standard of vital resistance to heat can be shown to be higher than it was formerly supposed to be, any single positive result when Schwann's experiment has been legitimately performed, is of far more importance towards the settlement of the question in dispute than five hundred negative results. It would tend to show that in the particular fluid employed, organisms might be evolved *de novo*.

The experiments of Schwann have been commonly believed by many to be altogether in favour of the views of the panspermatists. Those who read his memoir will find, however, that he did not fail to obtain living organisms in *all* his experimental fluids. When the fluids were such as were capable of undergoing the alcoholic fermentation on exposure to the air, living organisms were, in spite of all precautions, sometimes found within his flasks. And although many other investigators had subsequently obtained living things, even when other infusions were employed, M. Pasteur was quite inclined to believe for a time, on the strength of his own experiments, that Schwann's precautions, properly carried out, were adequate to prevent the occurrence of organisms in the experimental fluids. These early investigations were made with sweetened yeast-water, concerning which M. Pasteur says[1], 'I have certainly had occasion to repeat the experiment more than fifty times, and in no case has this fluid, otherwise so changeable, shown a vestige of organism when in the presence of calcined air.' But after a time M. Pasteur began to employ an entirely different fluid, and in all these experiments living organisms were invariably present in the previously boiled fluids from recently opened flasks. Formerly he used 'l'eau de levûre sucrée,' but now he employed milk—a complex and highly nutritive fluid. There was no necessary contradiction in these results. Facts which had been thoroughly established with regard to the one fluid might not necessarily hold good for the other. A consideration so obvious as this ought to have been entertained by any unbiassed experimenter, but it was not even hinted at by M. Pasteur. As on other occasions, when his experiments admitted of two interpretations, M. Pasteur spoke only of one. He completely ignored an equally possible interpretation—the very existence of which he left his readers to ascertain for themselves. Thus, speaking of his experiments with boiled milk and calcined air in closed vessels, he

[1] Loc. cit., p. 36, note (1).

says[1]:—'Je n'ai jamais vu se former dans le lait ainsi traité autre chose que des Vibrions, et des Bacteriums, aucune Mucédinée aucune Torulacée aucun ferment végétal. Il n'y a pas de doute que cela tient à ce que les germes de ces dernières productions ne peuvent résister à 100° au sein de l'eau, ce que j'ai d'ailleurs constaté par des expériences directes. Et de même nous allons reconnaitre que, *si le lait se putréfie dans les circonstances précédentes, c'est que les germes des Infusoires dont nous venons de parler peuvent résister à la température humide de* 100°, *lorsque le liquide où on les chauffe jouit de certains propriétés.*' But the passage which I have placed in italics has not been demonstrated by any direct evidence: it is in fact entirely opposed to all such evidence [2].

[1] Loc. cit., p. 60.
[2] Prof. Jeffries Wyman very aptly says (American Jour. of Science and Arts, vol. xliv. Sept. 1867):—'The study of organisms living in thermal springs is of great importance in connection with the investigation of the limits of vital resistance. Having become adapted through a long series of years to their surroundings, such organisms may be supposed to live under circumstances the most favourable possible for sustaining life at a high temperature. It is a well-known physiological fact that living beings may be slowly transferred to new and widely different conditions without injury; but if the same change is suddenly made they perish.' Even in these most favourable cases, however, no living things have ever been found in springs at the temperature of boiling water, though certain *Conferva* were found by M. Descloizeaux in a hot spring in Iceland which was registered at 208° F. No more extreme case than this can, I believe, be quoted. As Prof. Wyman points out, however, the question which it concerns us to settle is, at what temperature the organisms met with in our infusions perish—these being accustomed to live at ordinary atmospheric temperatures, and not being steeled against the action of heat by long custom and habit.

He came to the conclusion that if fluids with an alkaline reaction were raised to the temperature of boiling water, the organisms contained in them were not all destroyed, because such fluids were subsequently found by him to yield living things when experimented with in the manner adopted by Schwann; and similarly he believed that the organisms in these fluids were destroyed when the fluids had been raised for however short a time to a temperature of 110° C (230° F), because after such treatment no organisms were to be met with in the flasks to which calcined air alone had been admitted.

The conclusions drawn by M. Pasteur from his researches on the subject at present under discussion, may be summed up thus:—(1) When acid solutions of organic matter are employed, no living things are to be met with in repeating Schwann's experiments, because all pre-existing organisms are destroyed, and living things are believed to be incapable of arising *de novo*; but (2) when neutral or slightly alkaline solutions are made use of, organisms may be met with if such infusions are merely raised to the temperature of 100° C, though (3) they are never to be seen when similar infusions have been raised to a temperature of 110° C. On account of these supposed facts, and on the strength of a chain of indirect evidence, M. Pasteur assumes, that whilst *Bacteria* are destroyed in acid fluids at a temperature of 100° C, their hypothetical 'germs' are not destroyed in a neutral or slightly alkaline fluid at 100° C, though they do cease to live in such a fluid after it has been exposed to 110° C.

In the next chapter I shall endeavour to show how far the particular results of M. Pasteur's experiments are entitled to be taken as the basis for any general conclusions on the great question of the Origin of Life, and how far his assumptions were warrantable in the face of existing evidence.

CHAPTER IX.

THE EXPERIMENTAL PROOF. UNTENABILITY OF PASTEUR'S CONCLUSIONS.

Different results obtainable by Schwann's method of experimentation. M. Pasteur's conclusions. Presence of air in flasks not essential. Evolution *in vacuo* previously thought impossible. New method of experimentation. Results with acid infusions. Abundance of living organisms. Experiments with acid saline solutions. These not often yielding *Bacteria*, but rather *Torula* or *Fungi*.

M. Pasteur does not adequately consider the nature of the fluid employed. Thinks too exclusively about the germ-killing powers of acid or alkaline fluids. Pays no attention to opposing views. Negative results equally capable of explanation on either hypothesis. Importance of positive results. M. Pasteur not entitled to his conclusion about germs in alkaline solutions. His indirect evidence negatived by direct evidence. Other explanations more probable. Difference in degree of fermentability between acid and neutral states of same solution. Experiments in illustration. Differences seen with solutions fully exposed to air and germs. Similar in kind to those quoted by M. Pasteur. Fluids most favourable for growth also most favourable for evolution. Fertility of any given solution often in the inverse ratio to its acidity. Effect of acidity intensified by high temperatures. Improbability of M. Pasteur's explanations in face of these results.

THE experiments most frequently cited as adverse to the possibility of the *de novo* origination of living things, have been stated to be those of Schwann, or repetitions of them by other experimenters. And yet, as already mentioned, Schwann's results were by no means universally adverse to this possibility. Sometimes living organisms were met with in his flasks, when the fluids employed were such as underwent the vinous fermentation. Many other observers have also found organisms in fluids from hermetically-sealed flasks which had been strictly subjected to the conditions prescribed by Schwann; and that not unfrequently when the change which the fluid had undergone was of a putrefactive rather than of a fermentative character. Amongst those who have obtained these positive results may be named Mantegazza, Pouchet, Joly, Musset, Wyman, Bennett, Child, and others—including even Pasteur himself[1].

But, as soon as M. Pasteur discovered that organisms were undoubtedly to be met with under these conditions, and irrespective of the limitations established by Schwann, he sought to include all such exceptional cases under a new general rule. After further experiments he came to the conclusion that living organisms might be encountered in almost any suitable neutral or slightly alkaline solution, which had been submitted to Schwann's conditions, though, on the contrary, they were not to be met with when the solutions employed had an acid reaction. This rule was represented by M. Pasteur to be absolute. And, although the results of

[1] As it would be impossible to give any adequate account of all these valuable experiments, we must refer the reader to the works, already cited, in which they are detailed.

the investigators above mentioned did not permit them to come to a similar conclusion, still M. Pasteur's reputation as an exact and brilliant experimenter has been all-powerful, and the majority of readers have, apparently, been only too willing to believe implicitly in conclusions which they may have found to be compatible with their own theories or prejudices. They have not hesitated to explain away results of a contradictory nature, on the ground that those who made the experiments had not taken sufficient care to perform them in a thoroughly stringent manner, or else on the supposition that the organisms which they had found in their experimental fluids were not living. 'Was it certain that the flasks had been hermetically sealed? Had the air been sufficiently calcined? Were the organisms which had been seen really alive?' Such were the questions and doubts that were continually addressed to persons who chanced to get results at all different from those of M. Pasteur. His experiments and reasonings have again and again been quoted as alike unanswerable. Nevertheless, I hope to be able to show that his conclusions are rendered untenable in the face of further experiments, and that M. Pasteur was not even entitled to draw the conclusions which he did draw from his own experiments. Assumptions have occasionally been inserted, in his chain of reasoning, as though they were established facts, and his whole argument has, therefore, been rendered weak and vulnerable.

Although the presence of air within the closed flasks has generally been considered essential, still it had been shown by Fray[1], even before the time of Schwann, that atmospheric air might be replaced by other gases, such as hydrogen or nitrogen, and that even then (with the method of closing the vessels at the time in vogue) living organisms were subsequently to be met with in the infusions. More recently Prof. Mantegazza[2] and M. Pouchet[3] showed that oxygen gas might be successfully substituted for atmospheric air, in experiments which in other respects complied with Schwann's conditions; whilst Dr. Child[4] has also shown that organisms are to be met with when either oxygen or nitrogen is substituted for atmospheric air in similar experiments. He failed to get any positive results, however, in the presence of carbonic acid or hydrogen gases.

On the other hand, it was thought by Burdach[5] that organisms were not procurable unless the hermetically-sealed flasks contained a certain amount of air. He says :—'Gruithuisen discovered that infusions, otherwise very prolific (those of hay, for example), did not yield infusoria in glass vessels in which the stopper touched the surface of the fluid.' In a comparatively

[1] 'Essai sur l'origine des corps organisés et inorganisés.' Paris, 1821, pp. 5-8.
[2] 'Giornale. dell. R. Istituto Lombardo,' t. iii., 1851.
[3] 'Compt. Rend.' (1858), t. xlvii.
[4] 'Essays on Physiol. Subjects,' 2nd ed., 1869, p. 114.
[5] 'Traité de Physiologie' (Transl. by Jourdan), 1837, L. I p. 16.

recent paper by Prof. Wyman[1], also, in giving an account of experiments which were more than usually productive, he says, 'The amount of infusion used was from one-twentieth to one-thirtieth of the whole capacity of the flask;' the object of employing this comparatively small quantity of fluid being, as he adds, 'to have the materials exposed to as large a quantity of air as possible.' These facts and reasonings were consistent enough with the view that putrefactive and fermentative changes were incited in the organic fluids under the influence of the oxygen in the air above them[2]: and this has been the doctrine most in vogue amongst those who have believed in the possibility of the *de novo* origination of living things.

It had been stated by Spallanzani that whilst organisms were procurable from hermetically-sealed flasks in which the air was somewhat rarified, they were not to be met with when the rarefaction was extreme, or where a vacuum existed[3]. Although this was a conclusion which seemed to be generally accepted[4], still, on re-

---

[1] 'American Journal of Science,' vol. xxxiv., July, 1862.

[2] Thus Gerhardt says ('Chimie Organique,' 1856, t. iv. p. 537):—'Cet oxygène est en effet la cause première de tous les phénomènes de fermentation et de putréfaction.' Dr. Child's experiments, showing that organisms might be found even in presence of pure nitrogen gas, were made two or three years subsequently to those we are now alluding to by Prof. Wyman.

[3] See 'Obs. et exp. sur les Animalcules,' p. 140.

[4] M. Pouchet, for instance, rejected as preposterous the notion that organisms could be expected to occur under such conditions, in some experiments made by M. Milne-Edwards (see 'Nouvelles Experiments,'

flection, it appeared to me to be one which might very possibly be erroneous.

Putrefactive or fermentative changes might not always be initiated by contact of organic matter with oxygen or any other gas,—it might occasionally be dependent upon the inherent instability of the organic matter itself. Independently of the fact, therefore, that the sealing of the flask after all the air had been expelled and during ebullition of the fluid, was a much simpler process than having to admit calcined air and sealing the flask after it had cooled, it seemed likely that the presence of a vacuum might, for other reasons, sometimes prove to be a great advantage. It appeared quite possible that the diminution of pressure in the early stages of the experiment might favour the initiation of rearrangements amongst the molecules of the dissolved organic substances, whilst the absence of air might permit these changes to go much further than they could have done if calcined air had been present, because the vacuum would afford a space into which residual gases might collect without at once inducing an undue amount of pressure within the flask[1]. Ex-

---

1864. p. 12, note); whilst on another page he says:—'La présence de l'air paraît être l'une des conditions fondamentales de la fermentation. Plus il est abondant plus elle semble active. Si on le confine, ou s'il manque, cet acte chimique est paralysé ou absolument entravé.' (p. 156.)

[1] I was actually led to adopt this important modification, perhaps, by a mere chance. In the spring of last year Mr. Temple Orme, of University College, had kindly undertaken to perform some experiments with me bearing upon this subject. One day, however, he told me he

cessive pressure certainly does occur, and occasionally it has been so extreme as to cause a rupture of the vessel[1]. The tension within the flask was thought likely to be especially unfavourable to the occurrence of fermentation or putrefaction, since it had been experimentally proved by Mr. Sorby[2] that pressure does undoubtedly influence 'chemical changes taking place slowly,' and which are therefore 'probably due to weak or nearly counterbalanced affinities.' This influence of pressure in checking chemical change is more especially seen in cases where the chemical actions are accompanied by the evolution of a gas. So that, as Mr. Sorby adds, 'it may cause a compound to be permanent, which would otherwise be decomposed.' For these reasons I was led to adopt the following method of experimentation:—

After each flask had been thoroughly cleaned with

had boiled an infusion of hay for four hours, and had then hermetically sealed the neck of the flask whilst ebullition continued. In this way a more or less perfect vacuum was procured. This he did as a sort of tentative experiment; but it was then, on thinking over the subject, that I resolved to give the plan a thorough trial, as it appeared to me that by so doing I should be working under conditions which were most in accordance with the theory of evolution. I performed four experiments at that time in concert with Mr. Temple Orme, with hay infusions, which had been boiled for four hours, and had then been sealed up *in vacuo*. In each of these fluids, organisms were found after a comparatively short time. These were the first experiments performed under such conditions. In my subsequent work I have not had the benefit of Mr. Orme's personal assistance, although I have frequently profited by suggestions which he has made.

[1] 'Essays on Physiological Subjects,' 2nd ed., 1869, pp. 113, 114.
[2] Bakerian Lecture 'On the Direct Correlation of Mechanical and Chemical Forces.' (Proceed. of Royal Society, 1863, pp. 546 and 539.)

boiling water, three-fourths of it was filled with the fluid which was to be made the subject of experiment. With the aid of a small hand blow-pipe and the spirit-lamp flame, the neck of the flask[1], about three inches from its bulb, was then drawn out till it was less than a line in diameter. The neck having been cut across in this situation, the fluid within the flask was boiled continuously for a period of from ten to twenty minutes. At first, ebullition was allowed to take place rapidly (till some of the fluid itself frothed over) so as to procure the more thorough expulsion of the air; then the boiling was maintained for a time at medium violence over the flame of a spirit-lamp, whilst the greatly attenuated neck of the flask was heated in the flame of another spirit-lamp placed at a suitable elevation. The steam for a time poured out violently into the flame of the lamp; and whilst my assistant slightly moved the other lamp, so as to diminish still further the violence of the ebullition, I directed the blow-pipe flame upon the narrow neck of the flask, and sealed it hermetically. When the orifice was closed, the heat was immediately withdrawn from the body of the flask.

After a little practice I soon became able to procure in this way a tolerably perfect vacuum. Even though the vessels were so small, momentary ebullition could generally be renewed again and again for the space of

[1] They were generally small, capable of containing from three-quarters of an ounce to one ounce and a half of fluid.

five minutes after they had been hermetically sealed, by the mere application of one of my fingers, which had been dipped in cold water, to a portion of the glass above the level of the fluid. The water-hammer effect was also very obvious, in those which were tested in this fashion.

I believe that an almost perfect vacuum can be produced in this way. During the first violent ebullition the air is driven out of the flask by the fluid, and as ebullition is continuously kept up after this till the flask is hermetically sealed, there is always an outpouring of heated vapour, and no opportunity for re-ingress of air. But even, if in any given case, the vacuum should not prove to be absolute, it does not seem to me that there would be any material abatement from the severity of the conditions which strict experimentation would demand. If, on the one hand, absolutely the whole of the air had not been expelled from the flasks during the process of ebullition, what remained would necessarily be mixed up with a very much larger quantity of continually renewed steam, and the effect would probably be that any living things would be just as effectually and destructively heated in this as if they were lodged in the boiling solution itself; whilst if, on the other hand, the boiling had been arrested for one or two seconds before the complete closure of the almost capillary orifice at the mouth of the flask, and any air had entered, it would have had first to pass through the blow-pipe flame, and then through the white-hot capillary orifice—it would, in fact, have been calcined as in Schwann's experiment. The conditions of the experiment would thus have been no less severe, and the only effect would be that the vacuum (with which I prefer to work) would have been rendered by so much the less complete. These remarks are made with the view of meeting possible criticism. It should be remembered, however, that M. Pasteur always adopted this method when he wished to preserve solutions for a time *in vacuo* [1].

After the flasks had been prepared in the way above mentioned, they were kept in a warm place in which the temperature could be maintained at night. Some have been suspended in the air, whilst others have been immersed in a water-bath heated by a spirit-lamp. So far as I have been able to ascertain, the temperature to which they have been subjected has mostly ranged

---

[1] Whenever he desired to make comparative trials with the air of different localities, the solutions which had been prepared in this way were considered by him to be contained *in vacuo*. The necks of the flasks were broken in the several localities, in order that they might become filled with the ordinary air of the respective places. After this had been done the flasks were re-sealed and kept for future observation of their contained fluids. M. Pasteur, M. Pouchet, and others who adopted this method, carried away their experimental fluids *in vacuo*, during a two or three days' journey to the Alps or to the Pyrenees, and it never seemed to have occurred to either of them that evolutional changes might be taking place during the interval. M. Pasteur, in fact, habitually shut his eyes to all such possibilities; they did not come within the range of what he considered possible. Such thoughts might, however, have suggested themselves to M. Pouchet and others, had they not imagined that evolution *in vacuo* was an impossibility.

between 75°–86° F (23°–29°C), though occasionally it has been even higher than this. Sometimes the flasks have been exposed to the lower temperature and sometimes to the higher, and I suspect that a variation of this kind may perhaps be more favourable for the production of evolutional changes than maintenance at a constant temperature.

In detailing the results of the following experiments, I shall not enter into any minute description of the organisms found. The main object throughout has been to obtain evidence on the subject as to whether a *de novo* evolution of living things could or could not take place. Occasionally only small portions of the experimental fluids have been examined. If, for instance, what was found in the first few drops of the fluid left no doubt in my mind as to the nature and abundance of some living things contained therein, the remaining portions of the fluid were frequently not scrutinized.

Seeing that M. Pasteur and others admit that organisms are to be met with in neutral or slightly alkaline fluids, treated in the manner adopted by Schwann [1], I will only mention the fact that neutral solutions of hay, mutton, beef, and other substances have also readily yielded organisms in the course of a few days when treated in the manner just described. With respect to acid solutions, however, M. Pasteur's verdict

---

[1] M. Pasteur's explanation of this fact will be subsequently considered.

is different. 'These,' he says, 'are uniformly sterile; and the sterility is to be accounted for by the fact that all the lower organisms and their germs are destroyed in an acid fluid raised to the boiling point.'

The latter statement seems to be quite true; the former, however, is one which has been negatived by the experience of others, and which now may be shown to be altogether erroneous. Alterations in the nature of the fluid employed, or in the method of experimentation—either singly or in combination—easily show the untenability of M. Pasteur's conclusion with respect to the sterility of acid fluids.

A.—Experiments in which the fluids were raised to a temperature of $212°F$ for from 10 to 20 minutes, and in which the flasks were hermetically sealed whilst the fluids were still boiling.

SERIES a.—*Fluids employed being filtered infusions, containing organic matter in solution and having an acid reaction.*

Experiment 1. A closed flask containing a very strong infusion of hay (boiled for five minutes), to which had been added $\frac{1}{70}$th part of carbolic acid, was opened twelve days after it had been hermetically sealed.

The solution remained quite clear for the first four days, but on the fifth day a small quantity of a powdery sediment was observed, and also one small, grey, flake-like mass. On the seventh day more minute flakes were noticed, and also a slight general turbidity of the fluid. The turbidity and deposit having slightly increased, the flask was opened on the twelfth day. The vacuum was found to have been only very slightly impaired; and the reaction of the fluid was still very strongly acid.

On microscopical examination of some of the deposit there were found, amongst granular flakes and aggregations, a large number of *Torula* cells of most various shapes and sizes; also, in the midst of granule-heaps, many large, rounded or ovoidal, densely granular,

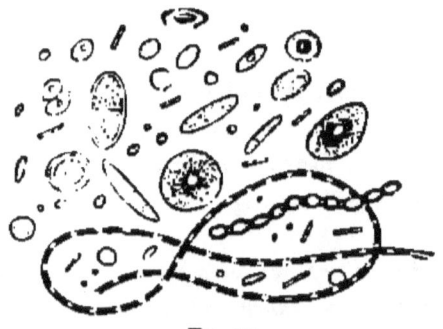

Fig. 23
Organisms found in an Infusion of Hay, plus one-twentieth part of Carbolic Acid. (× 850.)

nucleated bodies—whose average size was $\frac{1}{1800}''$ in diameter, though there were many much larger, and others even less than half this size. Intertwined amongst the granular matter also were a large number of algoid filaments $\frac{1}{70000}'$ in diameter, containing segmented protoplasmic contents. There were also in the fluid itself a number of medium-sized, unsegmented *Bacteria*, whose movements were somewhat languid [1].

Experiment 2. A closed flask containing a filtered infusion [2] of turnip, was opened five days after it had been hermetically sealed.

On the second day after the flask had been sealed, the previously clear solution began to exhibit a cloudy appearance. The next day a reticulated scum was seen on the surface of the fluid, which gradually became more manifest on the two following days. When the neck of the flask was opened, its contents were found to emit a most fœtid, sickly odour.

Microscopical examination revealed *Bacteria*, and a very large number of *Vibriones*—mostly without joints—some straight and others bent, some motionless and others exhibiting languid movements. These, mixed up with a thickly interlaced network of *Leptothrix*

---

[1] This experiment was one of a series of six, in which the same hay solution was employed (see Appendix C, pp. xlii-xlvi). A flask in which the hay solution had been boiled without any addition of carbolic acid, and which had been sealed after the solution had become cool and the flask was full of ordinary air, yielded no organisms.

[2] This and other infusions of a similar nature have been prepared by cutting a portion of white turnip into small thin slices, and then pouring warm water upon them (in a suitable vessel) up to rather above the level which they alone had reached. The infusions were then allowed to stand near a fire for three or four hours, so as to keep them at a temperature of from 110°-130° F. Nothing is easier than to obtain negative results in such experiments: it is only necessary to use weak infusions, more especially if, during their preparation, they have been kept for a prolonged period at a temperature near to that of boiling water, instead of at a heat which can be supported by the finger.

filaments, constituted the reticulated pellicle which was seen on the surface. The *Leptothrix* fibres were partly plain, and partly segmented; they presented—except in respect of their length—an appearance almost pre-

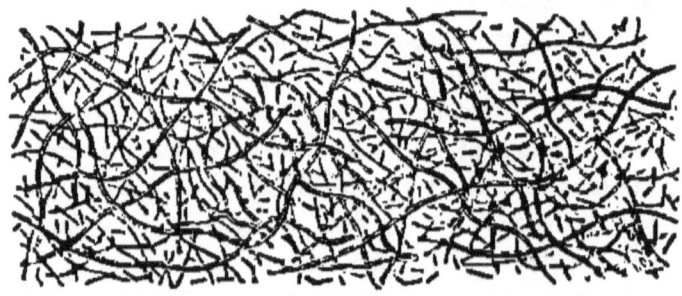

Fig. 24.

Bacteria, Vibriones, and *Leptothrix* filaments met with in a Turnip Infusion which had been only five days *in vacuo*. (× 800.)

cisely similar to the *Vibriones*. The long filaments seemed, in fact, to be only developed forms of the shorter rod-like bodies.

Experiment 3. A closed flask containing an infusion of turnip[1], was opened seventeen days after it had been hermetically sealed.

The fluid never exhibited any distinct turbidity, and no pellicle formed on the surface; there was, however, an irregular covering of the bottom of the flask by fine granular matter, with here and there a small patch of filamentous-looking substance. No bad odour was perceived when the flask was opened.

[1] See note 2, p. 357.

Unfortunately, just as I was proceeding to examine the contents microscopically, nearly all the fluid was lost, including the filamentous-looking masses. Examination of a few drops of the fluid which remained showed a very large number of plastide-particles and *Bacteria*.

Experiment 4. A closed flask containing an infusion of turnip was opened seven days after it had been hermetically sealed.

The solution itself was much clouded, and its surface was covered by a thick gelatinous pellicle.

On microscopical examination of the fluid it was found to contain a multitude of plastide-particles and very active *Bacteria*. The thick gelatinous pellicle was also made up of an aggregation of these in the usual transparent mucoid material. In very many situations this uniform pellicle was undergoing a process of *heterogenetic organization*, such as will be more fully described hereafter.

Experiment 5. A flask containing a very strong infusion of turnip was opened fifteen days after it had been hermetically sealed.

The solution itself was very cloudy, and there was on its surface a thick coriaceous sort of pellicle marked by more closely-set aggregations or islets of denser growth.

On microscopical examination the fluid was found to contain a multitude of plastide-particles and very active *Bacteria*. The *Bacteria* were almost more active than any I had before seen, and there were many different kinds.

Some exhibited rapid serpentine movements, accompanied by flexions of the two segments of which they are composed; whilst the movements of others were rapidly progressive in straight or curved lines.

The pellicle was made up mainly of simple *Leptothrix* filaments (mostly without joints or evidences of segmentation); and the thicker islets were found to be produced by a more luxuriant growth in these situations of densely interwoven filaments.

The pellicle was found to be so tough and elastic that some of it could only be mounted as a microscopical specimen after it had been compressed for an hour or two, by placing a small weight on the covering glass.

It would be useless to quote other experiments of the same kind, though many others have been made with similarly positive results. Those in which a hay infusion acidified by carbolic acid has been employed are most especially interesting. In no case has a properly prepared infusion of turnip failed to yield an abundance of living organisms in the course of from two to six days, although the reaction of the infusion has always been decidedly acid. A distinct pellicle, however, only forms occasionally. If a clear solution becomes turbid in a few days, with or without the formation of a thick pellicle, and if on microscopical examination the cause of the turbidity or the constituents of the pellicle have been found to be *Bacteria, Vibriones,* or *Leptothrix* filaments, no fair critic could reasonably object to the inference that the organisms found were living, simply because they only exhibited languid movements more or less indistinguishable from mere molecular or Brownian movements. The property of reproduction is a fundamental attribute of living things; the power of performing extensive movements is not. That reproduction has taken place must be obvious to all. How else could a clear fluid, within an hermetically-sealed vessel, become turbid owing to the presence of myriads of *Bacteria*? How else could a thick pellicle form on such a solution composed of densely interlaced *Bacteria*, *Vibriones*, and *Leptothrix* filaments? And, moreover, although in the fluid from some of the flasks the movements of the contained *Bacteria* were so languid as to be scarcely distinguishable from Brownian movements, in that of others (as, for instance, in Exps. 4 and 5) the movements were very active and unmistakeably vital. That the vessels were in no way cracked, and that the vacuum was in some cases still partially preserved, I have thoroughly satisfied myself[1]. For the rest, the

---

[1] This is easily done by carefully heating the end of the neck of the flask (before breaking it), and then softening it with the blow-pipe flame. The insinking of the softened glass is a sure sign that the vacuum is still more or less preserved. The amount of gas liberated in different cases varies very much. In many instances it is not sufficient to establish an equilibrium with the external atmospheric pressure, though occasionally (even when the fluids were originally contained *in vacuo*) the internal tension from liberated gases exceeds the external atmospheric pressure.

experiments can be easily repeated by any one who is desirous of seeing such results for himself.

In the next series of experiments, ammoniacal and other saline solutions have been employed. At present, we have to do with these simply as *acid* solutions in which living organisms have been procured. The presence of living organisms in such solutions, after ebullition and other proper precautions, being, in accordance with the admissions of M. Pasteur, only compatible with the *de novo* origination of those which first appear.

I was induced to employ saline solutions for various reasons. In the first place, after having read M. Pasteur's statements, concerning the growth and development of Fungi which had been *placed* in saline solutions[1], it occurred to me that it would be a subject of much interest to determine whether any evidence could be obtained, tending to show that organisms might even be evolved *de novo* in certain fluids of a similar character. This, in fact, seemed to be a problem of very great importance; for, if otherwise suitable, the employment of such saline solutions would be attended by certain advantages. It appeared likely that the saline materials in solution would be far less injured by the high temperature of 212°F than organic substances. We should thus, also, best prepare ourselves to be brought face to face with the problem—Whether the pre-existence of organic matter, which has been elabo-

[1] Loc. cit., p. 100.

rated in pre-existing organisms, is, at present, absolutely necessary for the *de novo* origination of living things; or whether, in fact, these may arise, more or less directly, by changes taking place in an aggregation of new-formed molecules of an organic type [1].

At present, however, no special precautions have been taken to ensure the purity of the chemical substances employed. These may, and sometimes did undoubtedly contain organic impurities, so that the following experiments are simply quoted as instances in which more or less *acid* fluids, containing at all events a very large proportion of saline ingredients, have proved productive of living organisms when treated in the way already described.

SERIES *b.*—*Saline Solutions having an acid reaction.*

Experiment 1. A closed flask containing a solution of ferric and ammonic citrate[2] in distilled water (gr. x. to ℥j.) was opened 29 days after it had been hermetically sealed.

A small amount of powder-like sediment had gradually collected at the bottom of the flask, though there was no general turbidity of the fluid. Before the flask was opened it was ascertained that the vacuum was still

---

[1] These having themselves arisen by the combination of some of the dissociated elements of the saline substances employed.

[2] Some of the purest that could be obtained, from Messrs. Hopkin and Williams.

partially preserved. The reaction of the fluid was found to remain slightly acid.

On microscopical examination of the sediment, *Bacteria* were found, having moderately active movements though they were not very numerous. There were many granular aggregations, from the midst of which were growing *Leptothrix* filaments, though the organisms

Fig. 25.

Torula, *Leptothrix*, and *Bacteria* found in simple Solution of Ferric and Ammonic Citrate. (x 800.)

which were most abundant were *Torula* cells of different sizes, many of which were provided with a segment across their short diameter, whilst each half contained a nuclear particle. These *Torula* cells had a uniform very faint greenish hue, and homogeneous contents. They often existed in groups of 12–20, or more.

Experiment 2. A closed flask containing a solution of ferric and ammonic citrate, together with a few minute fibres of deal wood (much less than half a grain), was opened 42 days after it had been hermetically sealed.

The fluid continued clear and there was no pellicle on the surface, though, after the first two weeks a slight deposit began to collect at the bottom of the flask, which slowly increased in quantity.

On opening the flask the reaction of the fluid was found to be still slightly acid; and on microscopical examination of the deposit several different kinds of organisms were discovered in and amongst the granular aggregations of which it was in great part composed. Many minute fragments of deal wood—dotted ducts, &c.—were also intermixed.

Amongst the organisms were perfectly-formed *Bacteria*, about $\frac{1}{7000}''$ in length, which were very numerous and *extremely active*; several long unsegmented *Leptothrix* filaments, $\frac{1}{15000}''$ in diameter; many oat-shaped *Torula* corpuscles, about $\frac{1}{1000}''$ in length; three or four spherical

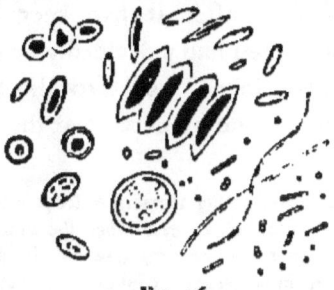

Fig. 26.

Bacteria, Leptothrix, Torulæ, and other organisms found in a Solution of Ferric and Ammonic Citrate, plus some minute fragments of deal wood. (× 800.)

or ovoid fungus-spores, each having a large central nucleus, and others rather smaller, having granules within instead of a distinct nucleus; also, partly imbedded in one of the granular aggregations was a distinct cellular body, $\frac{1}{1000}''$ in diameter, having a sharply-defined border and finely-granular contents, in the midst of which was a large nucleus. A thick hyaline capsule seemed to shut it off from the granular matrix in which it was imbedded. And, lastly, there were a number of bodies closely resembling one of the simplest kinds of Desmids. Some of them were single ovoidal bodies, about $\frac{1}{1000}''$ in length, consisting of an oat-shaped mass of faintly greenish protoplasm within a larger delicately hyaline envelope. Others were composite, and one mass was seen composed of four much larger segments[1].

Experiment 3. A closed flask containing a solution of potash-and-ammonia alum, and of tartar emetic[2], was opened 28 days after it had been hermetically sealed. The fluid then had a decidedly acid reaction.

The solution continued clear throughout; there was no trace of a pellicle and no deposit at the sides, though

---

[1] Organisms closely resembling these have frequently been met with in solutions similar to the above, even when the solutions have been exposed to much higher temperatures (see vol. ii. chap. x. *Exps.* 8, 9, 11 and 12). And in a flask containing an inoculated solution of ammonic tartrate and sodic phosphate, which had been heated to 140° F. and subsequently kept for eleven weeks, bodies somewhat similar were encountered. In this case, however, they were colourless, and were associated with a number of more ordinary-looking *Torula* cells. The green organisms of the iron solutions bear some resemblance to the Desmids of the genus *Arthrodesmus*, and to the Pediastrem of the genus *Scenodesmus*.

[2] The quantities were, unfortunately, not measured. The water used was not distilled, but was a pure drinkable water.

a whitish flocculent mass was seen at the bottom of the flask after the first fortnight, which gradually increased, and at last formed a mass about $\frac{1}{8}"$ in diameter.

On microscopical examination, the white mass was found to be made up of aggregations of colourless particles, varying much in size and shape, and imbedded (*b*) in a distinct hyaline jelly-like material. The granules were highly refractive, altogether irregular in shape, and they varied in size from $\frac{1}{3000}"$ to $\frac{1}{8000}"$ in diameter. Though most of them were

Fig. 27.

Fungus met with in a solution containing Potash-and-Ammonia Alum, with Tartar Emetic. (× 600.)

motionless and imbedded in the jelly, very many were seen exhibiting active and independent movements; some of these were in the form of little double spherules (*d*), and a very few others resembled *Bacteria* about $\frac{1}{8000}"$ in diameter, though they did not possess the accustomed joint.

Three fungus-spores with thick double walls were seen. Each of these was about $\frac{1}{3500}''$ in diameter. Within one of them there were only a number of granular particles (*c*), but within each of the other two there was a large and somewhat irregular nuclear mass.

In addition there was found the complete fungus which is represented in the figure (*a*), with all its spores, and in a portion of one of the granular aggregations, a mass of about thirty spores seemed to be undergoing evolution, by a differentiation of mucoid material through which some fine granules were disseminated.

Experiment 4. A closed flask containing a solution of neutral ammonic tartrate and neutral sodic phosphate[1] was opened on the 75th day after it had been sealed[2].

Before the opening of the flask it was ascertained[3] that the vacuum had been well preserved. The reaction of the fluid was still slightly acid. For a long time the contents of the flask seemed to remain unaltered, though for the last few weeks a very small amount of greyish deposit had collected at the bottom of the vessel.

When examined microscopically this deposit was found to be principally made up of amorphous granules,

---

[1] In the proportion of gr. xv. of the former to gr. v. of the latter in one ounce of distilled water.

[2] The flask having been kept during this time in a warm water-bath which was constantly maintained at a temperature of 95–90° F.

[3] By the inbending of the neck of the flask when heated. It had been kept with its neck immersed in the fluid, so that if this had become cracked the bath fluid would have been sucked into the flask.

colourless and irregular in size, amongst which were a number of minute *Torula*-cells, scattered here and there

Fig. 28.

Torula obtained from a Solution of Ammonic Tartrate and Sodic Phosphate. (× 800.)

both singly and in groups. No other kind of living thing was met with.

Some of this granular matter with *Torula* was mounted as a microscopical specimen, in a mixture of glycerine and carbolic acid (16 : 1), and in the course of two weeks it was found that the *Torula* had notably increased in size and in number beneath the cemented covering-glass.

Experiment 5. A flask containing a solution of ammonic tartrate and sodic phosphate was opened twenty days after it had been hermetically sealed. The reaction of the fluid was then decidedly acid.

The fluid itself showed no signs of turbidity, and there was no trace of scum on its surface. Small whitish flocculent shreds had, however, been seen at the bottom of the flask for the last twelve or fourteen days, during which time they seemed very slowly to increase in size. Some smaller sedimentary particles were also seen.

On microscopical examination, some of the white shreds were found to be composed of comparatively large masses of small, colourless, algoid filaments; whilst others were made up of aggregations of fungus-spores with an abundant mycelium which had been developed from them. The spores were rounded or oval, thick-walled bodies, varying very much in size. The largest of them were about $\frac{1}{1000}$" in diameter. Some of them were about to germinate, and these exhibited a rudimentary truncated outgrowth at one extremity [1], whilst others had germinated into a fungus of the *Penicillium* type. In one mass the mycelium had produced four or five much larger filaments, terminating in artichoke-like heads of different sizes, bearing naked spores [2]. All gradations in size

[1] Some of my critics speak of this as a 'hilum,' and look upon its presence as unmistakeable evidence that the spore came from a parent *Fungus*. At all events, such a 'hilum' is not presented by very many spores, and its absence from any of them does not seem reconcilable with this hypothesis. Other evidence shows unmistakeably that it is a rudimentary outgrowth, representing merely the first commencement of the mycelial filament which ultimately develops.

[2] Other critics seem to think it impossible that such heads of fructification could be developed in a fluid, and therefore express ominous doubts about my statements. Fungi of this type, however, were described several years ago by M. Pouchet (' Nouvelles Expériences,' Paris, 1864, p. 180), who says :—' Parmi les espèces submergées, celle à laquelle je donne le nom de *Penicillium submersum* est assurément la plus commune. Elle offre un mycélium à filaments très-fins, très long, rameux, articulés, fistuleux. Les pédicelles sont simples, excessivement grêles, articulés, long et offrent cinq à six cloisons. Le pinceau terminal est petit, peu rameux, et produit une énorme quantité de spores arrondies. . . . . Cette espèce n'est nullement décrite, ni dans les œuvres de Bulliard, ni dans celles de Paulet ou de Corda.'

and appearance existed between the algoid-looking filaments and those which were more obviously of a mycelial nature.

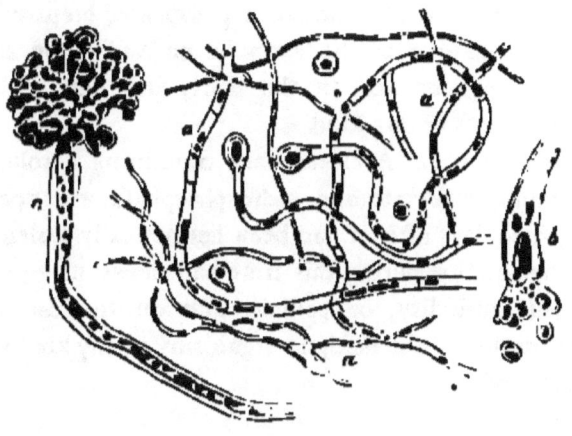

Fig. 19.

Fungus found in a Solution containing Ammonic Tartrate and So Phosphate. Transitions between small Conferva-like filaments and well-developed Mycelium. (× 600.)

A small number of granules and particles of various shapes were seen, though, as in the last solution, there was nothing resembling a *Bacterium*. Spherules which seemed to represent different stages in the development of the fungus-spores were met with, varying in size from that of an almost inappreciable speck to that of the perfect spore—which itself varied considerably in size even at the time that it began to germinate. In one of these fungus-spores which was about halfgrown, the nuclear particle within was seen actively moving from end to end of the cell.

Experiment 6. A flask containing a saturated solution of ammonic tartrate and sodic phosphate, prepared in the same manner as the last solution and at the same time, though opened on the thirty-fifth day, yielded no organisms of any kind.

Experiment 7. A closed flask containing a solution of ammonic acetate and sodic phosphate was opened forty-two days after it had been hermetically sealed.

The solution during this time had shown no signs of deposit, turbidity, or pellicle, and on microscopical examination of the fluid, no organisms of any kind were discovered.

All the fluids in the experiments hitherto related were subjected to a temperature of 212°F. It has been previously ascertained that none of the lower organisms which had been so treated and afterwards examined were able to survive an exposure for a few seconds to such a degree of heat. They had nearly all been destroyed, in fact, at a temperature many degrees short of this[1]. Many different kinds of organisms have been submitted to this test, and without the occurrence of any exceptions[2]

---

[1] See pp. 325-336.
[2] No exceptions, that is, amongst such organisms as are met with in infusions. The only known exceptions to that rule being met with in the case of seeds, naturally provided with a hard *testa*, which had undergone an extreme amount of desiccation (see p. 314, note 1).

such a degree of heat has always proved fatal to them. Looking therefore, on the one hand, at the uniformity in the experimental evidence, which has itself extended over a wide basis, and on the other, at the comparative uniformity in fundamental nature and property existing between all the lowest kinds of living things—which are almost wholly made up of a more or less naked living matter or protoplasm—it is only reasonable for us to conclude, until direct evidence can be adduced to the contrary, that that which holds good for the many without exception, may prove to be a rule of universal application. Therefore it was that the commission appointed by the Société de Biologie (and M. Pasteur himself for a long time) assumed that none of the lower kind of organisms could survive in a fluid which was raised to a temperature of 212°F.

No evidence has as yet been adduced which is capable of shaking the validity of this conclusion, so that the experiments just related afford strong evidence in favour of the view that the organisms found in my experimental fluids were there evolved *de novo*. Other experiments with negative results, in the face of these, cannot prove the impossibility of such a mode of evolution. And yet the experiments of Schwann and others were deemed by many to have conclusively upset the doctrines of the evolutionists. The particular fluids with which they experimented were only exposed to a temperature of 212°F, but they worked under a set of conditions which are considered by many to be particularly adverse to the occurrence of fermentation, so that they often found no organisms when their flasks were opened. But on subjecting other experimental fluids to the same temperature, though exposing them subsequently to quite different conditions—supposed by myself to be more favourable for the occurrence of fermentative changes —I do find organisms in the fluids when the flasks are opened.

It must then never be lost sight of that the negative results of Schwann, M. Pasteur, and others, may be only applicable to the particular fluids and the particular conditions under which they worked; but the multitudes of positive results legitimately obtained by myself and other experimenters, must have a most important bearing upon the settlement of the general doctrine.

As previously stated, M. Pasteur himself for a long time obtained only negative results in repeating the experiments of Schwann. In his earlier investigations he had generally made use of 'l'eau de levûre sucrée,' of urine, or of some other fluid which was naturally unfitted to undergo fermentative changes of marked intensity, or even to nourish the higher infusorial organisms [1]. But there came a time when M. Pasteur chanced

---

[1] Whether the organisms found in a given fluid have been actually produced therein, or have only undergone development in it, we may, for the sake of argument, measure the evolutional capacity of a fluid by the amount and kinds of organisms which are produced in a given quantity of it, in a definite time, and at a given temperature. We certainly must not judge of the evolutional qualities of a fluid by its mere tendency to emit a bad odour in a short space of time. A certain fluid

to repeat his experiments, using precisely the same precautions as before, and yet the results were quite different—organisms were now found in his solutions. There was one important difference, it is true. In these latter experiments, M. Pasteur had made use of milk. Now the quantity of organic matter contained in milk is, of course, very great; it is a highly nutritive and complex fluid. It might, therefore, and ought, perhaps, to have suggested itself to M. Pasteur that the different results of his later experiments were possibly explicable on the supposition that the restrictive conditions—the boiling of the solution, and the closed vessel already containing air—were too potent to be overcome by the organic matter in the one solution, whilst they were not too potent, and could not prevent fermentative changes taking place in that of the other.

—urine, for instance—judged by these qualities, may be disagreeably putrescible, though its evolutional tendencies may be quite low. By many experimenters this difference has not been appreciated, and they seem to imagine that in employing urine they make use of a fluid which is very favourable for such experiments—forgetting, apparently, that urine is an effete product containing comparatively stable compounds, which have already done their work in the body. It may after a short time swarm with *Bacteria*, and these may be followed by fungi; but there is no comparison even as to the actual quantity of these organisms, that may be developed in equal amounts of milk and urine respectively—when both are exposed to the air for the same time in similarly-shaped vessels, and under the same bell-jar. The milk soon becomes actually solid with fungus growths. M. Pasteur's 'l'eau de levûre sucrée,' by his own confession (loc. cit. note, p. 58), is never found to contain any of the higher ciliated infusoria, and though it produces fungi, they are met with in much smaller quantity than in an equal bulk of milk under similar conditions.

For if, in accordance with the belief of the evolutionists, different organic fluids have different initial tendencies to undergo fermentation (leading to the evolution of living things), it may be easily understood, that as the conditions favourable to fermentation are more and more restricted, certain of these fluids may altogether cease to undergo such changes, others may manifest them to a meagre extent, and others still, only a little more fully[1]. When subjected to a pressure of one atmosphere, do we not find that water boils at 212° F, alcohol at 173° F, and ether at 96° F? The restrictive condition, or atmospheric pressure, is here in each case the same, only, having to do with differently constituted fluids, it is natural enough to look for different results under the influence of like incident forces. Ether raised to a temperature of 100° F would rapidly disappear in the form of vapour, though no such result would follow the heating of water to the same extent. And similarly, whilst milk might be capable of yielding organisms in Schwann's apparatus, another fluid less rich in organic matter might fail to do so. It seems almost incredible that such considerations should not

[1] Referring to repetitions of Spallanzani's experiments made in concert with Prof. Oehl, Prof. Cantoni says (*Gaz. Med. Ital. Lombard.* t. i. 1869):—' E in fatto, preparando diversi palloni, egualmente scaldati a 100°, con sugo di carne a vario grado di diluzione, riconoscemmo che, mentre in alcune s' aveva un pronto e ricco sviluppo di infusorj, in altre esso era tardo e scarso, ed in altre ancora mancava affatto ancor dopo molti giorni dalla preparazione.' And even the strongest solution will yield similarly varying results, when exposed to successively lower atmospheric temperatures.

have suggested themselves to M. Pasteur; but yet we have no mention of them, or any evidence that they had been considered [1]. He explains the discrepancy between his earlier and his later experiments by reference to a completely different supposition, and, as on other occasions, he does not even suggest to the reader that any different explanation is possible from that which he adduces. He at once assumes that the *Bacteria* and *Vibriones* which were ultimately found in the milk used in these experiments had been derived from 'germs' of such organisms which either preexisted in, or had obtained access to this fluid before it had been heated, and also (contrary to the general rule which had been previously admitted) he assumed that such supposed preexisting germs were capable of resisting the influence of the heat which causes milk to boil. No direct proof of the latter assumption was ever attempted, though M. Pasteur did afterwards endeavour to bring the cases in which organisms were to be met with under a general law: he supposed that the results obtained were due to the absence of acidity in the fluids employed. Neutral or slightly alkaline fluids might yield positive results in repeating Schwann's experiments, because, as he alleged, the 'germs' of *Bacteria* and *Vibriones* were not destroyed by the temperature of 212°F in such fluids.

[1] The experiments and reasonings to which I now allude are detailed in pp. 58-66 of M. Pasteur's Memoir ('Ann. de Chim. et de Phys.' 1862).

Such was the very definite statement made by M. Pasteur on the faith of a chain of evidence of which almost every link is ambiguous. He did not even allude to the desirability of making direct observations upon this subject. They lend not the least support to his assumption, however; on the contrary, they go to confirm the rule which had hitherto been generally admitted, as to the inability of any of these lower organisms to live after an exposure for even a few seconds in a fluid raised to a temperature of 212° F. I have again and again boiled neutral and alkaline infusions containing very active *Bacteria* and *Vibriones*, and the result has always been a more or less complete disruption of the *Vibriones*, and the disappearance of all unmistakeable signs of life in the *Bacteria*[1]. All their peculiarly vital movements have at once ceased, and it has been shown by the evidence detailed in the last chapter, that these organisms and any 'germs,' visible or invisible[2], by which they multiply, have been really killed by an exposure to even a much lower degree of heat.

[1] The results with neutral hay infusions have not seemed to differ at all from those which were obtained with slightly acid turnip infusions, or solutions of ammonic tartrate and sodic phosphate. See p. 318 and p. 332, note 1. It seems a vague supposition to imagine that either *Bacteria* or *Vibriones* have germs which are in any way differently endowed from themselves. In common with other primitive living things, they are only known to multiply by *fission* or *gemmation*. The separated portions, however minute, would always resemble the parent structure, of which, indeed, they are unaltered fragments.

[2] See p. 332.

M. Pasteur approached the solution of the discrepancy in this way. His attention was arrested by the fact that milk was an alkaline fluid, because he afterwards ascertained that other alkaline fluids also yielded positive results when submitted to the conditions involved in Schwann's experiments. But having satisfied himself of this, it was necessary for M. Pasteur to offer some explanation, if he was not prepared to yield his assent to the doctrine which he had formerly rejected. He soon found, truly enough, that the mere alkalinity or acidity of the solution was a matter of great importance in these experiments; he ascertained, for instance, that his sweetened yeast-water, naturally a faintly acid fluid, was always unproductive when submitted to Schwann's conditions unaltered, though it was, on the contrary, always productive if it had previously been rendered neutral or slightly alkaline by the addition of a little carbonate of lime. Facts of this kind were observed so frequently as to make him come to the conclusion that whilst acid solutions were never productive in Schwann's apparatus, any neutral or alkaline fluids might be, if they were otherwise suitable for such experiments. Then came the question as to how this was to be explained.

It should be remembered that M. Pasteur was engaged in investigating the problem of the mode of origin of certain low organisms in organic fluids, concerning which so much controversy had taken place. In this controversy hitherto, it had been contended on the one hand, that the living things met with derived their origin from pre-existing 'germs' that had survived all the destructive conditions to which the media supposed to contain them had been subjected; whilst, on the other hand, it was contended that if the media had been subjected to conditions which (by evidence the most direct and positive) had been shown to be destructive to the lowest living things, then any such living things as were subsequently discovered in these fluids must have been evolved *de novo*. It was a question, therefore, on the one hand, as to the degree of 'vital resistance' to heat which might be displayed by the lowest living things; and on the other, as to the strength of the tendency in the organic matter of the solution to undergo changes of a fermentative character, coupled with the degree to which this molecular mobility could persist in spite of the disruptive agency of the heat to which the organic matter had been subjected. Whatever fluids are employed, if after they have been boiled and exposed to a given set of conditions, organisms are not found, their absence is explicable in one of two ways—that is, in accordance with either of the two opposing views. Either the heat has proved destructive to all living things in the solutions; or else the restrictive conditions to which the organic matter in these solutions has been exposed have been such as to prevent the occurrence of fermentative changes. Any person seriously wishing to ascertain the truth, and competent to deal with such a subject, of course, would not fail to see that he was bound to give equal attention to each of these possibilities. He would have no right to *assume* that the probabilities were greater in favour of the one mode of explanation than they were in favour of the other; this was the very subject in dispute—this it was which had to be proved. When, therefore, it was definitely ascertained by M. Pasteur that acid solutions employed in Schwann's experiments yielded negative results as far as organisms were concerned, the establishment of this fact was in reality no more favourable to the one view than to the other. It is what the panspermatists might have expected, it is true, because—regarding it only as a question of the destruction or non-destruction of germs —even they had convinced themselves that calcining the air and boiling the fluids were adequate to destroy all living things contained in these media. But on the other hand, it was equally open to the evolutionists to say, that the restrictive conditions employed were so severe that they also were not surprised at the fermentative changes being stopped and at the consequent non-appearance of organisms in the solutions. When positive results were obtained, however, the case became altogether different. The rule with regard to the inability of living things to survive in solutions which had been raised to the boiling temperature for a few minutes was absolute, so far as it had gone, and being founded on good evidence, to which M. Pasteur and others had assented, no one should have attempted to set it aside, except upon evidence equally direct and equally positive, though more extensive than that upon which the rule had been originally founded. Certainly, no one should have attempted to set it aside on the strength of indirect evidence, which, though equally capable of explanation in accordance with either one of the two opposing views, was tacitly represented to be explicable only in accordance with one of them. Such, however, was the course pursued by M. Pasteur. It will, perhaps, scarcely be credited by many that the investigations of M. Pasteur, which have had so much influence, and which have been looked upon by many as models of scientific method, should really contain such fallacies. On other important occasions, however, his reasoning has been similarly defective, though he himself claimed and was believed by many to have 'mathematically demonstrated' what he had so plausibly appeared to prove.

In the present case, after his experiments with milk in Schwann's apparatus, M. Pasteur ascertained that in other alkaline or neutral fluids, even when they had been subjected to all the conditions above mentioned, inferior organisms might be found more or less quickly. But he also discovered that even such solutions no longer yielded organisms, if instead of being subjected to a heat of 212° F they were exposed for a few minutes to a temperature of 230° F. And it was on the strength of two or three other links of such evidence as this that M. Pasteur sought to upset the rule with regard to the inability of inferior organisms to resist the destructive influence of a moist temperature of 212°F. On such evidence as this he attempted to raise the possible limit of vital resistance by 18°F, and sought to establish the rule that living organisms might survive in neutral or alkaline solutions, which had been raised to any temperature short of 230°F. He did not seem to appreciate the fact that he had less warrant for the assumption that the organisms met with in these neutral or alkaline fluids had been derived from 'germs' which had resisted the temperature of 212°F, than he or his opponents would have had in falling back at once upon the counter assumption, that the evolutional tendencies of neutral or alkaline fluids exposed to high temperatures were greater than those of similar fluids when in an acid state [1]; such neutral or alkaline fluids being, as was now seen, capable of overcoming the restrictive conditions in Schwann's experiments and of giving

[1] This omission on the part of M. Pasteur is all the more remarkable in the face of facts which must have been well known to such an accomplished chemist. Thus, Gerhardt says ('Chimie Organique,' t. iv. p. 547):— 'Beaucoup de matières qui seules ou à l'état humide ne s'oxydent pas à l'air, éprouvent une combustion dès qu'elles se trouvent en contact avec un alcali. Ainsi l'alcohol pur se conserve à l'air indéfiniment et sans s'aigrir; mais, si l'on y verse un peu de potasse, il absorbe promptement de l'oxygène et se convertit en vinaigre et en une matière brune résineuse. Il est clair, d'après cela, que la potasse doit favoriser certaines fermentations, puisqu'elle favorise l'absorption de l'oxygène et que la présence de celui-ci développe les ferments.' He also says (loc. cit. p. 556):—'On sait, que les viandes et les substances végétales mariées dans le vinaigre sont preservées de la décomposition, au moins pour un certain temps . . . . La plupart des acides produisent le même effet que le vinaigre.'

birth to organisms, by permitting the occurrence of life-evolving changes amongst the colloidal molecules contained therein. He had less right to explain the facts as he did, than the evolutionist would have had to explain them as above mentioned, because in so doing he was attempting to upset previously admitted facts on insufficient evidence, whilst the reasonings of the evolutionist would have been in every way legitimate. And yet M. Pasteur left his readers to imagine that the explanation which he had adduced was that which was alone admissible; he did not refer to the existence of any other mode of explanation, but at once attempted to set aside the old rule. And similarly, when he ascertained that such alkaline or neutral fluids were no longer found to contain organisms if they had been previously submitted to a temperature of 230° F, he was entitled to draw no conclusion from such facts. Nevertheless, M. Pasteur did assume that such ambiguous evidence entitled him to come to the conclusion that the hypothetical 'germs' contained in these solutions—those which were not killed, as he supposed by a temperature of 212° F—were destroyed by a temperature of 230° F. Such two-faced evidence is, however, worthless for raising the standard of 'vital resistance' to heat; and to ignore the possible differences which may exist, from the evolutionist's point of view, between acid and alkaline solutions, as M. Pasteur did, is about as reasonable as if he had imagined that because water does not boil at the temperature of 100° F., the same rule must necessarily hold good for ether.

Much evidence, indeed, can be brought forward to show that even at ordinary temperatures, and under conditions in which there is a moderately free exposure to the air (and where there is therefore every facility for the entrance of germs), organisms are not only found in a neutral or slightly alkaline solution more quickly, but they are found to exist in it in much greater variety than in solutions which are slightly acid, but in other respects similar. Any of the higher forms of Ciliated Infusoria *may* appear in different neutral or slightly alkaline solutions, though they rarely if ever present themselves in those having an acid reaction, either in a developed or undeveloped condition—dead or living.

The amount of difference that is capable of being produced by the mere acidity of a solution was well seen by me a few months ago. Having prepared[1] a mixture of white sugar and ammonic tartrate, with small quantities of ammonic phosphate and sodic phosphate in distilled water, whose reaction was found to be neutral, two similar, wide-mouthed bottles, of about three ounces capacity, were filled with this fluid. Both were kept side by side in a tolerably warm place, the mouths of the bottles being merely covered in each case by a piece of glass—after glycerine had been smeared over the rim on which the cover rested. Although not

[1] Dec. 23, 1869. The weather being very cold and frosty.

hermetically sealed, these solutions were thus sufficiently protected, to prevent the access of much dust from the neighbouring fire. The fluid in one of the bottles was allowed to remain neutral, whilst to that of the other four or five drops of acetic acid were added, so as to make it yield a faintly acid reaction to test paper. The results were quite different in the two cases. Towards the end of the fourth day the originally unaltered neutral solution began to assume a cloudy appearance; this increased in amount during the next day, and at the close of the sixth day a thin pellicle was found on the surface, and beneath it there were some irregular, flocculent, whitish masses buoyed up by small air bubbles. Examined microscopically, the pellicles and also the flocculent masses beneath were found to be made up of medium-sized plastide-particles and *Bacteria*, mixed with crystals of triple phosphate. There were also many scattered cells of a *Torula*, varying from $\frac{1}{5000}''$ to $\frac{1}{10000}''$ in diameter. By this time (close of the sixth day), however, the companion solution which had been slightly acidified, had undergone scarcely any appreciable change. It was still quite clear and transparent, and there was no pellicle on the surface, though there was a very slight whitish flocculent stratum at the bottom of the bottle. Even on the twenty-first day this solution continued in much the same condition—still showing no trace of a pellicle. The fluid itself was clear, and there had been only a very slight increase in the thickness of the white flocculent layer at the bottom of the bottle. This, on microscopical examination, was found to be made up mainly of a granular matter having no definite character — though a small number of minute but well-formed *Bacteria* were mixed with it. The acid solution had remained throughout in the same warm place, but the bottle containing the neutral fluid had not (after the examination on the sixth day) been replaced in its original situation near the fire: it had continued since this time in a part of the room altogether away from the fire, and yet when this was also examined on the twenty-first day, it was found to present a very cloudy, whitish appearance throughout. There was also a thick flocculent stratum at the bottom, and a very consistent, well-marked pellicle on the surface of the fluid, made up almost entirely of large and well-formed *Torula*-cells.

Although the results here detailed, as occurring in the neutral and the acidified solutions respectively, are so strikingly different, still they are by no means singular or peculiar to the particular kind of solution which was employed in this experiment. Phænomena essentially similar in kind may be observed when almost any neutral or slightly alkaline organic infusion is employed. I will quote only one out of many experiments bearing upon this point. A short time ago, having prepared a pretty strong infusion of mutton, about an ounce and a half was put, after filtration, into each of two similar flasks. One portion of the infusion was allowed to remain neutral, whilst to the other three drops of strong acetic acid were added, so as to make the whole yield a faintly acid reaction to test paper. The two flasks were then exposed side by side to a temperature of 75° to 80° F during the day. In twenty-four hours the neutral solution was clouded, and more or less opaque, whilst the portion which was acid appeared perfectly unchanged. It was as clear as ever; and so it continued even to the end of forty-eight hours, although by this time the neutral solution was quite opaque and muddy-looking, with a pellicle on its surface and also some flocculent deposit at the bottom of the flask. A microscopical examination of two or three drops of this fluid showed that it was teeming with plastide-particles, and most actively moving *Bacteria* and *Vibriones*; whilst a similar examination of the acid fluid, showed not a trace of these or of any other kind of organisms[1].

The difference between the results in these two sets of cases was thus extremely well marked, and the results themselves are well worth our serious attention. We had to do with equal bulks of fluid, placed under similar conditions and similarly constituted, with the exception that in each set a few drops of acid had been added to the one fluid, whilst the other was allowed to remain neutral. And it must be acknowledged that the difference encountered was very similar in kind to that which was observed by M. Pasteur when he made use

---

[1] The reverse results, which may be produced by neutralising the acidity of a naturally acid fluid, will be exemplified farther on.

of acid, or of neutral or alkaline solutions respectively, in repeating the experiments of Schwann. But here we had nothing to do with the destructive agency of heat, and germs were as free to enter or develop in the one solution as they were in the other; so that the differences actually observed would seem now, at all events, simply due to the different qualities of the fluids themselves. Of course such results cannot be adduced as evidence that the evolutional property of the neutral solution was higher than that of the acid solution. It may not be a case of *de novo* origination at all, but simply one of growth and development. The results, however, show plainly enough that the neutral solution was the one most favourable to the growth and development of living things. And if, starting from this fact which cannot be denied, the evolutionists see reasons which induce them to assume the possibility that an actual origination of living things may have taken place *de novo*, in addition to mere growth and development; they would also be likely to suppose that the neutral fluid was more favourable to such evolution than that which had been acidified[1]—a supposition which

[1] Taking it only for what it is worth, it is at least deserving of mention that no reason seems assignable for the presence of *Torula* in the one saline solution and not in the other. They were both equally exposed to the advent of 'germs.' It can scarcely be imagined that the *Torula*-germs obtained access to both solutions, but that they perished in that which was faintly acid, for, as a matter of fact, *Torulæ* are much more frequently met with in acid solutions than in those which are alkaline. And for the same reason one can scarcely imagine that any germs of *Torula* which preexisted in the fluids were unable to develop in one of them merely on account of its slight acidity.

seems fully borne out by facts already cited. The solution which was found favourable for the processes of growth and development might also, reasonably enough, be considered favourable for Archebiosis. A process would most likely be *initiated* where the conditions were suitable for its continuance. And surely the same factors would be at work in the initiation of a living thing that would be called into play during its growth. The presumption, therefore, is a fair one, that solutions which are favourable to the growth and development of certain organisms, may also be favourable to the occurrence of evolutional changes which more especially lead to the initiation of such living things.

Seeing, then, that the question of the occurrence or non-occurrence of Archebiosis is the very matter in dispute, it is certainly most imperative that all those engaged in investigations bearing on the subject should appreciate (when weighing the evidence) that these are possibilities whose probability ought to be assumed as equal. We may well be surprised, therefore, to find such an investigator as M. Pasteur completely ignoring one of these points of view, interpreting all his experiments by the light of a foregone conclusion, and looking *solely* upon the different solutions employed, as fluids which are destructive or not destructive at a given temperature to hypothetically-existing 'germs.'

It should not be understood that we are to regard all acid solutions as having a low evolutional or fermentative tendency. On the contrary, evidence has already been adduced in this chapter to show that *some* acid solutions are most prone to undergo evolutional changes of a certain kind. These do not result in the production of living things of a high type, but rather in an abundance of organisms of a comparatively low type. It seems to me, however, after careful observation and experiment, that a neutral or slightly alkaline solution to which a few drops of acid have been added is almost always found, after a given time, to contain a notably smaller number of organisms than an equal bulk of the unaltered solution. And conversely, having an acid solution whose productiveness is known, the number of organisms found in equal bulks under similar conditions can almost always be notably increased in either one of them by the mere addition of a few drops of *liquor potassæ*, so as to render it neutral or slightly alkaline. This, as previously pointed out, *may* be interpreted as an indication that alkalinity or neutrality of the fluids is more favourable than their acidity for the occurrence of fermentative changes. And thus the fact that organisms were never met with when an acid 'eau de levûre sucrée' was used in repeating the experiments of Schwann, though they were met with, on the contrary, in other experiments where portions of this same fluid had been used which had been rendered slightly alkaline by the addition of chalk, may be explained without the aid of that supposition which alone seems to have occurred to M. Pasteur.

But, after reflection on this subject, it seemed to me quite within the range of probability, that the difference between acid and alkaline solutions as regards the number of organisms which are to be found in them, when they have been simply exposed to ordinary atmospheric conditions, might be exaggerated after they had been subjected to the temperature at which water boils. It seemed quite possible that high temperatures might be more destructive to organic matter contained in acid solutions than when it existed in alkaline solutions. Since the acid seems to exercise a certain noxious influence even at ordinary temperatures, so it may be conceived that this influence, whatever its nature, may be increased in intensity with the rise of temperature, and with the consequent greater facility for the display of chemical affinities. Hot acids will frequently dissolve metals which would remain unaffected by them at ordinary temperatures; and chemical affinities generally, are notably exalted by an increased amount of heat. Since the addition of an acid, therefore, to a previously neutral or slightly alkaline fluid containing organic matter in solution, appears to alter its character in some mysterious way, we may assume that its action upon the unstable organic molecules goes on increasing in intensity, as the fluid becomes hotter. Thus, when two portions of a solution containing organic matter—the one neutral and the other acid—have been raised to a temperature of 212° F, the organic matter of the one has been injured only by the mere action of heat; whilst that of the other solution, which has been acidified, has not only had to submit to the deleterious influence of the high temperature, but also to the increased activity of the acid at this temperature. The result would be that the amount of difference existing between the two solutions before they had been heated, would be found more or less increased after they had been exposed to the high temperature, in direct proportion to the increase in intensity of the action of the acid produced by such high temperature. What we know concerning the precipitation of albumen in urine is quite in harmony with this view. When albumen is present, and the fluid has an alkaline reaction, mere boiling does not cause its precipitation; though, if the reaction is acid [1], the albumen present would be precipitated, when, or even before the temperature of the fluid was raised to the boiling point. Or a similar result might have been induced by the addition of a small quantity of acid to a portion of a neutral or alkaline albuminous urine, which had just been boiled without a precipitation of the albumen having been brought about. Thus the addition or presence of a small quantity of acid, in conjunction with an elevated temperature, is seen to be capable of bringing about results which cannot be produced by the mere elevated temperature alone. But the fact that an isomeric

[1] Provided this was not due to the presence of a mere trace of nitric acid.

transformation of albumen can be brought about in this way—that albumen can be transformed so as to be no longer capable of remaining in solution—shows that a molecular change has been induced by the influence of the acid working at high temperatures, which neither the acid nor the heat, working alone, are capable of effecting.

With the view of throwing further light on this subject, I made the following experiment on March 27, 1870:—A tolerably strong infusion of white turnip was prepared and subsequently filtered [1]. This had a decidedly *acid* reaction. It was then divided into two portions, one of which was allowed to remain unaltered, whilst to the other a few drops of *liquor potassæ* were added, so as to give the fluid a very faintly alkaline reaction. This addition produced a slight alteration, even in the naked-eye appearance of the fluid; the faintly whitish opalescence which formerly existed disappeared, and was replaced by an equally faint brownish tinge. About an ounce of each of the two fluids was then placed separately in two small flasks. The fluids were not heated at all, but a piece of paper having been placed loosely in the neck of each, so as to exclude dust, they were exposed side by side to a temperature varying from 75° to 85° F. After twenty-four hours [2], the unaltered acid infusion merely showed

---

[1] The turnip at this season of the year was, however, very poor and dry as compared with that which was employed in some of my earlier experiments (Experiments 2–5) during the winter months.

[2] During the whole of this time the heat only varied between the limits mentioned.

a more decided opalescence approaching to cloudiness; though that which had been rendered faintly alkaline had a distinctly opaque whitish colour, and there was also a distinct pellicle, covering more than one-half of the surface of the fluid. In the three or four succeeding days the amount of opacity, of pellicle, and of deposit increased in both the fluids, though each of these continued to be more manifest in the alkaline than in the acid solution. After a week, however, the difference was scarcely appreciable, though on the whole, for about two weeks afterwards, the quantity of new matter seemed to be greater in the alkaline than in the acid solution.

But, on the same morning that these two portions of the acid and alkaline infusions had been set aside for observation, I had placed with them vessels containing two other specimens of the same fluids. These had been previously treated in the following manner. The acid and the alkaline fluid were placed in their respective flasks, and after the necks of these had been drawn out the fluids were boiled for ten minutes. At the expiration of this time, and whilst ebullition was still continuing, the drawn-out necks of the flasks were hermetically sealed in the blow-pipe flame. These experiments were undertaken in order to show, by comparison with the other two, whether the difference produced by mere acidity or alkalinity of the solutions at low temperatures was or was not intensified by the action of heat. The flasks were all suspended in a group at the same time, and were, thenceforward, subjected to the same temperature. The results were as follows: After twenty-four hours the slightly alkaline fluid which had been boiled showed a slight though decided opalescence; it was, in fact, very similar in appearance to the acid solution which had not been boiled. The boiled acid solution was, however, as clear as when the flask was first suspended, and it remained apparently quite unaltered, after it had been suspended a week; though the boiled alkaline solution had by this time become decidedly opaque, and also showed some flocculent matter lying at the bottom of the vessel. And after they had been suspended rather more than three weeks, the acid solution still remained almost transparent, presenting only the faintest cloudiness, though with no pellicle or deposit at the bottom[1]. The boiled alkaline fluid, however, exhibited a totally different appearance; it was whitish and quite opaque, there was a very thick pellicle covering part of its surface, and also some whitish sediment at the bottom of the flask.

Thus the difference which already exists between alkaline and acid solutions at ordinary temperatures was seen to be most notably intensified after similar alkaline and acid solutions have been raised to a temperature of

[1] This solution was, therefore, much more backward in exhibiting signs of change than were the others which had been used in Experiments 2 to 5—a difference probably explicable by the poorer quality of the turnip used in this last experiment (see p. 394, note 1).

212° F. And whilst these differences tend strongly to confirm the truth of the mode of explanation which I have suggested of the discrepancies observed by M. Pasteur when he repeated Schwann's experiments with acid and alkaline organic infusions respectively, they may also be considered to strengthen the probabilities in favour of my assumption that an acid fluid is less prone to undergo those molecular changes which lead to the evolution of living things, than a fluid, otherwise similar, whose reaction is neutral or faintly alkaline. And yet, this explanation was utterly ignored by M. Pasteur; he leads his readers to believe that the before-mentioned discrepancies were explicable only in one way; and he moreover illogically attempted to set aside a rule, concerning the limits of 'vital resistance' to different degrees of heat, to which he had previously assented, on the strength of evidence which was most ambiguous and inconclusive.

One finds M. Pasteur, as a chemist, engaging himself in a controversy concerning one of the most important questions in the whole range of biological science; and yet he assumes the attitude of a man who is so convinced beforehand of the error of those who are of the opposite opinion, that he will not abide by ordinary rules of fairness; he will not even, at first, assume the possibility of the truth of the opinions which are opposed to his own. Ambiguous evidence is explained as though it were not ambiguous; conclusions based upon good evidence are attempted to be set aside in favour of conclusions based upon evidence which is comparatively worthless: and, by such illogical methods, M. Pasteur proclaims that he has 'mathematically demonstrated' the truth of his own views. Unfortunately for the cause of truth, many have been only too much blinded by his skill and precision as a mere experimenter.

An attempt has been made to show the inconclusiveness of M. Pasteur's mode of reasoning on this point, principally with the view of preventing similar deductions being drawn from observations and experiments of the same nature by subsequent workers. Otherwise it would not have been at all necessary. For so far from there being any truth in M. Pasteur's assumption that *Bacteria* and their germs are not killed in slightly alkaline or neutral fluids raised to a temperature of 212° F, we have found that experiment and observation alike seem to show that they are killed when such fluids are raised for two or three minutes to a temperature of 140° F. Nay, more, taking M. Pasteur even upon his own ground—using boiled acid infusions, in which he admits that all germs of preexisting life are killed—we find, nevertheless, as others have found, that such infusions, contained within heated and hermetically-sealed flasks, will speedily become turbid, owing to the presence of multitudes of living organisms.

There being no valid reasons, therefore, for our belief in the assumption that *Bacteria*, *Vibriones*, and their germs, are not killed in slightly alkaline or neutral solutions which have been boiled, very many of the experiments of M. Pasteur with such fluids may be cited amongst many others by Schwann, Mantegazza, Pouchet, Joly, Musset, Wyman, Hughes Bennett, Child, Cantoni, and other experimenters, in addition to those recorded in the present work, as testifying to the reality of the process of Archebiosis, and to the erroneousness of the doctrines concerning Fermentation, of which he is the advocate.

CHAPTER X.

PHYSICAL AND VITAL THEORIES OF FERMENTATION.

Questions as to Cause of Fermentation and Origin of Life intimately associated. Pasteur's researches undertaken to establish a 'vital theory' of Fermentation. Fermentable substances and Ferments. Nature of latter. Doctrine of Liebig and others. Influence of the discovery of the yeast-plant. Vital theories of Schwann, Pasteur, and others. Upholders of Physical theory admit the facts of the Vitalists. Interpretations of latter too narrow. Pasteur's experiments inconclusive in themselves. His conclusions wider than were legitimate. Vital theory opposed to known facts. Manufacture of Vinegar. Continuous series of chemical changes in dead muscle. Transformation of starch into glucose. Communicability of molecular movements. No line of demarcation between fermentative and non-fermentative chemical changes. Two degrees of fermentability. Oxygen not always the *primum movens* in Fermentations. Action of diminished pressure in some cases. Preservation of Meats. Differences between these processes and my experiments. Observations of Gruithuisen. Reconciliation of results. Conclusions.

THE lower organisms being so very frequently met with in fermenting fluids, and being invariably present in some of them, it so happens that the problem as to the cause of fermentation has come to be inseparable from the question as to the possibility of the *de novo* origin of living things. Thus it is that the most important problem in biology is one towards the solution of which many distinguished chemists have been induced to devote much time and labour. The ground is in fact common to biologists and chemists, and the question is so obscure and difficult that it stands much in need of the double illumination. Important, however, as are the considerations which the chemist brings towards its solution, and valuable as are the methods which he employs, the problem is, nevertheless, so all-important in its biological aspects that it cannot with advantage be wholly relegated to him.

M. Pasteur frankly tells us that, having formed certain views concerning the cause of fermentations in general, he found himself compelled to come to an opinion 'sur les questions des générations spontanées.' And here some words of explanation seem needed, in order to show more fully how the two problems are so inseparably related, and as well that the reader may comprehend the nature of the doctrines which are held by many other chemists, in opposition to those of M. Pasteur.

We are now becoming better acquainted with a set of remarkable changes that certain compound substances are apt to undergo, and which have usually been known by the generic name of 'Fermentations[1].' The prevailing opinion had been that for the occurrence of such a

[1] Those which are accompanied by the evolution of fœtid gases (see p. 266, note 1) have usually been spoken of as putrefactions. The old view of Mitscherlich ('Ann. Chem. Pharm.' xlviii. p. 126) was that 'fermentation is caused by a plant organism, and putrefaction by an animal organism.' No such distinction can, however, be drawn.

process two things are necessary: in the first place, there must be a *fermentable* substance—a body capable of undergoing chemical change—and, in the second place, there must be a *ferment*, or substance capable of initiating such a change. According to MM. Pelouze and Frémy, 'the decomposition of organic substances under the influence of a body which acts only by its mere presence is called fermentation.' What, then, is the nature of the ferment? It has generally been regarded as some nitrogenous substance, belonging to the albumenoid type, though subject to much variation in actual composition. Gerhardt even says that 'a ferment is not a body *sui generis*, but rather any substance in a state of decomposition.'

In the opinion of some chemists — followers of Gay-Lussac—the mere presence of the ferment in company with the fermentable substance is not sufficient. Even its activity must be excited before it can act upon the fermentable substance: a result generally brought about by the action of the oxygen contained in the air with which the ferment is in contact [1]. But according to other chemists—and more especially to Liebig [2]—it is only necessary to have a body which decomposes, perhaps spontaneously, in the presence of another (fermentable substance) whose elements are held together by a feeble affinity. The more changeable substance, by virtue of its own inherent instability,

---

[1] So that, as Gerhardt says, 'L'oxygène de l'air, comme nous l'avons dit, est donc le *primum movens* des fermentations.' Loc. cit. p. 540.

[2] 'Annales de Chimie et de Physique,' 2nd série, t. lxxi. p. 178.

may initiate molecular movements in even a large amount of a less unstable substance with which it is brought into contact; and to this latter set of changes the name 'fermentation' is applied. Liebig's explanation of this process, which is accepted by Gerhardt and many other chemists, is thus described in Gerhardt's *Chimie Organique*[1]:—'Every substance which decomposes or enters into combination is in a state of movement—its molecules being agitated; but since friction, shock, mechanical agitation, suffice to provoke the decomposition of many substances (chlorous acid, chloride of nitrogen, fulminating silver), there is all the more reason why a chemical decomposition, in which the molecular agitation is more complete, should produce similar effects upon certain substances. In addition, bodies are known which, when alone, are not decomposed by certain agents, but which are attacked when they exist in contact with other bodies, incapable of resisting the influence of these agents. Thus platinum alone does not dissolve in nitric acid, but when allied with silver, it is easily dissolved; pure copper is not dissolved by sulphuric acid, but it does dissolve in this when it is allied with zinc, &c. According to M. Liebig it is the same with ferments and fermentable substances; sugar, which does not change when it is quite alone, changes—that is to say, ferments—when it is in contact with a nitrogenous substance undergoing change, that is, with a ferment.'

[1] Tom. iv. p. 539.

But since the discovery by Cagniard-Latour and Schwann, in 1836, of the yeast-plant, which invariably reveals itself during the vinous fermentation; and since the recognition of the existence of a similar relationship between other fermentations and other organisms, there have always been persons who have inclined to the notion that the associated organism was the actual *cause* of the fermentation itself. For three or four years after the discovery of the yeast-plant, it was warmly advocated by Cagniard-Latour, Turpin, Mitscherlich, and others, that living organisms alone were capable of initiating the changes known as fermentations—that they, in fact, were the only true ferments. According to the notions of Liebig, Gerhardt, and others, fermentations are separated by no hard and fast line from chemical changes in general; here, however, a limitation was sought to be established; a hard and fast line was to be drawn, and fermentations were to be supposed to differ from chemical changes in general, by the fact that they could only be initiated by the presence and influence of living organisms. Such a limitation seemed of itself to necessitate the supposition that the chemical changes occurring in living things were wholly different from all other chemical changes—that the changes, in fact, constituting fermentations were initiated by occult 'vital' influences.' This is the doctrine which M. Pasteur has revived, and which he has sought to establish upon a firm foundation. He says:—' Je trouvais que toutes les fermentations proprement dites, visqueuse, lactique, butyrique, la fermentation de l'acide tartarique, de l'acide malique, de l'urée . . . ., étaient toujours corrélatives de la présence et de la multiplication d'êtres organisés. Et, loin que l'organisation de la lêvure de bière fut une chose gênante pour la théorie de la fermentation, c'était par là au contraire, qu'elle rentrait dans la loi commune, et qu'elle était le type de tous le ferments proprement dits. Selon moi, les matières albuminoïdes n'étaient jamais des ferments, mais l'aliment des ferments. Les vrais ferments étaient des êtres organisés.' (Loc. cit. p. 23.)

Thus it may be seen that there are two principal doctrines as to the nature of a 'ferment,' each having its several supporters; so that two distinct theories of fermentation at present divide the world of chemists. Some now believe in the exclusive view resuscitated by M. Pasteur[1], that (1) all ferments are living organisms—these being upholders of what may be called a 'vital theory of fermentation;' whilst others maintain (2) that certain not-living albumenoid substances are also capable of acting as ferments, so that they may be classed as believers in a 'physical theory of fermentation.' Of those who maintain the latter opinion, the great majority believe with Gay-Lussac, that the presence of oxygen is necessary in order to arouse the activity of the ferment; though my

[1] Liebig says:—'It is impossible to detect any fundamental difference between the views of Turpin and those of Pasteur.'

own experiments[1] tend to show that a ferment may begin to operate, independently of the disturbing influence of oxygen, so long as other conditions are favourable for the initiation of molecular movements amongst its delicately-balanced constituent elements.

In reference to the doctrine revived by M. Pasteur, that *all* ferments are living organisms, it should be clearly understood that those who reject this notion by no means deny the almost invariable association of organisms with *some* fermentations. They maintain however that other real fermentations exist with the occurrence of which organisms are not associated; and that in all those fermentations in which organisms are encountered, these are concomitant formations or results, rather than causes of the fermentative changes. The facts cited by Pasteur, even granting that his statements are perfectly correct, are obviously open to a double interpretation. Although it is true that such constant association of particular organisms with particular fermentations would occur if the changes in question were initiated by pre-existing omnipresent organisms, some of which found in each fermentable substance a nidus suitable for their development and multiplication; still the same constancy of association ought also to occur if the changes which initiated the process of fermentation were purely chemical in nature, and led to the evolution of living things as concomitant

[1] In addition to those detailed in the last Chapter, they are recorded in Chapters xii. and xiii., and in Appendix C.

results. The same substance would decompose in the same way on different occasions, if placed under the influence of similar conditions, so that if certain kinds of organisms arose *de novo* on any occasion during the occurrence of such changes, similar organisms ought also to be produced whenever these changes were repeated. Therefore, whether the organisms which are undoubtedly to be met with in association with certain fermentations are to be regarded as causes or as concomitant results, is a question which can only be settled by having recourse to experiment. If living things are shown to be capable of arising *de novo*, then the doctrine that fermentations cannot be initiated without the agency of living things must receive its death-blow.

M. Pasteur did appeal to experiment to support him in maintaining this particular doctrine of fermentation, which, as the reader should not forget, is repugnant to the teachings of many chemists equally eminent with himself. We have endeavoured to show that the experimental evidence on which M. Pasteur relies in support of his doctrine is insufficient and inconclusive—nay, more, that many other careful experimenters, who have no theory whatever to support, have failed to get results similar to those which he has recorded. We have, moreover, attempted to explain why his own results cannot fairly receive the interpretation that he has applied to them. Thus, not only has M. Pasteur been unable to establish his point with reference to the nature of the relation existing between organisms and those fermentations with which they are undoubtedly associated, but it may fairly enough be said that he is the advocate of a doctrine which is irreconcilable with many other facts generally admitted by chemists, and of one which is thought by some of the most eminent of them to be adverse to the best chemical knowledge of the day. They hold the opinion (1) that fermentations cannot be definitely and sharply discriminated from other chemical changes not usually placed in this category; and (2) that amongst those chemical changes which are generally considered to be real fermentations, there are some whose occurrence is not necessarily associated with the presence of organisms.

If fermentative changes were, in reality, only to be brought about through the agency of living organisms or particles, how could we then account for the fact that precisely such changes as are effected occasionally when the influence of living particles might be predicated, are at other times occasioned when no such predication is tenable? Thus, although pancreatin and pepsine convert starch into sugar, a precisely similar change may be brought about by dilute sulphuric acid; and although saliva or emulsin may cause a breaking-up or fermentation of salicine, here again dilute sulphuric acid is capable of effecting a similar change.

To take another instance, the production of acetic acid is due to a process of fermentation, in which alcohol is first converted into aldehyde and then into the acid in question. This fermentative change, according to M. Pasteur, is brought about by a living organism, the vinegar-plant (*Mycoderma aceti*); but, as we are reminded by Baron Liebig, acetic acid may be similarly derived from alcohol through the agency of finely-divided platinum, as was first pointed out by Döbereiner. The finely-divided platinum has the power—and many organic substances have a similar property—of absorbing oxygen from the air, and bringing it into a condition in which it can unite with other substances with which it would not otherwise enter into combination at low temperatures. So that, when alcohol is subjected to the influence of finely-divided platinum, it is first converted into aldehyde, owing to the oxidation of its hydrogen, whilst aldehyde, by a further oxidation, is converted into acetic acid. And, according to Liebig, the method introduced by Schutzenbach in 1823, for the manufacture of vinegar, is based upon this theory. He says[1]:—'In this operation wood shavings or fragments of charcoal are used for determining the oxidation. At one of the largest vinegar factories in Germany, the dilute alcohol receives no admixture during the whole operation; besides air, and wood shavings, or charcoal, there is no other substance concerned, and the fresh supply of dilute alcohol is only mixed with a little of the unfinished vinegar from a previous operation. The proprietor of these works, Hy. Riemerschmied, sent me

[1] On Acetic Fermentation, translated in 'Pharmaceutical Journal,' Aug. 13, 1870, p. 124.

some of the beech-wood shavings which had been used uninterruptedly for twenty-five years; and in reply to my enquiry whether the *Mycoderma aceti* took part in the production of vinegar, he states that, so far as can be seen, the shavings that have been thirty years in use are quite free from the fungus[1].' Although, therefore, the vinegar-plant is capable of causing the conversion of alcohol into acetic acid, this conversion can be otherwise achieved without the intervention of a living organism. The process is one of oxidation merely, so that even when it does take place by the agency of the vinegar-plant, the effective action is in all probability none the less purely chemical in nature[2]. Baron Liebig says:—'Analyses of the air discharged from the vessels where the vinegar is made, show that the oxygen consumed in the oxidation of alcohol is taken from the air, so that the only part taken by

[1] It appears, however, that 'the production of the fungus is a continual source of hindrance in factories where *beer-wort* is used [instead of dilute alcohol], since the interstices of the wood shavings are gradually stopped up by its growth, and thus free circulation of air is prevented so far as to stop the formation of vinegar.'

[2] The *Mycoderma aceti* is, also, only an occasional instrument in bringing about the acetous fermentation: it is not a necessary concomitant, as yeast-cells seem to be of the vinous fermentation. The acetic fermentation may occur without the presence of the vinegar-plant, though the vinous fermentation never occurs without the appearance of yeast. When produced, yeast is, as we all know, capable of initiating the vinous fermentation in other suitable liquids, though the vinous fermentation is also capable of originating without the influence of pre-existing yeast. In fermentations which commence in this way yeast arises *de novo*, as one of the results of the process. (See Pouchet's 'Nouvelles Expériences,' Paris, 1864, pp. 190–191.)

the vinegar plant in the process is that of determining the absorption of oxygen; it is active only in virtue of this chemical property, and it can be replaced by a large number of dead materials or parts of plants.'

Again, in a continuous series of chemical changes, why should an arbitrary division be made? Why should some changes, which are admitted to be 'spontaneous,' be artificially separated from others, when these latter follow in an uninterrupted sequence? Baron Liebig says[1]:—'From the moment that a piece of muscle is separated from the living body it begins to undergo alteration; after some hours it acquires an alkaline reaction; the coagulable substances are coagulated, the contents of the muscular tubes become more solid and acquire a clouded appearance, with a thickish consistence. The muscle contracts and thickens, or *rigor mortis* takes place; then, after some time, the stiffness ceases, the acidity augments, and offensively-smelling products make their appearance. . . . . . If organized ferments have nothing to do with the formation of the first products that appear in the muscles up to the occurrence of *rigor mortis*—and I believe there is no physiologist who thinks they have—then it is difficult to understand how the further alterations can be determined by them.'

The transformation of starch into glucose by the agency of sulphuric acid, to which we have already referred, is a process that cannot logically be

---

[1] Loc. cit., p. 123.

separated from the fermentations; whilst the change which occurs when sugar is added to a mixture of yeast and dextrine, is probably no less truly chemical in nature, even though a living organism does take part in the process. A solution of dextrine does not undergo fermentation when it is mixed with beer-yeast alone; though, when a certain quantity of sugar is added to the mixture, a great part of the dextrine shares the same fate as the sugar itself, and is converted into alcohol and carbonic acid. 'In this case,' Liebig says, 'the influence of the motion communicated to the sugar atoms by the action of the yeast appears very evidently to have been extended to the dextrine upon which yeast itself has no action.' Facts like these—and many others which might be mentioned, showing how the different kinds of fermentation are influenced and modified by the presence of different chemical substances—lead most strongly to the conclusion that fermentations are themselves, in essence, nothing more than definite processes of chemical change which certain complex bodies are apt to undergo, either by virtue of their own inherent instability, or by reason of the action upon them of other bodies (ferments) which are at the time in a state of molecular flux, or *motor-decay*.

Such processes are, moreover, separated by no well-defined line from other chemical changes. It can no longer be maintained that they are chemical processes which are only capable of being initiated by the contact-influence of the changes taking place in living things. Observation and experiment alike are absolutely opposed to such a limitation, and even had it not already been shown to be utterly erroneous, it is a doctrine which ought only to have found favour with those who are professed 'vitalists.' Consistent believers in the physical doctrine of life could scarcely be expected to do other than mistrust a doctrine which would have them believe either that the molecular changes taking place in living things were not essentially chemical in nature, or else that they were chemical changes absolutely *sui generis*. It would be almost impossible, indeed, to frame a true and distinctive definition of fermentative changes. Just as we have previously urged, that the living thing differs from the not-living thing in degree and not in kind, since the properties of both are dependent upon their molecular composition and structure; so does the fermentative chemical change differ from the not-fermentative chemical change merely in degree —though even to a less extent, because these two kinds of chemical change are now actually known to merge almost insensibly into one another. It is almost impossible to say where the one ends and the other begins.

As we have already intimated, in the opinion of Gay-Lussac and also of many chemists in the present day, oxygen is needed to initiate the changes which the ferment undergoes. According to Baron Liebig, however, all that is essential in order that fermentation may occur, is that a complex substance should undergo changes of a particular kind, either by reason of its own instability, or on account of the greater instability of some more mobile substance with which it is brought into contact. He says:—'Many organic compounds are known which undergo, in presence of water, alteration and metamorphosis having a certain duration, and ultimately terminating in putrefaction; while other organic substances that are not liable to such alterations by themselves, nevertheless suffer a similar displacement or separation of their molecules when brought into contact with the former[1].'

[1] 'Pharm. Journal,' 1870. This statement is illustrated by Gerhardt when he says ('Chimie Organique,' t. iv. p. 474):—'En présence de l'eau, le gluten s'altère continuellement; si on le delaye dans l'eau et qu'on l'abandonne dans cet état à la température ordinaire, il se gonfle peu à peu en dégageant beaucoup de gaz acide carbonique mélangé d'hydrogène non carbone, et d'hydrogène sulfuré; en même temps il se ramollit et se fluidifie entièrement; l'eau qui le recouvre devient alors acide, et contient de la leucine, du phosphate et de l'acétate d'ammoniaque; finalement le gluten se fonce de plus en plus et se dissout presque entièrement. . . . . Pendant les différentes phases de sa transformation le gluten possède la propriété d'agir comme ferment à la manière des autres substances albuminoides. Avant de subir lui-même la fermentation putride, il possède la propriété de faire subir une métamorphose remarquable à la matière amylacée. En effet lorsqu'on ajoute de la farine de blé à de l'empois d'amidon delayé dans l'eau et qu'on expose ce mélange, pendant quelques heures, à une température de 60 a 70° C, il perd sa consistance, se fluidifie, et finalement devient entièrement sucré; la matière amylacée se trouve alors convertie soit en dextrine, soit en glucose.' It should be observed that the temperature at which this change takes place, 60-70° C (140°-158° F), precludes the possibility of its being brought about by living organisms, since *Bacteria* and *Torula* are uniformly killed by exposure for a few minutes to a temperature of 140°F. The recent researches of Hoppe-Seyler ('Med. Chem. Unters,' 1871, pp. 557-581), also show that living ferments are killed by temperatures which do not destroy the virtues of dead ferments.

In the great majority of cases oxygen may be the initiator of the molecular change which the fermentable substance or the ferment undergoes; it would seem scarcely probable, however, that in the absence of free oxygen, no other conditions would be adequate to disturb the delicate balance existing between the elements of a highly unstable substance.

In considering such a subject it is of great importance always to bear in mind the various degrees of molecular mobility of different substances, and also the fact that some substances will easily decompose under the influence of conditions which do not affect other compounds of equal complexity. Individual differences or peculiarities cannot be ignored. Under the influence of any particular set of conditions, therefore, organic substances may be ranged under two distinct categories, with respect to their degree of fermentability. Substances which are to be placed in the *first* class are so unstable that they decompose 'spontaneously' and without the aid of a separate ferment; whilst those which possess only the *second* degree of fermentability cannot by themselves be made to initiate a fermentative change —require to be brought into contact with a more unstable substance whose *motor-decay* may impart the needful molecular movement. Once initiated, the process of change is afterwards easily maintained, even in those bodies which possess only the second degree of fermentability. This distinction is one of a most important nature, and will subsequently help us to explain the results of many experiments, in a manner different from that which has been generally accepted.

Those experiments which I have already detailed tend to show, in opposition to the widely-accepted views of Gay-Lussac, that the presence of free oxygen is not necessary even for the initiation of certain processes of fermentation or putrefaction, since such processes may occur *in vacuo*. Dr. Child, however, had previously shown that fermentation might take place in a closed flask containing nothing but freshly-prepared nitrogen gas in contact with the fermentable fluid (see p. 347).

My experiments have been conducted, to a certain extent, in accordance with a method which is in daily use for the preservation of meats and various kinds of provisions. Curiously enough, Gay-Lussac, Gerhardt, and other chemists came to the conclusion that oxygen was necessary for the initiation of fermentation and putrefaction, because meats or vegetables can only be preserved by a process somewhat similar to that which I have adopted in my experiments—that is, by sealing them hermetically in vessels from which all air has previously been expelled by heat. So prepared, the most changeable meats or vegetables will often preserve all their freshness for many years—a fact which has been attributed principally to the absence of oxygen gas. Now, however, by a certain modification of the experiment, I find that fermentation and putrefaction will occur *in vacuo*, and am consequently led to the opposite conclusion—that oxygen is not always necessary for the initiation of such processes.

This announcement, made on a former occasion[1], seems quite to have paralysed the understandings of some of my readers. The effect produced would have been laughable had it not been rather pitiable. Instead of repeating such simple experiments as I have described with infusions of hay or turnip, and satisfying themselves as to the truth of what had been said, the scientific world and the public generally have been authoritatively told by more than one of them, that such statements are unworthy of attention; and the excellence of many meats, which have been preserved for years in airless and hermetically-sealed tins, has been said to afford a practical denial of the truth of my assertions.

The differences between the two kinds of experiments are, however, sufficiently notable to account for the apparently discordant results. When provisions are preserved, it is in a tin case that is almost filled, and then hermetically sealed, after all air has been expelled by a prolonged ebullition of its fluid contents[2]. What small space there may be at first between the top of the tin and the upper surface of the provisions, is speedily lessened by the insinking of the top, owing to atmospheric pressure. The meats are thus enclosed in

---

[1] 'Nature,' Nos. 35, 36, 37, 1870.
[2] Very frequently the closed tins are immediately submitted, for half an hour or more, to a much higher temperature—even to 258°–260° F.

a vessel which is full—nay, more, in one in which they are cut off from all access of light. My flasks, on the contrary, have been only half filled with the fermentable infusions, and these have been subjected to any disturbing influences which may have been derivable from the influence of light, at the same time that they have been purposely exposed to a warm temperature.

What, then, is the explanation to be given of the results which I have obtained? Quite early in the present century Gruithuisen discovered, as we have previously quoted from Burdach, that 'infusions, otherwise very prolific (those of hay, for example), did not yield infusoria in glass vessels in which the stopper touched the surface of the fluid.' Under such circumstances [1], no space is left for the liberation of waste gases; pressure rapidly increases, and fermentative or putrefactive changes, if they chance to be initiated at all, are generally checked at their very onset [2]. When

---

[1] Even Gay-Lussac was also aware of a similar fact with regard to urine. And, moreover, urine may often be preserved, in this way, when it has not been previously boiled.

[2] A microscopical examination of the surface of some preserved meats which are sold as being 'perfectly good,' and whose taste ratifies the truth of this description, has occasionally revealed the presence of a number of *Bacteria* and *Leptothrix* filaments, which, though extremely small in quantity and not numerous enough to affect the quality of the provisions, would seem to have been developed in the situation in which they are found, because the meats in their original condition do not present even this amount of organisms, and because other cases of meats are found to be perfectly free from organisms ('Nature,' No. 48, p. 433). Thus a change seems to commence in certain cases, which is, however, so speedily stopped (owing to the unfavourable nature of the

this liberation or emission (which is almost always one of the accompaniments of a fermentative change) has taken place to a slight extent, the meats are in the very best condition for preservation. There is an absence of free oxygen, an utter absence of light, and also an absence of that diminished pressure which my experiments seem to show[1] is favourable to the promotion of many kinds of fermentative change. It would seem that fluids whose fermentation or putrefaction is hindered by increased pressure, and favoured by diminution of pressure, may be placed under conditions which are successively more favourable than the last for the occurrence of such changes, by putting a gradually smaller and smaller quantity of fluid into a flask, to which calcined air is admitted[2]. Whilst, if the stimulus of free oxygen is not absolutely needed in order to incite fermentation in the fluid employed, the conditions may often be still further improved by only half filling the flask, and procuring a more and more perfect vacuum before it is hermetically sealed.

If any one wishes, therefore, to understand why I have been enabled to bring about putrefaction and to obtain living organisms in my flasks, whilst preserved meats do not usually change *in vacuo*, let him repeat

'conditions' to which the fermentable substances are exposed), as to cause no appreciable detriment to the provisions. In other rare cases, the change does proceed, and the contents of the tin become more or less putrid.

[1] See *Appendix* C, *Exps.* ix and xv., *Exps.* xxxiii. and xxxvi., etc.
[2] See p. 348.

Gruithuisen's experiment and one of my own with the same fluid. Let him fill a stoppered bottle with a boiled infusion of hay or turnip and then close it hermetically, and he will almost certainly find, as I and others have found, that such an infusion will keep for an indefinite time without exhibiting any trace of turbidity [1]. Let him, at the same time, treat some of the same boiled infusion of hay or turnip in a different manner: let it only half fill a hermetically-sealed flask from which all air has been expelled. He will then learn, better than by any amount of mere idle conjecturing, whether there is any real contradiction between the results of my experiments, and generally admitted facts.

The conclusions to which I have been compelled to arrive, therefore, on the subject of Fermentation, are these. The 'Vital theory' is untrue on account of its exclusiveness; *some* organisms are ferments, though *all* ferments are not organisms. Organisms may be either

---

[1] Although hay and other infusions will yield these results—which are comparable with the majority of cases in which provisions are properly preserved in tins—still it has been shown by M. Pouchet ('Nouvelles Expériences,' Paris, 1864, p. 190), that beer-wort which has been boiled will undergo change even in a full vessel, and give rise to an abundance of yeast-cells. This, therefore, is an example which is comparable with those exceptional cases in which meats undoubtedly become putrid in spite of every care in their preparation, and notwithstanding the fact of their being contained in filled-tins which are hermetically closed. Some fermentations are doubtless attended by a less copious emission of waste gases than that which characterizes other fermentations; and some fermentations will progress in spite of an amount of pressure which, in other cases, would quite put a stop to the process.

absent, occasional instruments, or necessary concomitants in processes of fermentation. Thus there are (*a*) chemical changes which are essentially fermentative in nature, with which organisms are never known to be associated: to this class belongs the conversion of cellulose into dextrine and glucose under the influence of heat and sulphuric acid. There are other (*b*) fermentations that may be initiated by ordinary physical or chemical agencies alone, or which may be brought about by the agency of living organisms. Examples of such changes are the conversion of salicin into glucose and saligenin, which may be produced either by contact with dilute sulphuric acid or by the influence of yeast (*Torula*); and also the acetous fermentation, which may be induced either by bringing alcohol into contact with certain dead oxidising agents, or by subjecting it to the influence of a living fungus (*Mycoderma*). Whilst there is a third set (*c*) of changes in which the transformative processes are invariably associated with the presence of organisms; the most familiar examples of this class being the putrid and vinous fermentations. Although these latter may be initiated by the agency either of dead or of living ferments, living matter is one of the invariable products of the fermentative changes[1]: during their progress

---

[1] 'Schlossberger observed that many juicy fungi (for example *Agaricus russula*, &c.), when kept in narrow-mouthed, open flasks, underwent vinous fermentation spontaneously, and that alcohol could be obtained from the expressed liquid on distillation; *meanwhile true yeast-cells were*

growth and reproduction of the old, goes on simultaneously with the production of new living matter.

Looked at from a chemical point of view, the most essential feature of these changes seems to be that they are successive, similar changes, induced by mere contact with another body[1]. As we have previously stated, however, such changes do not form a group apart, they blend insensibly into chemical actions in general. To speak of certain chemical changes, therefore, as fermentations, as though they were different in kind from other chemical changes, may be convenient, though it must be acknowledged to be a mere arbitrary distinction, and not justifiable from a philosophical point of view. Limiting ourselves, however, to such processes as seem best entitled, in the opinion of Liebig and others, to be included in this category, it appears to me that, from one important point of view, they may be included under three principal groups[2].

formed.' (Liebig on *Alcoholic Fermentation*, loc. cit.) When a small quantity of yeast is added to a simple solution of sugar, there can be no new production of yeast either by growth or evolution, if no nitrogen exists.

[1] See the definition of Pelouze and Frémy at p. 402. Liebig says:—' We can resolve with a given quantity of sulphuric acid unlimited quantities of alcohol into ether and water; we can, by the help of the same acid, convert a quantity of starch into grape sugar, without the acid being neutralized in either case. These effects are utterly distinct from the effects produced when sulphuric acid acts on metals or metallic oxides; but it is quite absurd to ascribe them to a peculiar cause, altogether different from chemical affinity.' (Letters on Chemistry, 1851, p. 263.)

[2] These views are submitted, with all deference, to the consideration of chemists.

I. (*Synthetic Fermentations.*) In this group the changes that occur are wholly synthetic, leading to the evolution of compounds which have a higher molecular complexity. Thus, as Schmitz and Glutz have observed, contact with strong hydrochloric acid causes the conversion of cyanogen into oxamide ($C^2 N^2 + 2 H^2 O = C^2 O^2 N^2 H^4$), by bringing about a combination between the elements of cyanogen and those of water. This is one of the simplest examples, though a large number of such changes might be cited [1].

II. (*Analytic Fermentations.*) In these cases we find that a more or less complex body breaks up into two or more simpler products, as when starch and water, in contact with sulphuric acid, is converted into dextrin and glucose; or when salicin, in contact with the same acid, breaks up into saligenin and glucose.

III. (*Analytico-synthetic Fermentations.*) In this group the two processes occur simultaneously—the fermentable substance breaks up into simpler compounds, and at the same time gives origin to higher and more complex products [2]. As a simple instance of such a change may be cited the fact, that tartaric acid, when heated, not only yields such lower derivatives as water and carbonic acid, but also the decidedly more com-

---

[1] See vol. II. chap. xii. p. 24.
[2] This is an occasion most favourable for the production of higher compounds. Elements or compounds always unite most freely ' when one or both are in the act of separating from some previous combination. The state in which they are at that moment is called by chemists the *status nascens*, or nascent state.' (Liebig.)

plex body known as pyrogallic acid. Here, all the products are still mere ordinary chemical compounds. But in those processes which are most familiarly known as fermentations, some of the higher products constitute what we know as 'living' matter, and soon separate from the solution in the form of visible specks or particles[1]. This is what occurs in the vinous, and all those more or less putrid fermentations of animal and vegetable substances with which living matter is invariably and necessarily associated. These are all of them exceedingly complex processes[2], which are as yet very imperfectly understood. The results of the experiments of many investigators, however, compel us to believe that living matter is one of the products, in these fermentations.

Double simultaneous changes of a synthetic and analytic character are familiar enough to chemists. When olefiant gas (C^2H^4), or the vapour of alcohol or ether, is passed through red hot tubes, a complex body known as naphthalene ($C^{10}H^6$) is obtained in addition to such lower products as marsh gas (CH^4), carbon and hydrogen. Several acids when heated yield water and a di-acid: thus tartaric acid yields di-tartaric acid, whilst glycol yields di-glycol, and even tri- and tetra-glycol. More notable, however, than the oc-

---

[1] See pp. 77-79.

[2] Even in the vinous fermentation there are, as Pasteur has shown, non-volatile products, in addition to such derivatives as succinic acid, glycerine, alcohol, and carbonic acid.

currence of all such reactions is the fact that simultaneous processes of analysis and synthesis are continually taking place in all growing forms of living matter. This dependence of life on decomposition is a subject which has been much dwelt upon by Dr. Freke[1] and Mr. Hinton[2]; and, quite apart from the special relations to which I have just been alluding, Baron Liebig has, on other and broader grounds, pointed out the striking analogies that exist, between processes of fermentation and those nutritive changes which occur within the living body during the acts of assimilation and growth. After alluding to the retrogressive theories of Pasteur[3], he adds:—' I have regarded the phenomena of fermentation and putrefaction from a totally different point of view, and have considered their elucidation as the bridge by means of which we may arrive at a more exact knowledge of the processes taking place in the bodies of animals and plants[4]. Who can at the present time fail to perceive the significance of these facts, in regard to the conception and explanation of many vital processes? If a

---

[1] On Organization, 1848.
[2] 'Life in Nature,' 1862, pp. 51-54, and 229-258.
[3] In the following terms:—' Inasmuch as Pasteur has again diverted the study of fermentation and putrefaction by microscopists into the old objectless path, the result has been, that the general aspect of these processes has been disregarded, the phenomena that are common to all of them have been overlooked. Observation has been directed to the search for mere details, and it has thus become incoherent.' (*On Alcoholic Fermentation*, Pharmac. Jrnl. Aug. 6, 1870, p. 104.)
[4] 'Ann. Chem. Pharm.' lxii. p. 263.

change in the locality and relative position of the elementary particles of animal substances[1], outside the organism, be capable of exerting a very definite influence upon a number of organic substances which are brought in contact with them; if those substances are thereby decomposed, while new compounds are formed from their elements; and if it be considered that the class of substances susceptible of such changes as take place in fermentation, comprises all those which are the constituents of the food of man and animals, who can doubt that the same causes act one of the most important parts in the vital process, or that they have a powerful share in the alterations which the materials of food undergo when they are converted into fat, blood, or constituents of organs[2]? We know, indeed, that there is in all parts of the "living" animal body an incessant change going on; that living particles of this body are eliminated; that their constituents, whether fibrin, albumen, gelatin, or whatever else they may be, rearrange themselves as new compounds; that their elements unite to form new products. In accordance with our experience, we must presume that in virtue of this activity, there is at all places where it obtains, and corresponding to its direction and intensity, a parallel alteration in the character and composition of con-

---

[1] Belonging to the class known as 'ferments.'

[2] This view was very clearly expressed by Mr. Hinton in his 'Life in Nature,' pp. 41, 42—an interesting work, which I have only seen since this Chapter was in type.

stituents of the blood or of food, coming in contact with such changing particles—that consequently the animal metamorphosis is itself a main cause of the alterations that the food undergoes, and a determining condition of the nutritive process.'

The breadth and suggestiveness of these views of Liebig are most striking, and we venture to hope that they may be considered to derive additional support from our own experiments—all of which tend to show the essential similarity of the influences that occasion both the 'genesis' and the 'growth' of living matter. Chemical affinities, variously modified by physical agencies, are the causes of those fermentations which lead to the production of living matter; and chemical affinities similarly modified, are again all powerful in continuing the growth of the matter thus initiated. Nutritive processes are closely allied to fermentative processes, and both sets of phenomena are due to common causes. In other words, the same forces which are operative in the production of the subsequent units of living matter are potential in the initiation of the first unit. The occurrence of living matter is, like the formation of crystalline matter, the result of inherent molecular affinities and of immutable natural laws.

CHAPTER XI.

ADDITIONAL PROOFS OF THE OCCURRENCE OF ARCHEBIOSIS.

Uniformity of natural phenomena. Influence of Heat upon Living Matter. Equally uniform appearance of *Bacteria* and *Torulæ* within super-heated, closed Flasks. Their *de novo* origin alone reconciles such apparently contradictory Facts. Difficulties with which the Experimenter has to contend. Nature works with Unboiled Materials, and under freer Conditions. Further deleterious Action of increased Heat. Living, Colloidal, and Crystalloidal Matter. Diminishing Molecular Complexity goes with diminishing destructibility by Heat. Limits within which Archebiosis is possible. Life and Death are but Transitions.

Experiments with still Higher Temperatures. Those of Mantegazza, Wyman, and Cantoni. Author's experiments. Mode of preparation. Sealed flasks heated to 270°–275°F. Living *Torulæ*, *Protamœbæ*, and *Monads*. Sealed flasks heated to 293°F. *Bacteria*, *Leptothrix*, and chlorophyll-containing Organisms found. Sealed flasks heated to 295°–307°F for four Hours. *Bacteria*, *Fungus* spores, and *Fungi* found. Other experiments in which Flasks were heated to 327°F and 464°F. Charring of Organic Matter most extensive. Action of high temperatures upon Living Organisms. They not only kill but disintegrate. Experiments conclusively in favour of the occurrence of Archebiosis.

THE regularity of natural phenomena is proverbial, and is tacitly recognized by each one of us in our daily actions. Even where the succession of events seems less constant, they are none the less the natural resultants of a more complex set of antecedent conditions. Chance finds no recognized place where law, or uniformity of result, is eternal. New doctrines must, therefore, before their period of general acceptance, be shown to rest upon phenomena that are easily obtainable. Facts which can be attested by all are not to be gainsayed by any amount of theorizing, or mere affirmation of opposite 'mental convictions.'

The uniformity in the properties of living matter, as it exists in the simplest living things, is recognized by all biologists. All minute, naked, living organisms with which experiment has been made, have been killed by being immersed for a few minutes in water raised to the temperature of 140° F; so that, judging from this known uniformity, there is very good reason for believing that such an amount of heat would prove destructive to all similar, minute, naked portions of living matter. With regard to the higher temperature of 212° F, however, there is the most unanimous agreement (amongst all those who are best entitled to speak upon the subject) as to the fact that such an amount of heat is destructive to all the lower forms of life which are to be met with in infusions.

On the other hand, the labours of very many experimenters have now placed it beyond all question of doubt or cavil, that living *Bacteria*, *Torulæ*, and other low forms of life, will make their appearance and multiply within hermetically-sealed flasks (containing organic infusions), which had been previously heated to

212° F, even for one or two hours. This result is now so easily and surely obtainable, as to make it come within the domain of natural law[1]. All pre-existing living matter and organisms having been killed within the closed flasks, how can new living things appear therein save by a process of Archebiosis—or new origination of living compounds? The explanations which are adduced may be criticized, the phraseology employed may be objected to, but the great fact remains that the new living matter must have originated by the occurrence of some combinations similar in kind to those which

---

[1] In a very large number of trials I have never had a single failure when an infusion of turnip has been employed, and from what I have more recently seen of the effects produced by the addition of a very minute fragment of cheese to such an infusion (see *Appendix* C, pp. xxxiv—xxxviii), I fully believe that in 999 cases out of 1000, if not in every case, a positive result could be obtained. Having made use of this infusion most frequently, I am able to speak more positively concerning it than about others, many of which would, I doubt not, if sufficient care were taken, yield equally unmistakeable results. It must indeed never be forgotten, that the obtaining of positive results or not, in such experiments, depends not a little upon the strength of the solutions employed. A weak infusion will often yield no trace of living things, whilst a stronger infusion—prepared at the same time, and treated in the same manner—will, after a similar period, be found to swarm with living organisms. The original access of germs having been equally possible in each case, and the destructive influences to which they had been submitted being similar, the subsequent presence of living organisms in the one solution and their absence from the other, seems only consistent with the supposition, that an increased quantity of organic matter in a solution acts in the same way as the addition of a very fermentable fragment (cheese), and suffices to produce an increased tendency towards the occurrence of those fermentative changes during which there is a correlative production of new-born living matter.

take place in plants during every moment of their growth—even though such chemical combinations occur 'spontaneously,' or independently of the influence of any pre-existing living protoplasm.

It may be easily understood, however, that he who investigates this subject has to work under the influence of a set of conditions which are of the most unfavourable description. What he wishes to ascertain is whether in the wide field of nature—in its ponds, its lakes, its rivers, and its ocean beds, where there is the freest play of cosmical forces upon the most suitable materials—any *de novo* origination of living matter is taking place. And with the view of answering this portentous question, he is compelled (if he would avail himself of experimental conditions which shall be free from all chances of error) to resort to a poverty of conditions, which seems but a mockery of the wealth of nature. In the one case we have ponds, containing in solution an abundance of protein materials whose virtues have not been impaired by the blighting influence of heat, and which are freely exposed to air, light, and all those other known or unknown cosmical agencies which stimulate the growth of living matter. Whilst, in the other case, the experimenter has to content himself with boiled organic infusions, shut up within the narrow confines of a small, hermetically-sealed flask. Seeing, however, that conclusive results are still obtainable in spite of these unpromising conditions, the subject is one on which science may be congratulated. Had the natural tendency to the formation of living compounds in certain solutions been much less potent than it seems to be[1], the problem to which we have been referring could never have been solved. As it is, that which we are absolutely compelled to believe takes place within the closed flasks, may illuminate our mental vision concerning all the richer probabilities which are possibly being realized from moment to moment in such freer sites as ponds, lakes, rivers, and ocean beds.

Looking, however, again at the experimental aspects of the question, it will be easily understood that by increasing the stringency of the 'conditions,' we may ultimately succeed in stifling the voice of nature.

That combination of properties which we generalize and include under the word 'Life' being the result of a fine and subtle molecular combination in the matter by which it is manifested, it is easy to understand that a certain amount of heat may be adequate to destroy these more delicate combinations, and so put an end to the 'vital' manifestations with which they are associated. Such is the action of heat when it just suffices to convert a living thing into a dead organism. Though it is no longer living, however,—though, in common parlance, its 'life' has departed—the body may still remain as an organic aggregate. If allowed to continue in water, it gradually disintegrates, and becomes more or less dissolved—yielding

[1] See Vol. ii. pp. 27-32.

an organic solution in which colloidal substances are dissolved.

But just as the combinations which constitute living matter are superior in complexity to, and more destructible by heat than, colloidal compounds, so are colloidal compounds themselves broken up and more or less destroyed, by an amount of heat which will leave many crystalloids unaltered. The degree of heat necessary to decompose different complex colloids is, of course, subject to an amount of variation which does not admit of previous predication. As a rule, however, the more intense the heat to which a solution has been subjected, the more has the complex composition of the dissolved substances been impaired, and the less is the solution calculated to be one in which the new combinations initiative of living matter could arise. The *de novo* origin of living matter in a solution is possible at any period, after the destruction of all its pre-existing living things, provided the heat employed has not been so extreme as to break up its colloidal compounds, or such other unstable combinations as may be capable of conjointly yielding so high a product. The number of successful results, however, naturally diminishes, according as one employs, either more destructible compounds or higher temperatures and less destructible compounds.

So that however meagre the chances may seem for the occurrence of nature's subtlest material combinations within even ordinary experimental flasks (as compared with those which favour their induction in the outside world), the chances become far less when still higher temperatures are made use of, with or without longer periods of exposure. And, ultimately, a limit must be attained, at which the degrading influence of heat produces effects that suffice to render the experimental vessel a dreary and lifeless tomb, in which no living thing can subsequently arise. The transition from the not-living to the living, is an ascent in molecular complexity which may not be possible under such conditions—where the much-altered matter exists, though shorn of its finer virtues.

> 'Nec perit in tanto quicquam (mihi credite) mundo,
> Sed variat, faciemque novat : nascique vocatur,
> Incipere esse aliud, quam quod fuit ante ; morique,
> Definere illud idem.'

Although no additional evidence is actually required to prove that living matter can and does arise *de novo*, still my own experiments, and those of others, in which very much higher temperatures have been resorted to, and successful results have yet been obtained, ought to be cited, because of the great additional surety which they supply that no pre-existing living matter was left within the experimental flasks.

In 1851, Prof. Mantegazza[1], of Pavia, introduced a decoction of lettuce into a strong glass tube, and then hermetically sealed it in the flame of a lamp. One-

[1] 'Giornal dell R. Istituto Lombardo.' Esp. iii.

third of the tube was occupied by the fluid, and the remaining two-thirds contained ordinary air. It was exposed for thirty minutes to a temperature of 212°F, and for forty minutes to 284°F (140°C), in a bath saturated with carbonate of potash. Fifty-nine hours after having taken the tube from the bath (during which time it had been maintained at a temperature of about 75°F), it was divided by a file, and the fluid was submitted to a microscopical examination. In the fluid, Prof. Mantegazza says he found living specimens of *Bacterium termo.*

In 1862, Prof. Jeffries Wyman, of Cambridge, U.S., performed, and subsequently recorded the following experiments [1]. 'Exp. xxxiv. (3.) March 27th. Juice of mutton, in a hermetically sealed flask, was boiled five minutes in a Papin's digester, under a pressure of two atmospheres [120·6°F]. A film formed on the fourth day. It was opened several days later in the presence of Prof. Gray, and found to contain Vibrios and Bacteriums, some of them moving with great rapidity.'

The next experiment was also made with the same kind of solution [2]. It is thus recorded :—' Exp. xxxv. (3.) The same as the preceding, and boiled in Papin's digester ten minutes, and under the pressure of five

---

[1] 'American Journal of Science and Arts,' July, 1862.

[2] In two other experiments, in which beef juice was employed instead of mutton juice, and in which the flasks were raised to the same temperatures for fifteen minutes, no organisms were found.

atmospheres [152·2°F]. No film was formed. The flask was opened on the forty-first day. Monads and Vibrios were found, some of the latter moving across the field. No putrefaction; the solution had an alkaline taste.'

In 1868, Prof. Cantoni, of Pavia, also made some experiments in concert with Profs. Balsamo and Maggi, in which hermetically sealed flasks containing various organic solutions or infusions were heated to temperatures ranging from 100°–117°C (212°–242·6°F), in a Papin's digester[1]. Amongst other fluids they tried a solution of yolk of egg, and with reference to this Prof. Cantoni says[1]: 'We began by observing that this solution, enclosed with plenty of air in a flask hermetically sealed and heated to 105°–110°, produced a large number of Vibrios in two days. We heated it in different experiments to 112°, 114°, 116°, 117°, and *always obtained the same result*, if the temperature of the air was from 25° to 27°.' Experiments were similarly conducted with other organic fluids, which led to the following results:—' The juice from meat sufficiently concentrated produces Vibrios if heated to 112°, but not if heated to 114°; cow's milk of good quality produces them if heated to 113·5°, and remains unpro-

[1] I was for a long time unable to procure a sight of Prof. Cantoni's valuable papers, but he has lately been kind enough to send them to me. Having merely seen references to them in journals, I was led on a former occasion ('Nature,' No. 48, 1870, p. 432) to state that he had obtained positive results at 242·6°C, instead of 242·6°F. I much regret that the mistake should have occurred.

[2] 'Gazzetta Medica Italiana-Lombardia.' Serie VI. t. 1, 1868.

ductive from 114·5°; a decoction of pumpkin[1] produces them at 110° and not at 112°; the albumen of an egg is productive at 112°, and at 113° commences to show signs of disintegration; and the decoction of hay gives, moreover, Vibrios at 110°, but cannot when subjected to a higher temperature[2].' These experiments were all comparable with one another, from the fact that they were performed during the months of July and August, when the atmospheric temperature remained pretty constantly at from 25°–27°C (77°–80°F)[3].

Thinking it very desirable to ascertain the highest point to which some solutions might be heated without being rendered unproductive; and also wishing

---

[1] Heated to any extent short of 110°C, this fluid is said by Prof. Cantoni to produce *Vibrios* with astonishing rapidity.

[2] Solutions of Liebig's soup were also found, on another occasion, to be unproductive at and above this point, though they were productive after exposure to temperatures a little lower, providing the daily atmospheric temperature remained high.

[3] Prof. Cantoni naturally enough asks, why it should be, if the *Vibriones* are in all cases produced from germs, that these germs should be killed at such different temperatures in different fluids; and why the germs (which nobody has seen) should require such a very much higher temperature to kill them, than suffices to destroy their parents? The latter he, also, believes to be destroyed by a temperature of about 60° C. Then, again, there is the fact that the amount of heat which is necessary in order to stop the productivity of the fluid (other things being equal), becomes lower and lower as the temperature of the air diminishes—so that the yolk of egg, for instance, which, with a temperature of 25°C, will produce after being heated even to 117°C, will not produce after being heated only to 110° if the temperature of the air continues at 20°, whilst when it is still further reduced to 15° (59°F) the fluid ceases to be productive after it has been exposed to 105° or even 100°.

to ascertain what amount of evidence was obtainable as to the possibility of living matter being produced *de novo*, from changes taking place, in the main, amongst inorganic or mineral elements, I made during the present and the past year many experiments, some of which I will now detail. With the exception of Prof. Mantegazza's one experiment, and of one by Prof. Wyman, all the flasks in my experiments have been raised to temperatures higher than any which had previously been resorted to.

In those which have been productive, the hermetically closed flasks have been exposed to temperatures ranging from 270°–307°F (132°–153°C), though in other unproductive experiments the flasks have been heated to 327°F and 464°F. As on other occasions, the solutions were heated *in vacuo*, so that the experiments also differed in this respect from those of Mantegazza, Wyman, and Cantoni, who adhered to the method pursued by Spallanzani and Needham.

In some of my earlier experiments, I had the benefit of Prof. Frankland's assistance, though subsequently he kindly placed his digester at my disposal[1].

The mode of preparation of the flasks and the instrument employed for heating them were thus described by Prof. Frankland:—

[1] Of the Experiments now about to be recorded, those in which the flasks were heated under Dr. Frankland's superintendence are Nos. *g, h, j, k, s, u, w,* and *y,* whilst those which were executed alone by me in University College are Nos. *a, b, c, d, e, f, l, m, n, o, p, q, r, t, v, x,* and *z.*

'Each liquid was placed in a glass tube about three-quarters of an inch in diameter, nine inches long, and closed at one end by fusion of the glass. The open end of the tube was then drawn out so as to form a thick capillary tube, which was afterwards connected with a Sprengel's mercurial pump. The action of the pump soon produced a tolerably good vacuum, when on gently warming the liquid, the latter began to boil, its vapour expelling the last traces of air from the apparatus. After the boiling had been continued for several minutes, the tube was hermetically sealed at the capillary part.

'The tubes were now placed in the wrought iron digester, described by me in the Philosophical Transactions for 1854, p. 260. It consists essentially of a cylindrical iron vessel, with a tightly-fitting cover, which can be securely screwed on to it. Through the centre of the cover passes an iron tube, which descends half way down the centre of the cylinder. This tube is closed at bottom, and contains a column of mercury about an inch long, and a thermometer plunged into the mercury shows the temperature of the liquid inside the digester.

'Water being now poured into the digester until it covered the tubes, and the cover having been screwed on, heat was applied by means of a gas stove.

'The temperature was allowed to rise to about 150°C, and was maintained between 146° and 153°C for four hours[1], and it is almost needless to say that every part of the sealed tubes and their contents was exposed to this temperature during the whole time. The glass tubes, though of moderately thick glass only, ran no risk of fracture, because the pressure inside them was approximately counterbalanced by the pressure of steam outside.'

In all the subsequent experiments which I performed alone, an approximate vacuum was procured, as in my former experiments, by boiling the fluids and sealing the flasks hermetically during ebullition. The vacuum may have been somewhat less perfect in these cases than when it was procured by means of the Sprengel pump, though this circumstance does not in the least diminish the value of the experiments. The vacuum was not desired, because, by working under these conditions, all atmospheric 'germs' might be abstracted— since in all cases the flasks were exposed to a temperature which is acknowledged to be destructive of living things whether in air or in fluids. In the experiments of Mantegazza, Wyman, and Cantoni, the portions of the closed flasks above the level of the fluids were filled with ordinary air. If, therefore, the vacuum may not have been quite so complete in some of my latter experiments as in those in which I had the benefit of Prof. Frankland's assistance, it is a matter

---

[1] This prolonged period of exposure was subsequently only resorted to in some of the experiments. In others they were exposed for shorter periods, as will be seen from the different headings.

of no importance, and does not in the least affect their value.

Solutions exposed in airless and hermetically sealed flasks to 270°–275° F (132°–135°C) for twenty minutes, and subsequently maintained at a temperature of 70°–80° F. These flasks were also exposed to direct sunlight for eight days [1].

Experiment a. A strong infusion of turnip, rendered very faintly alkaline by liquor potassæ, to which a few muscular fibres of a cod-fish were added.

When taken from the digester the fluid was found to have assumed a pale brownish colour. The flask was kept in a warm place, in addition to being exposed to direct sunlight. The vacuum having been ascertained to be partially preserved, the neck of the flask was broken two months after the date of its preparation. The reaction of the fluid was then decidedly *acid*, and the odour (differing altogether from that of mere baked turnip) was sour, though not at all fœtid. The fluid was very slightly turbid, and there was a well-marked sediment consisting of reddish-brown fragments, and a light flocculent deposit. On microscopical examination, the fragments were found to be portions of altered muscular fibre, whilst the flocculent deposit was composed,

---

[1] The solutions and flasks were exposed to a temperature of from 110°–135°C for *one hour*, if we include the twenty minutes' exposure, and also the period which elapsed till the fluid in the digester cooled down to 110°C. The subsequent exposure to direct sunlight was, for several hours daily, during some very fine weather in the month of March.

for the most part, of granular aggregations and *Bacteria*. In the portions of fluid and deposit which were examined,

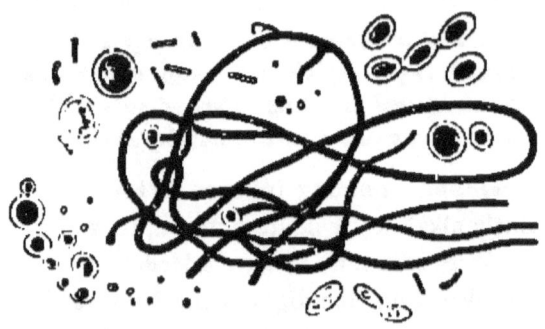

Fig. 30.

Bacteria, Torula, Fungus-mycelium, and Spores of different sizes, from a neutralized Turnip Infusion. (× 800.)

there were thousands of *Bacteria* of most diverse shapes and sizes, either separate or aggregated into flakes. There were also a large number of monilated chains[1] of various lengths, though mostly short; a large number of small spherical *Torula* cells with mere granular contents, and a smaller number of ovoid, vacuolated cells. There were, in addition, a considerable number of brownish nucleated spores, gradually increasing in size from mere specks about $\frac{1}{30000}$" in diameter, up to bodies $\frac{1}{1800}$" in diameter; and also a small quantity of a mycelial filament, having solid protoplasmic contents,

---

[1] Similar to those found in other turnip infusions which have been slightly acid and not fœtid. See *Appendix* C, *Experiments* xxi. and xxvi.

broken at intervals, and bearing bud-like projections, each of which was capped with a single spore.

Experiment b. An infusion of common cress (*Lepidium sativum*), to which a few of the leaves and stalks of the plant were added.

This was kept in the same way as the last solution, and was similarly exposed to sun-light for a few days.

After nine weeks, and before the neck of the flask was broken, the vacuum was found to be well preserved. The reaction of the fluid was distinctly acid, but there was no notable odour of any kind. The fluid itself was tolerably clear and free from scum, though there was a considerable quantity of a dirty-looking flocculent sediment at the bottom of the flask, amongst the débris of the cress. On microscopical examination of portions of these fragments, most of the cells in the stalks were found crowded with very actively-moving granules. In some of the leaves the chlorophyle was not much altered, whilst in others it presented various stages of decomposition—being in some cells wholly replaced by a blackish-brown granular material. Large quantities of such matter also existed, either dispersed or aggregated, amongst the sediment; and in some of it three minute and delicate *Protamœbæ* were seen, creeping with moderately-rapid, slug-like, movements and changes of form. They contained no nucleus, and presented only a few granules in their interior. Partly in the same drop, and partly in others, there were also seen more than a dozen very active *Monads*, $\frac{1}{1000}''$ in diameter—each being provided with a long rapidly-

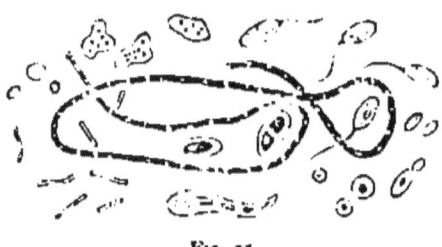

Fig. 31.

Bacteria, Torulæ, Protamoba, Monads, &c., from an infusion of Common Cress. (× 800.)

moving flagellum, with which neighbouring granules were lashed about [1]. There were many smaller motionless spherules, of different sizes, whose body-substance presented a similar appearance to that of the *Monads*. There were also several unjointed *Bacteria*, presenting most rapid progressive movements, accompanied by rapid axial rotations; many *Torula*-cells of different kinds, and coarser fungus spores, some of them with segmented protoplasmic contents; and lastly, some mycelial or algoid filaments, containing tolerably equal blocks of colourless protoplasm within an investing sheath.

[1] A drop containing several of the Monads was placed for about five minutes on a glass slip, in a warm-water oven maintained at a temperature of 140° F. All the movements of the Monads ceased from that time; and they never again showed any signs of life.

Experiment c. An infusion of beef with some muscular fibres, prepared at the same time, similarly exposed, and also opened after nine weeks, was not found to contain any living things, though there was an abundance of mere moving granules. Some of the muscular fibres had preserved their natural appearance, whilst others had lost it, and had become completely granular.

Experiment d. An infusion of cod-fish muscle, similarly prepared and exposed, also proved quite sterile.

Experiment o. A solution containing ten grains of potash and ammonia alum, three grains of tartar emetic, and half a grain of new cheese to an ounce of distilled water.

The vacuum having been ascertained to be still partly preserved, this flask was opened at the end of the seventh week. The fluid was odourless, and its reaction neutral. There was a considerable quantity of dirty-looking deposit, and some oily matter on the surface, though the fluid itself was tolerably clear. The deposit was, for the most part, composed of dark granules, together with mucoid flakes also containing granules. Mixed with the moving granules were a considerable number of *Bacteria*—partly of the ordinary shape, and partly of the monilated variety—the movements of which were tolerably extensive. They travelled over small areas, and danced around one another, in a manner quite different from the mere granules with which they were intermixed.

There were no traces of *Torula* or *Leptothrix* filaments.

Experiment f. A solution containing ten grains of ammonic tartrate and three grains of sodic phosphate, with half a grain of new cheese, to an ounce of distilled water.

The vacuum having been ascertained to be well preserved, the flask was opened in the early part of the sixth week. The fluid was found to have a neutral reaction, and there was a well-marked, whitish deposit at the bottom of the vessel. On microscopical examination, no *Bacteria*, *Torula*, or Fungi were found, but there were a great number of fibres, exactly like unsegmented *Leptothrix* filaments, growing from the midst of aggregations of the irregular particles of which the deposit was composed. Other filaments were seen having a close resemblance to the spiral fibres met with in somewhat similar solutions which were exposed to a lower temperature [1]. They were, however, in smaller masses, the spirals were less marked, and transitional states existed between them and the fibres which resembled *Leptothrix* [2].

[1] See *Appendix* A, pp. v—ix.

[2] Since this was written I have seen *Leptothrix* (or *Spirulina*) filaments, growing so as to form quite irregular, spirally-disposed masses of different sizes. These were obtained from the surface of water, in which a few young twigs of the common elder had been immersed for five or six days. All stages were seen, also, between such spiral masses and more ordinary *Bacteria* and *Vibrio* forms. As the latter elongated they gradually became curved. Segmentations were seen, at intervals, in the internal solid protoplasm of which they were principally composed.

Solutions exposed in airless and hermetically-sealed flasks to 293°F (145°C), for from five to twenty minutes; and subsequently maintained at a temperature of 70–80°F.

Experiment g. A turnip infusion rendered very faintly alkaline by liquor potassæ.

The flask was opened after nine weeks, when the vacuum was found to be partially preserved. The fluid was still of the same light brown colour as when it was taken from the digester. Its reaction was now decidedly acid, though the odour was slightly sour and not fœtid. There was a small quantity of granular scum on some parts of the surface, and a distinct brownish flocculent sediment, but the bulk of the fluid was tolerably clear. On microscopical examination of the deposit, a number of minute *Torula*-cells were found, both singly and in groups. They varied from the minutest specks up to bodies $\frac{1}{1000}$" in breadth, and were mostly with-

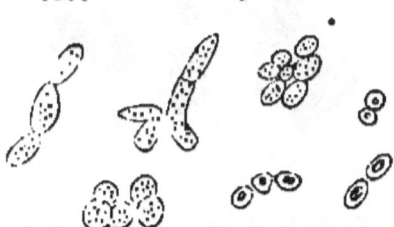

FIG. 32.
Various kinds of *Torulæ* from a neutralized Infusion of Turnip. (× 600.)

out nuclei or vacuoles. Some were growing out into mycelial filaments. Other small, nucleated, spores were also met with, singly and in groups; and in addition, a thick-walled body with granular contents, $\frac{1}{1375}''$ in diameter. No distinct *Bacteria* were seen, though there were numerous acicular crystals, some solitary, and others in peculiar bundles having constrictions at intervals. A number of minute octohedral and prismatic crystals were also present [1].

Experiment h. A solution containing seven grains of iron and ammonic citrate (mixed with a few very minute fibres of deal wood), seven grains of ammonic tartrate, and three grains of sodic phosphate, to one ounce of distilled water.

When taken from the digester this solution was found to have become fluorescent—being blackish by reflected, and olive-green in colour by transmitted light. After a time, some cloud-like flakes appeared, and also an increasing quantity of sediment. After eight months,

Fig. 33.

Bright green Organisms resembling *Pediastrea*, from a Solution containing Iron and Ammonic Citrate and other ingredients. (× 800.)

the vacuum being still well preserved, the neck of the flask was broken and its contents examined micro-

---

[1] Only three drops of the fluid were examined.

scopically. The sediment contained a few wood fibres and ducts, and very much granular matter together with actively-moving particles, though no distinct *Bacteria*. There were also very many ovoid cells (single, and in groups of two to eight), about $\frac{1}{1000}$" in length, with somewhat granular and rather bright green contents —in which a vacuole existed. Other somewhat similar bodies were seen in groups of four, each segment of which was surrounded by a hyaline envelope. In one group the protoplasm within the hyaline envelope was seen to have undergone segmentation.

Some of this fluid was put on one side in a small corked tube, and when examined after six weeks, the cells had lost all their green colour—the contents having assumed a dirty yellowish brown hue [1].

Experiment J. A solution containing fifteen grains of iron and ammonic citrate (mixed with a few minute fibres of deal wood), in one ounce of distilled water.

The vacuum having been ascertained to be well preserved, the neck of the flask was broken eight months after its preparation. The fluid, which was still very faintly acid, was not fluorescent, though there had been a notable amount of sediment for some time. On microscopical examination, the latter was found to consist of dotted ducts and minute portions of woody fibre, mixed with large quantities of granular matter

[1] A certain general resemblance exists between the organisms met with in this experiment, and those of *Experiments j, l,* and *m,* as well as those of *Experiment* 2, recorded at p. 365.

(aggregated into flakes), and a great multitude of very actively-moving particles. Some of them had a figure-of-8 shape, and others were well-formed *Bacteria*. There were also a few monilated chains, as well as simple, unsegmented *Leptothrix* filaments. The most

Fig. 34.

Bacteria, different kinds of *Leptothrix*, and green Organisms resembling Desmids, from a Solution of Iron and Ammonic Citrate. (× 800.)

notable products, however, were a great number of single and aggregated organisms, resembling certain simple Desmids and *Pediastreæ*. Like them, also, they exhibited slow oscillations or partial slight rotations. Their contents were decidedly greenish, though the hue was not so bright as that of the organisms found in the last solution. Some were single, and others were in groups of four or eight [1].

Two drops of the solution, containing some of the sediment, were placed in a clean animalcule-cage,

---

[1] The organisms in this solution more closely resembled those of *Experiment* 2 (p. 365) than those of *Experiments* l and m. *Bacteria* were contained in both, and the solutions themselves were also more similar —neither of them had become fluorescent.

which was kept at a temperature of 85°—90°F in a developing oven. After twenty-four hours the groups and single Desmid-like bodies were still seen undergoing partial rotations, and the number of *Bacteria* had increased in quantity. After forty-eight hours, a group of eight cells, in addition to solitary and smaller groups, was seen distinctly oscillating; and there were two or three elongated bodies (containing segmented blocks of protoplasm), which seemed to have resulted from the development of single organisms; there were also several *Leptothrix* filaments, and a great increase had taken place in the number of *Bacteria*, which showed very active movements of translation. After this period the contents of the Desmid-like bodies began to fade, and they seemed gradually to die; though the *Bacteria* lived and increased for several days, during which the specimen was kept under observation.

Experiment k. A solution containing ten grains of ammonic sulphate, and ten minims of dilute liquor ferri perchloridi in one ounce of distilled water.

A thick scum formed on the surface after about two months. The flask was opened at the expiration of the third month, the vacuum being still well preserved. On microscopical examination, no trace of living things was to be seen amongst the amorphous deposit at the bottom of the flask. The pellicle was found to present a cellular arrangement (Fig. 39). It polarized light, however, and was obviously crystalline in constitution. It was very heavy—sinking at once in the watch-glass as soon as its upper surface was wetted. This solution contained no carbon (see *Appendix* A, p. x).

Experiment 1. A solution containing twelve grains of iron and ammonic citrate (mixed with a few very minute fibres of deal wood) in one ounce of distilled water.

The flask was opened at the commencement of the seventh week from the date of preparation. It was exposed to sunlight for about eight days during the last fortnight, though previous to this the amount of sediment had gradually increased. After the second or third exposure the previously dark brown fluid became fluorescent—black to reflected, but olive-coloured to transmitted light. There was also a brownish deposit on one side of the tube. When the flask was opened it was found that the vacuum was almost wholly impaired, by an internal evolution of gas. On microscopical examination of a drop of the fluid (containing sediment), multitudes of granules, separate and aggregated into flakes, were seen. There were no distinct *Bacteria*, though large numbers of the rounded and ovoid organisms similar to those met with in *Exps.* 9 and 12, were intermixed with the granules. They were partly separate, partly in groups of fours and eights. They varied considerably in size, and also in colour—some being decidedly greenish, and others quite yellow and faded. In the granular aggregations, different stages in the growth of these Desmid-like bodies were to be recognized. What appeared to be short *Leptothrix* filaments issued from some of the granular masses.

Experiment m. Some of the same solution as was employed in the last experiment, similarly exposed and rendered similarly fluorescent. After the exposure to sunlight, however, the tube was kept in ordinary daylight for two weeks, so that it was not opened till the commencement of the ninth week.

It was then found that the vacuum was impaired as in the last experiment. On microscopical examination of the sediment the same kind of granules (separate and aggregated) were seen, and also great multitudes of the Desmid-like organisms. These existed more abundantly than in the last solution. Here also there was the same fresh appearance of some, and faded look of others, and also great variations in size—the largest being $\frac{1}{1100}''$ in length, whilst many were not more than $\frac{1}{1000}''$ in length. Several groups of four were seen, in

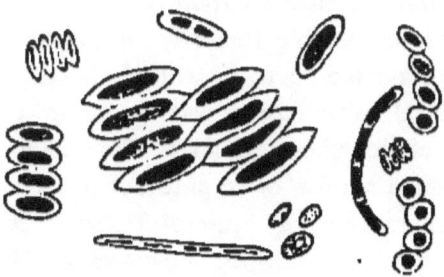

Fig. 35.

Greenish, Desmid-like Organisms of different kinds, and *Torulæ*, found in a fluorescent solution of Iron and Ammonic Citrate. (× 800.)

which the separate elements were spherical instead of ovoid. There were also many straight, or slightly curved bodies, having blocks of protoplasm within—which apparently resulted from a longitudinal growth of single frustules. The groups of organisms, as well as those which were single, exhibited the same slow partial rotations, forwards and backwards, which had been observed in those produced in other solutions.

Some of this solution was put into a corked tube, and when it was examined two months afterwards, all the frustules had lost their greenish colour, and were apparently quite dead.

Experiment n. A solution containing ten grains of ammonic carbonate, and three grains of sodic phosphate in one ounce of distilled water.

The flask was opened in the commencement of the twelfth week from the date of preparation, the vacuum having been previously ascertained to be well preserved. The reaction of the solution was slightly *alkaline*. There was no notable turbidity of the fluid, though there was a small amount of whitish deposit, which on microscopical examination was found to be mostly composed of amorphous granules. The fluid itself contained a small number of minute but distinct *Bacteria*, and also a number of figure-of-8 shaped bodies—all of which exhibited sluggish movements. They were very faint in colour, so that on this account and owing to their small size, although plentiful enough, they were somewhat difficult to recognize. A drop of the solution, on the application of the covering glass, had been immediately cemented, and when examined after twenty-four hours, both varieties of *Bacteria* had notably increased in quantity, and had become somewhat larger, though their movements were not at all more active.

Experiment o. An infusion of hay, which had become slightly darker by the exposure to heat, and in which a fine flocculent sediment had been thrown down.

The flask was opened at the end of the seventh week, the vacuum being still well preserved. The reaction of the fluid was then found to be acid, and its odour was hay-like though somewhat altered in character. No organisms of any kind were discovered in the fluid, or amidst the minutely granular deposit.

Experiment p. An infusion of turnip (not neutralized but in its natural slightly acid condition) was found to have assumed the colour of pale sherry when removed from the digester. There was also a small amount of light flocculent sediment.

The flask was opened eight weeks afterwards; the vacuum having been well preserved. The reaction of the fluid was still acid, and its odour was that of baked turnip. There was a considerable quantity of granular matter at the bottom of the flask, but after careful microscopical examination, no organisms of any kind could be detected [1].

[1] Compare the results of this experiment with those of Nos. *a* and *g*. The very slight addition of dilute liquor potassæ to the latter fluids seems to have been the immediately determining cause of their productiveness (see p. 383). Some other experiments recorded in

After it had been examined, the remainder of the fluid was left in the open flask. Six weeks afterwards it was accidentally noticed, and a bluish-green fungus was seen covering the surface of the fluid. On microscopical examination of the sediment which had collected at the bottom of the flask, multitudes of *Torula* cells were found, though there was a complete absence of *Bacteria* [1].

Solutions exposed in airless and hermetically-sealed flasks to a temperature of 295°—307°F (146°—153°C) for four hours, and subsequently maintained at a temperature of 70°—80°F.

Experiment q. An infusion of turnip which had been much charred by the high temperature. It had become brown in colour, and in addition there was a

---

Appendix C, also point to the desirability of neutralizing a turnip infusion if we wish to increase the chances of finding organisms within the flasks. In *Exps.* o and g the odour was not that of mere baked turnip, and the solutions had become acid—fermentation had in fact taken place.

[1] I have also on other occasions (see *Appendix* C, *Exp.* xviii.) frequently found, when the fermentability of certain fluids is lowered by the influence of heat, that they yield nothing but slowly-growing *Torulæ*, although a portion of the same fluid, unheated and standing beneath the same bell-jar, would speedily become turbid and yield myriads of *Bacteria* without *Torulæ*. Facts of this kind are very interesting, and serve to throw light upon the morphological differences which exist between *Bacteria* and *Torulæ*. Crystals which are produced rapidly, are always smaller and less perfect in form than those of slower growth.

blackish-brown deposit of charred matter, which, after it had thoroughly settled, was about equal to one-twelfth of the bulk of the fluid.

The flask was opened at the end of the eighth week, when the vacuum was found to be well preserved. The odour of the fluid was for the most part that of baked turnip, and its reaction was acid. The deposit was composed of amorphous granules, and also of a multitude of reddish or claret-coloured spherules of various sizes, but no organisms of any kind could be discovered.

Experiment r. An infusion of turnip rendered slightly alkaline by the addition of dilute liquor ammoniæ, was affected in almost precisely the same way as in the last experiment.

The flask was prepared at the same time, and opened after the same interval. The deposit, in its microscopical characters, resembled that found in the last experiment, and there was a similar absence of all organisms [1].

Experiment s. A tube containing an unaltered infusion of turnip was opened at the end of the twelfth day.

When received from Dr. Frankland, the fluid had been changed to a decided but light brown colour, and there was some quantity of a blackish-brown granular

---

[1] Considering the results which were obtained in *Exps.* a and g, I think that a turnip infusion neutralized by liquor potassæ rather than liquor ammoniæ, is one of the most favourable combinations for producing organisms after exposure to high temperatures.

sediment, though the infusion had been quite free from all deposit when placed in the digester. After this tube was suspended in a warm place, as the others had been, it remained in the same position till it was taken down to be opened. A slight scum or pellicle, which partially covered the surface, was observed on the sixth day. During the succeeding days it did not increase much in extent, though it became somewhat thicker. Although very great care was taken, still the slight movement of the flask, occasioned in knocking off its top, caused the pellicle to break up and sink [1].

The contents of the flask emitted a somewhat fragrant odour of baked turnip, and the reaction of the fluid was still slightly acid. On microscopical examination, a great deal of mere granular *débris* and irregular masses of a brownish colour were found, and also a very large number of dark, and apparently homogeneous reddish-brown spherules, mostly varying in size from $\frac{1}{1800}''$ to $\frac{1}{10000}''$ in diameter, partly single and partly in groups of various kinds. There were no distinct *Bacteria*, though in one of the drops examined there was a delicate tailed-monad in active movement—a specimen of *Monas lens*, in fact, $\frac{1}{1800}''$ in diameter, having

[1] It was owing to the appearance of the pellicle and the seeming likelihood of its breaking up and sinking to the bottom of the vessel, as others had done, if allowed to remain, that I was induced to open this tube so early. I thought it possible that nothing else might form afterwards, and felt anxious to examine the pellicle before it became mixed with the granular deposit.

a distinct vacuole in the midst of the granular contents of the cell, and a rapidly-moving flagellum.

Experiment t. An infusion of hay. When taken from the digester there was a considerable quantity of brownish-black, charred, organic matter at the bottom of the flask, though the fluid itself was clear and of a dark sherry colour.

The flask was opened on the fourteenth day; and for six or seven days previously a slight scum had been seen covering part of the surface of the fluid, the solution itself remaining clear. The fluid was found to be quite strongly acid, whilst its odour was sour and not at all hay-like. The scum was found to be composed of mere charred granules and globules, and no trace of organisms could be found either in the fluid or amongst the deposit [1].

Experiment u. A solution containing fifteen grains of ammonic carbonate, and five grains of sodic phosphate, in one ounce of distilled water.

When taken from the digester the glass of the tube was found to be considerably corroded, and there was

---

[1] This infusion had been evidently wholly altered in quality by the high temperature to which it had been exposed; and from the fact that it was left in an open flask for more than a week, and was still found to be free from any trace of living things, its original sterility cannot be wondered at. It is easy enough to believe that the different organic compounds existing in different infusions would be differently capable of resisting the destructive influence of heat; so that some infusions may be much more favourable than others for experiments in which high temperatures are resorted to.

a whitish deposit as a result of this. After a few weeks many bluish cloudlike masses became visible in the fluid, dotted here and there with minute whitish spots, but no pellicle made its appearance on the surface. The flask was opened at the end of the fifteenth week, no apparent change having taken place. On microscopical examination the flakes were found to have a very minutely granular composition, and the whitish spots on them consisted of aggregations of minute linear crystals, about $\frac{1}{30000}$" in length. The deposit was composed of amorphous particles and spherules, but there was no trace of the existence of living things[1].

Experiment v. A solution of eight grains of ammonic carbonate and three grains of sodic phosphate in one ounce of distilled water.

When taken from the digester the glass was not in the least corroded. The tube was opened at the expiration of eight weeks, when the vacuum was found to be well preserved. There was a very small amount of whitish deposit at the bottom and sides of the tube, though there never had been any trace of scum on the surface. When examined microscopically the deposit was found to be composed of more or less rounded refractive particles, imbedded in a homogeneous colourless matrix. There were also very many motionless rod-

---

[1] This tube was one of English glass. The quality of the solution must have been altogether altered by the corrosion—a great part, if not the whole, of the phosphoric acid being precipitated in the form of insoluble phosphate of lead.

like bodies from $\frac{1}{8000}''$ to $\frac{1}{1800}''$ in length (crystalline?), but no trace of living things, either amongst them or suspended in the fluid itself.

Experiment w. A solution containing an unweighed quantity of ammonic carbonate and sodic phosphate in distilled water.

The fluid was at first somewhat whitish and clouded. From the twentieth to the thirtieth day a thin pellicle had been seen gradually accumulating on its surface; and in the latter four or five days this increased much in thickness, and gradually assumed a distinct mucoid appearance. The fluid itself was tolerably clear, though an apparent turbidity was given by the presence of a fine whitish deposit on the sides of the glass.

The flask was opened on the thirtieth day, and the reaction of the fluid was then found to be neutral. When submitted to microscopical examination portions of the pellicle were seen to be made up of large, irregular, and highly-refractive particles, imbedded in a transparent jelly-like material. The particles were most varied in size and shape, many of them being variously branched and knobbed. Several very delicate perfectly hyaline vesicles about $\frac{1}{1000}''$ in diameter, altogether free from solid contents, were seen; and, in addition, there were a number of figure-of-8 bodies, exhibiting tolerably active vibrations, each half of which was about $\frac{1}{10000}''$ in diameter.

A subsequent careful examination, on the same evening, of a quantity of the granular matter of the pellicle (which had been mounted on two microscope-slips, and at once protected by surrounding the covering glasses with cement), revealed five spherical or ovoid spores, the average size of which was about $\frac{1}{3300}''$ in diameter. They all possessed a more or less perfectly-

Fig. 36.

Spore-like bodies, and figure-of-8 particles, from a solution of Ammonic Carbonate and Sodic Phosphate. (× 600.)

formed nucleus, and all showed a most distinct doubly-contoured wall. One of the smaller of them showed that it had reached a stage when it was about to germinate. In addition, a small mass of *Sarcina*-like material was seen, which was not very distinctly defined, owing to its being still in a somewhat embryonic stage.

Experiment x. A solution containing eight grains of ammonic carbonate and three grains of sodic phosphate.

The vacuum having been ascertained to be well preserved, the tube was opened in the beginning of the eleventh week. There was no pellicle or scum of any kind, and no turbidity, though there was a very small amount of deposit at the bottom of the vessel. The reaction of the fluid was decidedly though not strongly alkaline. On microscopical examination, the deposit was found to be principally made up of mere amorphous granules—separate, as well as forming aggregations of various sizes. Here and there, however, there were granules, both separate and aggregated, of a much less refractive character, and more closely resembling organic particles. Short homogeneous filaments, having all the appearance of *Leptothrix*, were seen to project from two or three of the granule heaps.

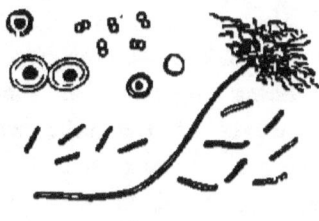

Fig. 37.

Bacteria, Leptothrix, and Spore-like bodies found in a Solution of Ammonic Carbonate and Sodic Phosphate. (× 800.)

Several *Bacteria*, some of medium size, and others somewhat large and unjointed, were observed, flitting across the field of view with quite rapid undulating movements, whilst others were seen rapidly rotating on their long axis. There were also many figure-of-8 shaped bodies which showed distinct and slightly progressive movements—quite different from those which are called 'Brownian'—though many single particles were seen which soon ceased to exhibit movements of any kind. In addition, there were several spore-like bodies having doubly-contoured walls, which were also similar to those of the last solution.

Experiment y. A solution containing an unweighed quantity of ammonic tartrate and sodic phosphate in distilled water.

The solution in this tube was at first quite colourless, clear, and free from visible deposit. About the fifth or sixth day, however, after it had been suspended in a warm place, a number of small, pale, bluish-white flocculi made their appearance throughout the solution, and continued always in the same situation except when the fluid was shaken,—owing apparently to their specific weight being the same as that of the fluid itself. The contents of the tube were repeatedly scanned with the greatest care with the aid of a lens, though nothing else could be seen until about the expiration of a month. Then there was observed, attached to one of the flocculi, about $\frac{1}{4}''$ from the bottom of the vessel, a small, opaque, whitish speck, scarcely bigger than a pin's point. This seemed to increase very slowly in size for the next three or four weeks, and then another smaller mass was also perceived. At the expiration of this time the larger mass was more than $\frac{1}{8}''$ in diameter. Both could be, and were, seen by several people with the naked eye. During the three weeks immediately preceding the opening of the flask, it was often remarked that the mass did not appear to have undergone any increase in size.

It was found that the tube acted as a water-hammer only to a trifling extent before it was opened, though, when the narrow end of the tube was broken off, there was a slight dull report, and a quantity of small particles of glass were swept by the in-rush of air into the fluid. There had still, then, been a partial vacuum in the tube. The reaction of the fluid was found to be slightly acid.

This tube was opened in Dr. Sharpey's presence. He had examined the white masses previously with a pocket-lens, and when the vessel was broken the larger white mass issued with some of the first portions of the fluid, which were poured into a large watch-glass. It was at once taken up on the point of a penknife and transferred to a clean glass slip, where it was immersed in a drop of the experimental fluid and then protected by a thin glass cover. On microscopical examination, we at once saw that the whitish mass was composed of a number of rounded and ovoidal spores, with mycelial filaments issuing from them, in all stages of development. The spores varied much in shape and dimensions; the prevalent size being about $\frac{1}{8800}''$ in diameter, though one was seen as much as $\frac{1}{2000}''$ in diameter. They all possessed a single and rather large nucleus, which was mostly made up of an aggregation of granular particles. Some were just beginning to develop mycelial filaments; others had already given origin to such filaments, which were about $\frac{1}{1800}''$ in diameter, and in which were scattered some colourless protoplasmic granules, but no vacuoles. Contiguous to these fresh and evidently living portions of the plant, there were other parts in all stages of decay, in which

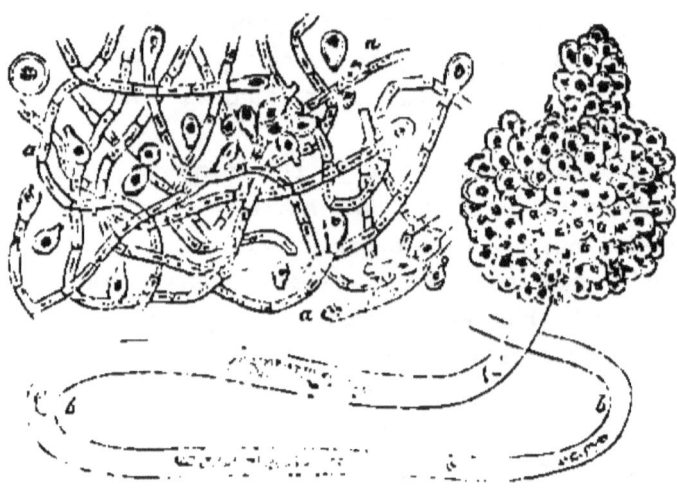

Fig. 38.

Fungus found in a solution of Ammonic Tartrate and Sodic Phosphate. (× 600.)

the remains of the filaments were seen in the form of more or less irregular rows of brownish granules—representing the altered protoplasmic contents of a previous filament, whose walls were now often scarcely visible. Subsequently the smaller white mass was picked out, and this was found to contain some living mycelium and spores, and also a considerable patch of decaying filaments, in connection with which there was a long and broader filament bearing at its distal extremity a large aggregation of more than 100 spores, quite naked, and very similar in character to those from which the mycelial thread arose. This plant was evidently a *Penicillium*, quite similar to what had been obtained from other ammonic tartrate and sodic phosphate solutions[1]. The delicate flocculi that first made

[1] I have ascertained that the life of this particular fungus is destroyed by exposure for a few minutes to the influence of boiling water. Placed even in a mere corked flask, containing an ammonic tartrate solution, the boiled fungus does not grow, whilst an unboiled specimen will slowly increase and grow in all directions. (The *extremely slow growth* of the fungus in this solution is very remarkable, when compared with the rapidity with which other minute fungi increase in organic solutions.) A specimen which had been boiled for 5″ was kept under observation for nearly three months, and it showed not the slightest signs of growth. Mere exposure to the influence of boiling water for a few minutes suffices to break up and disperse such heads of fructification as are represented in Fig. 38, and also to produce some amount of disorganization of the filaments. How much more, therefore, does it seem likely that an exposure to 146-153°C for four hours, should prove destructive even to mere organic forms? With the view of answering this question, I placed a quantity of a small fungus, consisting of mycelial filaments and multitudes of spores (closely resembling, although not quite so delicate as those which were met with in the saline mixtures), into a solution, of the same strength as that which had been previously employed, of tartrate of ammonia and phosphate of soda in distilled water, and then handed it over to Dr. Frankland with the request that he would kindly treat this in the same way as he had done the other solutions. Accordingly, on May 11, a vacuum having been produced within the flask before it was hermetically sealed, the solution was submitted in the same digester to a temperature of 146-153°C for four hours. When taken from the digester, the previously whitish mass of fungus filaments and spores had assumed a decidedly brownish colour, and it was in great part converted into mere *débris*. On the following morning the flask was broken, and some of the remains of the fungus and its spores were

their appearance in the solution, and which persisted throughout, were gelatinous and made up of aggregations of the finest granules. These, however, became almost invisible when mounted in glycerine and carbolic acid.

Experiment 8. A solution containing eight grains of ammonic tartrate, and three grains of sodic phosphate, in one ounce of New River water (from the tap).

On dissolving the crystals in this water, a small amount of fine white precipitate was produced. After the tube was taken from the digester a fine white deposit soon subsided. No cloud-like flocculi appeared, and no further change was discovered in the solution. The tube was opened on the sixty-sixth day, after the vacuum had been ascertained to be still well preserved. The fluid had a neutral reaction, and on microscopical examination no living things could be found, either in it or amongst the amorphous granules of the sediment [1].

In addition to the experiments now recorded, I have performed twenty others in which the tubes and solu-

examined microscopically. *The plant was completely disorganised: not a single entire spore could be found*; they were all broken up into small and more or less irregular particles, and the filaments were more or less empty—containing no definite contents, and being only represented by torn tubular fragments of various sizes.

[1] New River water was used in this case with the view of seeing how the results would be modified. It probably contained too much lime-salts and other saline constituents. Germs, of course, may have been present in abundance, and yet no living things were subsequently to be found.

tions were exposed to still higher temperatures. In fourteen of these they were heated to a temperature ranging as high as 327°F (164°C) for four hours, whilst in the other six they were maintained at a temperature of 464°F (240°C) for one hour[1]. Some only of each set have been opened, but all of these were wholly devoid of living things. The infusions of hay and turnip which have been heated to the lower temperature of 327°F were almost hopelessly changed by this amount of heat. When taken from the digester, the previously clear and colourless turnip infusions, for instance, were of a brownish-black colour; owing to the abundant presence of granules and flakes of charred organic matter, which, after complete subsidence, occupied a space equal in bulk to one-fourth of the supernatant brown fluid. Infusions of hay were

[1] The latter tubes had been sealed in the blow-pipe flame during the ebullition of their contained fluids. Each was then placed in a very thick iron tube, whose internal diameter was only slightly larger than the glass, and into which some of the experimental fluid was also poured. Each iron tube was fitted with a screw-cap, which was firmly fastened by means of long iron wrenches, whilst the tube itself was secured in a vice. The hermetically sealed glass tube was thus enclosed within a hermetically closed iron tube, and by putting the same kind of fluid within each, an equal pressure was ensured upon the inner and the outer surfaces of the glass. All the tubes were then placed in an iron vessel containing five quarts of the very best French Colza oil, which was maintained, by means of gas burners, at a temperature of 464°F for one hour. Although the oil did not boil, the vapours which were given off at this temperature were most disagreeable and suffocating, and made me feel faint and giddy for several hours afterwards. Oils of inferior quality are not available, because they actually boil at much lower temperatures.

charred to a similar extent. Infusions of mutton, however, were scarcely altered in colour by this temperature or by the higher one of 464°F, and only a small amount of a light flocculent precipitate was thrown down. But on opening these flasks, the mutton infusion in each case presented a very strongly ammoniacal and otherwise unpleasant odour, and was also alkaline in reaction. The organic compounds had, therefore, been differently decomposed in these cases—in the hay and turnip infusions more or less pure carbon had been liberated, whilst the mutton solution probably broke up, in the main, into ammonia and carbonic anhydride. Seeing that the organic matter was so thoroughly destroyed in these infusions, there was not much chance that any mere shreds of it should have escaped uninjured in the tubes which contained various saline solutions. And in those experiments in which the tubes and their solutions were raised to the temperature of 464°F, all the disadvantages were further augmented by the extreme amount of corrosion of the tubes, which took place even when the hardest Bohemian glass was employed.

Confining ourselves, therefore, to a consideration of the experiments in which the closed flasks containing the experimental fluids have been heated to temperatures ranging from 270°–307°F, the results arrived at must be looked at from two or three different points of view.

Living organisms have, undoubtedly, been obtained from hermetically sealed flasks which had been heated for various periods to such temperatures; and many persons have been not a little surprised at the comparatively high forms of life which have presented themselves. This of itself has been deemed by some to be a difficulty of so serious a nature as to make them hesitate to accept the results of the experiments—principally on account of a preconceived notion that such organisms could not arise *de novo* and without ordinary parentage. Although willing to concede that the very simplest organisms might so arise, they are quite indisposed to believe that some of the higher forms which I have represented could have had an independent origin. I will not, however, at present enter upon this question, but will merely state that such difficulties are likely to disappear on a more thorough consideration of the subject—as it is hoped the reader will perceive after a perusal of Chaps. xiii. xiv. and xv.

Limiting ourselves at present to the fact that specks of living matter must either have been born in the experimental fluids after they had been exposed to the heat, or else (having pre-existed in the fluids) have braved its influence, we have merely again to consider which of these alternatives is the more probable. A choice must be made, and yet, as Prof. Wyman has pointed out, it does not appear at first sight that a profitable resort can be made to arguments from analogy.

He says [1]:—'If, on the one hand, it is urged that all organisms, in so far as the early history of them is known, are derived from ova, and therefore from analogy, we must ascribe a similar origin to these minute beings whose early history we do not know; it may be urged with equal force, on the other hand, that all ova and spores, in so far as we know anything about them, are destroyed by prolonged boiling: therefore from analogy we are equally bound to infer that Vibrios, Bacteriums, &c., could not have been derived from ova, since these would all have been destroyed by the conditions to which they have been subjected. The argument from analogy is as strong in the one case as in the other.'

We do not think, however, that the analogical arguments are so nearly balanced as Prof. Wyman appears to consider them. Whilst it would contradict all our previous experience, and violate the uniformity of natural laws, if certain pre-existing germs had been able to survive the exposure to which they must have been subjected in my experimental flasks, it would in no way outrage our experience if we found that specks of living matter might form *de novo* in some fluids, just as specks of crystalline matter form in other fluids—especially as they do actually appear, under the microscope, to arise in this way. The physical doctrines of life which are now so widely believed in, speak unhesi-

---

[1] 'American Journal of Science and Art,' July, 1862.

tatingly in favour of the latter possibility. So that we have an analogical argument of great force, and, in addition, most overwhelming experimental evidence, tending to oppose a mere dogma (*omne vivum ex vivo*) which many erroneously believe to be a legitimate inference from every-day experience. I say that this inference is erroneous, because, whilst we do know something about the ability which most organisms possess of reproducing similar organisms, we cannot possibly say, from direct observation, that *every* organism which exists has had a similar mode of origin. The cases in which organisms may have originated *de novo* are the very cases in which their mode of origin must elude our observation; for it can actually be shown that some organisms make their appearance in fluids after precisely the same fashion as crystals—that is to say, they can be seen to arise independently of all pre-existing visible germs [1].

Germs, therefore, which cannot be seen, and which nobody knows, are not only presumed to exist, but (contrary to all evidence) they are to be deemed capable of resisting the influence of far higher tempe-

---

[1] Having made this announcement on a previous occasion, and having had the satisfaction of finding it pooh-poohed as an idle statement, I, still believing in its truth, am glad to ascertain that others hold the same opinion. Dr. Burdon Sanderson says in a recent Memoir (Thirteenth Report of the Medical Officer of the Privy Council, p. 62):—'From the most careful and repeated examinations of water known to be zymotic, we have learnt that such waters often contain no elements or particles whatever which can be detected by the microscope.'

ratures than those which, on other occasions, are uniformly found to be fatal to all germs with which experiment is made, whether visible or invisible. And, moreover, some would have us give credence to these assumptions and improbabilities, in order to stave off a belief in the occurrence of something which would be thoroughly harmonious with all the best biological knowledge of the day.

Let the reader finally consider the extent of the contradictions which would be involved by the acceptance of the hypothesis, that the results of my experiments are to be explained by the assumption that some preexisting germs escaped death within the closed flasks, during the fiery ordeal to which they had been submitted.

It has been previously shown that *Bacteria* and *Torulæ*—as well as their germs, both visible and invisible [1]—are killed by exposure for ten minutes to a temperature of 140° F, and that they are even destroyed by a heat of 125° F, when it is prolonged for four hours. It is, moreover, admitted by all persons who have paid an adequate attention to the subject, that all such low organisms as may be met with in the experimental fluids, are unable to resist the destructive influence of boiling water. And yet now, in addition to all the evidence previously detailed, we again find living organisms occurring in closed flasks which have been

[1] See pp. 331-333.

exposed to 270°F, and 293°F, and even in others which have been heated to 295°-307°F for four hours. Of these experiments none have, perhaps, yielded more striking results than No. b. Here active *Protamœba* and ciliated *Monads* were taken from an hermetically sealed flask which, eight weeks previously, had been exposed to a temperature of 270°-275°F; and these very organisms were killed by the same temperature (140°F) as that which has been found to prove fatal to all other *Monads* and *Protamœba*.

It seems scarcely possible to present experimental evidence which could speak more plainly in favour of the occurrence of Archebiosis.

BEDFORD STREET, COVENT GARDEN, LONDON,
April 1872.

MACMILLAN & Co.'S CATALOGUE of WORKS in MATHEMATICS and PHYSICAL SCIENCE; including PURE and APPLIED MATHEMATICS; PHYSICS, ASTRONOMY, GEOLOGY, CHEMISTRY, ZOOLOGY, BOTANY; PHYSIOLOGY, ANATOMY and MEDICAL WORKS generally; and of WORKS in MENTAL and MORAL PHILOSOPHY and Allied Subjects.

MATHEMATICS.

Airy.— Works by G. B. AIRY, Astronomer Royal :—

ELEMENTARY TREATISE ON PARTIAL DIFFERENTIAL EQUATIONS. Designed for the Use of Students in the Universities. With Diagrams. Crown 8vo. cloth. 5*s.* 6*d.*

It is hoped that the methods of solution here explained, and the instances exhibited, will be found sufficient for application to nearly all the important problems of Physical Science, which require for their complete investigation the aid of Partial Differential Equations.

ON THE ALGEBRAICAL AND NUMERICAL THEORY OF ERRORS OF OBSERVATIONS AND THE COMBINATION OF OBSERVATIONS. Crown 8vo. cloth. 6*s.* 6*d.*

In order to spare astronomers and observers in natural philosophy the confusion and loss of time which are produced by referring to the ordinary treatises embracing both branches of probabilities (the first

Airy (G. B.)—continued.

relating to chances which can be altered only by the changes of entire units or integral multiples of units in the fundamental conditions of the problem; the other concerning those chances which have respect to insensible gradations in the value of the element measured), this volume has been drawn up. It relates only to errors of observation, and to the rules, derivable from the consideration of these errors, for the combination of the results of observations.

UNDULATORY THEORY OF OPTICS. Designed for the Use of Students in the University. New Edition. Crown 8vo. cloth. 6s. 6d.

The undulatory theory of optics is presented to the reader as having the same claims to his attention as the theory of gravitation,—namely, that it is certainly true, and that, by mathematical operations of general elegance, it leads to results of great interest. This theory explains with accuracy a vast variety of phenomena of the most complicated kind. The plan of this tract has been to include those phenomena only which admit of calculation, and the investigations are applied only to phenomena which actually have been observed.

ON SOUND AND ATMOSPHERIC VIBRATIONS. With the Mathematical Elements of Music. Designed for the Use of Students of the University. Second Edition, revised and enlarged. Crown 8vo. 9s.

This volume consists of sections, which again are divided into numbered articles, on the following topics:—General recognition of the air as the medium which conveys sound; Properties of the air on which the formation and transmission of sound depend; Theory of undulations as applied to sound, etc.; Investigation of the motion of a wave of air through the atmosphere; Transmission of waves of soniferous vibrations through different gases, solids, and fluids; Experiments on the velocity of sound, etc.; On musical sounds, and the manner of producing them; On the elements of musical harmony and melody, and of simple musical composition; On instrumental music; On the human organs of speech and hearing.

A TREATISE ON MAGNETISM. Designed for the Use of Students in the University. Crown 8vo. 9s. 6d.

As the laws of Magnetic Force have been experimentally examined, *with philosophical accuracy, only in its connection with iron and steel, and in the influence exerted by the earth as a whole, the accurate portions of this work are confined to the investigations connected with these metals and the earth. The latter part of the work, however, treats in a more general way of the laws of the connection between Magnetism on the one hand and Galvanism and Thermo-Electricity on the other. The work is divided into Twelve Sections, and each section into numbered articles, each of which states concisely and clearly the subject of the following paragraphs.*

Ball (R. S., A.M.)—EXPERIMENTAL MECHANICS. A Course of Lectures delivered at the Royal College of Science for Ireland. By ROBERT STAWELL BALL, A.M., Professor of Applied Mathematics and Mechanics in the Royal College of Science for Ireland (Science and Art Department). Royal 8vo. 16s.

The author's aim in these twenty Lectures has been to create in the mind of the student physical ideas corresponding to theoretical laws, and thus to produce a work which may be regarded either as a supplement or an introduction to manuals of theoretic mechanics. To realize this design, the copious use of experimental illustrations was necessary. The apparatus used in the Lectures and figured in the volume has been principally built up from Professor Willis's most admirable system. In the selection of the subjects, the question of practical utility has in many cases been regarded as the one of paramount importance, and it is believed that the mode of treatment which is adopted is more or less original. This is especially the case in the Lectures relating to friction, to the mechanical powers, to the strength of timber and structures, to the laws of motion, and to the pendulum. The illustrations, drawn from the apparatus, are nearly all original and are beautifully executed. "In our reading we have not met with any book of the sort in English."—Mechanics' Magazine.

Bayma.—THE ELEMENTS OF MOLECULAR MECHANICS. By JOSEPH BAYMA, S.J., Professor of Philosophy, Stonyhurst College. Demy 8vo. cloth. 10s. 6d.

Of the twelve Books into which this treatise is divided, the first and second give the demonstration of the principles which bear directly on the constitution and the properties of matter. The next three books contain a series of theorems and of problems on the laws of motion of elementary substances. In the sixth and seventh, the mechanical constitution of molecules is investigated and determined: and by it the general properties of bodies are explained. The eighth book treats of luminiferous ether. The ninth explains some special properties of bodies. The tenth and eleventh contain a radical and lengthy investigation of chemical principles and relations, which may lead to practical results of high importance. The twelfth and last book treats of molecular masses, distances, and powers.

Boole.—Works by G. BOOLE, D.C.L., F.R.S., Professor of Mathematics in the Queen's University, Ireland :—

A TREATISE ON DIFFERENTIAL EQUATIONS. New and revised Edition. Edited by I. TODHUNTER. Crown 8vo. cloth. 14s.

Professor Boole has endeavoured in this treatise to convey as complete an account of the present state of knowledge on the subject of Differential Equations, as was consistent with the idea of a work intended, primarily, for elementary instruction. The earlier sections of each chapter contain that kind of matter which has usually been thought suitable for the beginner, while the latter ones are devoted either to an account of recent discovery, or the discussion of such deeper questions of principle as are likely to present themselves to the reflective student in connexion with the methods and processes of his previous course.

A TREATISE ON DIFFERENTIAL EQUATIONS. Supplementary Volume. Edited by I. TODHUNTER. Crown 8vo. cloth. 8s. 6d.

This volume contains all that Professor Boole wrote for the purpose of enlarging his treatise on Differential Equations.

THE CALCULUS OF FINITE DIFFERENCES. Crown 8vo. cloth. 10s. 6d.

In this exposition of the Calculus of Finite Differences, particular attention has been paid to the connection of its methods with those of the Differential Calculus—a connection which in some instances involves far more than a merely formal analogy. The work is in some measure designed as a sequel to Professor Boole's Treatise on Differential Equations.

Cambridge Senate-House Problems and Riders,
WITH SOLUTIONS:—

1848–1851.—PROBLEMS. By FERRERS and JACKSON. 8vo. cloth. 15s. 6d.
1848–1851.—RIDERS. By JAMESON. 8vo. cloth. 7s. 6d.
1854.—PROBLEMS AND RIDERS. By WALTON and MACKENZIE. 8vo. cloth. 10s. 6d.
1857.—PROBLEMS AND RIDERS. By CAMPION and WALTON. 8vo. cloth. 8s. 6d.
1860.—PROBLEMS AND RIDERS. By WATSON and ROUTH. Crown 8vo. cloth. 7s. 6d.
1864.—PROBLEMS AND RIDERS. By WALTON and WILKINSON. 8vo. cloth. 10s. 6d.

These volumes will be found of great value to Teachers and Students, as indicating the style and range of mathematical study in the University of Cambridge.

Cambridge and Dublin Mathematical Journal.
The Complete Work, in Nine Vols. 8vo. cloth. 10l. 10s.

Only a few copies remain on hand. Among contributors to this work will be found Sir W. Thomson, Stokes, Adams, Boole, Sir W. R. Hamilton, De Morgan, Cayley, Sylvester, Jellett, and other distinguished mathematicians.

Cheyne.—Works by C. H. H. CHEYNE, M.A., F.R.A.S.:—

AN ELEMENTARY TREATISE ON THE PLANETARY THEORY. With a Collection of Problems. Second Edition. Crown 8vo. cloth. 6s. 6d.

In this volume, an attempt has been made to produce a treatise on the Planetary theory, which, being elementary in character, should be so far complete as to contain all that is usually required by students in the University of Cambridge. This Edition has been carefully revised. The stability of the Planetary System has been more fully treated, and an elegant geometrical explanation of the formula for the secular variation of the node and inclination has been introduced.

THE EARTH'S MOTION OF ROTATION. Crown 8vo. 3s. 6d.

> *The first part of this work consists of an application of the method of the variation of elements to the general problem of rotation. In the second part the general rotation formulæ are applied to the particular case of the earth.*

Childe.—THE SINGULAR PROPERTIES OF THE ELLIPSOID AND ASSOCIATED SURFACES OF THE Nth DEGREE. By the Rev. G. F. CHILDE, M.A., Author of "Ray Surfaces," "Related Caustics," &c. 8vo. 10s. 6d.

> *The object of this volume is to develop peculiarities in the Ellipsoid; and, further, to establish analogous properties in the unlimited congeneric series of which this remarkable surface is a constituent.*

Dodgson.—AN ELEMENTARY TREATISE ON DETERMINANTS, with their Application to Simultaneous Linear Equations and Algebraical Geometry. By CHARLES L. DODGSON, M.A., Student and Mathematical Lecturer of Christ Church, Oxford. Small 4to. cloth. 10s. 6d.

> *The object of the author is to present the subject as a continuous chain of argument, separated from all accessories of explanation of illustration. All such explanation and illustration as seemed necessary for a beginner are introduced either in the form of foot-notes, or, where that would have occupied too much room, of Appendices.*

Earnshaw (S., M.A.)—PARTIAL DIFFERENTIAL EQUATIONS. An Essay towards an entirely New Method of Integrating them. By S. EARNSHAW, M.A., of St. John's College, Cambridge. Crown 8vo. 5s.

> *The peculiarity of the system expounded in this work is, that in every equation, whatever be the number of original independent variables, the work of integration is at once reduced to the use of one independent variable only. The author's object is merely to render his method thoroughly intelligible. The various steps of the investigation are all obedient to one general principle; and though in some degree novel, are not really difficult, but on the contrary easy when the eye has become accustomed to the novelties of the notation. Many of the results of the integrations are far more general than they were in the shape in which they appeared in former Treatises, and many*

Equations will be found in this Essay integrated with ease in finite terms, which were never so integrated before.

Ferrers.—AN ELEMENTARY TREATISE ON TRILINEAR CO-ORDINATES, the Method of Reciprocal Polars, and the Theory of Projections. By the Rev. N. M. FERRERS, M.A., Fellow and Tutor of Gonville and Caius College, Cambridge. Second Edition. Crown 8vo. 6s. 6d.

The object of the author in writing on this subject has mainly been to place it on a basis altogether independent of the ordinary Cartesian system, instead of regarding it as only a special form of Abridged Notation. A short chapter on Determinants has been introduced.

Frost.—THE FIRST THREE SECTIONS OF NEWTON'S PRINCIPIA. With Notes and Illustrations. Also a Collection of Problems, principally intended as Examples of Newton's Methods. By PERCIVAL FROST, M.A., late Fellow of St. John's College, Mathematical Lecturer of King's College, Cambridge. Second Edition. 8vo. cloth. 10s. 6d.

The author's principal intention is to explain difficulties which may be encountered by the student on first reading the Principia, and to illustrate the advantages of a careful study of the methods employed by Newton, by showing the extent to which they may be applied in the solution of problems; he has also endeavoured to give assistance to the student who is engaged in the study of the higher branches of mathematics, by representing in a geometrical form several of the processes employed in the Differential and Integral Calculus, and in the analytical investigations of Dynamics.

Frost and Wolstenholme.—A TREATISE ON SOLID GEOMETRY. By PERCIVAL FROST, M.A., and the Rev. J. WOLSTENHOLME, M.A., Fellow and Assistant Tutor of Christ's College. 8vo. cloth. 18s.

Intending to make the subject accessible, at least in the earlier portions to all classes of students, the authors have endeavoured to explain completely all the processes which are most useful in dealing with ordinary theorems and problems, thus directing the student to the selection of methods which are best adapted to the exigencies of each problem. In the more difficult portions of the subject, they have considered themselves to be addressing a higher class of students; and they have there tried to lay a good foundation on which to build, if any reader should wish to pursue the science beyond the limits to which the work extends.

Godfray.—Works by HUGH GODFRAY, M.A., Mathematical Lecturer at Pembroke College, Cambridge:—

A TREATISE ON ASTRONOMY, for the Use of Colleges and Schools. 8vo. cloth. 12s. 6d.

This book embraces all those branches of Astronomy which have, from time to time, been recommended by the Cambridge Board of Mathematical Studies: but by far the larger and easier portion, adapted to the first three days of the Examination for Honours, may be read by the more advanced pupils in many of our schools. The author's aim has been to convey clear and distinct ideas of the celestial phenomena. "It is a working book," says the Guardian, *"taking Astronomy in its proper place in the Mathematical Sciences. . . . It is a book which is not likely to be got up unintelligently."*

AN ELEMENTARY TREATISE ON THE LUNAR THEORY, with a Brief Sketch of the Problem up to the time of Newton. Second Edition, revised. Crown 8vo. cloth. 5s. 6d.

These pages will, it is hoped, form an introduction to more recondite works. Difficulties have been discussed at considerable length. The selection of the method followed with regard to analytical solutions, which is the same as that of Airy, Herschel, etc., was made on account of its simplicity; it is, moreover, the method which has obtained in the University of Cambridge. "As an elementary treatise and introduction to the subject, we think it may justly claim to supersede all former ones."—London, Edinburgh, and Dublin Phil. Magazine.

Green (George).—MATHEMATICAL PAPERS OF THE LATE GEORGE GREEN, Fellow of Gonville and Caius College, Cambridge. Edited by N. M. FERRERS, M.A., Fellow and Tutor of Gonville and Caius College. 8vo. 15s.

The publication of this book may be opportune at present, as several of the subjects with which they are directly or indirectly concerned have recently been introduced into the course of mathematical study at Cambridge. They have also an interest as being the work of an almost entirely self-taught mathematical genius. The Papers comprise the following:—An Essay on the application of Mathematical Analysis to the Theories of Electricity and Magnetism—On the Laws of the Equilibrium of Fluids analogous to the Electric Fluid—On the Determination of the Attractions of Ellipsoids of variable Densities—On the Motion of Waves in a variable Canal of small depth and width—On the Reflection and Refraction of Sound—On the Reflection and Refraction of Light at the Common Surface of two Non-Crystallized Media—On the Propagation of Light in Crystallized Media—Researches on the Vibrations of Pendulums in Fluid Media. "It has been for some time recognised that Green's writings are amongst the most valuable mathematical productions we possess."—Athenæum.

Hemming.—AN ELEMENTARY TREATISE ON THE DIFFERENTIAL AND INTEGRAL CALCULUS. For the Use of Colleges and Schools. By G. W. HEMMING, M.A., Fellow of St. John's College, Cambridge. Second Edition, with Corrections and Additions. 8vo. cloth. 9s.

"*There is no book in common use from which so clear and exact a knowledge of the principles of the Calculus can be so readily obtained.*"—Literary Gazette.

Jackson.—GEOMETRICAL CONIC SECTIONS. An Elementary Treatise in which the Conic Sections are defined as the Plane Sections of a Cone, and treated by the Method of Projections. By J. STUART JACKSON, M.A., late Fellow of Gonville and Caius College. Crown 8vo. 4s. 6d.

This work has been written with a view to give the student the benefit of the Method of Projections as applied to the Ellipse and Hyperbola. When this method is admitted into the treatment of Conic Sections there are many reasons why they should be defined, not with reference to the focus and directrix, but according to the original definition from which they have their name, as Plane Sections of a Cone. This method is calculated to produce a material simplification in the treatment of these curves and to make the proof of their properties more easily understood in the first instance and more easily remembered. It is also a powerful instrument in the solution of a large class of problems relating to these curves.

Morgan.—A COLLECTION OF PROBLEMS AND EXAMPLES IN MATHEMATICS. With Answers. By H. A. MORGAN, M.A., Sadlerian and Mathematical Lecturer of Jesus College, Cambridge. Crown 8vo. cloth. 6s. 6d.

> This book contains a number of problems, chiefly elementary, in the Mathematical subjects usually read at Cambridge. They have been selected from the Papers set during late years at Jesus College. Very few of them are to be met with in other collections, and by far the larger number are due to some of the most distinguished Mathematicians in the University.

Newton's Principia.—4to. cloth. 31s. 6d.

> It is a sufficient guarantee of the reliability of this complete edition of Newton's Principia that it has been printed for and under the care of Professor Sir William Thomson and Professor Blackburn, of Glasgow University. The following notice is prefixed:—"Finding that all the editions of the Principia are now out of print, we have been induced to reprint Newton's last edition [of 1726] without note or comment, only introducing the 'Corrigenda' of the old copy and correcting typographical errors." The book is of a handsome size, with large type, fine thick paper, and cleanly-cut figures, and is the only recent edition containing the whole of Newton's great work.

Parkinson.—Works by S. PARKINSON, D.D., F.R.S., Fellow and Tutor of St. John's College, Cambridge :—

AN ELEMENTARY TREATISE ON MECHANICS. For the Use of the Junior Classes at the University and the Higher Classes in Schools. With a Collection of Examples. Fourth Edition, revised. Crown 8vo. cloth. 9s. 6d.

> In preparing a fourth edition of this work the author has kept the same object in view as he had in the former editions—namely, to include in it such portions of Theoretical Mechanics as can be conveniently investigated without the use of the Differential Calculus, and so render it suitable as a manual for the junior classes in the University and the higher classes in Schools. With one or two short exceptions, the student is not presumed to require a knowledge of any branches of Mathematics beyond the elements of Algebra, Geometry,

Parkinson (S.)—*continued.*

and Trigonometry. *Several additional propositions have been incorporated in the work for the purpose of rendering it more complete, and the collection of Examples and Problems has been largely increased.*

A TREATISE ON OPTICS. Third Edition, revised and enlarged. Crown 8vo. cloth. 10s. 6d.

A collection of Examples and Problems has been appended to this work, which are sufficiently numerous and varied in character to afford useful exercise for the student. For the greater part of them, recourse has been had to the Examination Papers set in the University and the several Colleges during the last twenty years.

Phear.—ELEMENTARY HYDROSTATICS. With Numerous Examples. By J. B. PHEAR, M.A., Fellow and late Assistant Tutor of Clare College, Cambridge. Fourth Edition. Crown 8vo. cloth. 5s. 6d.

This edition has been carefully revised throughout, and many new Illustrations and Examples added, which it is hoped will increase its usefulness to students at the Universities and in Schools. In accordance with suggestions from many engaged in tuition, answers to all the Examples have been given at the end of the book.

Pratt.—A TREATISE ON ATTRACTIONS, LAPLACE'S FUNCTIONS, AND THE FIGURE OF THE EARTH. By JOHN H. PRATT, M.A., Archdeacon of Calcutta, Author of "The Mathematical Principles of Mechanical Philosophy." Fourth Edition. Crown 8vo. cloth. 6s. 6d.

The author's chief design in this treatise is to give an answer to the question, "Has the Earth acquired its present form from being originally in a fluid state?" This edition is a complete revision of the former ones.

Puckle.—AN ELEMENTARY TREATISE ON CONIC SECTIONS AND ALGEBRAIC GEOMETRY. With numerous Examples and Hints for their Solution; especially designed for the Use of Beginners. By G. H. PUCKLE, M.A., Head Master of

Windermere College. New Edition, revised and enlarged. Crown 8vo. cloth. 7s. 6d.

> *This work is recommended by the Syndicate of the Cambridge Local Examinations, and is the text-book in Harvard University, U.S. The* Athenæum *says the author "displays an intimate acquaintance with the difficulties likely to be felt, together with a singular aptitude in removing them."*

Routh.—AN ELEMENTARY TREATISE ON THE DYNAMICS OF THE SYSTEM OF RIGID BODIES. With numerous Examples. By EDWARD JOHN ROUTH, M.A., late Fellow and Assistant Tutor of St. Peter's College, Cambridge; Examiner in the University of London. Second Edition, enlarged. Crown 8vo. cloth. 14s.

> *In this edition the author has made several additions to each chapter: he has tried, even at the risk of some little repetition, to make each chapter, as far as possible, complete in itself, so that all that relates to any one part of the subject may be found in the same place. This arrangement will enable every student to select his own order in which to read the subject. The Examples which will be found at the end of each chapter have been chiefly selected from the Examination Papers which have been set in the University and the Colleges in the last few years.*

Smith's (Barnard) Works.—See EDUCATIONAL CATALOGUE.

Smith (J. Brook.)—ARITHMETIC IN THEORY AND PRACTICE. By J. BROOK SMITH, M.A., LL.B., St. John's College, Cambridge; Barrister-at-Law; one of the Masters of Cheltenham College. Crown 8vo. 4s. 6d.

> *Writers on Arithmetic at the present day feel the necessity of explaining the principles on which the rules of the subject are based, but few as yet feel the necessity of making these explanations strict and complete; or, failing that, of distinctly pointing out their defective character. If the science of Arithmetic is to be made an effective instrument in developing and strengthening the mental powers, it ought to be worked out rationally and conclusively; and in this work the author has endeavoured to reason out in a clear and accurate*

manner the leading propositions of the science, and to illustrate and apply those propositions in practice. In the practical part of the subject he has advanced somewhat beyond the majority of preceding writers; particularly in Division, in Greatest Common Measure, in Cube Root, in the chapters on Decimal Money and the Metric System, and more especially in the application of Decimals to Percentages and cognate subjects. Copious examples, original and selected, are given.

Snowball.—THE ELEMENTS OF PLANE AND SPHERICAL TRIGONOMETRY; with the Construction and Use of Tables of Logarithms. By J. C. SNOWBALL, M.A. Tenth Edition. Crown 8vo. cloth. 7s. 6d.

In preparing the present edition for the press, the text has been subjected to a careful revision; the proofs of some of the more important propositions have been rendered more strict and general; and a considerable addition of more than two hundred examples, taken principally from the questions set of late years in the public examinations of the University and of individual Colleges, has been made to the collection of Examples and Problems for practice.

Tait and Steele.—DYNAMICS OF A PARTICLE. With numerous Examples. By Professor TAIT and Mr. STEELE. New Edition. Crown 8vo. cloth. 10s. 6d.

In this treatise will be found all the ordinary propositions, connected with the Dynamics of Particles, which can be conveniently deduced without the use of D'Alembert's Principle. Throughout the book will be found a number of illustrative examples introduced in the text, and for the most part completely worked out; others with occasional solutions or hints to assist the student are appended to each chapter. For by far the greater portion of these, the Cambridge Senate-House and College Examination Papers have been applied to.

Taylor.—GEOMETRICAL CONICS; including Anharmonic Ratio and Projection, with numerous Examples. By C. TAYLOR, B.A., Scholar of St. John's College, Cambridge. Crown 8vo. cloth. 7s. 6d.

This work contains elementary proofs of the principal properties of Conic Sections, together with chapters on Projection and Anharmonic Ratio.

Todhunter.—Works by I. TODHUNTER, M.A., F.R.S., of St. John's College, Cambridge :—

"*Perspicuous language, vigorous investigations, scrutiny of difficulties, and methodical treatment, characterize Mr. Todhunter's works.*"—Civil Engineer.

THE ELEMENTS OF EUCLID; MENSURATION FOR BEGINNERS; ALGEBRA FOR BEGINNERS; TRIGONOMETRY FOR BEGINNERS; MECHANICS FOR BEGINNERS.—See EDUCATIONAL CATALOGUE.

ALGEBRA. For the Use of Colleges and Schools. Fifth Edition. Crown 8vo. cloth. 7s. 6d.

This work contains all the propositions which are usually included in elementary treatises on Algebra, and a large number of Examples for Exercise. The author has sought to render the work easily intelligible to students, without impairing the accuracy of the demonstrations, or contracting the limits of the subject. The Examples, about Sixteen hundred and fifty *in number, have been selected with a view to illustrate every part of the subject. The work will be found peculiarly adapted to the wants of students who are without the aid of a teacher. The Answers to the Examples, with hints for the solution of some in which assistance may be needed, are given at the end of the book. In the present edition two New Chapters and* Three hundred *miscellaneous Examples have been added.* "*It has merits which unquestionably place it first in the class to which it belongs.*"—Educator.

KEY TO ALGEBRA FOR THE USE OF COLLEGES AND SCHOOLS. Crown 8vo. 10s. 6d.

AN ELEMENTARY TREATISE ON THE THEORY OF EQUATIONS. Second Edition, revised. Crown 8vo. cloth. 7s. 6d.

This treatise contains all the propositions which are usually included in elementary treatises on the theory of Equations, together with Examples for exercise. These have been selected from the College and University Examination Papers, and the results have been given when it appeared necessary. In order to exhibit a comprehensive view of the subject, the treatise includes investigations which are not found in all the preceding elementary treatises, and also

Todhunter (I.)—*continued.*

some investigations which are not to be found in any of them. For the second edition the work has been revised and some additions have been made, the most important being an account of the Researches of Professor Sylvester respecting Newton's Rule. "A thoroughly trustworthy, complete, and yet not too elaborate treatise."
—Philosophical Magazine.

PLANE TRIGONOMETRY. For Schools and Colleges. Fourth Edition. Crown 8vo. cloth. 5s.

The design of this work has been to render the subject intelligible to beginners, and at the same time to afford the student the opportunity of obtaining all the information which he will require on this branch of Mathematics. Each chapter is followed by a set of Examples: those which are entitled Miscellaneous Examples, *together with a few in some of the other sets, may be advantageously reserved by the student for exercise after he has made some progress in the subject. In the Second Edition the hints for the solution of the Examples have been considerably increased.*

A TREATISE ON SPHERICAL TRIGONOMETRY. Third Edition, enlarged. Crown 8vo. cloth. 4s. 6d.

The present work is constructed on the same plan as the treatise on Plane Trigonometry, to which it is intended as a sequel. In the account of Napier's Rules of circular parts, an explanation has been given of a method of proof devised by Napier, which seems to have been overlooked by most modern writers on the subject. Considerable labour has been bestowed on the text in order to render it comprehensive and accurate, and the Examples (selected chiefly from College Examination Papers) have all been carefully verified. "For educational purposes this work seems to be superior to any others on the subject."—Critic.

PLANE CO-ORDINATE GEOMETRY, as applied to the Straight Line and the Conic Sections. With numerous Examples. Fourth Edition, revised and enlarged. Crown 8vo. cloth. 7s. 6d.

The author has here endeavoured to exhibit the subject in a simple manner for the benefit of beginners, and at the same time to include in one volume all that students usually require. In addition, therefore, to the propositions which have always appeared in such

Todhunter (I.)—*continued.*

treatises, he has introduced the methods of abridged notation, *which are of more recent origin: these methods, which are of a less elementary character than the rest of the work, are placed in separate chapters, and may be omitted by the student at first.*

A TREATISE ON THE DIFFERENTIAL CALCULUS. With numerous Examples. Fifth Edition. Crown 8vo. cloth. 10s. 6d.

The author has endeavoured in the present work to exhibit a comprehensive view of the Differential Calculus on the method of limits. In the more elementary portions he has entered into considerable detail in the explanations, with the hope that a reader who is without the assistance of a tutor may be enabled to acquire a competent acquaintance with the subject. The method adopted is that of Differential Coefficients. To the different chapters are appended Examples sufficiently numerous to render another book unnecessary; these Examples being mostly selected from College Examination Papers. This and the following work have been translated into Italian by Professor Battaglini, who in his Preface speaks thus:—
"*In publishing this translation of the Differential and Integral Calculus of Mr. Todhunter, we have had no other object than to add to the books which are in the hands of the students of our Universities, a work remarkable for the clearness of the exposition, the rigour of the demonstrations, the just proportion in the parts, and the rich store of examples which offer a large field for useful exercise.*"

A TREATISE ON THE INTEGRAL CALCULUS AND ITS APPLICATIONS. With numerous Examples. Third Edition, revised and enlarged. Crown 8vo. cloth. 10s. 6d.

This is designed as a work at once elementary and complete, adapted for the use of beginners, and sufficient for the wants of advanced students. In the selection of the propositions, and in the mode of establishing them, it has been sought to exhibit the principles clearly, and to illustrate all their most important results. The process of summation has been repeatedly brought forward, with the view of securing the attention of the student to the notions which form the true foundation of the Calculus itself, as well as of its most valuable applications. Every attempt has been made to explain those

Todhunter (I.)—*continued.*

difficulties which usually perplex beginners, especially with reference to the limits of integrations. A new method has been adopted in regard to the transformation of multiple integrals. The last chapter deals with the Calculus of Variations. A large collection of Exercises, selected from College Examination Papers, has been appended to the several chapters.

EXAMPLES OF ANALYTICAL GEOMETRY OF THREE DIMENSIONS. Second Edition, revised. Crown 8vo. cloth. 4s.

A TREATISE ON ANALYTICAL STATICS. With numerous Examples. Third Edition, revised and enlarged. Crown 8vo. cloth. 10s. 6d.

In this work on Statics (treating of the laws of the equilibrium of bodies) will be found all the propositions which usually appear in treatises on Theoretical Statics. To the different chapters Examples are appended, which have been principally selected from University Examination Papers. In the Third Edition many additions have been made, in order to illustrate the application of the principles of the subject to the solution of problems.

A HISTORY OF THE MATHEMATICAL THEORY OF PROBABILITY, from the Time of Pascal to that of Laplace. 8vo. 18s.

The subject of this work has high claims to consideration on account of the subtle problems which it involves, the valuable contributions to analysis which it has produced, its important practical applications, and the eminence of those who have cultivated it; nearly every great mathematician within the range of a century and a half comes under consideration in the course of the history. The author has endeavoured to be quite accurate in his statements, and to reproduce the essential elements of the original works which he has analysed. Besides being a history, the work may claim the title of a comprehensive treatise on the Theory of Probability, for it assumes in the reader only so much knowledge as can be gained from an elementary book on Algebra, and introduces him to almost every process and every special problem which the literature of the subject can furnish.

RESEARCHES IN THE CALCULUS OF VARIATIONS, Principally on the Theory of Discontinuous Solutions: An Essay

Todhunter (I.)—*continued.*

to which the Adams' Prize was awarded in the University of Cambridge in 1871. 8vo. 6s.

The subject of this Essay was prescribed in the following terms by the Examiners:—"A determination of the circumstances under which discontinuity of any kind presents itself in the solution of a problem of maximum or minimum in the Calculus of Variations, and applications to particular instances. It is expected that the discussion of the instances should be exemplified as far as possible geometrically, and that attention be especially directed to cases of real or supposed failure of the Calculus." While the Essay is thus mainly devoted to the consideration of discontinuous solutions, various other questions in the Calculus of Variations are examined and elucidated; and the author hopes he has definitely contributed to the extension and improvement of our knowledge of this refined department of analysis.

Wilson (W. P.)—A TREATISE ON DYNAMICS. By W. P. WILSON, M.A., Fellow of St. John's College, Cambridge, and Professor of Mathematics in Queen's College, Belfast. 8vo. 9s. 6d.

Wolstenholme.—A BOOK OF MATHEMATICAL PROBLEMS, on Subjects included in the Cambridge Course. By JOSEPH WOLSTENHOLME, Fellow of Christ's College, some time Fellow of St. John's College, and lately Lecturer in Mathematics at Christ's College. Crown 8vo. cloth. 8s. 6d.

CONTENTS:—*Geometry (Euclid)—Algebra—Plane Trigonometry—Geometrical Conic Sections—Analytical Conic Sections—Theory of Equations—Differential Calculus—Integral Calculus—Solid Geometry—Statics—Elementary Dynamics—Newton—Dynamics of a Point—Dynamics of a Rigid Body—Hydrostatics—Geometrical Optics—Spherical Trigonometry and Plane Astronomy. In some cases the author has prefixed to certain classes of problems fragmentary notes on the mathematical subjects to which they relate.* "*Judicious, symmetrical, and well arranged.*"—Guardian.

PHYSICAL SCIENCE.

Airy (G. B.)—POPULAR ASTRONOMY. With Illustrations. By G. B. AIRY, Astronomer Royal. Seventh and cheaper Edition. 18mo. cloth. 4s. 6d.

This work consists of Six Lectures, which are intended "to explain to intelligent persons the principles on which the instruments of an Observatory are constructed (omitting all details, so far as they are merely subsidiary), and the principles on which the observations made with these instruments are treated for deduction of the distances and weights of the bodies of the Solar System, and of a few stars, omitting all minutiæ of formulæ, and all troublesome details of calculation." The speciality of this volume is the direct reference of every step to the Observatory, and the full description of the methods and instruments of observation.

Bastian (H. C. M.D., F.R.S.)—THE MODES OF ORIGIN OF LOWEST ORGANISMS: Including a Discussion of the Experiments of M. Pasteur, and a reply to some Statements by Professors Huxley and Tyndall. By H. CHARLTON BASTIAN, M.D., F.R.S., Professor of Pathological Anatomy in University College, London, etc. Crown 8vo. 4s. 6d.

The present volume contains a fragment of the evidence which will be embodied in a much larger work—now almost completed—relating to the nature and origin of living matter, and in favour of what is termed the Physical Doctrine of Life. "It is a work worthy of the highest respect, and places its author in the very first class of scientific physicians. . . . It would be difficult to name an instance in which skill, knowledge, perseverance, and great reasoning power have been more happily applied to the investigation of a complex biological problem."—British Medical Journal.

Birks (R. B.)—ON MATTER AND ETHER; or, The Secret Laws of Physical Change. By THOMAS RAWSON BIRKS, M.A., Rector of Kelshall, Herts, formerly Fellow of Trinity College, Cambridge. Crown 8vo. 5s. 6d.

The author believes that the hypothesis of the existence of, besides matter, a luminous ether, of immense elastic force, supplies the true and sufficient key to the remaining secrets of inorganic matter, of the phenomena of light, electricity, etc. In this treatise the author endeavours first to form a clear and definite conception with regard to the real nature both of matter and ether, and the laws of mutual action which must be supposed to exist between them. He then endeavours to trace out the main consequences of the fundamental hypothesis, and their correspondence with the known phenomena of physical change.

Blanford (W. T.)—GEOLOGY AND ZOOLOGY OF ABYSSINIA. By W. T. BLANFORD. 8vo. 21s.

This work contains an account of the Geological and Zoological Observations made by the author in Abyssinia, when accompanying the British Army on its march to Magdala and back in 1868, and during a short journey in Northern Abyssinia, after the departure of the troops. Part I. Personal Narrative; Part II. Geology; Part III. Zoology. With Coloured Illustrations and Geological Map. "The result of his labours," the Academy says, "is an important contribution to the natural history of the country."

Cooke (Josiah P., Jun.)—FIRST PRINCIPLES OF CHEMICAL PHILOSOPHY. By JOSIAH P. COOKE, Jun., Ervine Professor of Chemistry and Mineralogy in Harvard College. Crown 8vo. 12s.

The object of the author in this book is to present the philosophy of Chemistry in such a form that it can be made with profit the subject of College recitations, and furnish the teacher with the means of testing the student's faithfulness and ability. With this view the subject has been developed in a logical order, and the principles of the science are taught independently of the experimental evidence on which they rest.

Cooke (M. C.)—HANDBOOK OF BRITISH FUNGI, with full descriptions of all the Species, and Illustrations of the Genera. By M. C. COOKE, M.A. Two vols. crown 8vo. 24s.

> *During the thirty-five years that have elapsed since the appearance of the last complete Mycologic Flora no attempt has been made to revise it, to incorporate species since discovered, and to bring it up to the standard of modern science. No apology, therefore, is necessary for the present effort, since all will admit that the want of such a manual has long been felt, and this work makes its appearance under the advantage that it seeks to occupy a place which has long been vacant. No effort has been spared to make the work worthy of confidence, and, by the publication of an occasional supplement, it is hoped to maintain it for many years as the "Handbook" for every student of British Fungi. Appended is a complete alphabetical Index of all the divisions and subdivisions of the Fungi noticed in the text. The book contains 400 figures. "Will maintain its place as the standard English book, on the subject of which it treats, for many years to come."*—Standard.

Dawson (J. W.)—ACADIAN GEOLOGY. The Geologic Structure, Organic Remains, and Mineral Resources of Nova Scotia, New Brunswick, and Prince Edward Island. By JOHN WILLIAM DAWSON, M.A., LL.D., F.R.S., F.G.S., Principal and Vice-Chancellor of M'Gill College and University, Montreal, &c. Second Edition, revised and enlarged. With a Geological Map and numerous Illustrations. 8vo. 18s.

> *The object of the first edition of this work was to place within the reach of the people of the districts to which it relates, a popular account of the more recent discoveries in the geology and mineral resources of their country, and at the same time to give to geologists in other countries a connected view of the structure of a very interesting portion of the American Continent, in its relation to general and theoretical Geology. In the present edition, it is hoped this design is still more completely fulfilled, with reference to the present more advanced condition of knowledge. The author has endeavoured to convey a knowledge of the structure and fossils of the region in such a manner as to be intelligible to ordinary readers, and has devoted much attention to all questions relating to the nature and present or prospective value of deposits of useful minerals.*

> Besides a large coloured Geological Map of the district, the work is illustrated by upwards of 260 cuts of sections, fossils, animals, etc. "The book will doubtless find a place in the library, not only of the scientific geologist, but also of all who are desirous of the industrial progress and commercial prosperity of the Acadian provinces."—Mining Journal. "A style at once popular and scientific. . . . A valuable addition to our store of geological knowledge."—Guardian.

Flower (W. H.)—AN INTRODUCTION TO THE OSTEOLOGY OF THE MAMMALIA. Being the substance of the Course of Lectures delivered at the Royal College of Surgeons of England in 1870. By W. H. FLOWER, F.R.S., F.R.C.S., Hunterian Professor of Comparative Anatomy and Physiology. With numerous Illustrations. Globe 8vo. 7s. 6d.

> Although the present work contains the substance of a Course of Lectures, the form has been changed, so as the better to adapt it as a handbook for students. Theoretical views have been almost entirely excluded: and while it is impossible in a scientific treatise to avoid the employment of technical terms, it has been the author's endeavour to use no more than absolutely necessary, and to exercise due care in selecting only those that seem most appropriate, or which have received the sanction of general adoption. With a very few exceptions the illustrations have been drawn expressly for this work from specimens in the Museum of the Royal College of Surgeons.

Galton.—Works by FRANCIS GALTON, F.R.S. :—

METEOROGRAPHICA, or Methods of Mapping the Weather. Illustrated by upwards of 600 Printed Lithographic Diagrams. 4to. 9s.

> As Mr. Galton entertains strong views on the necessity of Meteorological Charts and Maps, he determined, as a practical proof of what could be done, to chart the entire area of Europe, so far as meteorological stations extend, during one month, viz. the month of December, 1861. Mr. Galton got his data from authorities in every part of Britain and the Continent, and on the basis of these has here drawn up nearly a hundred different Maps and Charts, showing the state of the weather all over Europe during the above period. "If the various Governments and scientific bodies would perform for the

Galton (F.)—*continued.*

whole world for two or three years what, at a great cost and labour, Mr. Galton has done for a part of Europe for one month, Meteorology would soon cease to be made a joke of."—Spectator.

HEREDITARY GENIUS: An Inquiry into its Laws and Consequences. Demy 8vo. 12s.

"I propose," the author says, "to show in this book that a man's natural abilities are derived by inheritance, under exactly the same limitations as are the form and physical features of the whole organic world. I shall show that social agencies of an ordinary character, whose influences are little suspected, are at this moment working towards the degradation of human nature, and that others are working towards its improvement. The general plan of my argument is to show that high reputation is a pretty accurate test of high ability; next, to discuss the relationships of a large body of fairly eminent men, and to obtain from these a general survey of the laws of heredity in respect of genius. Then will follow a short chapter, by way of comparison, on the hereditary transmission of physical gifts, as deduced from the relationships of certain classes of oarsmen and wrestlers. Lastly, I shall collate my results and draw conclusions." The Times calls it "a most able and most interesting book;" and Mr. Darwin, in his "Descent of Man" (vol. i. p. 111), says, "We know, through the admirable labours of Mr. Galton, that Genius tends to be inherited."

Geikie (A.)—SCENERY OF SCOTLAND, Viewed in Connection with its Physical Geography. With Illustrations and a new Geological Map. By ARCHIBALD GEIKIE, Professor of Geology in the University of Edinburgh. Crown 8vo. 10s. 6d.

"We can confidently recommend Mr. Geikie's work to those who wish to look below the surface and read the physical history of the Scenery of Scotland by the light of modern science."—Saturday Review.
"Amusing, picturesque, and instructive."—Times.

Hooker (Dr.)—THE STUDENT'S FLORA OF THE BRITISH ISLANDS. By J. D. HOOKER, C.B., F.R.S., M.D., D.C.L., Director of the Royal Gardens, Kew. Globe 8vo. 10s. 6d.

> The object of this work is to supply students and field-botanists with a fuller account of the Plants of the British Islands than the manuals hitherto in use aim at giving. The Ordinal, Generic, and Specific characters have been re-written, and are to a great extent original, and drawn from living or dried specimens, or both. "Cannot fail to perfectly fulfil the purpose for which it is intended."—Land and Water. "Containing the fullest and most accurate manual of the kind that has yet appeared."—Pall Mall Gazette.

Huxley (Professor).—LAY SERMONS, ADDRESSES, AND REVIEWS. By T. H. HUXLEY, LL.D., F.R.S. New and Cheaper Edition. Crown 8vo. 7s. 6d.

> Fourteen Discourses on the following subjects:—(1) On the Advisableness of Improving Natural Knowledge:—(2) Emancipation—Black and White:—(3) A Liberal Education, and where to find it:—(4) Scientific Education:—(5) On the Educational Value of the Natural History Sciences:—(6) On the Study of Zoology:—(7) On the Physical Basis of Life:—(8) The Scientific Aspects of Positivism:—(9) On a Piece of Chalk:—(10) Geological Contemporaneity and Persistent Types of Life:—(11) Geological Reform:—(12) The Origin of Species:—(13) Criticisms on the "Origin of Species:"—(14) On Descartes' "Discourse touching the Method of using One's Reason rightly and of seeking Scientific Truth." The momentous influence exercised by Mr. Huxley's writings on physical, mental, and social science is universally acknowledged: his works must be studied by all who would comprehend the various drifts of modern thought.

ESSAYS SELECTED FROM LAY SERMONS, ADDRESSES, AND REVIEWS. Crown 8vo. 1s.

> This volume includes Numbers 1, 3, 4, 7, 8, and 14, of the above.

LESSONS IN ELEMENTARY PHYSIOLOGY. With numerous Illustrations. Fourteenth Thousand. 18mo. cloth. 4s. 6d.

> This book describes and explains, in a series of graduated lessons, the principles of Human Physiology, or the Structure and Functions of the Human Body. The first lesson supplies a general view of the subject. This is followed by sections on the Vascular or Venous System, and the Circulation; the Blood and the Lymph; Respira-

tion: *Sources of Loss and of Gain to the Blood; the Function of Alimentation; Motion and Locomotion; Sensations and Sensory Organs; the Organ of Sight; the Coalescence of Sensations with one another and with other States of Consciousness; the Nervous System and Innervation; Histology, or the Minute Structure of the Tissues. A Table of Anatomical and Physiological Constants is appended. The lessons are fully illustrated by numerous engravings.* " Pure gold throughout."—Guardian. " Unquestionably the clearest and most complete elementary treatise on this subject that we possess in any language."—Westminster Review.

Kirchhoff (G.)—RESEARCHES ON THE SOLAR SPECTRUM, and the Spectra of the Chemical Elements. By. G. KIRCHHOFF, Professor of Physics in the University of Heidelberg. Second Part. Translated, with the Author's Sanction, from the Transactions of the Berlin Academy for 1862, by HENRY R. ROSCOE, B.A., Ph.D., F.R.S., Professor of Chemistry in Owens College, Manchester.

"*It is to Kirchhoff we are indebted for by far the best and most accurate observations of these phenomena.*"—Edin. Review. " *This memoir seems almost indispensable to every Spectrum observer.*"—Philosophical Magazine.

Lockyer (J. N.)—ELEMENTARY LESSONS IN ASTRONOMY. With numerous Illustrations. By J. NORMAN LOCKYER, F.R.S. Eighth Thousand. 18mo. 5s. 6d.

The author has here aimed to give a connected view of the whole subject, and to supply facts, and ideas founded on the facts, to serve as a basis for subsequent study and discussion. The chapters treat of the Stars and Nebulæ; the Sun; the Solar System; Apparent Movements of the Heavenly Bodies; the Measurement of Time; Light; the Telescope and Spectroscope; Apparent Places of the Heavenly Bodies; the Real Distances and Dimensions; Universal Gravitation. The most recent Astronomical Discoveries are incorporated. Mr. Lockyer's work supplements that of the Astronomer Royal. " The book is full, clear, sound, and worthy of attention, not only as a popular exposition, but as a scientific 'Index.'"—Athenæum. " The most fascinating of elementary books on the Sciences."— Nonconformist.

Macmillan (Rev. Hugh).—For other Works by the same Author, see THEOLOGICAL CATALOGUE.

HOLIDAYS ON HIGH LANDS; or, Rambles and Incidents in search of Alpine Plants. Crown 8vo. cloth. 6s.

The aim of this book is to impart a general idea of the origin, character, and distribution of those rare and beautiful Alpine plants which occur on the British hills, and which are found almost everywhere on the lofty mountain chains of Europe, Asia, Africa, and America. In the first three chapters the peculiar vegetation of the Highland mountains is fully described; while in the remaining chapters this vegetation is traced to its northern cradle in the mountains of Norway, and to its southern European termination in the Alps of Switzerland. The information the author has to give is conveyed in a setting of personal adventure. "One of the most charming books of its kind ever written."—Literary Churchman. *"Mr. M.'s glowing pictures of Scandinavian scenery."*—Saturday Review.

FOOT-NOTES FROM THE PAGE OF NATURE. With numerous Illustrations. Fcap. 8vo. 5s.

"Those who have derived pleasure and profit from the study of flowers and ferns—subjects, it is pleasing to find, now everywhere popular—by descending lower into the arcana of the vegetable kingdom, will find a still more interesting and delightful field of research in the objects brought under review in the following pages."—Preface. *"The naturalist and the botanist will delight in this volume, and those who understand little of the scientific parts of the work will linger over the mysterious page of nature here unfolded to their view."*—John Bull.

Mansfield (C. B.)—A THEORY OF SALTS. A Treatise on the Constitution of Bipolar (two-membered) Chemical Compounds. By the late CHARLES BLACHFORD MANSFIELD. Crown 8vo. 14s.

"Mansfield," says the editor, "wrote this book to defend the principle that the fact of voltaic decomposition afforded the true indication, if properly interpreted, of the nature of the saline structure, and of the atomicity of the elements that built it up. No chemist will peruse this book without feeling that he is in the presence of an

original thinker, whose pages are continually suggestive, even though their general argument may not be entirely concurrent in direction with that of modern chemical thought."

Mivart (St. George).—ON THE GENESIS OF SPECIES. By ST. GEORGE MIVART, F.R.S. Crown 8vo. Second Edition, to which notes have been added in reference and reply to Darwin's "Descent of Man." With numerous Illustrations. pp. xv. 296. 9s.

The aim of the author is to support the doctrine that the various species have been evolved by ordinary natural laws (for the most part unknown) controlled by the subordinate action of "natural selection," and at the same time to remind some that there is and can be absolutely nothing in physical science which forbids them to regard those natural laws as acting with the Divine concurrence, and in obedience to a creative fiat originally imposed on the primæval cosmos, "in the beginning," by its Creator, its Upholder, and its Lord. Nearly fifty woodcuts illustrate the letter-press, and a complete index makes all references extremely easy. Canon Kingsley, in his address to the "Devonshire Association," says, "Let me recommend earnestly to you, as a specimen of what can be said on the other side, the 'Genesis of Species,' by Mr. St. George Mivart, F.R.S., a book which I am happy to say has been received elsewhere as it has deserved, and, I trust, will be received so among you." "In no work in the English language has this great controversy been treated at once with the same broad and vigorous grasp of facts, and the same liberal and candid temper."—Saturday Review.

Nature.—A WEEKLY ILLUSTRATED JOURNAL OF SCIENCE. Published every Thursday. Price 4d. Monthly Parts, 1s. 4d. and 1s. 8d.; Half-yearly Volumes, 10s. 6d. Cases for binding vols. 1s. 6d.

"Backed by many of the best names among English philosophers, and by a few equally valuable supporters in America and on the Continent of Europe."—Saturday Review. "This able and well-edited Journal, which posts up the science of the day promptly, and promises to be of signal service to students and savants."—British Quarterly Review.

SCIENTIFIC CATALOGUE.

Oliver.—Works by DANIEL OLIVER, F.R.S., F.L.S., Professor of Botany in University College, London, and Keeper of the Herbarium and Library of the Royal Gardens, Kew :—

LESSONS IN ELEMENTARY BOTANY. With nearly Two Hundred Illustrations. Twelfth Thousand. 18mo cloth. 4s. 6d.

This book is designed to teach the elements of Botany on Professor Henslow's plan of selected Types and by the use of Schedules. The earlier chapters, embracing the elements of Structural and Physiological Botany, introduce us to the methodical study of the Ordinal Types. The concluding chapters are entitled, " How to Dry Plants" and " How to Describe Plants." A valuable Glossary is appended to the volume. In the preparation of this work free use has been made of the manuscript materials of the late Professor Henslow.

FIRST BOOK OF INDIAN BOTANY. With numerous Illustrations. Extra fcap. 8vo. 6s. 6d.

This manual is, in substance, the author's " Lessons in Elementary Botany," adapted for use in India. In preparing it he has had in view the want, often felt, of some handy résumé of Indian Botany, which might be serviceable not only to residents of India, but also to any one about to proceed thither, desirous of getting some preliminary idea of the botany of the country. It contains a well-digested summary of all essential knowledge pertaining to Indian Botany, wrought out in accordance with the best principles of scientific arrangement."—Allen's Indian Mail.

Penrose (F. C.)—ON A METHOD OF PREDICTING BY GRAPHICAL CONSTRUCTION, OCCULTATIONS OF STARS BY THE MOON, AND SOLAR ECLIPSES FOR ANY GIVEN PLACE. Together with more rigorous methods for the Accurate Calculation of Longitude. By F. C. PENROSE, F.R.A.S. With Charts, Tables, etc. 4to. 12s.

The author believes that if, by a graphic method, the prediction of occultations can be rendered more inviting, as well as more expeditious, than by the method of calculation, it may prove acceptable to the nautical profession as well as to scientific travellers or amateurs. The author has endeavoured to make the whole process as intelligible as possible, so that the beginner, instead of merely having to follow directions imperfectly understood, may readily comprehend the meaning of each step, and be able to illustrate the practice by the theory. Besides all necessary charts and tables, the work contains a large number of skeleton forms for working out cases in practice.

ROSCOE.—Works by HENRY E. ROSCOE, F.R.S., Professor of Chemistry in Owens College, Manchester :—

LESSONS IN ELEMENTARY CHEMISTRY, INORGANIC AND ORGANIC. With numerous Illustrations and Chromolitho of the Solar Spectrum, and of the Alkalies and Alkaline Earths. New Edition. Thirty-first Thousand. 18mo. cloth. 4s. 6d.

It has been the endeavour of the author to arrange the most important facts and principles of Modern Chemistry in a plain but concise and scientific form, suited to the present requirements of elementary instruction. For the purpose of facilitating the attainment of exactitude in the knowledge of the subject, a series of exercises and questions upon the lessons have been added. The metric system of weights and measures, and the centigrade thermometric scale, are used throughout this work. The new edition, besides new woodcuts, contains many additions and improvements, and includes the most important of the latest discoveries. "*We unhesitatingly pronounce it the best of all our elementary treatises on Chemistry.*"—Medical Times.

SPECTRUM ANALYSIS. Six Lectures, with Appendices, Engravings, Maps, and Chromolithographs. Royal 8vo. 21s.

A Second Edition of these popular Lectures, containing all the most recent discoveries and several additional illustrations. "*In six lectures he has given the history of the discovery and set forth the facts relating to the analysis of light in such a way that any reader of ordinary intelligence and information will be able to understand what 'Spectrum Analysis' is, and what are its claims to rank among the most signal triumphs of science.*"—Nonconformist. "*The lectures themselves furnish a most admirable elementary treatise on the subject, whilst by the insertion in appendices to each lecture of extracts from the most important published memoirs, the author has rendered it equally valuable as a text-book for advanced students.*"—Westminster Review.

Stewart (B.)—LESSONS IN ELEMENTARY PHYSICS. By BALFOUR STEWART, F.R.S., Professor of Natural Philosophy in Owens College, Manchester. With numerous Illustrations and Chromolithos of the Spectra of the Sun, Stars, and Nebulæ. Second Edition. 18mo. 4s. 6d.

A description, in an elementary manner, of the most important of those laws which regulate the phenomena of nature. The active agents, heat, light, electricity, etc., are regarded as varieties of energy, and the work is so arranged that their relation to one another, looked at in this light, and the paramount importance of the laws of energy, are clearly brought out. The volume contains all the necessary illustrations. The Educational Times *calls this "the beau-ideal of a scientific text-book, clear, accurate, and thorough."*

Thudichum and Dupré.—A TREATISE ON THE ORIGIN, NATURE, AND VARIETIES OF WINE. Being a Complete Manual of Viticulture and Œnology. By J. L. W. THUDICHUM, M.D., and AUGUST DUPRÉ, Ph.D., Lecturer on Chemistry at Westminster Hospital. Medium 8vo. cloth gilt. 25s.

In this elaborate work the subject of the manufacture of wine is treated scientifically in minute detail, from every point of view. A chapter is devoted to the Origin and Physiology of Vines, two to the Principles of Viticulture; while other chapters treat of Vintage and Vinification, the Chemistry of Alcohol, the Acids, Ether, Sugars, and other matters occurring in wine. This introductory matter occupies the first nine chapters, the remaining seventeen chapters being occupied with a detailed account of the Viticulture and the Wines of the various countries of Europe, of the Atlantic Islands, of Asia, of Africa, of America, and of Australia. Besides a number of Analytical and Statistical Tables, the work is enriched with eighty-five illustrative woodcuts. "A treatise almost unique for its usefulness either to the wine-grower, the vendor, or the consumer of wine. The analyses of wine are the most complete we have yet seen, exhibiting at a glance the constituent principles of nearly all the wines known in this country."—Wine Trade Review.

Wallace (A. R.)—CONTRIBUTIONS TO THE THEORY OF NATURAL SELECTION. A Series of Essays. By

ALFRED RUSSEL WALLACE, Author of "The Malay Archipelago," etc. Second Edition, with Corrections and Additions. Crown 8vo. 8s. 6d. (For other Works by the same Author, see CATALOGUE OF HISTORY AND TRAVELS.)

Mr. Wallace has good claims to be considered as an independent originator of the theory of natural selection. Dr. Hooker, in his address to the British Association, spoke thus of the author: "Of Mr. Wallace and his many contributions to philosophical biology it is not easy to speak without enthusiasm; for, putting aside their great merits, he, throughout his writings, with a modesty as rare as I believe it to be unconscious, forgets his own unquestioned claim to the honour of having originated, independently of Mr. Darwin, the theories which he so ably defends." The Saturday Review says: "He has combined an abundance of fresh and original facts with a liveliness and sagacity of reasoning which are not often displayed so effectively on so small a scale." The Essays in this volume are:—I. "On the Law which has regulated the introduction of New Species." II. "On the Tendencies of Varieties to depart indefinitely from the Original Type." III. "Mimicry, and other Protective Resemblances among Animals." IV. "The Malayan Papilionidæ, as illustrative of the Theory of Natural Selection." V. "On Instinct in Man and Animals." VI. "The Philosophy of Birds' Nests." VII. "A Theory of Birds' Nests." VIII. "Creation by Law." IX. "The Development of Human Races under the Law of Natural Selection." X. "The Limits of Natural Selection as applied to Man."

Warington.—THE WEEK OF CREATION; OR, THE COSMOGONY OF GENESIS CONSIDERED IN ITS RELATION TO MODERN SCIENCE. By GEORGE WARINGTON, Author of "The Historic Character of the Pentateuch Vindicated." Crown 8vo. 4s. 6d.

*The greater part of this work is taken up with the teaching of the Cosmogony. Its purpose is also investigated, and a chapter is devoted to the consideration of the passage in which the difficulties occur. "A very able vindication of the Mosaic Cosmogony, by a writer who unites the advantages of a critical knowledge of the Hebrew text and of distinguished scientific attainments."—*Spectator.

Wilson.—Works by the late GEORGE WILSON, M.D., F.R.S.E., Regius Professor of Technology in the University of Edinburgh:—

RELIGIO CHEMICI. With a Vignette beautifully engraved after a design by Sir NOEL PATON. Crown 8vo. 8s. 6d.

"*George Wilson,*" *says the Preface to this volume, "had it in his heart for many years to write a book corresponding to the* Religio Medici *of Sir Thomas Browne, with the title* Religio Chemici. *Several of the Essays in this volume were intended to form chapters of it. These fragments being in most cases like finished gems waiting to be set, some of them are now given in a collected form to his friends and the public. In living remembrance of his purpose, the name chosen by himself has been adopted, although the original design can be but very faintly represented." The Contents of the volume are:*—"*Chemistry and Natural Theology.*" "*The Chemistry of the Stars; an Argument touching the Stars and their Inhabitants.*" "*Chemical Final Causes; as illustrated by the presence of Phosphorus, Nitrogen, and Iron in the Higher Sentient Organisms.*" "*Robert Boyle.*" "*Wollaston.*" "*Life and Discoveries of Dalton.*" "*Thoughts on the Resurrection; an Address to Medical Students.*" "*A more fascinating volume,*" *the* Spectator *says,* "*has seldom fallen into our hands." The* Freeman *says: "These papers are all valuable and deeply interesting. The production of a profound thinker, a suggestive and eloquent writer, and a man whose piety and genius went hand in hand.*"

THE PROGRESS OF THE TELEGRAPH. Fcap. 8vo. 1s.

"*While a complete view of the progress of the greatest of human inventions is obtained, all its suggestions are brought out with a rare thoughtfulness, a genial humour, and an exceeding beauty of utterance.*"—Nonconformist.

Winslow.—FORCE AND NATURE: ATTRACTION AND REPULSION. The Radical Principles of Energy graphically discussed in their Relations to Physical and Morphological Development. By C. F. WINSLOW, M.D. 8vo. 14s.

The author having for long investigated Nature in many directions, has ever felt unsatisfied with the physical foundations upon which some branches of science have been so long compelled to rest. The question, he believes, must have occurred to many astronomers and physicists whether some subtle principle antagonistic to attraction does not also exist as an all-pervading element in nature, and so operate as in some way to disturb the action of what is generally considered by the scientific world a unique force. The aim of the present work is to set forth this subject in its broadest aspects, and in such a manner as to invite thereto the attention of the learned. The subjects of the eleven chapters are:—*I. "Space." II. "Matter." III. "Inertia, Force, and Mind." IV. "Molecules." V. "Molecular Force." VI. "Union and Inseparability of Matter and Force." VII. and VIII. "Nature and Action of Force—Attraction—Repulsion." IX. "Cosmical Repulsion. X. "Mechanical Force." XI. "Central Forces and Celestial Physics." "Deserves thoughtful and conscientious study."*—Saturday Review.

Wurtz.—A HISTORY OF CHEMICAL THEORY, from the Age of Lavoisier down to the present time. By AD. WURTZ. Translated by HENRY WATTS, F.R.S. Crown 8vo. 6s.

"*The discourse, as a résumé of chemical theory and research, unites singular luminousness and grasp. A few judicious notes are added by the translator.*"—Pall Mall Gazette. "*The treatment of the subject is admirable, and the translator has evidently done his duty most efficiently.*"—Westminster Review.

WORKS IN PHYSIOLOGY, ANATOMY, AND MEDICAL WORKS GENERALLY.

Allbutt (T. C.)—ON THE USE OF THE OPHTHALMOSCOPE in Diseases of the Nervous System and of the Kidneys; also in certain other General Disorders. By THOMAS CLIFFORD ALLBUTT, M.A., M.D. Contab., Physician to the Leeds General Infirmary, Lecturer on Practical Medicine, etc. etc. 8vo. 15s.

The Ophthalmoscope has been found of the highest value in the investigation of nervous diseases. But it is not easy for physicians who have left the schools, and are engaged in practice, to take up a new

instrument which requires much skill in using; it is therefore hoped that by such the present volume, containing the results of the author's extensive use of the instrument in diseases of the nervous system, will be found of high value; and that to all students it may prove a useful hand-book. After four introductory chapters on the history and value of the Ophthalmoscope, and the manner of investigating the states of the optic nerve and retina, the author treats of the various diseases with which optic changes are associated, and describes the way in which such associations take place. Besides the cases referred to throughout the volume, the Appendix contains details of 123 cases illustrative of the subjects discussed in the text, and a series of tabulated cases to show the Ophthalmoscopic appearances of the eye in Insanity, Mania, Dementia, Melancholia and Monomania, Idiotcy, and General Paralysis. The volume is illustrated with two valuable coloured plates of morbid appearances of the eye under the Ophthalmoscope. "By its aid men will no longer be compelled to work for years in the dark; they will have a definite standpoint whence to proceed on their course of investigation."
—Medical Times.

Anstie (F. E.)—NEURALGIA, AND DISEASES WHICH RESEMBLE IT. By FRANCIS E. ANSTIE, M.D., M.R.C.P., Senior Assistant Physician to Westminster Hospital. 8vo. 10s. 6d.

Dr. Anstie is well known as one of the greatest living authorities on Neuralgia. The present treatise is the result of many years' careful independent scientific investigation into the nature and proper treatment of this most painful disease. The author has had abundant means of studying the subject both in his own person and in the hundreds of patients that have resorted to him for treatment. He has gone into the whole subject indicated in the title ab initio, and the publishers believe it will be found that he has presented it in an entirely original light, and done much to rob this excruciating and hitherto refractory disease of many of its terrors. The Introduction treats briefly of Pain in General, and contains some striking and even original ideas as to its nature and in reference to sensation generally.

Barwell.—THE CAUSES AND TREATMENT OF LATERAL CURVATURE OF THE SPINE. Enlarged from Lectures published in the *Lancet*. By RICHARD BARWELL, F.R.C.S.,

Surgeon to and Lecturer on Anatomy at the Charing Cross Hospital. Second Edition. Crown 8vo. 4s. 6d.

Having failed to find in books a satisfactory theory of those conditions which produce lateral curvature, Mr. Barwell resolved to investigate the subject for himself ab initio. The present work is the result of long and patient study of Spines, normal and abnormal. He believes the views which he has been led to form account for those essential characteristics which have hitherto been left unexplained; and the treatment which he advocates is certainly less irksome, and will be found more efficacious than that which has hitherto been pursued. Indeed, the mode in which the first edition has been received by the profession is a gratifying sign that Mr. Barwell's principles have made their value and their weight felt. Many pages and a number of woodcuts have been added to the Second Edition.

Corfield (Professor W. H.)—A DIGEST OF FACTS RELATING TO THE TREATMENT AND UTILIZATION OF SEWAGE. By W. H. CORFIELD, M.A., B.A., Professor of Hygiene and Public Health at University College, London. 8vo. 10s. 6d. Second Edition, corrected and enlarged.

The author in the Second Edition has revised and corrected the entire work, and made many important additions. The headings of the eleven chapters are as follow:—I. "Early Systems: Midden-Heaps and Cesspools." II. "Filth and Disease—Cause and Effect." III. "Improved Midden-Pits and Cesspools; Midden-Closets, Pail-Closets, &c." IV. "The Dry-Closet Systems. V. "Water-Closets." VI. "Sewerage." VII. "Sanitary Aspects of the Water-Carrying System." VIII. "Value of Sewage; Injury to Rivers." IX. "Town Sewage; Attempts at Utilization." X. "Filtration and Irrigation." XI. "Influence of Sewage Farming on the Public Health." An abridged account of the more recently published researches on the subject will be found in the Appendices, while the Summary contains a concise statement of the views which the author himself has been led to adopt: references have been inserted throughout to show from what sources the numerous quotations have been derived, and an Index has been added. "Mr. Corfield's work is entitled to rank as a standard authority, no less than a convenient handbook, in all matters relating to sewage."—Athenæum.

Elam (C.)—A PHYSICIAN'S PROBLEMS. By CHARLES ELAM, M.D., M.R.C.P. Crown 8vo. 9*s.*

> CONTENTS:—"*Natural Heritage.*" "*On Degeneration in Man.*" "*On Moral and Criminal Epidemics.*" "*Body v. Mind.*" "*Illusions and Hallucinations.*" "*On Somnambulism.*" "*Reverie and Abstraction.*" *These Essays are intended as a contribution to the Natural History of those outlying regions of Thought and Action whose domain is the debateable ground of Brain, Nerve, and Mind. They are designed also to indicate the origin and mode of perpetuation of those varieties of organisation, intelligence, and general tendencies towards vice or virtue, which seem to be so capriciously developed among mankind. They also point to causes for the infinitely varied forms of disorder of nerve and brain—organic and functional—far deeper and more recondite than those generally believed in.* "*The book is one which all statesmen, magistrates, clergymen, medical men, and parents should study and inwardly digest.*"—Examiner.

Fox.—Works by WILSON FOX, M.D. Lond., F.R.C.P., Holme Professor of Clinical Medicine, University College, London, Physician Extraordinary to her Majesty the Queen, etc. :—

> ON THE DIAGNOSIS AND TREATMENT OF THE VARIETIES OF DYSPEPSIA, CONSIDERED IN RELATION TO THE PATHOLOGICAL ORIGIN OF THE DIFFERENT FORMS OF INDIGESTION. Second Edition. 8vo. 7*s.* 6*d.*

> ON THE ARTIFICIAL PRODUCTION OF TUBERCLE IN THE LOWER ANIMALS, With Coloured Plates. 4to. 5*s.* 6*d.*
>
>> *In this Lecture Dr. Fox describes in minute detail a large number of experiments made by him on guinea-pigs and rabbits for the purpose of inquiring into the origin of Tubercle by the agency of direct irritation or by septic matters. This method of inquiry he believes to be one of the most important advances which have been recently made in the pathology of the disease. The work is illustrated by three plates, each containing a number of carefully coloured illustrations from nature.*

> ON THE TREATMENT OF HYPERPYREXIA, as Illustrated in Acute Articular Rheumatism by means of the External Application of Cold. 8vo. 2*s.* 6*d.*

The object of this work is to show that the class of cases included under the title, and which have hitherto been invariably fatal, may, by a judicious use of the cold bath and without venesection, be brought to a favourable termination. Minute details are given of the successful treatment by this method of two patients by the author, followed by a Commentary on the cases, in which the merits of the mode of treatment are discussed and compared with those of methods followed by other eminent practitioners. Appended are tables of the observations made on the temperature during the treatment; a table showing the effect of the immersion of the patients in the baths employed, in order to exhibit the rate at which the temperature was lowered in each case; a table of the chief details of twenty-two cases of this class recently published, and which are referred to in various parts of the Commentary. Two Charts are also introduced, giving a connected view of the progress of the two successful cases, and a series of sphygmographic tracings of the pulses of the two patients. "A clinical study of rare value. Should be read by every one."—Medical Press and Circular.

Galton (D.)—AN ADDRESS ON THE GENERAL PRINCIPLES WHICH SHOULD BE OBSERVED IN THE CONSTRUCTION OF HOSPITALS. Delivered to the British Medical Association at Leeds, July 1869. By DOUGLAS GALTON, C.B., F.R.S. Crown 8vo. 3s. 6d.

In this Address the author endeavours to enunciate what are those principles which seem to him to form the starting-point from which all architects should proceed in the construction of hospitals. Besides Mr. Galton's paper the book contains the opinions expressed in the subsequent discussion by several eminent medical men, such as Dr. Kennedy, Sir James Y. Simpson, Dr. Hughes Bennet, and others. The work is illustrated by a number of plans, sections, and other cuts. "An admirable exposition of those conditions of structure which most conduce to cleanliness, economy, and convenience."
—Times.

Harley (J.)—THE OLD VEGETABLE NEUROTICS, Hemlock, Opium, Belladonna, and Henbane; their Physiological Action and Therapeutical Use, alone and in combination. Being the Gulstonian Lectures of 1868 extended, and including a Complete Examination of the Active Constituents of Opium. By JOHN HARLEY, M.D. Lond., F.R.C.P., F.L.S., etc. 8vo. 12s.

*The author's object throughout the investigations and experiments on which this volume is founded has been to ascertain, clearly and definitely, the action of the drugs employed on the healthy body in medicinal doses, from the smallest to the largest; to deduce simple practical conclusions from the facts observed; and then to apply the drug to the relief of the particular conditions to which its action appeared suited. Many experiments have been made by the author both on men and the lower animals; and the author's endeavour has been to present to the mind, as far as words may do, impressions of the actual condition of the individual subjected to the drug. "Those who are interested generally in the progress of medical science will find much to repay a careful perusal."—*Athenæum.

Hood (Wharton).—ON BONE-SETTING (so called), and its Relation to the Treatment of Joints Crippled by Injury, Rheumatism, Inflammation, etc. etc. By WHARTON P. HOOD, M.D., M.R.C.S. Crown 8vo. 4s. 6d.

*The author for a period attended the London practice of the late Mr. Hutton, the famous and successful bone-setter, by whom he was initiated into the mystery of the art and practice. Thus the author is amply qualified to write on the subject from the practical point of view, while his professional education enables him to consider it in its scientific and surgical bearings. In the present work he gives a brief account of the salient features of a bone-setter's method of procedure in the treatment of damaged joints, of the results of that treatment, and of the class of cases in which he has seen it prove successful. The author's aim is to give the rationale of the bone-setter's practice, to reduce it to something like a scientific method, to show when force should be resorted to and when it should not, and to initiate surgeons into the secret of Mr. Hutton's successful manipulation. Throughout the work a great number of authentic instances of successful treatment are given, with the details of the method of cure; and the Chapters on Manipulations and Affections of the Spine are illustrated by a number of appropriate and well-executed cuts. "Dr. Hood's book is full of instruction, and should be read by all surgeons."—*Medical Times.

Humphry.—THE HUMAN SKELETON (including the joints). By G. M. HUMPHRY, M.D., F.R.S. With 260 Illustrations, drawn from nature. Medium 8vo. 28s.

PHYSIOLOGY, ANATOMY, ETC.

In lecturing on the Skeleton it has been the author's practice, instead of giving a detailed account of the several parts, to request his students to get up the descriptive anatomy of certain bones, with the aid of some work on osteology. He afterwards tested their acquirements by examination, endeavouring to supply deficiencies and correct errors, adding also such information—physical, physiological, pathological, and practical—as he had gathered from his own observation and researches, and which was likely to be useful and excite an interest in the subject. This additional information forms, in great part, the material of this volume, which is intended to be supplementary to existing works on anatomy. Considerable space has been devoted to the description of the joints, because it is less fully given in other works, and because an accurate knowledge of the structure and peculiar form of the joints is essential to a correct knowledge of their movements. The numerous illustrations were all drawn upon stone from nature; and in most instances, from specimens prepared for the purpose by the author himself. "Bearing at once the stamp of the accomplished scholar, and evidences of the skilful anatomist. We express our admiration of the drawings."—Medical Times and Gazette.

Huxley's Physiology.—See p. 24, preceding.

Journal of Anatomy and Physiology.
Conducted by Professors HUMPHRY and NEWTON, and Mr. CLARK of Cambridge, Professor TURNER of Edinburgh, and Dr. WRIGHT of Dublin. Published twice a year. Old Series, Parts I. and II., price 7s. 6d. each. Vol. I. containing Parts I. and II., Royal 8vo., 16s. New Series, Parts I. to IX. 6s. each, or yearly Vols. 12s. 6d. each.

Lankester.—COMPARATIVE LONGEVITY IN MAN AND THE LOWER ANIMALS. By E. RAY LANKESTER, B.A. Crown 8vo. 4s. 6d.
This Essay gained the prize offered by the University of Oxford for the best Paper on the subject of which it treats. This interesting subject is here treated in a thorough manner, both scientifically and statistically.

Maclaren.—TRAINING, IN THEORY AND PRACTICE. By ARCHIBALD MACLAREN, the Gymnasium, Oxford. 8vo. Handsomely bound in cloth, 7s. 6d.

*The ordinary agents of health are Exercise, Diet, Sleep, Air, Bathing, and Clothing. In this work the author examines each of these agents in detail, and from two different points of view. First, as to the manner in which it is, or should be, administered under ordinary circumstances; and secondly, in what manner and to what extent this mode of administration is, or should be, altered for purposes of training; the object of "training," according to the author, being "to put the body, with extreme and exceptional care, under the influence of all the agents which promote its health and strength, in order to enable it to meet extreme and exceptional demands upon its energies." Appended are various diagrams and tables relating to boat-racing, and tables connected with diet and training. "The philosophy of human health has seldom received so apt an exposition."—Globe. "After all the nonsense that has been written about training, it is a comfort to get hold of a thoroughly sensible book at last."—*John Bull.

Macpherson.—Works by JOHN MACPHERSON, M.D. :—

THE BATHS AND WELLS OF EUROPE; Their Action and Uses. With Hints on Change of Air and Diet Cures. With a Map. Extra fcap. 8vo. 6s. 6d.

*This work is intended to supply information which will afford aid in the selection of such Spas as are suited for particular cases. It exhibits a sketch of the present condition of our knowledge on the subject of the operation of mineral waters, gathered from the author's personal observation, and from every other available source of information. It is divided into four books, and each book into several chapters:—Book I. Elements of Treatment, in which, among other matters, the external and internal uses of water are treated of. II. Bathing, treating of the various kinds of baths. III. Wells, treating of the various kinds of mineral waters. IV. Diet Cures, in which various vegetable, milk, and other "cures" are discussed. Appended is an Index of Diseases noticed, and one of places named. Prefixed is a sketch map of the principal baths and places of health-resort in Europe. "Dr. Macpherson has given the kind of information which every medical practitioner ought to possess."—*The Lancet. *"Whoever wants to know the real character of any health-resort must read Dr. Macpherson's book."—*Medical Times.

Macpherson (J.)—*continued.*

OUR BATHS AND WELLS: The Mineral Waters of the British Islands, with a List of Sea-bathing Places. Extra fcap. 8vo. pp. xv. 205. 3s. 6d.

> *Dr. Macpherson has divided his work into five parts. He begins by a few introductory observations on bath life, its circumstances, uses, and pleasures; he then explains in detail the composition of the various mineral waters, and points out the special curative properties of each class. A chapter on "The History of British Wells" from the earliest period to the present time forms the natural transition to the second part of this volume, which treats of the different kinds of mineral waters in England, whether pure, thermal and earthy, saline, chalybeate, or sulphur. Wales, Scotland, and Ireland supply the materials for distinct sections. An Index of mineral waters, one of sea-bathing places, and a third of wells of pure or nearly pure water, terminate the book. "This little volume forms a very available handbook for a large class of invalids."*—Nonconformist.

Maudsley.—Works by HENRY MAUDSLEY, M.D., Professor of Medical Jurisprudence in University College, London:—

BODY AND MIND: An Inquiry into their Connection and Mutual Influence, specially in reference to Mental Disorders; being the Gulstonian Lectures for 1870. Delivered before the Royal College of Physicians. Crown 8vo. 5s.

> *The volume consists of three Lectures and two long Appendices, the general plan of the whole being to bring Man, both in his physical and mental relations, as much as possible under the scope of scientific inquiry. The first Lecture is devoted to an exposition of the physical conditions of mental function in health. In the second Lecture are sketched the features of some forms of degeneracy of mind, as exhibited in morbid varieties of the human kind, with the purpose of bringing prominently into notice the operation of physical causes from generation to generation, and the relationship of mental to other diseases of the nervous system. In the third Lecture are displayed the relations of morbid states of the body and disordered mental function. Appendix I. is a criticism of the Archbishop of York's address on "The Limits of Philosophical Inquiry." Appendix II. deals with the "Theory of Vitality," in which the author en-*

Maudsley (H.)—continued.

deavours to set forth the reflections which facts seem to warrant. "It distinctly marks a step in the progress of scientific psychology." —The Practitioner.

THE PHYSIOLOGY AND PATHOLOGY OF MIND. Second Edition, Revised. 8vo. 16s.

This work is the result of an endeavour on the author's part to arrive at some definite conviction with regard to the physical conditions of mental function, and the relation of the phenomena of sound and unsound mind. The author's aim throughout has been twofold: I. To treat of mental phenomena from a physiological rather than from a metaphysical point of view. II. To bring the manifold instructive instances presented by the unsound mind to bear upon the interpretation of the obscure problems of mental science. In the first part, the author pursues his independent inquiry into the science of Mind in the same direction as that followed by Bain, Spencer, Laycock, and Carpenter; and in the second, he studies the subject in a light which, in this country at least, is almost entirely novel. "Dr. Maudsley's work, which has already become standard, we most urgently recommend to the careful study of all those who are interested in the physiology and pathology of the brain."—Anthropological Review.

Practitioner (The).—A Monthly Journal of Therapeutics. Edited by FRANCIS E. ANSTIE, M.D. 8vo. Price 1s. 6d. Vols. I to VII. 8vo. cloth. 10s. 6d. each.

Radcliffe.—DYNAMICS OF NERVE AND MUSCLE. By CHARLES BLAND RADCLIFFE, M.D., F.R.C.P., Physician to the Westminster Hospital, and to the National Hospital for the Paralysed and Epileptic. Crown 8vo. 8s. 6d.

This work contains the result of the author's long investigations into the Dynamics of Nerve and Muscle, as connected with Animal Electricity. The author endeavours to shew from these researches that the state of action in nerve and muscle, instead of being a manifestation of vitality, must be brought under the domain of physical law in order to be intelligible, and that a different meaning, also based upon pure physics, must be attached to the state of rest. "The practitioner will find in Dr. Radcliffe a 'guide, philosopher, and friend,' from whose teaching he cannot fail to reap a plentiful harvest of new and valuable ideas."—Scotsman.

Reynolds.—A SYSTEM OF MEDICINE. Vol. I. Edited by J. RUSSELL REYNOLDS, M.D., F.R.C.P. London. Second Edition. 8vo. 25s.

Part I. General Diseases, or Affections of the Whole System. § I.—Those determined by agents operating from without, such as the exanthemata, malarial diseases, and their allies. § II.—Those determined by conditions existing within the body, such as Gout, Rheumatism, Rickets, etc. Part II. Local Diseases, or Affections of particular Systems. § I.—Diseases of the Skin.

A SYSTEM OF MEDICINE. Vol. II. Second Edition in the Press. 8vo. 25s.

Part II. Local Diseases (continued). § I.—Diseases of the Nervous System. A. General Nervous Diseases. B. Partial Diseases of the Nervous System. 1. Diseases of the Head. 2. Diseases of the Spinal Column. 3. Diseases of the Nerves. § II.—Diseases of the Digestive System. A. Diseases of the Stomach.

A SYSTEM OF MEDICINE. Vol. III. 8vo. 25s.

Part II. Local Diseases (continued). § II. Diseases of the Digestive System (continued). B. Diseases of the Mouth. C. Diseases of the Fauces, Pharynx, and Œsophagus. D. Diseases of the Intestines. E. Diseases of the Peritoneum. F. Diseases of the Liver. G. Diseases of the Pancreas. § III.—Diseases of the Respiratory System. A. Diseases of the Larynx. B. Diseases of the Thoracic Organs. "One of the best and most comprehensive treatises on Medicine which have yet been attempted in any country."—Indian Medical Journal. "Contains some of the best essays that have lately appeared, and is a complete library in itself."—Medical Press.

Seaton.—A HANDBOOK OF VACCINATION. By EDWARD C. SEATON, M.D., Medical Inspector to the Privy Council. Extra fcap. 8vo. 8s. 6d.

The author's object in putting forth this work is twofold: First, to provide a text-book on the science and practice of Vaccination for the use of younger practitioners and of medical students ; secondly, to give what assistance he could to those engaged in the administration of the system of Public Vaccination established in England. For many years past, from the nature of his office, Dr. Seaton has had constant intercourse in reference to the subject of Vaccination, with medical men who are interested in it, and especially with that large part of the profession who are engaged as Public Vaccinators. All the varieties of pocks, both in men and the lower animals, are treated of in detail, and much valuable information given on all points connected with lymph, and minute instructions as to the niceties and cautions which so greatly influence success in Vaccination. The administrative sections of the work will be of interest and value, not only to medical practitioners, but to many others to whom a right understanding of the principles on which a system of Public Vaccination should be based is indispensable. "Henceforth the indispensable handbook of Public Vaccination, and the standard authority on this great subject."—British Medical Journal.

Symonds (J. A., M.D.)—MISCELLANIES. By JOHN ADDINGTON SYMONDS, M.D. Selected and Edited, with an Introductory Memoir, by his Son. 8vo. 7s. 6d.

The late Dr. Symonds of Bristol was a man of a singularly versatile and elegant as well as powerful and scientific intellect. In order to make this selection from his many works generally interesting, the editor has confined himself to works of pure literature, and to such scientific studies as had a general philosophical or social interest. Among the general subjects are articles on "the Principles of Beauty," on "Knowledge," and a "Life of Dr. Prichard;" among the Scientific Studies are papers on "Sleep and Dreams," "Apparitions," "the Relations between Mind and Muscle," "Habit," etc.; there are several papers on "the Social and Political Aspects of Medicine;" and a few Poems and Translations selected from a great number of equal merit. "A collection of graceful essays on general and scientific subjects, by a very accomplished physician."—Graphic.

WORKS ON MENTAL AND MORAL PHILOSOPHY, AND ALLIED SUBJECTS.

Aristotle.—AN INTRODUCTION TO ARISTOTLE'S RHETORIC. With Analysis, Notes, and Appendices. By E. M. COPE, Trinity College, Cambridge. 8vo. 14s.

This work is introductory to an edition of the Greek Text of Aristotle's Rhetoric, which is in course of preparation. Its object is to render that treatise thoroughly intelligible. The author has aimed to illustrate, as preparatory to the detailed explanation of the work, the general bearings and relations of the Art of Rhetoric in itself, as well as the special mode of treating it adopted by Aristotle in his peculiar system. The evidence upon obscure or doubtful questions connected with the subject is examined; and the relations which Rhetoric bears, in Aristotle's view, to the kindred art of Logic are fully considered. A connected Analysis of the work is given, and a few important matters are separately discussed in Appendices. There is added, as a general Appendix, by way of specimen of the antagonistic system of Isocrates and others, a complete analysis of the treatise called 'Ῥητορική πρὸς 'Αλέξανδρον, with a discussion of its authorship and of the probable results of its teaching.

ARISTOTLE ON FALLACIES; OR, THE SOPHISTICI ELENCHI. With a Translation and Notes by EDWARD POSTE, M.A., Fellow of Oriel College, Oxford. 8vo. 8s. 6d.

Besides the doctrine of Fallacies, Aristotle offers, either in this treatise or in other passages quoted in the Commentary, various glances over the world of science and opinion, various suggestions or problems which are still agitated, and a vivid picture of the ancient system of dialectics, which it is hoped may be found both interesting and instructive. "*It will be an assistance to genuine students of Aristotle.*"—Guardian. "*It is indeed a work of great skill.*"—Saturday Review.

Butler (W. A.), Late Professor of Moral Philosophy in the University of Dublin :—

LECTURES ON THE HISTORY OF ANCIENT PHILOSOPHY. Edited from the Author's MSS., with Notes, by WILLIAM HEPWORTH THOMPSON, M.A., Master of Trinity College, and Regius Professor of Greek in the University of Cambridge. Two Volumes. 8vo. 1*l.* 5*s.*

These Lectures consist of an Introductory Series on the Science of Mind generally, and five other Series on Ancient Philosophy, the greater part of which treat of Plato and the Platonists, the Fifth Series being an unfinished course on the Psychology of Aristotle, containing an able Analysis of the well known though by no means well understood Treatise, περὶ ψυχῆς. *These Lectures are the result of patient and conscientious examination of the original documents, and may be considered as a perfectly independent contribution to our knowledge of the great master of Grecian wisdom. The author's intimate familiarity with the metaphysical writings of the last century, and especially with the English and Scotch School of Psychologists, has enabled him to illustrate the subtle speculations of which he treats in a manner calculated to render them more intelligible to the English mind than they can be by writers trained solely in the technicalities of modern German schools. The editor has verified all the references, and added valuable Notes, in which he points out sources of more complete information. The Lectures constitute a History of the Platonic Philosophy—its seed-time, maturity, and decay.*

SERMONS AND LETTERS ON ROMANISM.—See THEOLOGICAL CATALOGUE.

Calderwood.—PHILOSOPHY OF THE INFINITE: A Treatise on Man's Knowledge of the Infinite Being, in answer to Sir W. Hamilton and Dr. Mansel. By the Rev. HENRY CALDERWOOD, M.A., LL.D., Professor of Moral Philosophy in the University of Edinburgh. Cheaper Edition. 8vo. 7*s.* 6*d.*

The purpose of this volume is, by a careful analysis of consciousness, to prove, in opposition to Sir W. Hamilton and Mr. Mansel, that man possesses a notion of an Infinite Being, and to ascertain the peculiar nature of the conception and the particular relations in which it is found to arise. The province of Faith as related to that of Knowledge, and the characteristics of Knowledge and Thought as bearing on this subject, are examined; and separate chapters are devoted to the consideration of our knowledge of the Infinite as First Cause, as Moral Governor, and as the Object of Worship. "A book of great ability . . . . written in a clear style, and may be easily understood by even those who are not versed in such discussions."—British Quarterly Review.

Elam.—A PHYSICIAN'S PROBLEMS. — See MEDICAL CATALOGUE, preceding.

Galton (Francis).—HEREDITARY GENIUS: An Inquiry into its Laws and Consequences. See PHYSICAL SCIENCE CATALOGUE, preceding.

Green (J. H.)—SPIRITUAL PHILOSOPHY: Founded on the Teaching of the late SAMUEL TAYLOR COLERIDGE. By the late JOSEPH HENRY GREEN, F.R.S., D.C.L. Edited, with a Memoir of the Author's Life, by JOHN SIMON, F.R.S., Medical Officer of Her Majesty's Privy Council, and Surgeon to St. Thomas's Hospital. Two Vols. 8vo. 25s.

The late Mr. Green, the eminent surgeon, was for many years the intimate friend and disciple of Coleridge, and an ardent student of philosophy. The language of Coleridge's will imposed on Mr. Green the obligation of devoting, so far as necessary, the remainder of his life to the one task of systematising, developing, and establishing the doctrines of the Coleridgian philosophy. With the assistance of Coleridge's manuscripts, but especially from the knowledge he possessed of Coleridge's doctrines, and independent study of at least the basal principles and metaphysics of the sciences and of all the phenomena of human life, he proceeded logically to work out a system of universal philosophy such as he deemed would in the main accord with his master's aspirations. After many years of preparatory labour he resolved to complete in a compendious form a work which should give in system the doctrines most distinctly Coleridgian. The result is these two volumes. The first volume

> is devoted to the general principles of philosophy; the second aims at vindicating à priori (on principles for which the first volume has contended) the essential doctrines of Christianity. The work is divided into four parts: I. "On the Intellectual Faculties and processes which are concerned in the Investigation of Truth." II. "Of First Principles in Philosophy." III. "Truths of Religion." IV. "The Idea of Christianity in relation to Controversial Philosophy."

Huxley (Professor.)—LAY SERMONS, ADDRESSES, AND REVIEWS. See PHYSICAL SCIENCE CATALOGUE, preceding.

Jevons.—Works by W. STANLEY JEVONS, M.A., Professor of Logic in Owens College, Manchester :—

THE SUBSTITUTION OF SIMILARS, the True Principle of Reasoning. Derived from a Modification of Aristotle's Dictum. Fcap. 8vo. 2s. 6d.

> "All acts of reasoning," the author says, "seem to me to be different cases of one uniform process, which may perhaps be best described as the substitution of similars. This phrase clearly expresses that familiar mode in which we continually argue by analogy from like to like, and take one thing as a representative of another. The chief difficulty consists in showing that all the forms of the old logic, as well as the fundamental rules of mathematical reasoning, may be explained upon the same principle; and it is to this difficult task I have devoted the most attention. Should my notion be true, a vast mass of technicalities may be swept from our logical text-books and yet the small remaining part of logical doctrine will prove far more useful than all the learning of the Schoolmen." Prefixed is a plan of a new reasoning machine, the Logical Abacus, the construction and working of which is fully explained in the text and Appendix. "Mr. Jevons' book is very clear and intelligible, and quite worth consulting."—Guardian.

ELEMENTARY LESSONS IN LOGIC.—See EDUCATIONAL CATALOGUE.

Maccoll.—THE GREEK SCEPTICS, from Pyrrho to Sextus. An Essay which obtained the Hare Prize in the year 1868. By

MENTAL AND MORAL PHILOSOPHY, ETC. 49

NORMAN MACCOLL, B.A., Scholar of Downing College, Cambridge. Crown 8vo. 3s. 6d.

This Essay consists of five parts: I. "Introduction." II. "Pyrrho and Timon." III. "The New Academy." IV. "The Later Sceptics." V. "The Pyrrhoneans and New Academy contrasted."—"Mr. Maccoll has produced a monograph which merits the gratitude of all students of philosophy. His style is clear and vigorous; he has mastered the authorities, and criticises them in a modest but independent spirit."—Pall Mall Gazette.

M'Cosh.—Works by JAMES M'COSH, LL.D., President of Princeton College, New Jersey, U.S.

"He certainly shows himself skilful in that application of logic to psychology, in that inductive science of the human mind which is the fine side of English philosophy. His philosophy as a whole is worthy of attention."—Revue de Deux Mondes.

THE METHOD OF THE DIVINE GOVERNMENT, Physical and Moral. Tenth Edition. 8vo. 10s. 6d.

This work is divided into four books. The first presents a general view of the Divine Government as fitted to throw light on the character of God; the second deals with the method of the Divine Government in the physical world; the third treats of the principles of the human mind through which God governs mankind; and the fourth is on Pastoral and Revealed Religion, and the Restoration of Man. An Appendix, consisting of seven articles, investigates the fundamental principles which underlie the speculations of the treatise. "This work is distinguished from other similar ones by its being based upon a thorough study of physical science, and an accurate knowledge of its present condition, and by its entering in a deeper and more unfettered manner than its predecessors upon the discussion of the appropriate psychological, ethical, and theological questions. The author keeps aloof at once from the à priori idealism and dreaminess of German speculation since Schelling, and from the onesidedness and narrowness of the empiricism and positivism which have so prevailed in England."—Dr. Ulrici, in "Zeitschrift für Philosophie."

THE INTUITIONS OF THE MIND. A New Edition. 8vo. cloth. 10s. 6d.

M'Cosh (J.)—continued.

The object of this treatise is to determine the true nature of Intuition, and to investigate its laws. It starts with a general view of intuitive convictions, their character and the method in which they are employed, and passes on to a more detailed examination of them, treating them under the various heads of "Primitive Cognitions," "Primitive Beliefs," "Primitive Judgments," and "Moral Convictions." Their relations to the various sciences, mental and physical, are then examined. Collateral criticisms are thrown into preliminary and supplementary chapters and sections. "*The undertaking to adjust the claims of the sensational and intuitional philosophies, and of the à posteriori and à priori methods, is accomplished in this work with a great amount of success.*"—Westminster Review. "*I value it for its large acquaintance with English Philosophy, which has not led him to neglect the great German works. I admire the moderation and clearness, as well as comprehensiveness, of the author's views.*"—Dr. Dorner, of Berlin.

AN EXAMINATION OF MR. J. S. MILL'S PHILOSOPHY: Being a Defence of Fundamental Truth. Crown 8vo. 7s. 6d.

This volume is not put forth by its author as a special reply to Mr. Mill's "Examination of Sir William Hamilton's Philosophy." In that work Mr. Mill has furnished the means of thoroughly estimating his theory of mind, of which he had only given hints and glimpses in his logical treatise. It is this theory which Dr. M'Cosh professes to examine in this volume; his aim is simply to defend a portion of primary truth which has been assailed by an acute thinker who has extensive influence in England. "*In such points as Mr. Mill's notions of intuitions and necessity, he will have the voice of mankind with him.*"—Athenæum. "*Such a work greatly needed to be done, and the author was the man to do it. This volume is important, not merely in reference to the views of Mr. Mill, but of the whole school of writers, past and present, British and Continental, he so ably represents.*"—Princeton Review.

THE LAWS OF DISCURSIVE THOUGHT: Being a Textbook of Formal Logic. Crown 8vo. 5s.

The main feature of this Logical Treatise is to be found in the more thorough investigation of the nature of the notion, in regard to

M'Cosh (J.)—*continued.*

which the views of the school of Locke and Whately are regarded by the author as very defective, and the views of the school of Kant and Hamilton altogether erroneous. The author believes that errors spring far more frequently from obscure, inadequate, indistinct, and confused Notions, and from not placing the Notions in their proper relation in judgment, than from Ratiocination. In this treatise, therefore, the Notion (with the term, and the Relation of Thought to Language) will be found to occupy a larger relative place than in any logical work written since the time of the famous Art of Thinking. "The amount of summarized information which it contains is very great; and it is the only work on the very important subject with which it deals. Never was such a work so much needed as in the present day."—London Quarterly Review.

CHRISTIANITY AND POSITIVISM: A Series of Lectures to the Times on Natural Theology and Apologetics. Crown 8vo. 7s. 6d.

These Lectures were delivered in New York, by appointment, in the beginning of 1871, as the second course on the foundation of the Union Theological Seminary. There are ten Lectures in all, divided into three series:—I. "Christianity and Physical Science" (three lectures). II. "Christianity and Mental Science" (four lectures). III. "Christianity and Historical Investigation" (three lectures). The Appendix contains articles on "Gaps in the Theory of Development;" "Darwin's Descent of Man." "Principles of Herbert Spencer's Philosophy." In the course of the Lectures Dr. M'Cosh discusses all the most important scientific problems which are supposed to affect Christianity.

Masson.—RECENT BRITISH PHILOSOPHY: A Review, with Criticisms; including some Comments on Mr. Mill's Answer to Sir William Hamilton. By DAVID MASSON, M.A., Professor of Rhetoric and English Literature in the University of Edinburgh. Crown 8vo. 6s.

The author, in his usual graphic and forcible manner, reviews in considerable detail, and points out the drifts of the philosophical speculations of the previous thirty years, bringing under notice the work of all the principal philosophers who have been at work during

Masson (D.)—*continued.*

that period on the highest problems which concern humanity. The four chapters are thus titled:—I. "A Survey of Thirty Years." II. "The Traditional Differences: how repeated in Carlyle, Hamilton, and Mill." III. "Effects of Recent Scientific Conceptions on Philosophy." IV. "Latest Drifts and Groupings." The last seventy-six pages are devoted to a Review of Mr. Mill's criticism of Sir William Hamilton's Philosophy. "We can nowhere point to a work which gives so clear an exposition of the course of philosophical speculation in Britain during the past century, or which indicates so instructively the mutual influences of philosophic and scientific thought."—Fortnightly Review.

BRITISH NOVELISTS.—See BELLES LETTRES CATALOGUE.

LIFE OF MILTON.—See BIOGRAPHICAL CATALOGUE.

Maudsley.—Works by HENRY MAUDSLEY, M.D., Professor of Medical Jurisprudence in University College, London :—

BODY AND MIND: An Inquiry into their Connection and Mutual Influence, specially in reference to Mental Diseases. See MEDICAL CATALOGUE, preceding.

THE PHYSIOLOGY AND PATHOLOGY OF MIND. See MEDICAL CATALOGUE, preceding.

Maurice.—Works by the Rev. FREDERICK DENISON MAURICE, M.A., Professor of Moral Philosophy in the University of Cambridge. (For other Works by the same Author, see THEOLOGICAL CATALOGUE.)

SOCIAL MORALITY. Twenty-one Lectures delivered in the University of Cambridge. 8vo. 14s.

In this series of Lectures, Professor Maurice considers, historically and critically, Social Morality in its three main aspects: I. "The Relations which spring from the Family—Domestic Morality." II. "The Relations which subsist among the various constituents of a Nation—National Morality." III. "As it concerns Universal Humanity—Universal Morality." Appended to each series is a chapter on "Worship:" first, "Family Worship;" second,

Maurice (F. D.)—*continued.*

"*National Worship;*" third, "*Universal Worship.*" " *Whilst reading it we are charmed by the freedom from exclusiveness and prejudice, the large charity, the loftiness of thought, the eagerness to recognise and appreciate whatever there is of real worth extant in the world, which animates it from one end to the other. We gain new thoughts and new ways of viewing things, even more, perhaps, from being brought for a time under the influence of so noble and spiritual a mind.*"—Athenæum.

THE CONSCIENCE: Lectures on Casuistry, delivered in the University of Cambridge. New and Cheaper Edition. Crown 8vo. 5s.

In this series of nine Lectures, Professor Maurice, with his wonted force and breadth and freshness, endeavours to settle what is meant by the word "Conscience," and discusses the most important questions immediately connected with the subject. Taking "Casuistry" in its old sense as being the "study of cases of Conscience," he endeavours to show in what way it may be brought to bear at the present day upon the acts and thoughts of our ordinary existence. He shows that Conscience asks for laws, not rules; for freedom, not chains; for education, not suppression. He has abstained from the use of philosophical terms, and has touched on philosophical systems only when he fancied "they were interfering with the rights and duties of wayfarers." The Saturday Review says: "*We rise from them with detestation of all that is selfish and mean, and with a living impression that there is such a thing as goodness after all.*"

MORAL AND METAPHYSICAL PHILOSOPHY. New Edition and Preface. Vol. I. Ancient Philosophy and the First to the Thirteenth Centuries; Vol. II. the Fourteenth Century and the French Revolution, with a glimpse into the Nineteenth Century. 2 Vols. 8vo. 25s.

This is an Edition in two volumes of Professor Maurice's History of Philosophy from the earliest period to the present time. It was formerly scattered throughout a number of separate volumes, and it is believed that all admirers of the author and all students of philosophy will welcome this compact Edition. The subject is one of the highest importance, and it is treated here with fulness and candour, and in a clear and interesting manner. In a long introduction to this Edition, in the form of a dialogue, Professor Maurice justifies some of his own peculiar views, and touches upon some of the most important topics of the time.

Murphy.—HABIT AND INTELLIGENCE, in Connection with the Laws of Matter and Force: A Series of Scientific Essays. By JOSEPH JOHN MURPHY. Two Vols. 8vo. 16s.

The author's chief purpose in this work has been to state and to discuss what he regards as the special and characteristic principles of life. The most important part of the work treats of those vital principles which belong to the inner domain of life itself, as distinguished from the principles which belong to the border-land where life comes into contact with inorganic matter and force. In the inner domain of life we find two principles, which are, the author believes, coextensive with life and peculiar to it: these are Habit and Intelligence. He has made as full a statement as possible of the laws under which habits form, disappear, alter under altered circumstances, and vary spontaneously. He discusses that most important of all questions, whether intelligence is an ultimate fact, incapable of being resolved into any other, or only a resultant from the laws of habit. The latter part of the first volume is occupied with the discussion of the question of the Origin of Species. The first part of the second volume is occupied with an inquiry into the process of mental growth and development, and the nature of mental intelligence. In the chapter that follows, the author discusses the science of history, and the three concluding chapters contain some ideas on the classification, the history, and the logic, of the sciences. The author's aim has been to make the subjects treated of intelligible to any ordinary intelligent man. "We are pleased to listen," says the Saturday Review, *"to a writer who has so firm a foothold upon the ground within the scope of his immediate survey, and who can enunciate with so much clearness and force propositions which come within his grasp."*

Thring (E., M.A.)—THOUGHTS ON LIFE-SCIENCE. By EDWARD THRING, M.A. (Benjamin Place), Head Master of Uppingham School. New Edition, enlarged and revised. Crown 8vo. 7s. 6d.

In this volume are discussed in a familiar manner some of the most interesting problems between Science and Religion, Reason and

MENTAL AND MORAL PHILOSOPHY, ETC.

Feeling. "*Learning and Science,*" says the author, "*are claiming the right of building up and pulling down everything, especially the latter. It has seemed to me no useless task to look steadily at what has happened, to take stock as it were of men's gains, and to endeavour amidst new circumstances to arrive at some rational estimate of the bearings of things, so that the limits of what is possible at all events may be clearly marked out for ordinary readers. . . . . This book is an endeavour to bring out some of the main facts of the world.*"

Venn.—THE LOGIC OF CHANCE; An Essay on the Foundations and Province of the Theory of Probability, with especial reference to its application to Moral and Social Science. By JOHN VENN, M.A., Fellow of Gonville and Caius College, Cambridge. Fcap. 8vo. 7s. 6d.

This Essay is in no sense mathematical. Probability, the author thinks, may be considered to be a portion of the province of Logic regarded from the material point of view. The principal objects of this Essay are to ascertain how great a portion it comprises, where we are to draw the boundary between it and the contiguous branches of the general science of evidence, what are the ultimate foundations upon which its rules rest, what the nature of the evidence they are capable of affording, and to what class of subjects they may most fitly be applied. The general design of the Essay, as a special treatise on Probability, is quite original, the author believing that erroneous notions as to the real nature of the subject are disastrously prevalent. "*Exceedingly well thought and well written,*" *says the* Westminster Review. *The* Nonconformist *calls it a* "*masterly book.*"

LONDON: R. CLAY, SONS, AND TAYLOR, PRINTERS, BREAD STREET HILL.

www.ingramcontent.com/pod-product-compliance
Lightning Source LLC
Chambersburg PA
CBHW031938290426
44108CB00011B/602